PAUL ART̲H̲U̲R̲ ̲ ̲ ̲ ̲ ̲ ̲ ̲ ̲ ̲ ̲ ̲ ̲ ̲ ̲ ̲ ̲U̲n̲i̲v̲e̲r̲s̲i̲t̲y of Ulster, and
Course D̲i̲r̲e̲c̲t̲o̲r̲ ̲ ̲ ̲ ̲ ̲ ̲ ̲ ̲ ̲ ̲ ̲ ̲P̲e̲a̲c̲e and Conflict
Studies. He is a frequent visitor to the USA in a professional capacity,
and in 1997–8 he was awarded a Senior Fellowship at the United States
Institute of Peace in Washington DC, where he had the opportunity to
work in the First Lady's Office. He is a regular contributor in the
capacity of political analyst to the local, national and international
media (the BBC, CNN, UTV, the *Irish Times*, the *New York Times* and
the *Sunday Times*).

SPECIAL RELATIONSHIPS

Britain, Ireland and the Northern Ireland problem

PAUL ARTHUR

THE
BLACKSTAFF
PRESS

BELFAST

First published in 2000 by
The Blackstaff Press Limited
Wildflower Way, Apollo Road
Belfast BT12 6TA, Northern Ireland

Typeset by Techniset Typesetters, Newton-le-Willows, Merseyside

Printed in Ireland by ColourBooks

A CIP catalogue record for this book
is available from the British Library

ISBN 0–85640–688–0

www.blackstaffpress.com

To my wife, Margaret
and to our children,
Louise, Kate and Daniel

CONTENTS

PREFACE

For those of us who carried out research on the conflict in Northern Ireland the temptation was always to procrastinate. Better, we thought, to wait until whatever current political initiative had played itself out. It seemed that we shared the fatalism of the people of Northern Ireland as a whole. Darker forces beyond our control seemed to be in play. That began to change when the President of Sinn Féin, Gerry Adams, met the British Prime Minister in Belfast on 14 October 1997. More symbolic was the picture of Adams and Martin McGuinness emerging from 10 Downing Street in December of that year. Less than seven years after the IRA attempted to mortar Downing Street when the cabinet was supposed to be in session, and more than seventy-five years after Arthur Griffith and Michael Collins met with the British Prime Minister, Lloyd George, in 1921, the politics of inclusion was back in vogue. History was being made and the population was sloughing off the dead weight of fatalism. Now was the time to take stock. That was the genesis of this book.

The research findings presented here have followed a circuitous route. In the early 1980s I began a project on the nature of direct rule in Northern Ireland. One of the obstacles I encountered was a lack of access to senior political and official actors. Some were prepared to co-operate but the picture was not complete. Officials in the Northern Ireland Office were erring on the side of caution. I turned my attention to Dublin – in part as a means of leverage on the Whitehall machine – and there I met with a more open system. It seemed to me that until both governments worked in harmony and proactively there would never be the beginnings of a solution. My interest switched from the narrow ground of direct rule to the larger arena of Anglo-Irish relations. In its turn that led to a concern with the nature of diplomacy and the impact of geopolitics. By the 1990s I was engaged with others in some efforts at unofficial diplomacy. There was a series of confidential workshops held well away from Northern Ireland with politicians from across the political divide. The cumulative effect of these meetings convinced me that we needed to separate the rhetoric of politicians from what they perceived to be 'doable'. In short, even when the public picture looked bleak there was some cause for optimism given favourable circumstances

The optimism is written into 'The Agreement Reached in Multi-party Negotiations' – to give the official title to the agreement signed on Good Friday 1998. Here was a triumph of Anglo-Irish diplomacy in the post–Cold War world. It was hailed as an example of how even the most intractable conflicts can be made more malleable given a fair wind. But it raises the question of why it took thirty years of intense conflict to reach an understanding of the problem before a solution could be implemented. That question suggested that we had to concern ourselves with a study of the mindsets and with the many mis-perceptions which have existed between the two islands for centuries. In essence the book became a study in *time* and *place* in Anglo-Irish relations. That is not to say that it is either a conventional study of intergovermental relations or a textbook on conflict resolution. Rather it is a work of synthesis drawing on several disciplines.

The book, decidedly, is not a chronology but a thematic study con-cerned with the nature of complexity in political relationships. Among other things it examines the life-span of a conflict – of potential inter-ventions by internal and external actors which may challenge conven-tional notions of state sovereignty; of choosing the moment when an intervention is most likely to succeed; of being conscious of geopoliti-cal change which allows for shifts in political discourse; and of ac-knowledging the role of interdependence. That enables us to look at the shifting patterns of Irish nationalism and Ulster unionism; at the role of diasporas in shaping (and resolving) conflicts; and being able to trace attitudinal change while allowing for such intangibles in politics as myth-making and symbolism.

The geography of the book needs some explanation. At the heart of it is the notion of three separate 'solitudes' represented by Belfast, Dublin and London. We need to trace the extent to which they grew apart and more recent efforts to bring them together. Thus the first three chapters centre mostly on the historic conflict within Northern Ireland up until the announcement of the two cessations of violence in 1994. Their concerns are with identity and with intra- as well as inter-ethnic conflict. Chapters 4 and 5 concentrate on the Dublin–London dimension until the 1980s. The following three chapters move beyond, and return to, the archipelago with attention being paid to the world system and to diaspora issues. Chapter 9 is centred firmly on political movement in the 1980s and the extent to which that laid foundations for the progress that was made in the 1990s. The last chapter examines the first tentative steps in implementing the peace process. It does not pretend to be anything more than a sketch because it is much too early to be definitive about the degree to which we have put our ancient quarrel behind us. It is guardedly optimistic in that it assumes that we have reached the beginning of the end.

ACKNOWLEDGEMENTS

I have been fortunate to work in a research-active department for the past quarter century. We worked on the assumption that active research informs good teaching. While we have concentrated on different aspects of the Northern Ireland question we have not always shared the same convictions. That has allowed for a robust diversity of opinion and a healthy pluralism. Thus I have benefited from the research of colleagues and former colleagues such as Arthur Aughey, Alan Bairner, Paul Bew, Paul Hainsworth, Keith Jeffrey, Duncan Morrow, Henry Patterson, and Carmel Roulston. My bibliography gives some indication of the debt of gratitude I owe to the wider academic community, none more so than Bernard Crick who has given me active encouragement throughout my academic career. The University of Ulster has contributed in many ways as well. The library staff at our Jordanstown and Magee campuses have been extremely helpful in meeting even the most trivial of requests. The Faculty of Humanities has been very generous in its support for my research, and I must thank in particular Tony Morris, Peter Roebuck, Tom Fraser, Alan Sharp and Terry O'Keefe. But above all it is our students who bear the brunt of our obsessions. I have been testing my ideas on our Master's degree in Peace and Conflict Studies for many years and I have learnt a great deal from their lively participation in these classes.

Particular individuals have been especially helpful with this project. I was fortunate to secure a Senior Fellowship in the Jennings Randolph Program for International Peace at the United States Institute of Peace in Washington DC from 1997 to 1998 to work on a project on unofficial diplomacy. That equipped me with an insider's view of the American political process as well as the space to reflect on the Anglo–Irish conflict from afar. The staff at USIP made my sojourn there most enjoyable. The Director of the Program, Joe Klaits, and his Program Officers, John Crist and Sally Blair, could not have been more helpful. The other Senior Fellows drawn from all corners of the world shared their insights with me in a series of seminars we organised jointly. My research assistant, Kimberley Cowell-Mayers, managed to bring some discipline and order into my work, and encouraged me to pursue this project. When I returned to the University of Ulster I moved into an office with the Initiative on Conflict Resolution and Ethnicity (INCORE) where I relied on the support of a number of research assistants. Desirée Neilsson from Sweden, who worked with me on a project on 'Memory and Forgiveness', gave me the freedom to pursue my Anglo-Irish interests and managed my administrative nightmare. Anna-Kaisa Kuusistsu from Finland assisted in the early stages of drafting the book, but, above all, Christer Grenabo from Sweden took on all the arduous and nit-picking details when I was up against a tight deadline. I owe Christer a huge debt of gratitude. My computer problems were handled with great tact and patience by Mike McCool and Norman Blair. Another group who made all of this possible were those private individuals, politicians and officials whom I interviewed in Belfast, Dublin, London, Washington and New York and who were very generous with their time and advice. Only a few are acknowledged in the text. The rest wished to preserve their anonymity but they know who they are.

Lastly none of this would have been possible without the tremendous help of Blackstaff. I took the idea of this book to Anne Tannahill late in the day. She took it on board immediately and has given me active support in the meantime. Patsy Horton brought her considerable editing skills and diplomatic abilities to the task; and as I approached the end Finber O'Shea set me very high professional standards, not all of which, alas, I attained. All of the above, of course, are professionals. They did not have to deal with the human side. My family had to bear that. For them the siege has been lifted. And it is to them – my wife, Margaret, and my children, Louise, Kate and Daniel – that I dedicate this book.

LIST OF ABBREVIATIONS

CSJ	Campaign for Social Justice
DUP	Democratic Unionist Party
EEC	European Economic Community
IFI	International Fund for Ireland
INC	Irish National Caucus
IRA	Irish Republican Army
NILP	Northern Ireland Labour Party
NIO	Northern Ireland Office
NORAID	Irish Northern Aid Committee
NSC	National Security Council
RAF	Royal Air Force
RUC	Royal Ulster Constabulary
SDLP	Social Democratic and Labour Party
UDA	Ulster Defence Association
UUP	Ulster Unionist Party
UUUC	United Ulster Unionist Council
UVF	Ulster Volunteer Force
UWC	Ulster Workers' Council
VUPP	Vanguard Unionist Progressive Party

1

THE THREE SOLITUDES

Lloyd George conjured [the Irish question] out of existence
with a solution which was accepted by all except rigorous
extremists in the IRA.

A. J. P. TAYLOR[1]

. . . after twenty years of study by hundreds of researchers, there is
still only partial agreement on the nature of the problem, and none at
all on the nature of the solution.

JOHN WHYTE[2]

. . . and now we are sadly the last imperial aspidistra in the
British window.

EDDIE McATEER[3]

Hindsight is not a particularly attractive device. It is easy to mock the
dictums of the Elders. Taylor's book was published in 1965, that is,
at a time of comparative peace in Northern Ireland. And it was self-
consciously *English*. The thrust of this chapter is to demonstrate the
patently self-obvious: that not only did the Irish 'settlement' of 1920–1
not work but it stored up problems for later generations. The consequences of the Government of Ireland Act of 1920 and the Anglo-
Irish Treaty of 1921 have had a malign impact on the politics of the
island of Ireland ever since. Three 'solitudes' – centred round Belfast,
Dublin and London – were created. They produced their own discrete
political cultures and their own competing mind-sets. In the late 1960s
when politicians had to revisit the problems that the Government of
Ireland Act was meant to have solved they discovered that there was no
political road-map to chart the way forward. They had to start from
scratch.

We will be looking at this seminal period of 1920–2 in some detail to place it in its political, temporal and spatial contexts. As an antidote to the Anglocentricity of the Taylor thesis our starting-point shall be the dynamics of 'British history', what J.G.A. Pocock speculatively calls 'the historiography of no single nation but of a problematic and un-completed experiment in the creation and interaction of several nations'.[4] We are concerned with that problematic and uncompleted experiment, with the 'unfinished business' of Northern Ireland, not in a narrow Irish nationalist sense, but as a reaction against navel con-templation. Some eighty years after the island was partitioned we shall see that the 'Northern Ireland problem' is but Anglo–Irish relations writ small; and that rather than concentrate solely on Belfast and the muddy byways of Fermanagh and Tyrone we shall be looking as well at Dublin and London, Brussels and (later) Washington. In short, this chapter will be concerned with a study in crisis management.

A more realistic approach to dealing with the conflict was the sign-ing of the Anglo–Irish Agreement on 15 November 1985 and of the 'Agreement Reached in the Multi-Party Negotiations' in Belfast on Good Friday 1998: for the latter I give the official title, its place of birth and the (religious) date of its signature in that order because all three titles – the 'Agreement', the 'Belfast Agreement' and the 'Good Friday Agreement' – are adopted as a form of ethnic shorthand. The signing of these two documents illustrated the extent to which both govern-ments had come to rely on each other and was some distance from the admonition which the British Foreign Secretary, Michael Stewart, de-livered to the Irish Minister for External Affairs, Patrick Hillery, in London on 1 August 1969 when, according to Hillery, he advised him that 'the matter [of Northern Ireland] was none of mine or my Government's business'.[5]

These two agreements form the backcloth of this book. They will be used to illustrate the significance of a proper sense of time-scales before one begins to speak of a 'solution'; to suggest that constitutional in-novation is a prerequisite for dealing with such a complex problem in the late twentieth/early twenty-first century; and, as a corollary, to argue that consent rather than territoriality should be the guiding principle in adjudicating such disputes. But before we consider these issues we need to pay some attention to the constituent parts re-presented by Belfast, Dublin and London, and to the peculiar form of governance inside the United Kingdom known as the 'Dual Polity'.

PARTITION

It is not too difficult to understand the optimism implicit in Taylor's remarks in 1965. Ireland had been enjoying its longest period of peace since the beginning of the nineteenth century. Superficially, relations between the two communities inside Northern Ireland appeared to be better than they had ever been; and (by the admittedly relaxed standards of a deeply conservative polity) the new Prime Minister, Captain Terence O'Neill, seemed to be a liberal. Relations between Dublin and London had never been better, and the British Prime Minister, Harold Wilson, conveyed the impression that he was sensitive to Irish needs.

But Taylor's analysis was based on the 1920s and not on the 1960s. Lloyd George's genius had been to manage to extricate Britain from the Irish imbroglio at minimum cost. By establishing two parliaments and governments in Ireland he had quarantined the Irish issue from British politics. At a stroke Irish representation at Westminster was reduced from 105 MPs to 46 (and then to 13 Northern Ireland MPs). British troops were withdrawn and control was left in the hands of indigenous forces. He had succeeded where no Prime Minister had succeeded before, and he could take some comfort from the fact that no successor would be placed in the invidious position in which Robert Peel found himself in 1829 when he remarked that 'in the course of the last six months, England being at peace with the whole world has had five-sixths of the infantry force of the United Kingdom occupied in maintaining the peace and in police duties in Ireland'.[6]

Insofar as we can speak of the 'settlement' embodied in the Government of Ireland Act and the Anglo-Irish Treaty as being a 'success' it was a British success but it did not deal with the fundamental problem. That much was recognised by Nicholas Mansergh when he made a devastatingly simple point in relation to the 1920–1 settlement: 'No reduction in the number of parties involved was achieved as a result of it. They remained as before, their conceptual approaches fundamentally unchanged, though now there were two sovereign states and a subordinate government where there had been a sovereign state, a national movement and a minority resistant to it.'[7] Not only were there still three parties to the conflict and not only did their fundamental beliefs hold but the very ambiguity of the settlement enabled them to indulge in self-delusion, self-pity and self-protection.

Part of the ambiguity lay in the transitional status of Ireland. At the second reading of the Government of Ireland Bill on 29 March 1920 the Chief Secretary for Ireland, James Ian Macpherson, held out the prospect of Irish unity at some future date: 'recent events, I am sorry to say, have only strengthened the view that an undivided Ireland for the purposes of legislation of this kind is in the meantime impossible. All of us hope that the division may be temporary only, and our arrangement has, therefore, been to frame the Bill in such a manner as may lead to a union between the two parts of Ireland.' He held out the prospect of a Council of Ireland which could become 'virtually a Parliament for all Ireland, and from that stage to complete union is but a very slight and very easy transition'.[8]

The 'temporary' arrangement slipped inexorably into permanence but there were doubts as to whether the 1920 Act was designed for permanent effect. Its provisions, Nicholas Mansergh asserts, 'were dictated with a view to political pacification rather than administrative efficiency. When Southern Ireland broke away from British rule, the Act was amended in form so as to be applicable to Northern Ireland alone. But it was not amended in substance. As a consequence, powers were delegated to Northern Ireland which had been drafted to meet a quite different situation. No regard was paid to the needs of the six counties as a political and economic unit.'[9] The absurdity of this administrative inefficiency could be seen in the 'very geographic irrationality' of a land boundary stretching more than three hundred miles which bisected 'villages, farms, fields and even on occasions shops and houses'.[10] The acceptance of this boundary caused immediate problems for unionists in Northern Ireland. It meant desertion of their fellow Ulster Protestants in counties Monaghan, Cavan and Donegal. It meant taking on board a Catholic minority in Northern Ireland proportionally larger than the unionist minority in Ireland as a whole: 'The border was not devised to keep two warring groups apart ... This brought the warring groups together more than it separated them.'[11] Therein lay the Northern Ireland problem.

But it created problems, too, for Dublin. Despite the rhetoric there is evidence that as early as mid-1922 influential figures in the Irish government realised that Northern Ireland was too solidly established to be easily overcome, and that a 'united Ireland' under a nationalist banner was to be relegated to 'the status of a comfortable aspiration'.[12] The creation of a Boundary Commission with the ostensible purpose of arriving at a more equitable settlement sent out the wrong signals. It reinforced the unionist sense of siege and raised nationalist expectations. The final outcome did little to soothe the former and reconfirmed an Irish sense of perfidious Albion.[13] Dublin engaged in precisely the same territorial game as had the unionists in 1920. In 1922 the Southern government organised the North-Eastern Boundary Bureau 'to make the case for the largest possible transfer of territory ... for over three years the Free State concentrated on achieving adjustments in the boundary by the use of propaganda and avoided the fundamental issues, notably the refusal of northern unionists to entertain any notion of either unity or the reduction of their territory'.[14] This concentration on territoriality ruled out any proper dialogue between North and South for over fifty years.

Partition was a fashionable enough device in the postwar world. The Austro-Hungarian Empire was partitioned by the victorious allies – with consequences, it should be noted, not dissimilar to those which arose with the creation of Northern Ireland.[15] Before submitting to the Boundary Commission the Dublin authorities had studied European precedents, particularly plebiscites in Silesia, Schleswig-Holstein and Hungary. But partition involved issues of territoriality and self-determination. In a study comparing the Irish case with that in Bohemia/Moravia and West Prussia/Posen Frank Wright concluded that the history of the three frontiers had shown that 'the legitimacy of head counting had been largely discounted . . . The new settlement in Europe was the work of the victors, and everywhere issues that could not be settled according to simple ethnic criteria were settled in accordance with strategic considerations.'[16]

Britain had long realised that it could not maintain the integrity of the United Kingdom of Great Britain *and* Ireland. It recognised (to quote Wright again) the 'limits of its power in the frontier where it could not govern without the support of the citizen peoples'. Unionists recognised the same: 'The hidden dimension of Ulster Unionist leadership was its role in disguising the essential weakness of British state power in the ethnic frontier between 1887 and 1912.'[17] Hence the partition of the island for strategic purposes, with unionists happily acting as collaborators. But it was a partition that was not evenhanded. In a survey of T.G. Fraser's *Partition in Ireland, India and Palestine* John Whyte comments that the British made some effort in India to find a compromise which would avoid the need for partition but that the dissident minority in Ireland was treated with indulgence: 'This lack of evenhandedness gave colour to the traditional nationalist argument that the unionists were encouraged to display an intransigence which they would not have shown if they had not been able to count on British support.'[18]

In all of these circumstances we can see that partition was simply an expedient which suited the British authorities and did little to deal with the real political problems it left behind in Ireland. Unionists did not lose their sense of siege – indeed up until the Boundary Commission deliberated in 1925 they could not even be certain of the boundaries of their territory – or nationalists their sense of betrayal. But besides this psychological backwash partition left a fundamental institutional inheritance whose import was not appreciated until the British and Irish authorities were confronted once again with the 'Northern Ireland problem' after 1968.

In short, partition created two solitudes (represented by Dublin and Belfast) overseen by an allegedly neutral arbiter (London), which was in essence another solitude: 'Two sovereigns exist where there was one, but their relationship has been marred by the residue of a long and bitter antagonism'[19] – that is their dispute over the third solitude. The object of the long and bitter antagonism was, of course, Northern Ireland. Reason suggested that Northern Ireland would seek shelter in the warm embrace of the Union: history dictated otherwise. Instead, like King Utopos in More's *Utopia* who had a channel dug to separate his kingdom from the mainland, Northern Ireland discovered that 'physical separation, of which insularity is the perfect avatar, creates favourable conditions for separate political development'.[20] Belfast and London shared a mutual accommodation but lasting relationships cannot be built on anything so instrumental. More strikingly there was even less accommodation between Dublin and London and, for that matter, between Belfast and Dublin. The solitudes went their separate ways – although it might be said that Dublin benefited from partition because, in Joseph Lee's felicitous phrase, it 'now saved the South from the most explosive internal problems subverting new states, race and religion, by the simple device of exporting them to the North'.[21]

THE BELFAST–DUBLIN AXIS

Beyond the facts that it was on the Liffey, that it was deficient
in industry, that it was addicted to drink, and that it contained
Guinness's brewery, there was little to be said about Dublin.

DENIS IRELAND[22]

It is not too startling to suggest that a cold war existed between North and South. They could not even agree on how to address each other. As early as 1922 the Provisional Government in Dublin spoke of 'North-East Ulster', and as late as 1969 official Irish government publications referred to the 'Six Counties'.[23] A mirror image could be found in Northern Ireland. Lord Craigavon's biographer, St John Ervine, suggested that the citizens of Éire be called 'Eireans', and in a futile attempt to wed Northern Ireland more closely to Great Britain Sir Wilfrid Spender, the Permanent Secretary of Northern Ireland's

Finance Ministry during the 1920s and 30s, suggested changing 'Northern Ireland' into 'North West Britain'.[24]

Cabinet papers for the years between 1947 and 1953 show Sir Basil Brooke, the Northern Ireland Prime Minister, to be obsessed about the whole question of terminology. There was even confusion in Whitehall: in 1947, for example, the Foreign Office confessed: 'Éire's anomalous position causes confusion even in our own ranks.' In 1949 a majority of a working party of senior Whitehall officials agreed with Brooke's suggestion that Northern Ireland's name be changed to 'Ulster' on the departure of the Republic of Ireland from the Commonwealth. The Prime Minister, Clement Attlee, rejected that proposal, as he did another suggestion from Brooke that the title 'Irish Republic' rather than 'Republic of Ireland' be used in the Ireland Act (1949) (since, it was alleged, the former gave credence to the Republic's territorial claim over Northern Ireland). In 1952, and again in 1953, the cabinet papers show that Brooke continued to fight old battles.[25]

It would be foolish to dismiss this simply as narrow-mindedness. Behind it all lay the more fundamental problem of status. After all, the settlement had created two sovereign states and a subordinate government. That government was reluctant to accept its inferior status and was irritated to learn that 'Westminster's overriding concern [was] to arrive at and maintain a peace with the South' and later to recognise 'the Provisional Government's need to survive in the South'.[26] Partition predated independence for the South by six months. Formally it began when the Northern Ireland Parliament was opened in June 1921. In December that year the Anglo-Irish Treaty was signed and unionists immediately denounced it as a betrayal and a disgrace: 'Unionist objections were threefold: to the principle of the Treaty, which theoretically included Northern Ireland in the Free State with the option of leaving; to the financial provisions which were thought likely to lead to high taxation and a tariff barrier, all to the detriment of Northern Ireland; and above all else, to the proposed Boundary Commission to look again at the North's territorial limits.'[27] In a damage limitation exercise the two respective leaders in Ireland, Sir James Craig and Michael Collins, held two meetings in London in January and March 1922. They concentrated on the Boundary Commission, on the Council of Ireland and on the removal of an economic boycott of the North by Dublin in return for Craig's undertaking to facilitate the return of Catholic workers to the Belfast shipyards. Here were all the ingredients of North–South conflict: claims of discrimination, concern with economic problems and fundamental difficulties over status. The last proved intractable. Craig had suggested that the Council of Ireland be replaced by joint meetings of both cabinets and that 'in all matters under the purview of the Council' each government consult each other 'on terms of equality'. Collins countered with a proposal for a meeting of all Irish representatives (to involve the Catholic minority in the North), and he feared that 'terms of equality' would give the unionists a veto.[28]

Dublin was consciously exploiting this asymmetrical relationship (just as it was conscious of its own asymmetrical relationship with London). Belfast's subordinate status was but one weapon in the campaign against partition. And the story of the next fifty years was an account of Dublin trying to distance itself still further from British dominance. That very struggle added to the distance between North and South. Following the outbreak of civil war in the South and the assassination of Michael Collins in August 1922 his successor, W.T. Cosgrave, met Craig in London on 10 November in one final attempt to solve their differences. They got on well together but it made absolutely no difference to the integrity of their quarrel. With the exception of a conference at Chequers in December 1925 to discuss the implications of the Boundary Commission there was no formal contact between the leaders of both parts of Ireland until Seán Lemass met Terence O'Neill at Stormont in January 1965 – although during 1949, the year that the Republic left the Commonwealth, Sean MacBride, the South's Minister for External Affairs, had two behind-the-scenes meetings with Sir Basil Brooke and three or four meetings with the Unionist Party Chief Whip, William Topping; and in 1957 the ennobled Lord Brookeborough (still Prime Minister) had low-level contact with J.C. Cole, a member of the Senate in Dublin.[29]

For the most part an iron curtain had descended in 1922 and contact between both parts of Ireland was kept to a minimum. That is not to say that there was no official contact – nor, for that matter, that social contacts were discouraged. But once the Northern Ireland government absorbed the powers of the Council of Ireland (in December 1925) there was no machinery, even in theory, for cross-border cooperation between the two governments other than the provision for the possibility of inter-governmental meetings on matters of common interest. They did not take place, although section 1 of the Northern Ireland Act (1947) removed territorial restrictions to enable Stormont to legislate and enter into agreement with the Irish government concerning cross-border schemes for electricity, transport and drainage. One such example was the Foyle Fisheries Commission which was established in 1952 with responsibility for protecting and conserving the Foyle drainage area that straddled the Derry–Donegal border. More structured arrangements emerged from the mid-1960s but it is only with the signing of the Anglo-Irish Agreement in 1985 that we can begin to speak of closer functional cooperation.

In addition the people of both parts of Ireland were badly served by the communications industry. In his perceptive analysis of 'Northern attitudes to the independent Irish state 1919–49' (to quote the subtitle of his book) Dennis Kennedy notes that 'the press was part of the mobilised Protestant community in the North' and yet none of the three major unionist newspapers, the *Northern Whig,* the *Belfast Telegraph* and the *News Letter,* had a staff correspondent based in Dublin. Only two annual events in the South – the General Synod of the Church of Ireland and the Dublin Horse Show – were reported on consistently by these newspapers. That is not to say that events in the South were ignored. Kennedy notes that during the entire period three Southern themes received substantial coverage and editorial comment in the Northern press: the constitutional evolution of the Irish Free State away from the position agreed in the Anglo-Irish Treaty of 1921; after 1932, Eamon de Valera's explicit moves to eliminate all vestiges and symbols of British rule; and the position of the Protestant or unionist minority in the Free State. We are not here concerned with a detailed analysis of these themes save to comment on the fact that their very choice (and the treatment they received) suggests a certain distortion of a more complex reality. Kennedy quotes from a Stormont parliamentary debate when a Unionist MP offered his views on the peoples of Ireland: 'There are two peoples in Ireland, one industrious, law-abiding and God-fearing, and the other slothful, murderous and disloyal.'[30] It does not take too much imagination to decode which was which, nor would it be too much to suggest that such an opinion would have received popular endorsement.

The Southern press was in no better position to deliver dispassionate analysis on the North. For example, Joseph Lee quotes from the *Irish Press* (1 April 1943): 'There is no kind of oppression visited on any minority in Europe which the Six County nationalists have not also endured' – which leads him to comment that that revelation 'would no doubt have helped the victims lining up for the Auschwitz gas chambers'. Similarly Lee quotes from directions to sub-editors from the editor of the *Irish Press* in which he warns them to be on 'guard against the habits of British and foreign news agencies who look at the world mainly through imperialist eyes'.[31] Irish journalism, either north or south of the border, could not be accused of such universality.

It is easy to exaggerate the lack of contact between North and South (especially at the political level). Where contact did arise – as, for example, during the IRA campaign of 1956–62 – it was often mediated through London. And the nature of that contact could be both controversial and contradictory. Successive Irish governments found that they could do little about the North except act as a kind of ombudsman for the Catholic minority. That was resented in the North where Dublin was perceived as being in a perpetual sulk, and, paradoxically, in the South where the Northern minority was often seen as being a burden on the South.[32] As a consequence the Irish political elite settled into a form of passivity. The picture was not quite so bleak in the private sector. In a survey of 898 private organisations operating throughout Ireland in 1983 John Whyte revealed that 'a substantial minority (174 bodies), or practically 20 per cent of the total, operate across the international frontier, either on an all-Ireland basis (116 bodies) or an all-archipelago one (58)'. He believed that that figure underestimated the extent of cross-border activity, and he noted that among these bodies all the major churches were represented, as were many youth and sporting organisations. Writing in 1983, that is at a time when the Anglo-Irish process was being revived, he concluded that the 'unusual degree to which the Anglo-Irish border is already permeated by private organisations may prove to have some, if limited, political significance'.[33]

Under the circumstances it is hardly surprising that Dublin was unprepared for the 'Troubles' after 1968. One reason lies in its stereotyping of the North, and in the fact that so much effort after 1922 had gone into state-building in the South to demonstrate its own autonomy. The historic 'nation' had to take a back seat in the interim. But another reason why Dublin could not respond rapidly and positively to the outbreak of the Troubles was that it had invested so much in highlighting the distinctiveness between North and South. What it failed to recognise was the degree of similarity in the two systems: that was something it shared with Belfast.

COMMONALITIES?

'L'Irlande est une île derrière une île.'

JEAN BLANCHARD[34]

In any global comparison both parts of Ireland suffer from the common disadvantage that an obvious reference point will always be Britain. Northern Ireland has been portrayed consistently as the poor relation of the United Kingdom, although two caveats need to be entered. The first is that 'the tendency has been to compare Northern

Ireland with either Britain or the United Kingdom as a whole to the inevitable disadvantage of the province'.[35] The second is that the comparison does not compare like with like. Northern Ireland was the only region within the United Kingdom to 'enjoy' devolution: 'Fundamentally, however, unlike the other poorer areas of the United Kingdom, the province was expected to live off the revenue generated within it.'[36] Tom Wilson takes that a stage further when he asserts: 'Over much the greater part of its half century of legislative devolution, the Province was treated *less* favourably than comparable regions in Great Britain. It was only on the eve of its dissolution that the Stormont government began to receive more equitable treatment and, even then, there was a substantial backlog, especially in deficient social capital, that had yet to be made good.'[37] An equally bleak picture of the Southern economy appears in the textbooks. Whyte's survey of the literature leads him to conclude that not only is the Republic a relatively poor society but it is also a relatively unequal one.[38] And yet, as Lee concedes, the South entered the task of state-building with many advantages: 'The Free State, then, inherited relatively strong economic, educational, social and political infrastructures'; however, over time, 'a native entrepreneurial cadre' failed to emerge. 'Irish-owned industry could not compete internationally. It could not even compete on the home market.'[39]

In David Fitzpatrick's survey of the two Irelands commonalities are found in terms of welfare, education and morality (and all to the detriment of both).[40] The two solitudes had a distorted and degraded view of each other,[41] and when all else failed England could always be blamed. Had they taken the trouble to look at each other dispassionately they would have discovered that they had not dissimilar political cultures.[42] Both were deeply conservative. Dennis Kennedy wonders, for instance, 'why there was no evolution of Unionism', and asserts that as a political philosophy it 'remained little more than a response to Irish nationalism' and as a political movement it was not equipped 'to present coherent policies on the areas of administration and government now being allocated to the devolved administration and government'.[43] The Minister for Home Affairs in the first Free State government, Kevin O'Higgins, told the Dáil in 1922: 'We were probably the most conservative minded revolutionaries that ever put through a successful revolution.'[44] Successive Dublin governments devised an educational system that was devoted to a defence of existing social (and religious) structures. And in the early years they pursued equally conservative budgetary policies.[45] The deep sense of religiosity on both sides of the border needs no comment at this stage. Both pursued rigid law and order policies and both shared common problems in relation to a narrow economic base.

Emigration presents a similarly depressing picture – the 'most poignant symbol of material failure' in the two Irelands, according to Fitzpatrick.[46] At one extreme its root cause was easy to detect. Lee quotes an unnamed Dáil deputy who said in May 1937 that 'without fear of contradiction' the 'main cause of that emigration, of all the poverty, and of anything else that is wrong politically, nationally and economically with the country is due to the partition of Ireland'.[47] That highlights the degree to which emigration has to be seen in emotional terms. Emigration created its own powerful sense of grievance, sometimes shared and sometimes divisive. Wright notes its contradictory hold over time:

> Just as the Famine came to be seen by nationalists as the start of a deliberate effort to scatter the Irish race, unionists came to represent the different experiences of the North as proof of Protestant industry and achievement. These ethnic reinterpretations of the Famine rubbed away the confused edges of shared experience, and the emigration question ceased to be the common experience that had held together the Land League–Liberal agitation of 1880–81. Once Unionist power was established in 1920 differential emigration rates became a malignant political focal point.[48]

Indeed 'Craig's government applauded it as a sign of imperial integration'.[49]

Kerby Miller draws attention to the negative aspects of emigration and argues that 'as the central experience of post-famine life, emigration demanded interpretation in political and religious contexts'. Central to this interpretation was

> emigration as exile, as *in*voluntary expatriation, which was obliged by forces beyond both individual choice and communal control: sometimes by fate or destiny, but usually by the political and economic consequences of 'British misgovernment', 'Protestant ascendancy' and 'landlord tyranny' . . . the misperception of emigration as political banishment was integral to Catholic Irishmen's sense of individual and collective identity.[50]

That same sense of collective grievance was brought to bear on post-partition Ireland (although, as usual, the evidence was used selectively). Generally, nationalists pointed to the fact that although Catholics were only one-third of the population in Northern Ireland they provided 55–8 per cent of the emigrants, while unionists have laid great political weight on the decline of Protestant numbers in the South since partition (although the 'Protestant emigration rate has actually been below the Catholic one – 50 per cent lower in the intercensal period 1961–71'[51]).

It is not our purpose to decode the competing propaganda claims but simply to make the point that emigration was a feature of life in both parts of Ireland and that it had a devastating effect on the maturing of the different polities: perhaps the most graphic quantative example is provided by Lee when he writes that four out of every five children born in Ireland between 1931 and 1941 emigrated in the 1950s.[52] (The traffic was not always one way: apparently there were 7,000 immigrants into Ireland in 1932 escaping from the depressed British and American economies,[53] and when the Irish economy picked up in the 1960s there was a huge return of the emigrants and their families.) Perhaps a more significant point – and one which pervades political culture on both sides of the border – is the extent to which emigration as a safety valve helped to produce a dependency mentality: the belief that there were others on whom we could rely on to look after our problems.

A final area which suggests a greater coincidence of method than either government might have been prepared to acknowledge lies in the conduct of security policy. Again, we must look to the pre-partition period to discover whether there has been a common strand. Since the nineteenth century Ireland can be seen as an ideal laboratory for testing the role of policing in crisis politics.[54] Its forces of law and order had been militia based. London relied on centralised rather than local forces. Ireland was left with a gendarmerie although that was repugnant to the English public mind. Law was to function as the expression of the impulse to order: between 1800 and 1921 there were 105 separate Coercion Acts dealing with Ireland and the suspension of habeas corpus was imposed on four separate occasions for a total of eleven years. In short, Ireland was being governed 'in answer to a British strategic imperative rather than any imagined duty to the people.'[55] The gamut of emotions and the mentality behind the enforcement of order in Ireland have been exposed by Townshend: 'the martial law problem', was 'a permanent underlying feature of Anglo-Irish relations. British rule in Ireland so often found itself paralysed because it could neither operate on English principles (because it did not have sufficient public co-operation) nor abandon English principles and govern by the direct application of force. It had to preserve the show and rhetoric of "civilisation".'[56]

When Northern Ireland came into existence it inherited these parameters of policing practice. By 1922 Northern Ireland had a ratio of one policeman to every six families so that the tradition of paramilitary-type policing held. Southern Ireland had more reason to be pleased with its policing practice after early scares. Its police were unarmed, a matter of justifiable pride. But as Eanna Mulloy reminds us the use of coercive measures in the South did not end with British administration.[57] Michael Farrell illustrates the point when he writes that since 'its birth in 1922, the Irish Republic and its predecessor, the Irish Free State, have scarcely ever been without emergency legislation on the statute book'.[58] Farrell acknowledges that there is a difference between legislation on the statute book and the uses to which it is put. And he provides some reasons why it is there: 'The State was born out of a compromise of the national aspiration that provoked a civil war ... Its legitimacy was slightly tainted, and there was always the plight of the Northern minority to act as a reminder ...'[59]

Just as we can establish that there was a commonality in their respective use of emergency legislation we would have to acknowledge, equally, that there was a difference of intensity in its use, North and South. The reason for that difference is, clearly, the distinction between a stable and a deeply divided society. But the reason for the retention of emergency legislation is also a consequence of partition and the British heritage. As they chose to ignore each other and address only their separate solitudes (and the British 'arbiter') perhaps what united them was this very dependency; and that as a result of partition 'Ireland's dual revolution had secured local power for the two dominant populist movements which had resisted British authority between 1912 and 1921'.[60]

THE DUAL POLITY

Northern Ireland's position inside the United Kingdom is easily – and frequently – misunderstood. It appears to be full of paradox: a successful implantation of the Westminster model which went horribly wrong; ultraloyal territory prepared to demonstrate its loyalty through acts of disloyalty; and a deeply conservative polity which (since 1972) has become an adventure playground for constitutional tinkering. To have any appreciation of its standing we need to adopt a fluid approach to an understanding of its historical evolution – and that presents another paradox since many of its unionist proponents insisted on a static model.

Again we return to Pocock's innovative attempt to open a debate on 'British' historiography where he explains that not only have 'the various peoples and nations, ethnic cultures, social structures, and locally defined communities, which have from time to time existed in the area known as "Great Britain and Ireland" ... acted so as to create the conditions of their several existences but [they] have also interacted so as to modify the conditions of one another's existence'.[61] The unionists of Northern Ireland have been too defensively introspective (especially in the Stormont years when they were left largely to their own devices) to recognise the significance of interaction.

They were more concerned with creating their own existence. And in any case they were bound in a straitjacket of 'Britishness', a liability not visited on their neighbours to the south. Independent Ireland had gone its own way to become the 'counterpolity of modern British history ... [a] political order created by assimilation to a parliamentary kingdom was used to establish a polity outside it'.[62] This section aims to examine the constraints (self?) imposed on unionism after 1920 by tracing its relationship with the mother country. Before proceeding down that road we must acknowledge the obvious. At its creation Northern Ireland was not a *tabula rasa*: it had its own psychology, its own culture and its own little place in the evolution of 'British' history; and it was encouraged to develop its sense of isolation by British politicians eager to keep their distance from Belfast.

Political science recognises the temporal as well as the spatial, and in an impressive overview Jim Bulpitt offers a simple definition of the structure of power in the United Kingdom. He dubs it the Dual Polity: 'a structure of territorial politics in which Centre and periphery had relatively little to do with each other', whereby 'until recently the Centre sought not to govern the United Kingdom but to manage it'. In terms of its management of the domestic environment, Bulpitt says that the Centre – which he defines as 'a political-administrative community composed of senior ministers and top civil servants' – 'will attempt to construct what can be labelled an external support system, that is to say, it will attempt to minimise the impact of external forces on domestic politics, or ensure that these forces are favourable to the maintenance of domestic tranquillity'.[63] He ranges widely over time and space in the search for 'a positive Unionist culture ... the idea that the United Kingdom was "one and indivisible" '.[64] He acknowledges the difficulties: that the political settlement worked out for the United Kingdom in the years following 1688 was 'highly ambiguous', and that the Union was based on its 'contractual' nature. And finally he accepts that Northern Ireland was/is the most extreme example of duality in the United Kingdom.[65]

Bulpitt's analysis serves as a good starting-point for the debate on territoriality and identity which has never been far from the surface in unionist politics. At times of relative tranquillity it was incipient, but at times of crisis – such as the period after 1910 or after the imposition of direct rule in 1972 or the signing of the Anglo-Irish Agreement in 1985 – it spilt over into the public domain. It can be studied on two levels: a philosophical debate on whether the Union is based on the 'classic "Whig" position [in which] one's relationship to the regime is defined by a social contract (more precisely, a "contract of government") by which the ruler and the ruled undertake certain obligations to each other';[66] or whether, as a practical consideration, the territory had developed, or could develop, a 'security community' which Karl Deutsch et al. define as a set of interrelationships 'in which there is a real assurance that the members of the community will not fight each other physically, but will settle their disputes in some other way'.[67]

Concepts of political obligation and the security community can be interrelated. Again Pocock is useful with his distinction between 'zones of law' and 'zones of war'. The former is defined by settled government and the latter is one in which the king or his subjects can make their presence effective only in arms. But it is possible that the king may rule 'a bifurcated realm or a realm having two faces: it is theoretically possible to distinguish between the "domain" where his writ runs and his clerks of justice assert his sedentary authority, and the "march" where his power is the sum of his relations with powerful military figures, feudatories or tributaries, subjects or aliens'.[68] Ulster (and later Northern Ireland) was a 'march' in search of a 'domain'.

As early as 1644 Ulster Protestants were engaged in contractarian social practice of long standing which had developed through 'the centuries of weak central government in the kingdom'; under this contractarian social practice the nobility and gentry 'had developed a tradition of entering into "bands" for mutual protection'. This tradition of 'public banding' became particularly pertinent for Protestant Ulster settlers unsure of their security in the Irish scheme of things:

> the Protestant tenantry were accustomed to being arrayed in arms under their landlords' leadership to maintain order ... The habit sustained in the Protestant community the sense that public order really derived more from their exertions than from the activities of the sovereign authority. Indeed, the central government might find itself bestowing its sanction on the militia only after the latter had in fact been constituted in the countryside.[69]

It was a practice that asserted itself especially during the final Home Rule crisis with the creation of the Ulster Volunteer Force (UVF) and the establishment of an Ulster provisional government under the leadership of Sir Edward Carson and Sir James Craig. Hence their reading of the 1920 settlement

> was that their state had come into existence by a process which seemed to conform to contractarian assumptions as to what was normal and right. A band had been entered into, its adherents had stood on their guard against the enemy, and in the end the sovereign authority seemed to have contracted with the banded community to exercise its sovereignty in the territory in question: to hold the pass against the king's enemies and their own.[70]

Even if we accept this version of events it raises questions about the nature of the relationship between the Centre (England) and the periphery, as well as the periphery's sense of its own identity. We have noted earlier Frank Wright's comment that the hidden dimension in the unionist leadership was its role in disguising the essential weakness of British state power in the ethnic state frontier between 1887 and 1912. But that was a dimension which had negative connotations because it suited the management of the Dual Polity. Unionists were ideal collaborators – 'stable, quiescent, efficient, and yet fundamentally weak in their relations with the Centre ... sustained by the Centre's indifference, not by peripheral strength'.[71] That was fine so long as the Centre remained indifferent. The 1920 Act can be read as the culmination of a process begun in Elizabeth I's reign of 'converting marches into colonies and colonies into polities operating within the framework of a subordinate parliamentary system'.[72] The devolved system in Northern Ireland was to be one such polity but by the time of the second Elizabethan reign questions were being asked about its status and stability. For that reason we need to spend some time trying to categorise (Protestant) Northern Ireland and its place in the scheme of things.

Peter Gibbon and J.C. Beckett allow for the emergence of an embryonic Ulster nationalism.[73] Richard Rose, applying social-psychological criteria, asserts that a case can be made for the 'creation of a nation-state' of Northern Ireland.[74] Tom Nairn writes of the 'peculiar fractured development of the Ulster-Protestant nationality' which is like 'a "mad" variable which falsifies every reasonable strategy of escape ... there is only one direction in which this change can now occur – that is, towards the formulation of a more than nominal "Ulster nationalism" '.[75]

That checklist could be lengthened. For the moment it serves a specific purpose: it demonstrates the difficulties encountered by policymakers in categorising one of the major actors. It is simple enough to describe them negatively; for example, Walker Connor quotes Max Weber approvingly: 'the sentiment of ethnic solidarity does not of itself make a "nation" '. Connor adds: 'To the degree that it represents a step in the process of nation-formation, it testifies that a group of people must know ethnically what they *are not* before they know what they *are*.'[76] To that could be added (borrowing again from Max Weber) that a sense of *ethnic honour*, that is, 'of the excellence of one's own customs and the inferiority of alien ones', grew up in Northern Ireland.[77] In place of the nation Ulster Protestants gathered behind a sense of ethnic honour. They assumed (without too much introspection) that they were British, but they compared their lot – especially after they were put in control of their own affairs – with the alien (and inferior) Catholic Irish.

They established their own existence by which they knew that they were not Irish – or, at least, not part of that Irish nation which had been fashioned by nineteenth-century Catholicism and a re-created Gaelic mythology. But it was an existence based, ultimately, on an illusion. That there had been an 'Ulster entity' in Ireland since at least the time of the introduction of the first Home Rule Bill (in 1886) could not be denied. But how to define it? David Miller has examined this process of definition and concludes that 'in the course of modernisation the Ulster protestant community developed feelings of nationality which were, at best, confused, ambivalent and fragile'. It was during these years that a Protestant *state* and a Protestant lack of a 'genuine feeling of co-nationality with the British people' emerged.[78]

In its own way the 1920 Act was as politically ambiguous as the 1688 settlement. It represented a political accommodation between the unionist leadership and a British government that wanted to quarantine the Irish issue from British politics. It did not rule out the possibility of eventual Irish unity; and over time it created a political unit which can best be described as 'a self-governing province with some of the trappings of sovereignty'.[79] We should recall the constitutional uncertainty surrounding the passage of the third Home Rule Bill. In February 1911 a powerful cabinet committee was formed to examine the whole question of devolution within the United Kingdom. It induced a debate which produced some highly original schemes – there was one suggestion that the Ulster counties be offered the option of joining a Scottish parliament instead of an Irish assembly; and the chairman, Lord Loreburn, wrote that Irish Home Rule should be treated as the first step towards Home Rule for all parts of the United Kingdom. A 'legislative enclave' would be created for Ulster so that laws affecting the four north-eastern counties could pass the Irish parliament only with the assent of a majority of the members representing those four counties – hence a form of Home Rule all round encompassing Home Rule within Home Rule.[80] What is interesting about the process as a whole is that it demonstrates some awareness of settling the 'Ulster' question in an overall United Kingdom context.

Britain's (unwitting?) strategy can be summarised as 'divide and depart', and a parallel can be drawn with the withdrawal from India. There, Jinnah, the Muslim leader, formulated the concept of two nations, Muslim and Hindu, since 'nations, unlike communities, negotiate as equals irrespective of size'. That is what he wanted to happen *before* power was transferred.' It provided him with 'at once a *rationale* for intransigence and a base from which to withstand Congress and British pressures for concessions'. The parallel with Northern Ireland is obvious except there 'the doctrine was at no point formulated in all its uncompromising bleakness'.[81]

It was a departure at a price because it enabled the Northern Ireland government to acquire delusions of grandeur through some of the trappings of sovereignty. But that was to take time. The putative Ulster state enjoyed few advantages at the outset. It had an administrative apparatus in place: the 'installation at Belfast of Sir Ernest Clark not only presaged partition four months before the 1920 Act became law, but initiated it in a practical way by the establishment of a central administrative apparatus working in the interests of the prospective Northern Ireland government. The British thus gave the Ulster Unionists their official blessing and active assistance in the process of building the wall of administrative partition.'[82]

On the other hand the 1920 Act withheld the instruments of physical force from the new governements (Dublin as well as Belfast) for a period of up to three years, at the discretion of the Westminster government. Miller writes that 'For five months Northern Ireland, if we consult only the statute book and the orders in council, did not constitute a state at all, but only a territory enjoying somewhat more extensive local government than an English county.' However he acknowledges that the reality was somewhat different because already the unionists had endowed themselves with the physical force necessary for the existence of the state, and the transfer of security powers on 22 November 1921 'was a mere formality'.[83] Indeed the following March the Chancellor of the Exchequer agreed to make a subvention to the Ulster Special Constabulary so long as it was buried in estimates making provision for unemployment and other services.

More worryingly, the administrative transition stopped short of a watertight definition of each entity, a fact acknowledged by Lloyd

George during the debate on the Government of Ireland Bill: 'Ulster is not a minority to be safeguarded. Ulster is an entity to be dealt with . . . I am not now going to enter into the question of whether there is one nation or two nations.'[84] But it was that precise problem which exercised the minds of Ulster Unionists before partition and, intermittently, ever since. It raised questions about their feeling of co-nationality with the British people so that they 'could not entrust their fate to "safeguards" which depended upon the willingness of that people to intervene in Irish affairs to rectify abuses'.[85]

In short, with the Government of Ireland Act (1920) unionists attained a measure of autonomy but not the requisite degree of self-confidence. Now they had to create their own existence. To some degree it was there already in their aggressive sense of isolation: 'Sinn Féin? Ourselves alone . . . It is we the Protestant people who have always stood alone. We have stood alone and triumphed, for we are God's chosen.'[86] It was an attitude of mind that drove unionists in on themselves. Even a former Northern Ireland Prime Minister could proclaim, 'Since I've become an Ulsterman I hate the English rather more.'[87] And collectively, in a 1968 survey, 66 per cent of Northern Ireland Protestants declared that they felt that 'their co-religionists in England . . . [were] much different from themselves'.[88]

DEVOLUTION AS ADMINISTRATIVE CONVENIENCE

Now that they had their own government and parliament Northern unionists were forced to address the question of how they treated with the Catholic minority, the Dublin government and the sovereign power in London. One interpretation of how this was handled is quoted at some length:

> Unionist politics in Northern Ireland between 1921 and 1972 was, in its character, a complex synthesis of both these elements ['sectarian exclusion' and 'liberal comprehension']. It exhibited a triumphalist, elitist group identity, and attempted to mould Ulster in an exclusive image. It also accommodated Ulster to the social democratic achievements of the British state. The motives for this were not just materialism and self-interest, though these were important enough; they were ideological as well. Unionist politics, for all its parochial stupidities, identified itself with the inherited if not always the current values of the British state. That is what British Ulster meant.[89]

It is not our purpose to dissect this (somewhat sweeping) statement but we can use it to examine the Britishness of Ulster by analysing the relationship between the governments in Belfast and London.

In terms of the administrative transition of 1920–2 it has been argued that each side got what it most desired: 'the South, sovereignty; the North, partition; the British, a settlement to the Ulster question, a constitutional withdrawal from the South and, for the moment, the preservation of the empire'.[90] This statement stands up only if we stress its transitional nature. Indeed the history of the following half-century was one whereby the Unionist Party turned Stormont into a fetish in an attempt to expand its own autonomy. Sir James Craig, Prime Minister from 1921 to 1940, ensured that local parliamentary institutions were not devalued: 'There must,' he declared in 1921, 'be a dignity about our Parliament and that Parliament must be very deeply rooted in Ulster soil, so that no opponent dare come forward at any time and say of that great structure . . . "that is only a small affair and we can easily sweep it to one side".'[91]

While some might question its dignity none would probe Stormont's grandeur. Completed in 1932 and opened by the Prince of Wales, this 'massive "official Classical" essay'[92] was a gift of the British government. The architectural historian of Belfast, Charles Brett diplomatically describes it as one of 'two architectural monuments of consequence, both too recent to be easily judged' – although, in placing them alongside other public buildings in the city, he writes that architecturally 'they constitute the corporate expression of embattled Unionism, and of an effort (perhaps largely unconscious) to convert a brash and sprawling industrial centre into a politico-religious capital city'.[93] Others are more sardonic. One commentator, Anthony Cronin, notes that Stormont was 'conceived on a giant scale and set upon the hill at the end of its astonishing avenue simply to prove that the Six County State was part of the eternal order of things'. He continues in this hyperbolic vein musing on Macaulay's New Zealander after he had hacked his way through the forest to gaze on this noble ruin: 'Surely he will think the Parliament Assembly that met here governed colonies and dependent territories, sent out battle fleets and pro-consuls to the farthest ends of the earth, deliberated the rewards of allies and decided the fates of subject people.'[94]

Architectural grandeur was matched by replication of procedure and ceremony. Stormont behaved as if it were Westminster across the water. All of this might be dismissed as imitation being the best form of flattery were it not that it led unionists into delusions about governing a sovereign state, a fact which was to have serious consequences after 1969 when the British government began to pay much closer attention to affairs in Northern Ireland and loyalists began to resent this British 'interference'. Northern Ireland's last Prime Minister, Brian Faulkner, criticised the illusions which had grown up around devolution because devolution 'created unspoken separatist tendencies. It also meant that devolution hit an unprepared Westminster right between the eyes.'[95] It is not our purpose to rehearse the record of devolution but we do need to consider why Westminster was unprepared in the late 1960s and what that tells us about the Dual Polity.

Superficially it would appear that relations between London and Belfast were benign, if not soporific. Very little time was spent at Westminster dealing with Northern Ireland matters. Constitutionally Stormont was a subordinate legislature subject to section 75 of the 1920 Act. It was expected 'to make laws for the peace, order and good government of the area subject to certain specific exceptions, reservations and restrictions'. Parliament could legislate only on matters within its own territory, unlike the British dominions, which could regulate the actions of their citizens while abroad. It had no power to legislate on 'excepted' matters such as the Crown and succession, the making of peace or war, the armed forces, foreign affairs, external trade, coinage and legal tender. A number of 'reserved' matters – the postal service, the Supreme Court, and certain reserved taxes including customs and excise, income tax, surtax and any tax on profits or capital levy – which it had been intended originally to transfer to an all-Ireland parliament were set aside. Put positively, the legislative powers transferred to Belfast have been summarised thus: 'the Northern Ireland Parliament may legislate on matters relating to law and order, to the police, to the courts other than the Supreme Court, to civil and criminal law, to local government, to health and social services, to education, to planning and development, to commerce and industrial development and internal trade, to agriculture and to finance'.[96] These were not inconsiderable powers and were to be exploited – perhaps not to the full in every department – by successive Northern Ireland governments. But there was always a degree of ambiguity. Thus unionists seemed to believe that usage and convention had placed section 75 in abeyance and were unaware of the limitations on security policy until British troops moved onto the streets of Belfast in 1969.

We should pause to consider the degree to which the 1920 Act made Stormont a 'subordinate' legislature. The meaning of section 75 seemed unambiguous but, as a former Permanent Secretary of the Northern Ireland civil service, Sir Kenneth Bloomfield, notes, the Westminster model does not permit one parliament to bind subsequent parliaments: after all the Act of Union of 1800 declared that the Union of Great Britain and Ireland was to be 'for ever', and 'for ever' lasted for 120 years. And in any case Westminster declined to exercise its authority under section 75 for almost fifty years. Further 'this openness of the legislative territory of Northern Ireland to invasion did *not* mean that the executive authorities in Northern Ireland, the Northern Ireland Cabinet and the Northern Ireland Departments, were also "subordinate" in the sense of being branches or outposts of White-hall'.[97] We shall see that this lack of 'subordination' created difficulties after 1969 when Westminster officials began to pay much closer attention to government and administration in Northern Ireland. In the meantime politicians and officials at Stormont probed the extent of Northern Ireland's autonomy.

If, as Mansergh asserts, the provisions of the 1920 Act were dictated with a view to political pacification rather than administrative efficiency we have some understanding of why London treated Belfast so leniently. Once civil war broke out in the Irish Free State London was no longer constrained to maintain the Provisional Government's credibility and, thus, unionists were given a hand to develop independent policies. There is not much evidence of Britain challenging Stormont's decisions with the obvious exception of the 1922 Local Government Bill which proposed the abolition of proportional representation for local council elections, a measure which was seen as endangering minority representation. Westminster withheld assent for two months but eventually capitulated after Sir James Craig declared that his government would resign if he did not receive satisfaction in the matter. After that there was little resistance from London to Belfast's actions. Indeed the record suggests that the Home Office enjoyed a complaisant relationship with successive unionist governments – a fact confirmed in 1955 by the Permanent Under-Secretary of State, Sir Frank Newsam, when he concluded smugly: 'Personal contacts which have been established between Home Office officials and their Northern Ireland colleagues have led to mutual understanding and good will in the handling of thorny problems, despite occasional differences of opinion.'[98]

Newsam did not elucidate on what the differences of opinion were and on whose opinion prevailed but we have no reason to believe that Northern Ireland governments were unhappy with the arrangements. On the contrary: so long as they could keep Northern Ireland in relative tranquillity the Home Office was prepared to let sleeping dogs lie, a doctrine which reached its apogee during the 1965 general election in Northern Ireland when the (Labour) Home Secretary, Sir Frank Soskice, sent the following message to unionism: 'From England we watch it, we admire it, and we rejoice in it.'[99] And that does not appear to have been an aberration. One of his fraternal colleagues in the

Northern Ireland Labour Party (NILP), Charles Brett, recalls a series of meetings to press for electoral reform with Labour Party officials after Harold Wilson's government was returned in 1964. The NILP delegation was graciously shown the door, and the 'Home Office officials were not only unhelpful, they were downright obstructive, and we had grounds for believing they were secretly furnishing Stormont with reports on our private representations to Labour Ministers.'[100] In these circumstances it was not altogether surprising that the Northern Ireland civil service was 'a complacent service' with a 'pleasant leisurely atmosphere, beguiling and deceptively easy going'.[101] That is not to say that its work rate should be dismissed or that it acted as a rubber stamp for Whitehall. As Birrell and Murie's exhaustive analysis of Northern Ireland's legislative output concludes:

> The evidence considered in this study supports the view that, in spite of the very real constraints, Northern Ireland and its government could and did diverge substantially from the standards and legislation operating in Great Britain and at Westminster. Independent action, different policies and substantially different legislation did emerge. Nor can this simply be explained as a freedom to do less. Even where identical policies were adopted in Northern Ireland it is demonstrably not true that they were adopted in a compliant or compulsory environment. There were real political decisions and choices made at every stage, and the steps taken were not always those which involved least conflict with Westminster or 'rocked the boat' to the smallest extent . . . The whole history of devolution since the Second World War is one of pushing back the constraints and creating room to exercise choice. It may be that this was not done vigorously enough. However, to imply that there was a fixed and permanent Stormont–Westminster relationship and that what could be done was predetermined by Westminster ignores the evidence about the process of government and policy-making.[102]

We do not intend to trace this tortuous path beyond revealing what it tells us about the Dual Polity. The best starting-point is the Department of Finance in Belfast. Sir Kenneth Bloomfield describes it as 'a powerful institution . . . because it was to that Ministry, and not to HM Treasury in London, that Northern Ireland Departments in the first place looked for those financial approvals and authorisations which are necessary whenever demands for resources far exceed any possible supply of them'.[103] And another former official, John A. Oliver, carries it a stage further when he writes that an important side 'to the work of the Finance officials lay in their handling of confidential relations with HM Treasury' (which he describes as 'an esoteric cult'). 'Suffice it now to say that those relations worked and worked well. Through good times and bad, in peace and in war, under Conservative, Labour or Coalition governments in London, no matter what the vicissitudes of fortune produced in Northern Ireland, the Ministry of Finance managed to make the system work to the great benefit of this province. No one can say otherwise.'[104]

It may be that Oliver exaggerates somewhat. He admits that the system came close to breakdown on two big issues: the need to carry out a general revaluation of all property in the North; and the contribution which local rates were making, or not making, to the cost of local education services. In any case, and 'contrary to the conventional view, the position of the Ministry [of Finance] in relation to other state apparatuses was in no way comparable to that of the Treasury. While its formal status was equivalent, its real control of other departments fell far short of its British equivalent.'[105] We shall see, too, that there were inevitable tensions between the Treasury and the Northern Ireland government.

Northern Ireland's viability was threatened by the financial restrictions of the 1920 Act, and in that respect the 'history of Northern Ireland's financial relations with Great Britain has been one of evading the consequences' of that Act.[106] Belfast was assisted in its evasion by London. First, there was the Colwyn Committee which was appointed in 1925 to decide on what was a 'fair' contribution to the imperial exchequer (for services such as the armed forces, defence, the national debt and other items falling on the British exchequer). Colwyn undermined two of the principles of the 1920 Act by providing a strong disincentive to the exercise of Northern Ireland's power to vary its own taxes and by envisaging that the imperial contribution might be reduced to vanishing point. A trend was set whereby Westminster's control over Stormont expenditure was minimised; as the 1973 report of the Kilbrandon Commission stated: 'Payments to Northern Ireland ... were covered by permanent statutory authority. They were made out of the Consolidated Fund, and the annual approval of Parliament was not required. The only exception to this were agricultural payments.'[107] Gradually Stormont built on these gains through the Unemployment Insurance Agreement (1926), Westminster's acceptance of the principles of parity (in 1938) whereby the UK ensured that Northern Ireland could have the same social services and the same standards as the mainland if their budget deficit was not the result of local extravagance; and in 1944 it was accepted that Northern Ireland needed social expenditure to make up a substantial leeway on services such as housing, schools and hospitals. Finally, the Social Services Agreement (1948) granted Northern Ireland special payments to meet national insurance and other benefits.

Much of the credit must go the first Prime Minister, Sir James Craig. He set great store 'in his ability to advance Northern Ireland's interests by direct and personal contacts with imperial ministers ... Craig acted less at times as Northern Ireland's Prime Minister than as its Ambassador in Britain.'[108] At home he built up a reputation as a profligate spender with electoral considerations in mind because he insisted that Westminster had a moral duty to bail the North out of any financial difficulties. That was not to the liking of the Treasury whose relations with Craig reached such a low point that he was effectively excluded from the financial negotiations between 1934 and 1938. As for his successor, J.M. Andrews, the Treasury considered him 'a dangerous demagogue'.[109]

Treasury animosity raises a more central issue. If Stormont was subordinate, to whom was it subordinate? There appears to have been no monolithic Westminster view about Northern Ireland. One Whitehall official drafted into Befast after the imposition of direct rule in 1972 described the local administation as 'a federation of baronies' with frequent contact being established between officials in London and Belfast on a department to department basis. There was no sustained generalist view in Whitehall – 'Until recently Northern Ireland was the divided responsibility of the Home Office, the Ministry of Defence, the Foreign Office and, sporadically, the Cabinet Office'[110] – and much depended on the exigencies of domestic politics and of British strategy. Thus the Dominions Office, concerned with wider imperial interests of international conciliation, was often hostile towards Stormont. Anglo–Irish negotiations during 1938 bear out this thesis.

During the 1930s Westminster was reluctant to introduce any controversial legislation in relation to Northern Ireland lest it open up problems at the Anglo–Irish level. The 1938 negotiations concerned, *inter alia*, trade and the treatment of the Northern minority. Both were sore points with unionist governments. The former drew attention to Free State economic policy and development which often threw the limited powers of the Northern Ireland government into sharp and unflattering contrast. Hence when negotiations opened Craig's government submitted a note claiming 'special attention' particularly on the matter of trade and tariffs. While there was general agreement that something had to be done to help Northern Ireland, the Permanent Secretary to the Treasury, Sir Warren Fisher, stretched the limits of that agreement when he advised that the North's prosperity would 'greatly gain from the termination of the present wholly uneconomic partition'. The statement highlighted the 'thread of inconsistency' which pervaded arguments about Northern Ireland: 'On the one hand British and Northern Ireland ministers were anxious to emphasise that she [Northern Ireland] was part of the United Kingdom economic system; on the other, they were attempting to secure some sort of special recognition for her in the Irish market.'[111]

The Northern Ireland government struck such a hard bargain so that 'as part of the price of Northern Ireland's acquiescence in the Anglo-Éire settlement of 1938 did the imperial government eventually accept, and then only in principle, the idea of a minus contribution'.[112] The Chancellor of the Exchequer Sir John Simon considered Northern Ireland's fears exaggerated and its demands outrageous: ' "Are we never to be allowed by Ulster to come to terms with the South", asked the Permanent Secretary at the Treasury, a lifelong critic of Ulster Unionism.'[113] Fisher was even more forthright when he presented a stark anti-unionist position at the negotiations: 'The real issue is whether Northern Ireland is to be allowed to veto a settlement between us and southern Ireland ... Blackmail and bluff (oddly enough called "loyalty") have for many years been the accepted methods of Northern Ireland. It is high time these parochial die-hards were made to face up to a touch of reality.'[114] It is only in very recent years that we encounter similarly brutal language from British sources in relation to their unionist 'allies'. What it demonstrates is the degree to which unionists relied on Home Office protection in particular. The simple fact of the matter was that so long as unionists insisted on remaining within the United Kingdom it was administratively convenient to let sleeping dogs lie.

DEVOLUTION AS POLITICAL CONVENIENCE

The provisional nature of devolution helps to explain why unionists sought as much political autonomy as they could hold. The fullest explanation of just how much that was comes from Birrell and Murie who write that Northern Ireland developed

> many of the characteristics of an independent state. Although it received continued and increasing financial and economic support from Westminster, it retained its own parliament, its own Civil Service and its own security forces, and it was able to pursue policies distinctly different from Britain in many politically controversial areas. Westminster supervision was slight, and ... it is arguable that in practice the status of the Stormont government was closer to the federal model than the devolution model – that is, that the two

governments were almost co-ordinate in powers with each other, each with its own sphere of influence.[115]

So slight was Westminster supervision that the first full-dress debate on the whole issue of Northern Ireland since the Treaty was not held until 1 June 1950. The bipartisan policy was maintained. One aspect of the debate is worthy of comment: the degree to which Westminster should – or could – interfere in Northern Ireland's affairs. The response was twofold: a form of moral blackmail and a journey round the constitutional niceties. The first was put none too subtly by the Unionist MP for North Down, Sir Walter Smiles: 'I sincerely hope that this debate will not lead to further bomb outrages or murders in Northern Ireland.' He was supported (more decorously) by Labour's Sir David Maxwell Fyfe: 'the exercise of restraint in the discussion of Irish affairs is still one of the primary needs and requirements of politicians'. The second was concerned with Northern Ireland's constitutional status: Conservative Earl Winterton wondered whether 'this is to be the prelude to a whole series of similar motions, in order to discuss, for example, *Apartheid* in South Africa or the position of Quebec in Canada'. The government, through the Home Secretary, James Chuter Ede, contented itself with the thought that 'Northern Ireland is in a slightly different position from that of a self-governing Dominion. I think it would be unwise of this House to exercise too meticulous a control over an area to which it has given self-government …'[116] So light was that control that when the next Labour government was returned it had little idea of what were the financial relations between London and Belfast. Richard Crossman, Secretary of State for Social Services, confirmed as much in his diary for 12 September 1968 after he attended a meeting of the cabinet's Steering Committee on Economic Policy: 'At this point I said, "I am an ignoramus; may I be told what is the exact financial arrangement?" Nobody could say. Neither Jack Diamond [Chief Secretary for the Treasury] nor the Chancellor knew the formula according to which the Northern Ireland Government gets its money.'[117]

Such was the control, such was the interest, exercised by successive British governments that when the time came to fulfil its responsibilities London encountered some resistance in persuading unionists to accept their subordination. And on those odd occasions when it *seemed* that Westminster *might* intervene unionism reconsidered its position. One such occasion occurred when the Labour Party won the 1945 general election. The two Nationalist MPs (who had been first elected to Westminster in 1935 but had not taken their seats) decided that they would participate because the new government would be good for Irish nationalism. The same perception mobilised the unionist community into conducting one of its perennial debates about the status of Northern Ireland within the United Kingdom. So the cabinet wondered, in the words of the Prime Minister Sir Basil Brooke, 'whether any changes could be made to avert such a situation [a constitutional clash between Belfast and London]. Two possibilities were dominion status for Northern Ireland and a return to Westminster.' But the cabinet soon realised that the British government was, in the words of Sir Basil Brooke, staffed by 'practical and experienced men who are personally friendly to Ulster'. The unionists recognised that their strength lay in their sense of regional identity and that they had secured the best of all possible worlds within the constraints imposed by economic dependence on the rest of the United Kingdom.[118] Their confidence was fulfilled in 1949 when Labour enacted the Ireland Act as a riposte to the South's declaration of a republic and its decision to leave the Commonwealth. Now unionists had a firm and specific guarantee of Northern Ireland's constitutional position in section 1 (2) of that Act: 'It is hereby declared that Northern Ireland remains part of His Majesty's dominions and of the United Kingdom and it is hereby affirmed that in no event will Northern Ireland or any part thereof cease to be part of His Majesty's dominions and of the United Kingdom without the consent of the Parliament of Northern Ireland.'

A surprising feature of the constitutional uncertainty was that total integration with the rest of the United Kingdom was not high on the agenda. After all it had been the unionist position before partition, and it was an issue which arose at Commonwealth level from time to time. It had the advantage of uniformity: 'There was of course one drastic way of thwarting such divergent evolution (within the Commonwealth, that is) and ensuring that colonies had "the perfect transcript" of Westminster: total assimilation by integration. Dependencies of the Crown could be directly represented in the King's imperial parliament – as maybe Edward I had wanted and many British and colonial politicians had urged since.'[119] Even in the mid-1950s and the later 1960s the inclusion of Maltese and Gibraltar members in the Commons was mooted. Northern Ireland may be one of the very rare examples where it was perceived that the Westminster model was exported *in toto*.

The unvarnished truth might be that unionists knew that they had the best of all possible worlds: integration in that the vast majority of Northern Ireland MPs at Westminster were Unionists who took the Conservative whip (hence the illusion of integration); and a devolution which appeared to broach little or no interference from Westminster.

In those circumstances it might not be that surprising that in 1956 the Maltese sought union with the United Kingdom on 'an Ulster basis', a proposal supported by 74 per cent of those Maltese who voted in a referendum in February of that year. But that amounted to only 45 per cent of the electorate and the plan was dropped eventually.[120] Malta went on to attain independence in September 1964 and become a republic within the Commonwealth on 13 December 1974. At present it is a member of the UN, the Commonwealth and the Council of Europe. With the advantage of hindsight perhaps Northern Ireland should have considered the 'Maltese option'. Events after 1968 and particularly after the imposition of direct rule in March 1972 illustrated that Northern Ireland had been presented with the simulacrum of independence in 1920. When Stormont mistook the shadow for the substance Westminster stepped in.

2

THE FATAL EMBRACE

It is as if two insane people, crazed with wrath, had decided to turn into a fatal embrace, the forced marriage from which they cannot free themselves. Forced to live together and incapable of uniting, they decide at last to die together.

ALBERT CAMUS[1]

When any community is subordinately connected with another, the great danger of the connection is the extreme pride and self-complacency of the superior, which in all matters of controversy will probably decide in its own favour.

EDMUND BURKE[2]

It was an old society, with a long memory, and no nose at all for the future.

PAUL THEROUX[3]

The union of Protestants and Catholics was never a happy marriage. It was marred from the outset by violence before it settled into a form of mutual contempt. But efforts were made to keep up appearances; and for a time it seemed that a reconciliation had been effected. Civilities were exchanged, local customs respected, the beginnings of mutual respect evident. There were some who believed that a new era was dawning – the loveless marriage might produce offspring. But it was not to be. Violence reasserted itself and dialogue barely rose above the level of recrimination. Now they are faced with a stark choice: self-immolation or seeking the advice of a marriage counsellor. The first would be to follow the habit of a lifetime, the second to contemplate one's own failings.

In retrospect we can see that the distance between the two

communities was always too great. They had not the space to grow together or to grow apart. A visitor from another planet would have been struck by their physical separation. Their territorial boundaries were marked by distinctive symbols: the Union Jack or the Irish Tricolour; wall murals celebrating local heroes or acting as warning signals to the other side; even, in some districts, kerbstones displaying party colours. It was a visual culture.[4] And it was an auditor's paradise in the shape of fifes and drums and marching men. The annual marching season produced approximately 3,500 parades in 1995, loyalist parades outnumbering republican by 9 : 1.

The poets, from different generations and traditions, encapsulate this distance between the two communities. Louis MacNeice writes of a gentler period in his autobiographical 'Carrickfergus':

> I was the rector's son, born to the anglican order,
> Banned for ever from the candles of the Irish poor[5]

And Seamus Heaney remembers the Christmas Eve delivery of a toy battleship crafted by his Protestant neighbour:

> And knew that if we met again
> In an Ulster twilight we would begin
> And end whatever we might say
> In a speech all toys and carpentry,
>
> A doorstop courtesy to shun
> Your father's uniform and gun,
> But – now that I have said it out –
> Maybe none the worse for that.[6]

This chapter will examine the culture that produced the need for recognising the neighbourly decencies alongside a desire to display raucous symbols. It will look at community as well as political levels, at religion, the arts and politics; and at the incestuous and exclusive habits they spawned. It is mindful of the proximity of political activity to imagination:

> man's political life is more intimately an expression of the general quality of his imaginative life than we are in the habit of noticing. And those who are concerned with man's imaginative life are therefore concerned with the area in which his political concepts are shaped. Are shaped: they do not shape themselves, but are shaped, in his imagination, not only by man's mortal destiny and the metaphysical questions to which it gives rise, but also by the particular contexts of nation, doctrine, class and race ... the study of politics must neither neglect the fact that man is an imagining and

myth-making animal, nor fail to make explicit allowances for the necessary entry of imagination and myth-making into the study itself.[7]

Not only does Northern Ireland present an ideal laboratory for the
study of myth-making but it highlights the deficiencies of a politically
moribund society. It was the literary critic Lionel Trilling who warned
that unless 'we insist that politics is imagination and mind, we will learn
that imagination and mind are politics, and of a kind that we will not
like'.[8] Events since 1969 have enabled some to fill the political vacuum
with dubious imaginative nostrums.

COMMUNITY

In the conclusion to his magisterial *Interpreting Northern Ireland* John
Whyte considers the research implications of his study and draws our
attention to the contrast between one part of Northern Ireland and
another: 'areas only a few miles from each other can differ enormously
– in religious mix, in economic circumstances, in the level of violence,
in political attitudes. This means that the nature and intensity of the
conflict can vary widely. That in turn means that the nature of a settlement likely to bring peace can vary widely too.'[9] Whyte allows that
his suggestion is only tentative but he touches on something which
helps us to understand the longevity of the quarrel: the sense of place, of
community, of territory – a sense which was there before partition but
which was reinforced by the incompleteness of the 1921 settlement
which concentrated on physical boundaries and questions of political
sovereignty. According to Oliver MacDonagh 'the Northern Ireland
of 1921 and later years was in a real sense the product of geographical
images, first that of a province, then that of a province less the least
harmonious blocks of what had been built'. That produced 'a new
mental geography. Once painted a different colour on the map
Northern Ireland became a pictorial entity in men's minds, with fresh
claims and counter-claims about territoriality. This reinforced the real
internal separation of Irish Protestant and Irish Catholic communities,
when they were divided between two states, and henceforth carried
along, to a degree, in the streams of two separate "national" histories.'
The Irish Catholic community found it easier to slot into one of those
'national' histories whereas the Northern Protestant community had to
invent its own myth: 'What northern Unionists really mean by
"place" and "people" is Protestant Ulster.'[10] In the meantime the
problem of the 'least harmonious blocks' had to be sorted out as
Catholic and Protestant communities were forced to live cheek by jowl

in an orange and green quilt.

One method of dealing with the lack of harmony was to resort to political violence in sporadic outbursts of intercommunal hostility. The worst of these occurred (before the present Troubles, that is) between December 1921 and May 1922 when 236 people were killed. By comparison most of the period from mid-1922 until late 1968 was relatively quiet. Economic historian D.S. Johnson attempts to put this into perspective by noting that during the 'whole period from mid-1922 to 1955 . . . there were 147 murders of which ninety-seven were political. The majority of the latter occurred in late 1922 and 1935. Thus in most years during the period there were two or three murders a year.' In contrast, England and Wales, with a population thirty times larger than Northern Ireland, had 'on average 150 murders per annum in the period 1920–50'. He draws the obvious conclusion that, seen in this light, 'Ulster society between the wars, while certainly sectarian, was far from being uniquely violent, and to dwell on the exceptional events of one or two years in one or two places undoubtedly created a distorted image of "normal" social conditions within the province.'[11]

But how normal was 'normal'? No one would dispute the figures but the culture which produced them repays careful scrutiny. In a particularly apt phrase Frank Wright comments that in place of what 'metropolitans call peace' Northern Ireland at best 'enjoyed a tranquillity of communal deterrence'.[12] It is a phrase to which we shall return because it enables us to place political violence in a wider perspective. It does this by allowing a longer time-span than the period since partition. John Darby has depicted a polity which operated under an intimidatory culture in which 'the power of intimidation springs from its essentially defensive nature. Local minorities were driven by violence and fear to move to other communities in which they could become part of a majority. They were often willing to encourage the expulsion of ethnic opponents from their new community.' Darby's empirical research is based on a study of three particular communities – two in Belfast and one in Cookstown, a rural area close to the geographical centre of Northern Ireland – which had suffered directly from the experience of intimidation. His theoretical aim is 'to examine how relationships are regulated, modified or extinguished between the protagonists after the period of direct confrontation has passed'. This enables him to produce a longitudinal analysis by drawing on nineteenth-century experience.

Darby notes eight periods of serious rioting in Belfast and two in Derry between 1835 and 1935, five of them sufficiently alarming to produce official inquiries (with all the valuable research material that

that entails). He arrives at the opinion that the culture of intimidation is more pervasive than we are willing to admit, but he also extracts positive messages:

> It will be argued that Northern Ireland's conflict is remarkable for the limitations on its violence rather than for the violence itself; that long familiarity with inter-community conflict within the north of Ireland has led to the evolution of effective mechanisms to control it; that these mechanisms arise from the mundane and essentially local accommodations reached in their own localities by people whose hostility has been modified by the need to carry on living in the same 'narrow ground'; and that the efficiency and variety of these mechanisms hold the key to explaining why a conflict of such duration has not produced more serious levels of violence. They have amounted, so far, to a major and effective control against the conflict expanding into a genocidal war.[13]

Belfast might not be Beirut but it is worth bearing in mind that Lebanon went through a sustained period of 'peace' before it broke down in gruesome violence in the 1970s and 1980s.[14] Similarly it might be said that politicians in Northern Ireland (and beyond) failed to take account of the considerable lulls in intercommunal conflict. We need to explore the nature of the 'tranquillity of communal deterrence' and the constraints which it placed on a willingness to negotiate a solution. We need to establish what sort of 'normal' society was Northern Ireland.

A useful starting-point is the issue (and variety) of boundaries – the international border between Northern Ireland and the Republic of Ireland; parliamentary boundaries which differed at Stormont, Westminster and European levels; the boundaries between local authorities; sports boundaries; ecclesiastical boundaries which in some cases cross the international border and which are not uniform between the churches; 'shatter zones', those urban points of sectarian contact where so many riots began. The list is by no means exhaustive but it does convey the significance of territory and the means whereby each side established its own.

Party parades were the manifestation of this sense of territoriality. David Miller asserts that in one period 'the crucial right of the citizen was the right of free expression through his state's territory', and that in ' "normal" times both sides tended to confine their rituals to accepted territorial boundaries'.[15] But the times were often far from 'normal' as the nineteenth-century riots testified. In that respect, 'Orangeism, with its parades and ritual, was a system of communal deterrence ... tranquillity depended on letting such marches take place.' But when they caused conflict 'all the various strands of justification of this practice – that it is not a vigilance practice only a tradition, that past Catholic acquiescence proved its acceptability and legitimacy, or that it is a vigilance practice and must be maintained – may converge on the same point. Communal deterrence practices may ritualise and conceal their origins in vigilance.'[16] In this instance 'tradition' can be read in two senses as it moved from its utilitarian base – the 'very longevity of a practice is an indicator of a consensus about its utility' – to being seen ideologically: 'there is a distinct element of enforcement, of reshaping the present consciously to fit the past'.[17]

Marches were highly visible manifestations of vigilance practices. Their impact might be felt across the North. More localised was the practice of 'exclusive dealing' (buying only from one's own kind) which was widespread by the 1880s. In her study of a rural community in the 1950s Rosemary Harris witnessed the same practice when she commented that such competition as there was over land 'was more often directed to its symbolic worth than its monetary value' because ownership of a farm 'meant the symbolic occupation of an area' but the 'renting of particular fields on short leases to the members of the other side' did not hold out the same threat.[18]

Reduced to the level of individual relations communal deterrence took the form of civility whereby matters of religion and politics were not discussed in 'mixed' company lest they offend. The result, as Wright observes, was that the clergyman 'who said that until he read the 1969 Cameron report he thought discrimination was simply a nationalist propaganda word speaks volumes about how civility acted as a barrier to empathy'.[19] In other words it encouraged ignorance of the other side and hence a lack of self-understanding – what Heaney calls 'a potent monocular vision'.[20] But it may have been shorthand for fear – and for revenge. The travel writer Paul Theroux recalls a conversation he had with someone who denied his religion when confronted with a drunken football fan on a train out of Belfast:

> and I thought how that denial must have hurt his pride, and it seemed to me that it was this sort of humiliation that made the troubles in Ulster a routine of bullying cowardice. It was all old grievances, and vengeance in the dark. That was why the ambush was popular, and the car bomb, and the exploding soap box, and the letter bomb. The idea was to deny what you stood for and then wait until dark to get even with the bugger who made you deny it.[21]

We must allow for some hyperbole but acknowledge that Theroux raises an important issue at the point where communal deterrence breaks out of its tranquillity. Why does it take such a violent turn?

How do individuals sustain their sense of self-esteem in these circumstances? Why do they persist with ancient prejudices? Again we turn to 'community'.

Raymond Williams writes that community, unlike all other terms of social organisation (state, nation, society, etc.) 'seems never to be used unfavourably'. To describe a social group as a community 'is to legitimize it'. But need it be so? What of communities who attempt, according to Geraint Parry, 'to solve the boundary problem – to, as it were, internalize externalities – [by redrawing] the boundaries in a restrictive way'? A community in this sense which ' "chooses" to maintain its traditions and customs necessarily excludes certain other ways of living'.[22] We are concerned with communities which (necessarily) exclude; which indulge in 'telling'; and which have the potential to resort to (reactive and proactive) violence. Social anthropologists have made a study of many (largely rural) communities[23] but our comments will centre on urban Belfast (and on the participant-observation research of sociologist Frank Burton).

Burton's research centres on 'Anro', an area in north Belfast which bore the brunt of much of the recent Troubles. He seeks to explain how the Troubles have been assimilated into the community's culture. He stresses a common sense of identity based on 'kin, class, religion and territory' which has produced a communal solidarity which in turn enables the community to withstand virtually any depredation:

> Precisely because the community manages to contain and disperse the troubles into its institutional framework, its normative structure and its symbolic universes, it manages to prevent the dominance of external social control. In turn, the community retains enough of its solidarity to allow the militant activists to continue the politics of violence ... The possibility of an IRA campaign is dependent in this respect on the social structure of its community being able to withstand the deleterious consequences that urban guerrilla activity creates.

One of the social consequences of the militant campaign has been 'the suspension of due process' which has 'seriously damaged the legitimacy of the law' in Catholic districts. 'Into this void of legitimacy the IRA have injected their own quest for moral acceptability. The political struggle in the community is precisely the attempt to gain authority for their own law and order.'[24]

One of the social skills employed to resist external control is the concept of 'telling', which is 'the pattern of signs and cues by which religious ascription is arrived at in the everyday interaction of Protestants and Catholics'. Burton explains: 'Telling is based on the social significance attached to name, face and dress, area of residence, school attended, linguistic and possibly phonetic use, colour and symbolism. It is not based on undisputed fact but as an ideological representation is a mixture of "myth" and "reality".'[25] Telling is part of the warp and woof of social life in Northern Ireland. The community has developed its own highly sensitive antennae whereby 'one of the other side' or a 'stranger' can be identified immediately. It is considered to be part of the survival package particularly for those living at the communal interface. It is like a sixth sense covering everything from the rhythm of speech to the distance between one's eyes. Heaney, for example, writes of trying 'to do justice to all the elements of heritage in my natural speech'.[26]

Telling is transmitted from generation to generation. In the late 1960s when generational conflict was a feature of life in most western societies commentators were struck by its absence in Northern Ireland. Sons joined fathers in the Orange lodges and families shared common experiences:

> Both political doctrines select historical events as claims to the moral superiority of their cause. This history is given vitality by the continuity of the troubles which has ensured that each generation has lived through and has stored violent experiences. Living memories stretch back to 1916, to the Black and Tans, the UVF resistance, the rioting 1930s, the 1956–62 IRA campaign, and right through to the present troubles. If the concept of a political generation can be used to explain the radicalism of particular age structures in certain situations, it would be a fair comment that in the Six Counties all generations are political generations.[27]

Gerry Adams' family background is a classic example of passing on the baton from one generation to the next. He came from a family of republican 'aristocrats':

> Both his father Paddy and his mother Anne were republicans. Paddy had been shot by the RUC in his youth, was a member of the IRA and had been imprisoned in the 1940s. His mother was a member of the Hannaway family, a well-respected, if not legendary, family among Belfast republicans. Adams' maternal grandfather had known the Irish socialist and revolutionary James Connolly and the forceful trade unionist Jim Larkin; he had campaigned for de Valera during the 1918 Irish elections . . . His paternal grandfather and in-laws were involved in the IRA.

An example of how the struggle crossed the generation gap was the fact that at one stage Adams' father Paddy, his brother Liam and two of his cousins, as well as his uncle Liam Hannaway, were all in the Maze prison.[28]

The senses of territorial integrity and of generational continuity are reinforced by a staple diet of self-imposed censorship. One either reads one's own newspaper or carries one's own prejudices when relying on 'neutral' sources such as television. The *News Letter* has an overwhelmingly Protestant readership which is matched on its side of the sectarian divide by the (Catholic) *Irish News*. Simon Winchester described them as 'the pepper and salt of Ulster journalism: they reported each day's events with about the coordination and agreement one might expect of the *Wall Street Journal* and the *Morning Star*'.[29] Only the evening *Belfast Telegraph*, both in readership and in (bland) content, holds out the potential as a cross-community integrator. These large provincial dailies are supplemented by thirty or so regional weekly newspapers, virtually all of them faithful to their readers' political outlook. Eamonn McCann's account of life in the Bogside stresses the role played by the *Derry Journal* in supplementing a prevailing ideology sustained by the Catholic Church, the schools and the Nationalist Party: 'bitterly anti-Unionist, passionately pro-Fianna Fáil, reverently Catholic and hysterically anti- communist. It never wrote "Northern Ireland", always " 'Northern' Ireland"; never "Londonderry", always " 'London'derry". Even the punctuation was patriotic.'[30]

The Troubles created their own outgrowth of community newspapers and political pamphlets, as if the usual sources of information were tainted. This flowering had the additional bonus of cementing communal solidarity. Some localities turned to pirate radio. Radio Free Belfast was established in the Falls Road area in August 1969 and the Shankill Road responded with Radio Orange which the Home Secretary James Callaghan considered 'pernicious'. It launched the careers of two voluble ladies, Orange Lily and Roaring Meg, who spewed out anti-Catholic invective. Pirate radios could heighten sectarianism and their very existence was another example of the necessity of relying on one's own interpretation of events.

There is some evidence to suggest that the main conduit of information in Northern Ireland, the BBC, was not always impartial in the manner in which it conducted its business. A historian of the BBC in Northern Ireland, Rex Cathcart, delineates three strategies which the corporation has used since the 1920s. During the pre-war period 'the BBC ignored the division and sought to prevent any of its manifestations from impinging on programmes. This was an abdication of social responsibility.' He produces impressive documentation which demonstrates that the BBC was beholden to the unionist establishment to such an extent that the broadcasters were perceived by the minority as a propaganda arm of government. On such sensitive issues as broadcasting Gaelic sports results on a Sunday, finding a place for the Irish language in the schedules or cooperating with the Irish broadcasting system, Radio Éireann, the BBC bowed to the wishes of the unionist government.

After World War II a new strategy emerged based on 'the positive aspects of community relations [with] the negative underplayed. A consensus emerged which had a false basis.' Unwittingly that contributed to the promotion of the false confidence which launched Prime Minister Terence O'Neill's reform programme. In turn that led to the formation of the civil rights movement, growing tensions inside the unionist 'family' and the spiral of political violence that ensued. That is not to suggest that the BBC must bear prime responsibility for the outbreak of the Troubles. The point is more delicate. In a divided society the BBC appeared to the minority to be part of an adversarial system when what was needed was a medium for promoting coalescent attitudes – not necessarily as a form of social engineering but simply as a recognition of the realities of political division. Because the newspaper industry was not homogenous and could reflect with a reasonable degree of proportionality the sectarian nature of society, it was not open to that charge. Nor could (or did) the BBC make an abrupt change. Since broadcasting is part of the political environment, power-sharing on the air would have been at odds with the adversarial political system. So the BBC's third and current strategy, honed in the hostile environment of incipient civil war, has been 'to reflect the whole of society as it is, in its negative and its positive aspects ... The price of the strategy is that neither community is satisfied, for each manifests exclusive political and cultural attitudes, and harbours the ultimate determination that the other community will not be seen or heard.'[31]

Those who came to visit Belfast usually left with a poor impression of the place. In the 1920s V.S. Pritchett described Belfast as 'that awful, rainy and smoky Presbyterian city'.[32] In 1941 from the vantage point of Donegall Place at the heart of commercial Belfast Sean O'Faolain wrote: 'You have before you an outline of Belfast's social structure. There is no aristocracy – no culture – no grace – no leisure worthy of the name. It all boils down to mixed grills, double whiskies, dividends, movies, and these strolling, homeless, hate-driven poor.'[33]

How accurate is the picture of Northern Ireland as a culture-free zone? We could say that such remarks about Northern Ireland could be applied to the island as a whole. It was the novelist Francis Stuart, describing himself as a 'ghetto writer', who castigated the 'soft centre of

Irish writing', those who reflected 'more flatteringly, its habits and thought modes . . . They quickly become integrated into their society and serve a civic function in the same way as do lawyers, doctors and civil servants . . . they might be said to preserve common cultural standards and present the national identity.'[34] Stuart cites Frank O'Connor as a typical representative. Seamus Deane adds to the list by condemning the aesthetic heritage of men like Yeats, Synge and Austin Clarke whose work 'clearly harbours the desire to obliterate or render nugatory the problems of class, economics, bureaucratic systems and the like, concentrating instead upon the essences of self, nationhood and Zeitgeist'.[35]

Northern Ireland's problem was that it did not have an agreed sense of nationhood and *Zeitgeist*. John Hewitt comments diplomatically that when 'we write of painting and sculpture in the North of Ireland, we are writing of a small area and a small population'. His commentary demonstrates a certain disdain for the level of civic taste in Belfast, and for a wider provincialism: 'The Festival of Britain, 1951, was not taken as an opportunity for the participation of a representative group of Ulster artists, the then Minister of Education at Stormont denying any sense of regional identity and insisting that Northern Ireland was as much part of Britain as the Yorkshire ridings.'[36] It had no national theatre to compare with the Abbey in Dublin although the Ulster Literary Theatre (formed in 1904) made its mark until about 1920 and then began a slow but perceptible decay. Theatre fulfilled an important role in Ulster social life but rarely was it challenging. When the working-class playwright Sam Thompson offered his account of sectarianism in the Belfast shipyards, *Over the Bridge*, to the Ulster Group Theatre in 1957 they rejected it for the extraordinary reason that they were 'determined not to mount any play which would offend or affront the religious or political beliefs or sensibilities of the man in the street of any denomination or class in the community and which would give rise to sectarian or political controversy of an extreme nature'.[37] There we have the problem of the arts in Ulster in a nutshell – safe, unquestioning, reinforcing fixed prejudices.

A composite picture emerges of an 'inarticulate' Ulster.[38] Curiously Catholic Ulster became much more self-confident. It moved beyond the self-doubt of Patrick Kavanagh:

> When Shakespeare, Marlowe and Johnson were writing
> The future of England, page by page
> A nettle-wild grave was Ireland's stage[39]

to the growing assertiveness of Heaney's generation:

> Those hobnailed boots from beyond the mountain
> Were walking, by God, all over the fine
> Lawns of elocution.

and

> Ulster was British, but with no rights on
> The English lyric[40]

It was Heaney again who highlighted the lack of an agreed culture when he wrote of the 'official British culture, if you like, ... at odds with the anthropological culture'.[41]

Some of the strongest criticism of Protestant Ulster came from within its own community. Perhaps its most searching critic was the poet John Hewitt. Always conscious of his own Protestant roots and what he called the 'distant bugle's echo' (the siren call back into the bosom of one's own community) he was merciless in his anatomy of his own people. In one essay he recalls the return in 1934 of one of Ulster's finest sons, Dr Alexander Irvine, author, journalist, preacher and founding member of the American Socialist party, who was on a speaking tour from California. He preached temperance at one gathering but then had the temerity to preach socialism and betrayal by the organised church at another: 'Of course, there was trouble afterwards. The popular smiling public man had turned traitor. He had savaged the ideals of his sponsors, the YMCA and the Presbyterian Church. He had violated the Rotarian code. He had taken the Lord's name in vain. He had consorted with atheists and communists; and the newspapers had reported it. So this was Irvine's last public appearance in the city.'[42] The incident highlighted one final aspect of community life – the influence of organised religion.

The link between religion and politics is generally considered to be perilously close in Ireland. Fundamentalist publications in the early days of Stormont used Unionist backbenchers like Thomas Moles and Wilson Hungerford to expose the hand of papal intrigue: *The Fellowship Forum* in 1923, for example, carried a headline which would be familiar to readers of the Reverend Ian Paisley's *Protestant Telegraph* in the 1960s: 'Irish Roman Catholics Flood Scotland in Papal Conspiracy. Member of Parliament Exposes Hand of Pope in Plot to Overcome Seat of Presbyterianism with Lowest Type of Erin Emigrant.'[43] But it is a mistake to lay too much emphasis on the extremes. Only 9 per cent of the population described themselves as 'evangelicals' in a 1978 survey, although 74.5 per cent gave fear of Rome as their reason for being unionist. Even the Free Presbyterian Church, whose membership had risen by over 30 per cent in a decade, had only 9,621 members in 1981.

In that same decade (1971–81) the three major Protestant denominations had decreased in membership by an average of about 17 per cent. Competition within Protestantism is one reason why religious influence is important in community life, if only because the Democratic Unionist Party (DUP) is led by the Free Presbyterian Moderator, Ian Paisley, and the Ulster Unionist Party (UUP) leadership contains such luminaries as the Presbyterian minister and former Orange Grand Master, the Reverend Martin Smyth. Competition was for constituents as well as souls.

One of the features which struck Rosemary Harris in her study of 'Ballybeg' was the intensity of interdenominational conflict among Protestants. But it should be seen in context. One astute and courageous observer has traced the growth of 'a collective Protestant self-understanding' since the second half of the nineteenth century; 'forged by theology and history', it is an 'alliance of Anglican, Methodist and Presbyterian people who believe that their interests have sufficient in common for them to come together in a coalition of loyalist convictions. The common factors were a fear of the Catholic Church and opposition to a united Ireland.' Scrutinising his own church, John Dunlop asserts that 'Presbyterian theology and Church life have, to a significant degree, been a reaction to Roman Catholicism'; indeed Presbyterians 'have become dependent on perceived Roman error for an understanding of Presbyterianism itself'. Beyond the theological, Protestants are suspicious of what they perceive as a highly centralised Catholicism: 'Presbyterian Churches have struggled for independence from state control, for democratic government in the Church, and for orthodoxy in theology.'[44] It is difficult to exaggerate the Protestant self-perception of its democratic foundation whereby it sees its structures as being 'bottom up' in contrast to the rigid hierarchical nature of Catholicism: 'The Protestant Reformation was profoundly democratizing in that its assertion of the sole authority of the Bible removed the need for properly ordained priests and reduced considerably their role.' Consequently Presbyterian Church government 'is a compromise between congregational independence and centralized government ... The pyramid of democratic centralism prevents anarchy. But the centralization is not strong because there is no doctrinal support for an authoritarian hierarchy.' The result is that in practice 'Presbyterianism permits local autonomy. Individual congregations do go their own way and there are no sanctions equivalent to the Catholic Church's power to excommunicate deviants.'[45]

Local autonomy can produce its own form of excommunication. One example concerns the unhappy experience of Presbyterian minister, David Armstrong, in the market town of Limavady. After he consorted with the local Catholic priest in 1983 a vendetta was conducted against him by a substantial part of his congregation, and his fellow ministers in the Route Presbytery failed to endorse his stance. He resigned early in 1985 and moved to England to train for the Anglican ministry.[46] For many people in Northern Ireland, Protestant and Catholic, the parish is their point of reference. It provides them with their self-esteem and their hierarchy of values. Community and parish merge in a society where religiosity is pervasive. That places an onus on ministers of religion who sometimes stray from the pastoral to the political – a factor recognised by John Dunlop when he acknowledges that Presbyterians 'have such compassion for the problems of our own people that we lack insight into the difficulties of our neighbours'. Translated into the political sphere this means that by providing 'an uncritical chaplaincy service to political ideologies we [Presbyterians] confer a quasi-religious character upon them. Necessary political compromise can then be portrayed as the betrayal of a religious trust. Politics need to be desacralised so that they become manageable and in the process the Churches will be set free to be the Church.'[47]

POLITY

In yet another study of the role of the churches Gallagher and Worrall argue that 'fundamentally the conflict was less one of religion or culture than of allegiance'.[48] Allegiance was to Britain or Ireland and, largely, it broke down into denominational components. Probably its most extreme manifestation could be found in the slogan of the eccentric loyalist paramilitary group Tara: 'We hold Ulster that Ireland might be saved and Britain be re-born.'[49] The remainder of this chapter will concentrate on the political but since it is a more familiar story we will pass over it quickly, addressing a number of the most salient features of Northern Ireland politics during the period.

Firstly, party politics cannot be separated from the community in Northern Ireland. For the most part politics was organised on a 'bottom up' basis through either the local Orange lodges or the Catholic Registration Association. The role of Orangeism inside unionism is too well known to need repetition. Catholics had their own system: 'the usual process for selecting candidates in nationalist constituencies was that the local clergy called a convention, with every Catholic organisation qualifying for two delegates. The system of keeping the register of Catholic voters up to date – to help gather all possible votes – depended on a collection in the Catholic churches. In Derry, the

Catholic Registration Office employed two people to plot where every Protestant and Catholic lived in the city, in red and green ink, while in country areas one volunteer would have this responsibility.'[50] Such a system invariably promoted localism.

Secondly, with, at one time or another, seventy-three local authorities (reduced to twenty-six in 1973), fifty-two members of the Stormont parliament, twelve MPs at Westminster (increased to seventeen in 1983) and three Members of the European Parliament Northern Ireland was overrepresented. The scramble for votes in such a small area produced intense electoral competition, an intensity which was propounded when proportional representation was in use – before 1929 and after 1972. Candidates were conscious of the debt they owed to their constituents. In a face-to-face society it was difficult not to be influenced by them. And the nature of that influence could be misunderstood. In a 1966 study of Belfast city politics Budge and O'Leary discovered that a majority of unionists wanted to make conciliatory moves towards Catholics 'which if carried through might have defused the imminent crisis. But moderate councillors were discouraged and conservatives strengthened by an overestimate of intransigence among the population: while the resultant failure of the moderate leaders to act strongly reinforced popular impressions of Unionist intransigence and immobility.'[51] In other words we are faced with the circular argument that politicians' misguided perceptions of their followers' bitterness led them to adopting more extreme positions than they held personally.

Thirdly, the Stormont government sought to maintain the loyalty of its supporters 'by developing an informal style of government inimical to long-term and overall planning and by discriminating in favour of Protestants and Unionists in respect of education and representation and, to a lesser extent, governmental employment and law and order'.[52] This informal style of government – personified by Sir James Craig's policy of frequently meeting deputations and, if necessary, overturning cabinet decisions to meet the delegations' wishes – may have been responsive and accessible but it did not make for good government. It was the politics of brokerage and patronage familiar throughout Ireland, with the important qualification in Northern Ireland that only one party ever had the means to distribute government largesse.[53]

Fourthly, Northern Ireland was a polity barren of political debate. The major opposition party, the Nationalists, often absented themselves from Stormont. Unionists awarded themselves an inordinately high number of executive posts. Nicholas Mansergh calculates that in 1933 some 27 per cent of Unionist MPs were in receipt of official salaries – 'at a disproportionally high level', he asserts – which revealed 'the probability of undue executive influence in a small legislature'.[54] Consequently there was little evidence of the usual cut and thrust of parliamentary debate. In the half-century of Stormont's parliamentary life the Nationalists succeeded in having only one piece of legislation accepted – an Act for the protection of wild birds in 1931. No efforts were made to woo Catholics to accept the political system although there was a section of the minority who were prepared to collaborate at the outset.[55]

And finally, the Northern Ireland party system was peculiar to Northern Ireland. It did not fit into the usual parameters of British political practice because 'in Ulster, the great permanent questions of political philosophy – the moral basis of authority, and of the right to resist authority, the relationship between law and force and that between nationality and political allegiance – were being debated'.[56] It was a fitful debate more noted for passion than for enlightenment. It made Northern Ireland an aberrant case in United Kingdom politics, a sort of Albania of the western world hermetically sealed from outside influences. It, too, encouraged notions of autonomy and even of sovereignty.

Several important consequences flowed. In the first place the major political parties were inert and deeply conservative. In terms of organisation the Nationalist Party did not exist. Until the 1960s it was without a party headquarters, party manifesto or professional staff. Writing in the 1930s Mansergh observed that the Nationalists were 'conservative by temperament. They emphasize the importance of home life, they believe in the benefits derived from the private ownership of property, their plan of social reform is inspired by Papal Encyclicals and not by Socialist thought.'[57] Little had changed by the 1960s except that now they were organised but even those who wanted to move things along more quickly such as the Campaign for Social Justice (CSJ) betrayed some of the same traits: 'the term adopted was not "civil rights" but "social justice", a term which was given a wide currency by Pope Pius XI in his encyclical, *Quadragesimo Anno*, of 1931. The adoption of this name said something about the background of the members of the CSJ, drawn as they were from the educated Catholic middle class, trained in Catholic schools and colleges.'[58]

We need not detain ourselves with an account of unionism in action. Its record speaks for itself and confirms its deeply conservative, if not reactionary, roots. And as for a bloc in the middle Frank Wright asserts that 'it is there, but it is exceedingly hard pressed to do more than provide cement for compromises made between elements in the main line blocs. The present-day Alliance party and the pre-1969 Labour party contained within them substantial diversity of opinion.'[59] Even the reintroduction of proportional representation in the early 1970s could not realise the emergence of a powerful middle ground. Combined with the presence of an intimidatory political culture the most significant aspect of the party system was its degree of political underdevelopment which manifested itself not in the two communities' 'inability to dominate' each other but their common vulnerability to internal factionalism; this in turn undermined their leadership's capacity to govern: 'Fraught with internal dissent and suspicion, each community is incapable of presenting leaders who can negotiate and institutions that can accurately represent the community's views.'[60] That is the real lesson of more than half a century of unionist rule. Political debate on the Westminster model was a luxury for which a parsimonious unionist leadership felt no need. They had controlled a political system which belied the political: since one party rule was inevitable, since both communities believed that they could rely on their external guarantors in moments of extreme crisis, and since they shared a sense of fatalism and (differing) senses of manifest destiny – for all these reasons they could ignore the first skill in political practice, the ability to negotiate. Even at societal level a sociologist has noted the debilitating effect of 'a taboo on political skills needed to *actively* negotiate solutions to the problems that divided them, even though many of them felt that their society was in need of political repair'.[61]

The absence of these skills was to become painfully evident in the years after the imposition of direct rule, and especially after unionists realised that they would have to negotiate an alternative to the Anglo-Irish Agreement in the 1990s.

3

THE DISTANT BUGLE'S ECHO

If Belfast had a contemporary novelist who decided to include
everything in one day, the pall of smoke, spreading gradually
upwards and outwards from its point of origin and visible from
everywhere else to all the characters whatever their concerns, might
well serve as his unifying device.

ANTHONY CRONIN[1]

... when I make what I think is a free act of choice, I still wonder
what distant bugle's echo is beckoning or in what mass movement I
shall shortly find myself.

JOHN HEWITT[2]

... bottled time turns sour upon the sill.

LOUIS MACNEICE[3]

On Friday 14 May 1971 'Ulster '71' was launched by the Lord Mayor
of London, Sir Peter Studd, on thirty-seven acres of exhibition park,
making it, according to the official programme, the largest exhibition
to be held in the UK for twenty years. It was, of course, a celebration of
fifty years of Northern Ireland but it was being held against a pall of
rising smoke and distant gunfire. The organisers paid some obeisance
to this uncongenial fact when they asserted that the whole concept was
a demonstration of faith in the ability of Northern Ireland to rise above
recent troubles. They even displayed some sensitivity: 'The term
"Ulster" is used, incidentally, as a convenient name for Northern
Ireland.' When it came to contemporary political realities their one
concession in an exhibition which celebrated the greatness of 'Ulster'
was the construction of a 'tunnel of hate', a polystyrene tunnel through
which visitors could wander and contemplate innocuous graffiti. In

short, it was a time of political innocence. Five hundred student demonstrators mounted what was considered to be a good-natured protest, and Sinn Féin did no more than complain that the whole charade was being financed out of the public purse to the tune of £800,000. It was the final act of whistling in the dark before the real dark descended on all the people of Northern Ireland and spread its wings into other corners of Britain and Ireland.

Already two Northern Ireland prime ministers, Captain Terence O'Neill and Major James Chichester-Clark, had departed as a result of the worsening political and security crisis; the political system was being thrown into chaos with the disappearance of old parties, the emergence of new ones and the disintegration of the unionist monolith; the Royal Ulster Constabulary (RUC) had been radically reformed (with, incidentally, its 'Inspector General' being replaced by a 'Chief Constable' – a tacit recognition that the paramilitary element of policing had to go); and, on one night in February 1971, the first Provisional had been shot in action and the IRA had retaliated by shooting the first British soldier – 'It was one apiece, and the war was on.'[4] But, with hindsight, we can see the beginnings of a collapse in authority and morale at all levels of society. This chapter is concerned with that collapse. We will not be examining the downward spiral into a maelstrom of violence in a chronological fashion. Rather we are concerned with the link *between* politics and violence, that is, we will discount the more conventional view that violence is necessarily the antithesis of politics and examine political activity in which political violence is at the extreme end of the continuum and peaceful co-existence at the other. The linkage between politics and violence manifested itself in several ways.

One of the most insidious was an evasion of language. The first government report on the violence was entitled *Disturbances in Northern Ireland*; the title of the second went one stage further when it referred to *Violence and Civil Disturbances in Northern Ireland in 1969*. The civilian population settled on the more comforting term 'The Troubles'. It was to be an era of the acronym with terms such as APCs, Armoured Personnel Carriers, commonly known as PIGS, and DMSUs and VCPs (standing for Divisional Mobile Support Units and Vehicle Check Points) being handy replacements for the instruments of state control. And when one of the chief holding centres for internees had been so discredited its original name Long Kesh (with its ancient Irish overtones) was replaced by its geographical location to become the Maze Prison. As the violence intensified a form of dehumanisation took over. A Sinn Féin distinction made between the 'Brits' – the 'occupying army and their RUC henchmen' – and 'our Protestant brothers and sisters' proved to be counterproductive. The 'Brits' in Britain – most notably their most strident political leader, Margaret Thatcher – embraced the term as a badge of valour, whereas the Protestant community simply matched the republican movement's words with its actions and concluded that the IRA was engaged in a form of fratricide. No similar evasion existed among Protestants/loyalists who prided themselves on 'plain speaking' although the utterings of their wilder shores indicated the extent to which all Catholics/nationalists were seen to belong in the 'disloyal' category. Perhaps the most crude example was a booklet entitled *Orange Loyalist Songs 1971*; one little ditty, 'I Was Born Under The Union Jack', concludes with the resonant message: 'If guns are made for shooting, then skulls are made to crack./ You've never seen a better Taig, than with a bullet in his back.'

From the outset linguistic evasion was part of the make-up of Whitehall officials sent across to Northern Ireland to clean out the 'Augean stables'.[5] They came 'out' to Northern Ireland as if it were somehow separate from the kingdom, maybe even extraterrestrial. We shall see that, with the passage of time as they dug themselves in for the long haul, they engaged in euphemism. Hence when they began to count the political cost of mounting army casualties in the mid-1970s they adopted a policy of 'Ulsterisation', that is they put local security forces in the front line and kept options open for military withdrawal. Equally 'normalisation' and 'criminalisation' were put in place in the vain hope that republican political violence would collapse under the weight of Catholic moral outrage at what was being done in the name of Ireland. And evasion translated itself into a distorted view of the nature of the UK in one section of the Prevention of Terrorism Act (1974) which permitted a system of internal exile whereby the Secretary of State for Northern Ireland had the power to exclude anyone, without a trial or without explanation of the evidence against them, from one part of the UK (Britain) and banish them to Northern Ireland or to the Republic.

A second manifestation of the link between politics and violence was a collapse of authority at the local level; this was to have a profound effect on the political process because it affected more than Stormont and Westminster. It can be seen in a report in the *New York Times* (24 January 1971) which describes a protest against the Catholic Bishop of Down and Connor, Dr William Philbin, after he had warned people away from the IRA while preaching in the west Belfast ghetto of Ballymurphy. One of the parishoners who went to the bishop's residence in a more salubrious part of Belfast commented: 'I bet nothing ever happens here. We're telling the Bishop he's completely out of touch with our problems.' Similar scenes occurred in other parts of Northern Ireland: in themselves they did not amount to much but their combined effect was to bring about the collapse of moral and political authority which in turn created a power vacuum. The political process (such as it was) became largely redundant. The institutional churches steered an uneasy line between the pastoral and the spiritual, and the pulpit was used too readily for political denunciation or military advice. In a demotic culture that vacuum was to be filled by the 'defenders' of the ghetto.

A third was the outbreak of confusion throughout the island with the collapse of the old order. One graphic example was the dismissal in May 1970 from the Fianna Fáil government of the Ministers for Agriculture, Neil Blaney, and the Minister for Finance, Charles Haughey, for their part in an alleged conspiracy to smuggle arms valued at £80,000 into the Republic for use, it was assumed, by beleaguered Catholics in the North. The details do not concern us here but the fallout does. The incident revealed atavistic feelings inside the largest party in the Republic (indeed on the island), feelings that had been contained so long as the Northern problem remained moribund. They were a symptom of a deeper fissure between North and South and within both polities as well as a manifestation of the lack of constructive thought on the national question; this can be found in the language emanating from Dublin at the outbreak of the violence. How to address the entity known as Northern Ireland? In the beginning the expression used was 'the Six Counties of Northern Ireland' with the emphasis on the diminutive. It was not until the signing of the Sunningdale Declaration in December 1973 (and in particular paragraph 5) that there was some form of official recognition of Northern Ireland by the government in the Republic. We shall see that the issue goes beyond nomenclature but, for the moment, the point is that non-recognition contributed to a climate where it was fashionable to engage in verbal republicanism and a (rhetorical?) call to arms.

A fourth was the deleterious effect on the physical environment of measures undertaken to counter the devastating IRA bombing campaign against the commercial heart of the North. It manifested itself in security gates, 'rings of steel', hideous concrete pillboxes, watch-towers constructed as if for some super Stalag bristling with sophisticated electronic technology, 'peace lines' and a distinctive Northern architecture to be found in public buildings which owed more to a concept of granite resistance than aesthetics. The zareba became the symbol of Protestant Ulster defiant in place of the competing symbols of unionism and nationalism – at least these symbols had some claims to a phoney folk art and to the cultural diversity of the north of Ireland. In its place a bland postmodernism attempted to 'reimage' city and town centres and to turn them into Northern variants of Croydon High Street. Taste played second fiddle to communal endurance and planning blight.

A fifth was the utter unpreparedness of the sovereign authority. The diaries of Richard Crossman expose the extent to which Northern Ireland had been seen as a place apart in British constitutional and political evolution. His first entry concerning Northern Ireland does not appear until 27 May 1968 – that is several months before the outbreak of communal disturbance – when he raises the issue of a government subsidy to the Belfast aircraft factory, Short Brothers.[6] And as the Troubles unfolded it became evident that London wanted to keep the problem at arm's length. Tony Benn records in his diary (19 August 1969) how Harold Wilson had told the cabinet that 'we want to be firm and cool and fair, but avoid a political row in the UK because he did not want to recall Parliament or take over the Government from Northern Ireland'.[7]

This has to be set against the unremitting problems faced by Labour after it had resumed power in 1964 for the first time in thirteen years: ongoing difficulties over sterling which culminated in devaluation in 1967; strife with the Left over the UK's supine role in Vietnam; the Rhodesian crisis; Czechoslovakia; the debilitating struggle to enter the European Economic Community (EEC). The list could be extended. Harold Wilson had signalled his intention that his premiership would be one of interventionist modernisation with major administrative reform: hence the reform of local government (the Redcliffe-Maud Report) and of the civil service (the Fulton Report). In addition with the election of a Plaid Cymru candidate at the Carmarthen by-election in 1966 and of a Scottish National Party candidate at Hamilton in 1967 the whole question of minority nationalisms within *Britain* moved up the agenda. The Prime Minister was forced to establish a Royal Commission on the Constitution – better known as the Kilbrandon Commission – whose task was to 'examine the present function of the central legislature and government in relation to the several countries, nations and regions of the United Kingdom'.[8] Even before that the Conservative leader, Edward Heath, had failed in his Perth declaration of May 1968 to persuade his Scottish colleagues to consider the case for an elected Scottish assembly.

Heath and Wilson were not moved by what was going on in Northern Ireland – because for all intents and purposes nothing was – but by the inescapable fact of inexorable economic decline. In the sober

and conservative opinion of Kilbrandon: 'there is probably some relationship between adverse economic conditions and the growth of
nationalist movements'.[9] Further examples of the new realism about
Britain's position in the postwar world and of the continuing search for
economies at home and abroad were the publication of the Plowden
Report in February 1964[10] and the Duncan Report in July 1969.[11]
Plowden led to the completion of the institutional merger of the Foreign Office and the Commonwealth Office in October 1968. The date
is significant in terms of the government's enforced renewed interest in
Irish affairs because until October 1968 the British embassy in Dublin
reported to the Commonwealth Office where matters tended to be
more relaxed. Hence, in terms of getting on top of the burgeoning
Northern Ireland problem through the acquisition of first-rate intelligence, the timing of the Foreign and Commonwealth Office merger was fortunate. But Duncan was not remotely about Irish affairs. It
was about Britain's diminishing influence in the world and its loss of
Empire. In all of these circumstances, domestic and external, it was not
altogether surprising that initially Northern Ireland was regarded as a
sideshow which 'from the point of view of the Government ... has its
advantages. It has deflected attention from our own deficiencies and the
mess of the pound. We have now got into something which we can
hardly mismanage.'[12]

Mismanage, they did. The British government was psychologically
and politically ill-equipped for the coming storm. It was forced to rely
on a unionist government which was perceived by the government as
being what the problem was about. If, following Richelieu, 'the true
business of government is to foresee problems and to administer appropriate remedies while time remains. This requires a combination of
imagination, information and judgement',[13] both the Westminster
and Stormont governments had failed on all counts.

THE DISINTEGRATION OF A 'PARANOCRACY'

Conventional wisdom suggests that the collapse of authority was inevitable after the rise of the civil rights movement. It need not necessarily have been so. Its demands were for the most part reasonable
and negotiable. Had the local government franchise been reformed
immediately to bring it in line with the rest of the UK it is conceivable
that the civil rights campaign would have run out of momentum and
that leadership would have fallen into the hands of more moderate
politicians. But one must remember the degree to which Northern
Ireland was not a democracy but a 'paranocracy' in which 'the basis of

power was the successful appeal to paranoid fears in the Protestant electorate about the political, social, philosophical and military potential of their Catholic neighbours'.[14] It was a 'relatively mild and insulated form of paranocracy [which] was impervious to economic and social failure, impervious to logical and political rebuttal, and [was] fuelled simply by regular doses of paranoia at appropriate moments in the social and political calendar'.[15] As we shall see in chapter 7 paranocracy re-emerged in terms of the international dimension to the conflict in the 1980s.

What led to the collapse of the old order was sustained attention from outside. Essentially Northern Ireland had been hermetically sealed from the wider world ever since partition. It had no external relations save through the Irish diaspora (both Catholic and Protestant). It seemed to enjoy a greater degree of autonomy than its constitutional position merited. And, above all else, successive British governments had demonstrated their desire to quarantine the issue of Northern Ireland from 'proper' politics at Westminster. There were formal links between individual government departments on both sides of the Irish Sea and the Home Office was responsible for political oversight. Within its General Department was one division which 'dealt with the Channel Islands, the Isle of Man, the Charity Commission and Northern Ireland, and this group of subjects was under the control of a staff of seven, of whom only one was a member of what was called the Administrative class'.[16] That individual had been in the post for something like twenty years. All of this suggested a certain intimacy, if not complacency, as we have seen earlier.

The Home Office was not in a position to offer knowledgeable and objective advice. Hence policy-makers worked on two false assumptions: that the conflict concerned only two parties – nationalist and unionist *or* republican and loyalist *or* Catholic and Protestant (the terms became interchangeable); and that a slight adjustment of institutional arrangements would furnish an acceptable political accommodation. The result was a reform programme relating to the local government franchise, the revision of local government areas, the allocation of houses, the creation of an ombudsman, machinery to consider citizens' grievances against other public authorities, and consideration of the role of the local security forces and their relationship to the army. All of this was contained within the Downing Street Declaration of August 1969, and in the fullness of time most of these reforms entered the statute-book.

But that was not the point. The Downing Street Declaration was about more fundamental matters as well. The first was to make the very firm assertion that 'Northern Ireland is entirely a matter of domestic jurisdiction. The United Kingdom Government will take full responsibility for asserting this principle in all international relationships.' It was as if London was acknowledging the constitutional implications *and* the international repercussions of its Northern Ireland policy. The second was that the declaration contained a statement that the Northern Ireland government would take the view of the British government into fullest account at all times 'especially in relation to matters affecting the status of citizens … and their equal rights and protection under the law'. The Home Secretary, James Callaghan, interpreted this as an acknowledgement by a Northern Ireland government 'for the first time since 1922' that London's views on civil and other rights must be listened to. This acknowledgement marked the turn of the tide in the relations between Westminster and Stormont. For forty years the unionist establishment had moved further and further away from the UK. Now, because they had to call on the UK for troops to sustain them, the reality of their position was uncovered, and eventually led to the suspension of Stormont itself.[17]

That last sentence leads us to the third fundamental point – and it proved to be a two-edged sword. If the Downing Street Declaration was a firm indication of Stormont's subordinate status it was also an illustration of the confusion which arose between the army and the RUC and between Westminster and Stormont over the division of control of security matters: 'In effect, it subordinated the Ulster security forces to the control of the General Officer Commanding (NI) who was responsible to the Ministry of Defence … [and the] GOC was committed to working "in the closest co-operation with the Northern Ireland Government and the Inspector-General of the RUC".'[18] Inevitably the result was professional rivalry between the army and the RUC at operational level, and this persisted until the late 1970s. Not only did this hamper the security effort but it added to London's embarrassment internationally when it was forced to explain its security policy. This occurred for example with the introduction of internment in August 1971 but especially after Bloody Sunday in January 1972.

Most commentators assert that Bloody Sunday made it inevitable that direct rule – that which London had striven so much to avoid – would be imposed, as it was in March 1972. Perhaps. There is another consideration. In the flurry of activity surrounding direct rule few recognised the significance of a legal decision which had arisen following the arrest under the Special Powers Act of two Stormont MPs (John Hume and Ivan Cooper) for refusing to obey the order of an army officer. The MPs won their appeal to the Northern Ireland High

Court on the grounds that section 4 (1) of the Government of Ireland Act 1920 did not permit the Special Powers Act to cover the actions of British troops. The matter was of considerable embarrassment to the authorities since it raised doubts about other major security operations and demonstrated that the legal basis of army operations had never been clarified. Precisely one month before the prorogation of Stormont the British government introduced the Northern Ireland Act which 'specifically authorised the Northern Ireland Parliament to legislate in respect of the armed forces of the Crown in so far as that was necessary to the maintenance of peace and order in Northern Ireland, and conferred *retrospective* validity on any actions taken before the passing of the act which would otherwise have been invalid'.[19] The bill became law within a matter of hours without a division on the second or third readings. The government's alacrity owed much to concerns about international opinion and demonstrated, finally, that it could not rule Northern Ireland by proxy.

In any case the collapse of the old order was visible for all to see. Between 1969 and March 1972 no less than three prime ministers – Terence O'Neill, James Chichester-Clark and Brian Faulkner – were replaced. The party system underwent a complete facelift following the civil rights campaign. The UUP was the only significant party to survive the upheaval but even it suffered from factionalism with the appearance of pro-O'Neill and anti-O'Neill candidates at the Stormont elections in February 1969. By the early 1970s its dominance of the Protestant community was being challenged by two new parties – the DUP led by the Reverend Ian Paisley and the Vanguard Unionist Progressive Party (VUPP) led by William Craig, the Minister of Home Affairs who had been sacked by Terence O'Neill in December 1968 for expressing ideas favouring a unilateral declaration of independence. What was euphemistically known as the 'middle ground' was now occupied by the Alliance Party, a biconfessional party of liberal unionists (with the emphasis very much on the lower-case 'u'). It attracted some support from former unionists and largely replaced the Ulster Liberal Party and the Northern Ireland Labour Party. But perhaps the biggest shift occurred with the demise of the Nationalist Party and the creation in 1970 of the Social Democratic and Labour Party (SDLP), the first disciplined and properly organised party to emerge from within the minority community since the foundation of the state.

In terms of the Northern Ireland party system such changes must have appeared cataclysmic. In reality they meant very little in terms of attitudinal change. Even with the introduction of proportional representation in 1973 the middle ground failed to materialise. In the local council elections on 30 May 1973 unionist or loyalist candidates fell into no less than thirteen categories, and in the one detailed study of voting transfers in the elections the authors comment on the very low transfers between parties across the sectarian divide: 'Of 171,772 transfers from non-centre parties, no more than 908 crossed from one side to the other [which] represents only one-half of 1 per cent of all transfers.'[20] These figures might suggest that the electorate was unsophisticated: on the contrary, it knew precisely the meaning of 'plumping', that is using the vote for one's own side only. Sixteen years later at the 1979 European Parliament elections 86 per cent of the DUP's surplus went to the UUP candidate and virtually none left the 'unionist family'. Hence the introduction of proportional representation had a paradoxical effect: it achieved its purpose of weakening the unionist monolith but failed to lay the foundations for a solid middle ground. One consequence for policy-makers attempting to fashion a solution to the Northern Ireland problem was the growing factionalism within unionism and its inability to produce a leader who could speak unequivocally for the Protestant people.

All of that was in the future. In the days before direct rule Westminster was confronted by the spectre of trying to rule through proxy. The Northern Ireland political establishment continued to go through the motions of governing overseen by two senior Whitehall officials dispatched to Belfast and occupying rooms adjacent to those of the Prime Minister and the Minister of Home Affairs with a remit to report directly to London. In addition joint working parties of officials of both governments were established to examine the extent and pace of a proposed reform package. This was to cause resentment within the Northern Ireland civil service. At the same time the local security forces were thoroughly demoralised. A committee under Lord Hunt which had been established to inquire into the structure of the RUC and B Specials reported in October 1969.[21] It led to the disarming of the RUC – although this was to be only temporary – and the disbandment of the B Specials. London also announced that Lord Scarman would lead a tribunal to inquire into particular acts of violence between March and August 1969. The tribunal's report made the interesting point that in a 'very real sense our inquiry was an investigation of police conduct'; it went on to find that, while a 'general case of a partisan force co-operating with Protestant mobs to attack Catholic people is devoid of substance', there were 'six occasions in the course of these disturbances when the police, by act or omission, were seriously at fault'.[22]

The escalation of violence between 1969 and 1972 was a further indication of political disintegration. In 1969 fourteen people lost their lives from political violence in Northern Ireland. That rose to 25 in 1970, 174 in 1971 and 470 in 1972 – the year which was to record the highest level of violence-related deaths. These figures say nothing about non-fatal incidents such as injury, rioting and explosions, nor do they tell us much about the culture that enabled violence to fester. The combined effect of all these factors was that the Conservative government was forced to prorogue Stormont and impose direct rule in March 1972. It was something that both major Westminster parties had resisted. In 1969 the Labour government was aware of its ignorance about the region and was uncertain of how direct rule would be interpreted by the RUC and the Northern Ireland civil service. Greater familiarity induced greater trepidation, and it was imposed only as the very last resort.

Reaction to its imposition was predictable. The Taoiseach, Jack Lynch, welcomed it as being sufficient to create the climate within which solutions to the Irish question could be found. After a matter of weeks the SDLP called on those Catholics who had withdrawn from public life as a protest against internment to return and (in effect) cooperate with the new administration. Unionists had reciprocated by withdrawing from public life. Their deposed Prime Minister, Brian Faulkner, supported a two-day loyalist strike which paralysed industry throughout the North. The broader Protestant community would have agreed with the statement from the Government Committee of the Presbyterian Church which 'deplored' the prorogation of Stormont.[23] A new democratic deficit had been created.

The Northern Ireland Office (NIO) was set up in 1972 as part of direct rule as a temporary measure to enable Northern Ireland politicians to reach a political accommodation. If the history of the NIO is the history of the Secretary of State for Northern Ireland then London was fortunate in the choice of William Whitelaw as the first incumbent of the post. He was conscious that he would have to move quickly to restore the conditions for stability because, as one well-informed commentator wrote some weeks later, when 'the Heath Government took over direct rule in Northern Ireland on March 30, private estimates in Whitehall of the amount of time that had been "bought" for a peaceful settlement ranged from three to six months'.[24] From the outset the Northern Secretary faced massive administrative and political problems. Administration was partially a question of structure: two locations, Belfast and London; two sets of departments and two civil services co-existing within the one ministry. The NIO had to be constructed incrementally and be sensitive to inherited animosities. The memoirs of two former Northern Ireland civil servants record tensions with the Home Office in the period prior to the imposition of direct rule, and within the Northern Ireland civil service in the period following direct rule.[25] One of Whitelaw's first tasks was to win the confidence of local officials.

A second was to come to terms with the intimacy of the local political system. Direct rule ministers were struck by the easy access of interest groups to centres of power which 'encouraged a style of instant politics that concentrates attention on the immediate without adequate concern for the future'.[26] Indeed after he became Northern Secretary in March 1974 Merlyn Rees issued an instruction to prevent elected representatives going direct to civil servants. Decisions such as this underlined the redundancy of the local political process, particularly for unionists who had seen the simulacrum of power disappear literally overnight. Many sought refuge in paramilitarism.

The Ulster Defence Association (UDA), formed in September 1971 with the ostensible aim of defending its territory from the IRA, 'grew enormously; a reasonable guess for the end of 1972 would be about 26,000 due-paying members. It also changed its structure to take on a deliberately military shape.'[27] In the immediate aftermath of the imposition of direct rule there was a rapid increase in what the authorities called 'motiveless murders', with eighty Catholics and thirty-eight Protestants being murdered before the end of 1972. Internment was applied to loyalists from early 1973. The IRA also rejected direct rule. Two senior SDLP members failed to persuade Seán Mac Stiofáin, Chief of Staff of the Provisional IRA, to call off the campaign of violence on 30 March, 1972, the day Stormont was prorogued and direct rule came into operation under the Northern Ireland (Temporary Provisions) Act 1972.

In these circumstances the creation of the NIO was a triumph over adversity. It was conceived as a temporary phenomenon and as an exercise in crisis management, and it was daily reminded of the impact of political violence with ensuing political uncertainty. It was staffed by officials mainly on loan from the Home Office, the Ministry of Defence and the Foreign Office and was paid for out of the Home Office budget. It was unlike any other territorial ministry in the UK if only because so much of its energy was consumed with security matters and (initially) constitutional innovation.

POLITICS AND VIOLENCE

Being 'second' to the Lebanon is an unenviable classification

O'LEARY AND McGARRY[28]

The cost of the conflict has been enormous in terms of deaths, injuries, compensation paid and human rights violations. The losers have been the people of Northern Ireland and, in terms of international prestige, the British government. 3,376 people were killed and over 42,000 people were injured in Northern Ireland as a result of political violence during the thirty years to 1999; this amounted to about 3 per cent of the population. This appalling level of violence took place despite 'the presence of moderately amicable relations between the relevant neighbouring states and regional powers, and in the absence of superpower rivalries'.[29] It meant that Northern Ireland was the most politically violent region within the EU; and that the UK topped the league table of nineteen western European societies in terms of deaths from political violence, the incidence of armed attacks, and successful assassinations.

The statistics are an inadequate reflection of the nature of the violence – of its intensity, of its locality, of the targets chosen and of the resources expended. They take no account either of the sophistication of the campaign of violence: 'In 1970 the IRA had to make an average of 191 attacks to kill a single member of the security forces; by 1984 18 attacks were sufficient.'[30] They cannot cover the depredations visited on communities, often by their alleged defenders. They do not allow for the dynamics of violence, for the messages which particular actions were intent in delivering, for the multi-layeredness of violence, for its political content, for its capacity to alter the political agenda. They cannot explore the levels of ambiguity that both communities shared in relation to their 'boys' or 'lads'. They fail to measure the distance between 'politics' and 'violence', and violence's lack of randomness. Above all, the figures mask the social costs. They do not explain why people tolerated it, why throughout the Troubles a place like the Bogside remained 'a community, not a war zone'.[31] In chapter 2 we explored Frank Burton's work which showed how the IRA were able to exploit the conditions in a working-class community in Belfast and adopt the role of 'defenders' in an effort to 'prevent the dominance of external social control'.[32] In this context political violence was not seen as aberrant, nor were the practitioners dismissed as outlaws.

THE 'NATURALNESS' OF VIOLENCE

Part of our purpose is to explain why political violence has been able to flourish; to raise the question whether there is a 'culture' of violence and, if so, whether it is confined to Northern Ireland; to establish the degree to which political violence has endangered the political process – in short, to make the link between politics and violence because searching for solutions is a meaningless exercise when there is not even agreement on the nature of the problem. What this approach should enable us to do is to go beyond conventional political discourse and explain the dynamics of politics and violence by exploring the role of 'history' and 'memory', the significance of symbolism and the power of myth-making – in other words the factors which invoked 'the distant bugle's echo' and persuaded ordinary men and women that it was not immoral to support the armed struggle.

Many contemporary democracies either have arisen through revolutionary violence or have been refined by political violence or the possibility of such. Some of the most stable societies tend to fall back on political prudery and forget the role that violence played in their own evolution. In Northern Ireland, Catholic communities were aware of the very real threat of loyalist paramilitarism and they had good reason to be wary of some aspects of official security policy. In addition they became more and more sceptical about the impartiality of British justice when they encountered cases like the Guildford Four and the Birmingham Six. They saw the formidable emergency powers adopted by the British state and they were aware of British violations of the European Convention on Human Rights. IRA violence impacted on the conduct of domestic politics to the detriment of British democracy. In short security reaction to Irish political violence was damaging the United Kingdom's reputation in the wider world and making it more difficult for any British government to fashion a solution for Northern Ireland since the Catholic community's trust in those governments diminished over time.

Terence O'Neill's premiership (1963–9) has been described as 'an era of good feelings' during which a 'majority of Protestants and Catholics in all kinds of localities agreed that relations were improving ... and very few anywhere thought they were getting worse'.[33] And yet no sooner had O'Neill been forced to resign – as much the result of the actions of some of his own 'followers' as of the increasing civil rights demands – than Northern Ireland spiralled into its worst period of violence since the establishment of the state. Commenting on the rapidity of the transition, one observer of republicanism has written that 'the whole process was so *natural* as to be beyond comment'. Attitudes were more important than weapons, and that was the key to the republican strategy: 'Nothing had to be imported, nothing fashioned by ideologues, nothing sold to the people, nothing secretly arranged because of events. All that was needed was to exploit the existing reality.'[34]

Despite the fact that Catholics continued to receive poor 'service' from their alleged protectors in the IRA, a sufficient number of them continued to vote for Sinn Féin or to give the IRA succour by other means to enable them to continue their campaign of destructive violence. All of this in spite of republicanism's incapacity for logical projection, encapsulated in Sean O'Faolain's comment that Sinn Féin's policy had 'since its foundation that simple formula: Freedom first; other things after'.[35] Ambiguity is evident in the remark of the nationalist MP, William O'Brien, at the end of the nineteenth century that violence is 'the only way of securing a hearing for moderation'. Commenting on its strategem of wrapping itself in ambiguity, Joseph Lee writes that it would be 'unnatural for any society enduring the traumas of nineteenth-century Ireland, including not only colonisation, but famine, depopulation, language loss and religious revival, not to have developed protective layers of ambiguity'.[36] These ambiguities are reflected in both Irish traditions, as is evident in the (loyalist) Solemn League and Covenant (1912) and in the First Dáil's Declaration of Independence (1919) where the same bald phrase, 'all means necessary', appears as a declaration of intent to use force of arms if necessary.

The attitude is based on a reading of history which emphasises victimhood and resistance: 'there is no place in Irish political culture for greatness outside the "heroic" model. Greatness is defined in terms of defiance of the external enemy.'[37] This dubious idea of patriotism is written into the canons of contemporary Irish nationalism. Compare for example the preamble to the present constitution of Ireland, Bunreacht na hÉireann, which was enacted in 1937:

> In the Name of the Most Holy Trinity, from Whom is all authority and to Whom, as our final end, all actions both of men and States must be referred,
>
> We, the people of Éire,
>
> Humbly acknowledging all our obligations to our Divine Lord, Jesus Christ, Who sustained our fathers through centuries of trial,
>
> Gratefully remembering their heroic and unremitting struggle to regain the rightful independence of our Nation,
>
> And seeking to promote the common good, with due observance of

> Prudence, Justice and Charity, so that the dignity and freedom of the individual may be assured, true social order attained, the unity of our country restored, and concord established with other nations,
>
> Do hereby adopt, enact, and give to ourselves this Constitution.

with the more graphic message which opens the 1916 Proclamation of the Republic:

> Irishmen and Irishwomen: In the name of God and of the dead generations from which she receives her old tradition of nationhood, Ireland, through us, summons her children to the flag and strikes for her freedom.

Both of those statements reveal the unfolding of a political culture with a profound sense of piety, a deep sense of history and of grievance, and an essential sense of the contemporaneity of the past overlaid with a fundamental religiosity secularised through a doctrine of manifest destiny. As late as 1972 a study of the Republic's political elite revealed that 45 per cent of that group had revolutionary experience and 18 per cent had participated in the 1916 Rising, including two who had became Taoiseach (Eamon de Valera and Seán Lemass) and two who had become President (Seán T. O'Kelly and de Valera).[38]

The symbolism and the psychology which enabled those to rise in 1916 appear in the 1937 preamble and are enlisted by the new generation of revolutionaries after 1969. A reading of Gerry Adams' *The Politics of Irish Freedom* (1986) confirms the degree to which his generation self-consciously donned the mantle of those earlier revolutionaries who, in turn, took their lead from the Fenians of the 1860s, the Young Irelanders of the 1840s and the United Irishmen of 1798. Indeed, the 1916 Proclamation refers to the fact that in the previous three centuries Ireland's right to independence had been asserted by force of arms on six occasions. Beyond the overtly political there was in Ireland a whole literary tradition devoted to the creation of moral and symbolic capital to be found in some of the poetry from the seventeenth century onwards, that is after the Elizabethan conquest with the disappearance of the old Irish aristocratic order and the transfer of 85 per cent of Irish land into the hands of new English colonists.[39]

In these circumstances republicans tended to invoke 'History'. In reality theirs was an appeal to the folk memory. A literary critic, reflecting on his own Irish background, makes the connection between history and memory: 'History is only one way of being significant. Memory gives the unofficial sense of history, effects an order not sequential but agglutinative. That is why we never ask our memories to line up rationally or sequentially, like soldiers on parade: they obey our orders, but not always or in the form we prescribe.'[40] That should be read alongside the words of the Polish Nobel laureate Czeslaw Milosz: 'It is possible that there is no other memory than the memory of wounds'.[41]

The catholics of west Belfast were only too conscious of loyalist incursions on to the Falls Road in August 1969 with what seemed suspiciously like official collusion, of the burning to the ground of Bombay Street, and of an army curfew (of dubious legality) imposed on the Lower Falls in June 1970 immediately after a Conservative government had assumed office. These people needed no lessons in history. Their elders could recall vividly earlier incursions in the 1930s and 1920s, and the fears were passed from one generation to the next. Adams personified that generational continuity. As we saw, he comes from a family of republican 'aristocrats'.

At a more profound level a (Catholic) narrative of oppression confronted settler vigilance with its emphasis on territoriality. Settler vigilance – in the form of either the mob or locally recruited militias (official and unofficial) – 'taught the natives that power and self-assertion were the property of those who could successfully inflict violence'. The result was a circularity of violence in which 'vigilance of power perpetually generates the symptoms of rebellion it purportedly guards against; while rebellion on the principle of collective responsibility validates the anxieties of the dominant'.[42] It was, as we saw earlier, a circularity which predated the establishment of Northern Ireland and has been traced through the tradition of 'public banding'.[43] and an intimidatory political culture.[44] In more recent times sections of the Protestant community in Northern Ireland perceived the civil rights campaign as a challenge to their very existence and entered into a form of public banding because they believed they could not rely on the state to protect their interests. In that situation the whole system becomes 'one of threatened violence in which the state is a feeble pivot between its ostensible supporters . . . and the natives'.[45]

This was a situation that the republican movement was able to exploit. It was the wholesale intimidation of some Catholic communities in 1969 that resurrected the IRA. It was able to reveal the state's hegemony in incidents like the introduction of internment in August 1971 when only republicans were interned. It demonstrated its capacity to resist compromise when the Northern Ireland government and parliament were prorogued in March 1972. Catholics noted the illegal Ulster Workers' Council (UWC) strike in May 1974; the 'constitutional stoppage' in 1977; the creation of a 'Third Force' in 1981; establishment insensitivity and the demeanour of Margaret Thatcher during the 1981 hunger strikes; the rise of the Ulster Clubs movement in 1985 and of Ulster Resistance in 1986. They noted the language of some loyalist politicians and charges of collusion between the security forces and loyalist paramilitaries from time to time. All of this was grist to the republican mill.

In 1969 republicans may have lacked weaponry and a ready-made infrastructure. Both of these problems could be overcome fairly easily. In any case they had the huge advantage that, unlike 1916, this was a genuinely popular uprising; it began among fearful Catholics in the ghettoes, and then, with the introduction of repressive legislation and internment and the events of Bloody Sunday, it widened into a growing Catholic disillusionment which crossed class barriers. One estimation in 1984 calculated that 60,000 mothers, wives and children were 'currently affected by the imprisonment of a near relative'.[46] Another study chronicles the disenchantment of the Catholic professional class in the period from internment onwards.[47] The younger generation, in both communities, took more direct action.

No remarks can do justice to the sheer human carnage of three decades of violence; no one who has not experienced the violence can even begin to fathom the hurt, despair and hopelessness of the victims' families and friends. In the beginning there were those who could recount every death, every incident – not as some ghoulish pastime but as a means of humanising the victims. But then the numbers overwhelmed us all and we turned away from the despotism of fact. We fell back on drawing up our own lists of those whom we could recall and the circumstances of their deaths – which became an unwitting form of erasure and of silence.[48] Others campaigned to maintain the primacy of life. Some, such as Gordon Wilson, engaged in acts of transcendence that may have had profound effects on dampening the cycles of violence. His immediate reaction to the murder of his daughter Marie in the Enniskillen Remembrance Sunday bombing in 1987 – 'I have lost my daughter and we shall miss her but I bear no ill will, I bear no grudge . . . Don't ask me, please, for a purpose. I don't have a purpose, I don't have an answer, but I know there has to be a plan' – was one such act of transcendence, 'connecting what violence had severed'.[49]

Gordon Wilson spent the rest of his life in a search for peace. He was appointed to the Irish Senate and held face-to-face talks with the IRA. But others have been forgotten – itself an indictment of the anonymity of widespread violence. Space permits only one example. Fourteen-year-old Stephen Parker, who was posthumously awarded the Queen's Commendation for bravery, was killed in a bomb explosion on 21 July 1972. He was one of nine killed and 130 injured in the IRA's Bloody

Friday bombs in Belfast. His father, a Protestant minister, the Reverend Joseph Parker, identified him by 'his hands, and by a box of trick matches he had in his pocket and by the scout belt he was wearing'. Three items – corporeal, trivial and sentimental – identified the lifespan of an innocent victim. His father conducted a service in November 1972 for the (then) 436 victims of the Troubles from every walk of life; a white cross was planted for each individual. The Reverend Parker went on to found the Witness for Peace Movement but he was a man before his time: 'We held services for everybody, soldiers, IRA, everybody, all the dead ... A lot of people in my own church didn't approve of what we were doing. I was asked by my bishop if I would confine my peace activities to my day off.'[50] The Parker family emigrated to Canada in 1974.

TWO DIMENSIONS OF POLITICAL VIOLENCE

I Communicative

[The Red Brigade's] actions are intended as 'armed propaganda' designed to illustrate new possibilities of political action, secure some form of political recognition for the group and provoke effects among opponents which will contribute to their own projects. By the systematic use of violence conveying the rejection of the current rules [the Red Brigades] establish a frame for communication between themselves and the political defenders of that order, whose actions and inactions cannot avoid interpretation as responses, direct or indirect, to the acts of violence

DAVID MOSS[51]

For 'Red Brigades' read IRA. There are two broad views of Irish political violence: it is mindless or psychopathic; or it has a rational purpose. We shall work on the second assumption. The IRA had to convince those in the Catholic ghettoes that 'if armed struggle did not exist there would be no hope of getting change'. They had to convince them that 'IRA volunteers are actually civilians, political people who decide for short periods in their lives to take part in armed action ... The reality is of people who have consciously decided that armed struggle is a political necessity.'[52] As the conflict continued it was not too difficult to persuade enough people that that was the case.

Burton's research in one Catholic ghetto in Belfast, 'Anro', identified the volatility of such communities: 'The area has been saturated by troops and is under constant surveillance. Hundreds of the district's inhabitants have been interned or detained or sentenced to prison. Such a violent affront upon the conventional activities of the community might well have resulted in anomic breakdown.' He goes on to explain how anomie – 'a condition in which our existing knowledge and beliefs are no longer able to cope with a radical new situation. A resulting struggle takes place to reconstruct both mental and moral worlds' – was contained: 'the existing culture of Anro stretches to accommodate the unknowable and unthinkable, reinterpreting events to sustain a sense of reality and striving to maintain coherence in the face of massive disturbance'.[53] Security responses to republican activity ensured the necessary coherence. No matter how horrendous particular IRA actions may have been there was no substantial desertion of the republican cause. The IRA had persuaded enough people to believe that theirs was the only way to release new possibilities of political action.

They also demonstrated a capacity for endurance and an ability to attract a sufficiently high calibre of volunteer. There was surprising endorsement of the latter by a British army report of 1979, 'Northern Ireland: Future Terrorist Trends', which concluded gloomily that there was no prospect in the military or political terrain of defeat of the IRA over the following five years.[54] So they had established a space to conduct a campaign of armed propaganda that was focussed, sustained and, by their own lights, generally restrained. When they pulled off 'spectaculars' – as with the bombing of the Conservative Party conference at Brighton in October 1984 when five people, including a Conservative MP, were killed – they displayed their propaganda skills. The IRA statement of admission was simplicity itself:

> The IRA claim responsibility for the detonation of 100lb of gelignite in Brighton against the British Cabinet and Tory warmongers. Mrs Thatcher will now realise that Britain cannot occupy our country and torture our prisoners and shoot our people on their own streets and get away with it. Today we were unlucky, but remember we only have to be lucky once – you will have to be lucky always. Give Ireland peace and there will be no war.[55]

It is difficult to overestimate the significance of the Brighton bomb. The IRA had displayed considerable ingenuity in planting a bomb in a maximum security area. They had targeted the Prime Minister and had ensured that the authorities would thereafter have to be on constant alert. They had increased the likelihood that repressive measures would be imposed on the Irish in Britain. Above all, they had secured maximum publicity around the world. The statistics on violence were not as important as the impact. Even when there was a lull in their campaign in 1980 a member of the IRA Army Council warned that the 'British are sliding into their 1977 mistake of predicting our defeat. They're fighting a statistical war. We're not. We're fighting a political war.'[56] More important than the damage that had been inflicted was the fact that the IRA had established the communicative dimension of political violence. To borrow from Moss again, their 'opponents had no exit, no opportunity simply to ignore acts of violence and thus to escape the communicative frame'.[57] Having established this communicative dimension the next challenge for the IRA would be to demonstrate to their own community that violent acts could have substantial political consequences. They would also have to ensure that the communicative frame did not become counterproductive; in other words, that their actions did not alienate their own followers.

II Symbolic

The IRA can hardly hope to achieve its aim by force of
argument, definition and reason. They must transcend the
terms of any such discourse. The only way to do that is to take
some morally intimidating course of action, something that
requires courage, passion and selflessness. Discourse can only
be transcended by action; inside a prison action can take only a
symbolic form, all the more potent for being irrational and in
every respect exorbitant. There is no gesture more compelling
than the hunger strike, and ideally the hunger strike to death.

DENIS DONOGHUE[58]

Donoghue was writing at the height of the second phase of the hunger strikes of 1980–1 when ten republican prisoners went to their deaths in protest against their status inside the Maze Prison. The awkward phrase 'went to their deaths' is deliberate because these acts discommoded the political and religious establishments, and led to questions about the nature of the deaths: suicide or self-starvation? The original pathologist's report had recorded 'self-imposed starvation'. After protests from the families the medical certificates were amended to record the cause of death as 'starvation'; and the coroner found the cause of death to be 'starvation, self-imposed'. In a deeply religious community the deaths led to a debate about the Thomist tradition and whether 'intention' was the crucial factor: 'To intend to terminate one's life – that is the distinguishing mark of the act of suicide. To bring about the termination of one's life by so arranging the circumstances that one dies but with the intention of bringing about some other state of affairs, is not suicide.'[59] The debate pointed up different theological interpretations between some of the hierarchy in England and Wales, and their colleagues in Ireland.

The hunger strike 'once again reaffirmed Protestants' sense of their own victimhood and helplessness, invalidating their grievances, making meaningless the deaths of their coreligionists who gave their lives for the protection of the state, reminding them of the perilous state of their existence'.[60] It proved to be a hollow victory for Margaret Thatcher. Even before it had come to an end the *New Statesman* (14 August 1981) was commenting on the IRA's tactical victory: 'By her continuing inflexibility over the H Blocks, Mrs Thatcher has achieved what the Provisional IRA always wanted. She has made politics in Northern Ireland into a straight confrontation between the British Government and the Provos, in which everyone else is rendered powerless or irrelevant.' Republican martyrology was reasserting itself and its deep sense of moral certitude.

The religious symbolism of the protest was not lost. Republicans had shifted their role from producers of violence to purveyors of *meaning*. Following the 1916 Rising posters had appeared around Dublin depicting the martyred Pearse supported by the mythic figure of Mother Erin in a *pietà* position and brandishing a Tricolour; the caption read 'All is Changed'. Precisely the same images and symbols reappeared in the aftermath of the hunger strike. And all ensured that the distant bugle's echo resounded once again. Furthermore, the growing support which the hunger strikers garnered in the wider Catholic community led them along the electoral path. And their success in that activity convinced Sinn Féin that indeed they had made the connection between politics and violence, that the armed struggle did have a positive political dimension.

CONCLUSION

The trouble with victimhood is that there is no sense of perpetration. It is always *they* who are to blame. Take the reaction of Gerry Adams to the murder by the UVF of a young Sinn Féin activist in October 1992. He condemned elements in the media, the churches and some political parties which 'demonise' Sinn Féin: 'You can censor us, call us thugs and murderers, call us fanatics and lunatics, refuse to speak to us, imprison us, extradite us, ban us, torture us and kill us, but there will always be enough of us to ensure that one day you will talk to us. No other party has suffered like Sinn Féin, but we are still here.' All parties to the conflict could have produced a variant of this statement. And all of them had something else in common – none of them were prepared to claim responsibility. But Adams' statement was significant in the context of this chapter. It was about making the link between politics and violence. It was about more than resistance. A graveside oration was used to send the message that inclusion would occur and that republicans would take their rightful place in the political process. The dead victim symbolised the valour of the republican movement and, as in the past, funerals were used to convey the sense of the risen people finding their place in the political sun.

The 1990s were to be about a politics of inclusion that altered the parameters of the problem. We have been concerned to illustrate the complexity, dynamics and unpredictability of political violence. Coming out of violence would present new challenges, not the least of which would be a culture of victimhood. It was one thing to replace the Armalite with the ballot box but it would be more difficult to create a climate of trust and reconciliation. Those who had vivid memories of the 'long war' knew that peace would not be embedded easily.

4

DARK ROSALEEN AND THE
MAIDEN AUNT

... for the outside world Dark Rosaleen has a sex appeal, whereas
Britain is regarded as a maiden aunt.

SIR JOHN MAFFEY[1]

Self-deprecation can either be a device of the vulnerable or be utilised
by those who wish to disarm criticism.[2] Sir John Maffey, the United
Kingdom's Representative to Ireland (1939–49), belongs in the latter
category. The above quotation appears in a lengthy memorandum,
'The Irish question in 1945', which he had prepared for the incoming
Labour government led by Clement Attlee. The tone is sanguine rather
than complacent and is based on a policy of functional cooperation: 'we
can now talk to Éire on a cold factual horse-trading basis, knowing
perfectly well that the cards are in our hands. All the really necessary
bridges between our two islands can be built on a clear economic basis,
and on this a happier and healthier relationship with the widest implications and associations can in time be established.'[3]

Maffey was a shrewd diplomat. He had a sense of the present (rea-
lising that Ireland's wartime neutrality had damaged its bargaining
power) as well as a sense of history – hence his concern with the outside
world. He would have appreciated (to borrow a more recent phrase)
the notion of 'the totality of relationships within these islands'. He
knew that the Dublin–London relationship could not be separated
from the Belfast–London axis or, for that matter, from the Belfast–
Dublin stand-off.

Any examination of these relationships must start from a simple, but
profound, position: Ireland is England's first colony, a fact which is
known to everyone in present-day Northern Ireland; and a fact which

allows for the contemporaneity of past whereby an act of 'heroism' today can be linked to the glorious deeds of 1916 or 1689 or 1641 or whenever:

> Ireland, far from being an oddity, was in many ways a classic example of the development of popular anti-colonial nationalism in a conquered country. Its peculiarities derive mainly from the fact that it was one of the first such cases, much as the oddities of the English Constitution derive in great part from the fact that England was the first true nation-state. Ireland was, perhaps, the first true colony of England, and therefore its tradition of anti-colonial nationalism may be one of the oldest in the world.[4]

Maffey believed that because Ireland's 'nationalist and separatist status is now definitely established' Britain was confronted with an Irish question 'in a simpler and more manageable form than ever before'. However, nothing is simple in Anglo-Irish affairs, as events between partition and the outbreak of war in 1939 had demonstrated. Indeed before Maffey retired from his post in 1949 he was to witness an unforeseen event when the South left the Commonwealth and became the Republic of Ireland. And his successors have been struggling mightily ever since the outbreak of the Troubles in 1968 to come to terms with the many ramifications which the *Northern* Ireland problem has had on Anglo-Irish relations. This chapter begins to confront some of those ramifications through a Dublin–London lens. It will be concerned with the evolving, asymmetrical Anglo-Irish relationship in the years after Irish 'independence' had been attained. It will examine how the junior partner, economically and psychologically stunted as it was, set about overcoming its subordinate status through the Commonwealth, the Irish diaspora and the anticolonial struggle. It will also examine the impact this had on British constitutional evolution and on the United Kingdom's (dubious) position as a major power in the world system.

THE PROSPERO COMPLEX

In 1950 the radical French historian Octave Mannoni argued that the coloniser has created a neurotic sense of inferiority in the colonised. He called it the Prospero complex.[5] This section will examine, in the context of Anglo-Irish relations, that sense of inferiority inherited by the independent Irish state after 1922 but it will assert that if inferiority was the property of one of the actors, guilt and a sense of immobilism belonged to the other.

One needs to be aware of the sheer effort in trying to manage – rather than govern – Ireland. The Act of Union (1800) 'was designed to permit British statesmen to devote less, not more, of their time to Irish Affairs',[6] yet as we have seen an enormous amount of time was spent in the security domain alone. In addition 'developments over the Irish question had, by 1911, thrown very grave doubt on the political system's capacity to contain irreconcilable conflict' between the Conservative and Labour parties.[7]

We need to remember that Britain had ruled over a world system and, in that respect, the 'Irish troubles are useful to us because they form a kind of intersection between the problems of empire and the problems of domestic British politics'.[8] Ireland attained dominion status at a time when the Chief of Imperial General Staff was writing: 'In no single theatre are we strong enough . . . not in Ireland, not in England, not on the Rhine, not in Constantinople, nor Batoum, nor Palestine, nor Mesopotamia, nor Persia, nor India.' He was writing during a period (1919–23) when expenditure on the army was cut by a half each year (amounting to a cumulative decrease from £395 million to £45 million), and when the Prime Minister, Andrew Bonar Law, was announcing that Britain could no longer be the policeman of the world. Notwithstanding the fact that 'it would be hard to find any more imperially-minded government in British history than Lloyd George's', the Irish Free State attained dominion status in this period.[9] That was far short of what the Irish revolutionaries sought:

> in 1922 by terms of the 'treaty' or 'agreement' imposed (according to de Valera) on Ireland, certain conditions and the wholly inappropriate status of Dominion (for Ireland was a mother country rather than a daughter nation which had evolved gradually to independence) were thrust upon Ireland: a category quite alien to its sense of nationality.[10]

In the meantime Ireland strove after a recognition of that nationality. But before we examine that we need to say how Ireland arrived at dominion status in 1922, and what were its consequences. The facts can be stated simply. Following the execution of the leaders of the 1916 Rising the Irish electorate abandoned the more moderate constitutional nationalists and threw in their lot with Sinn Féin. At the 1918 general election Sinn Féin won 73 of the country's 105 Westminster seats. They took this as a mandate for independence, and those who were not in prison or on the run, twenty-seven in all, established Dáil Éireann on 21 January 1919 charged with creating the Irish Republic that had been proclaimed in 1916. It was proscribed in September 1919;

meanwhile an Anglo-Irish war raged until 1921. Sinn Féin renewed its mandate in the general election of May 1921 which was held under the electoral provisions of the Government of Ireland Act (1920). On convening in August these Sinn Féin deputies constituted themselves the Second Dáil, and it was this body that ratified the Articles of Agreement for a Treaty which was concluded with British representatives in December 1921. The Treaty provided for the establishment of a self-governing dominion under the title of the Irish Free State for the whole island; however by presenting an Address to the Crown, Northern Ireland could retain its separate status under the 1920 Act: this option was exercised immediately. In October 1922 Dáil Éireann enacted the Constitution of the Irish Free State. It came into force, and the Irish Free State came into existence, on 6 December 1922. Partition was now a reality.

The Irish Free State was born into civil war. All Irish nationalists were conscious of the truncated nature of the state, and the Treaty signatories accepted that they had won only 'the freedom to achieve freedom'. Sinn Féin split in two on the question of the Treaty – into pro and anti camps – and the result was the Irish Civil War. The cost of the civil war – it began on 28 June 1922 – was horrendous. Fanning estimates that the military casualties alone were between 4,000 and 5,000, and that material damage and the cost of the civil war were immense: 'What is certain is that many more Irish nationalists were killed by other Irish nationalists in the civil war than were killed by British forces in the "five glorious years" of the revolutionary struggle.'[11]

It is difficult to assess the psychological damage done by the civil war but there can be no doubt that it shaped the Irish party political scene for the following half-century or more. Its legacy – 'civil war politics' – has diminished in recent decades, partly due to the continuing violence in Northern Ireland. That has imposed its own sobriety and has played some therapeutic role in Southern politics.

In any case the Prospero complex was already a fact of life. It can be examined at two levels: a collective mentality which strove after security; and a dependency syndrome which curbed the Irish psyche. Joseph Lee writes of a collective mentality of 'traditional' Ireland which can be traced far back in history. He looks at its manifestations only since the nineteenth century and sees it in an obsessive attachment to land which derived from the fact that land was equated with security:

> The concern with property rights was wholly natural in the light of the alternatives facing the holders of land or jobs. The price of failure was frighteningly high. It involved, for the vast majority of the

victims, far more than mere temporary unemployment ... [in] a
society characterised by intense population pressure in relation to
available employment opportunities ... Economic loss involved
psychic humiliation. The husband had failed his wife, the father his
children ... It was entirely rational in those circumstances for the
individual to prize security above all, and to abhor risk taking when
the price of failure was catastrophe.[12]

Lee notes, too, that there was very little discernible relationship – except for the very few – between effort and reward; and that the large
gains made by farmers in the nineteenth century (as a result of the Great
Famine of 1845–50 and the Land War of 1879–82) arose more from
collective political power than from individual economic performance.

But collective political power had its limitations, as was evident after
independence. Lee bemoans the lack of a programme for national development and sees this as a symbol of 'the dependency syndrome
which had wormed its way into the Irish psyche during the long centuries of foreign dominance':

The Irish mind was enveloped in, and to some extent suffocated by,
the English mental embrace. This was quite natural. A small occupied
country, with an alien ruling class, culturally penetrated by the language and many of the thought processes of the coloniser, was bound
in large measure to imitate the example of the powerful and the
prosperous.[13]

As we shall see the end result was that the revolutionaries inherited
much of the British legacy: 'Absorption in the English model gravely
limited Irish perspectives. When allied to the elusive but crucial psychological factors that inspired the instinct of inferiority, it shrivelled
Irish perspectives on Irish potential.'[14]

Another factor which may have shrivelled Irish potential was
something to which we referred in chapter 1 – emigration. Oliver
MacDonagh notes its influence: 'Emigration was the enemy of economic change, the solvent of economic conflict. More than any other
single force it was responsible for the immobility of Ireland – the politics of constitutional forms apart – in the opening decades of the
[twentieth] century.' He calculates that between 1850 and 1900 more
than two million Irish-born people were living overseas at a time when
the home population was dropping steadily. The social effects were
such that Ireland had 'a familial structure in which perhaps every second child migrated from country to town, from town to city or, most
commonly of all, beyond the seas. Children grew up in fear or hope,
the expectation or close certainty, of leaving home or homeland.' The
inevitable consequence, in MacDonagh's graphic phrase, was that 'a

certain air of impermanence pervaded Irish society: so much of it was provisional, preparatory'.[15] The same pattern repeated itself in independent Ireland.

An example of this lack of self-confidence can be seen in the evolution of Irish foreign policy. When asked what was Sinn Féin's foreign policy, the party's founder, Arthur Griffith, said: 'In any issue I find out where England stands. Ireland will be found on the other side.'[16] No doubt that was the astute answer for the audience to which it was addressed but unfortunately he meant every word he said. From the very first day of its existence the Irish Free State was obsessed with the complementary problems of partition and the quest for total independence from the United Kingdom. The English 'fact' was everything: 'the first question to be answered was less *what* foreign policy independent Ireland should pursue than whether the Irish Free State could establish *any* foreign policy genuinely independent of Britain'.[17] In 1923 the Dáil department which had been known as 'Foreign Affairs' changed its name to 'External Affairs' (until it reverted to 'Foreign Affairs' once again in 1971) allegedly to satisfy the British preference that dominion relations with non-Commonwealth countries be conducted through London.

The Department of External Affairs suffered from a problem of status from the outset. It was considered to be transient: diplomatic relations were slow in being established. Relations were established with Britain in 1923, with the United States in 1924, and then with the Holy See, France and Germany during the course of the 1920s. In the following decade Belgium, Spain, Italy and Canada were added, so that by 1939 the Free State had diplomatic relations with only nine states.

This relatively slow development indicates the tentative nature and narrow scope of policy-making in the earlier years of the state. So much depended on the relationship with Britain. Thus in 1937 Eamon de Valera desisted from naming the state 'Poblacht na hÉireann' (Republic of Ireland) in the new constitution because he feared British retaliation and he held out some limited hope that an association with the Commonwealth (and its link with the Crown) might assist in ending partition.[18] It is a moot point whether the obsession with partition added up to a foreign policy. Keatinge reminds us that 'the adjective "foreign" applies not only to what we do outside the boundaries of the state but to a wide variety of external forces which affect what we can do within the state'.[19] Since the government's primary motive was to expand the state to include the 'six lost counties' (of Northern Ireland) and since it seemed to believe that that 'must be sought in the larger general play of English interest'[20] it tended to take a rather restricted view of the content of foreign policy. A graphic example would be the contention of Frank Aiken, Minister for External Affairs, during the 1960s that the issues of membership of the EEC and that of Northern Ireland were 'constitutional issues' and therefore not primarily his business.[21]

We must not overstate the case. By 1952–3 Ireland was making payments to thirty-three international organizations and had some form of diplomatic representation in eighteen states, although some of their representatives were accredited to more than one state'.[22] As Ireland found its place in the international community it made its presence felt through, firstly, advancing the principle of equality of status among British Commonwealth members; secondly, playing a role in the League of Nations in an effort to distance itself from British influence;[23] and thirdly, identifying with the anti-imperialist struggle and the quest for world peace in the United Nations.[24] Over time the government came to view the UN as the principal framework for the conduct of Irish foreign policy and it became the forum in which Ireland encountered most of the major international issues of the day. One outstanding example of its influence in this forum was its 'prolonged and perspicacious effort' to secure a treaty on the non-proliferation of nuclear weapons, an initiative which 'appears to have been purely Irish' and which culminated in the unanimous adoption by the UN's General Assembly on 4 December 1961 of Ireland's draft resolution on the issue – 'a notable, if not historic, culmination of Ireland's unremitting efforts over four years'.[25]

In this context it is instructive to examine Irish self-doubt when the UN was created. The legal adviser in the Department of External Affairs suggested that 'in theory at least, it would look as though a small state joining the United Nations must irretrievably abandon its national security, not to say part of its sovereignty, to a Military Committee staffed by the Great Powers'.[26] We shall see that, with the passage of time, independent Ireland may have adopted a more realistic view of sovereignty than its dominant neighbour.

Contact with the wider world removed some of the obsessional nature – the overwhelming desire to end the internal hurt of partition – of Irish foreign policy, especially after Ireland joined the EEC in 1973, and Ireland began to appreciate the fundamental asymmetry in the Anglo-Irish relationship. It followed a policy of 'raising the sore thumb', that is availing of every opportunity at international forums to complain of the evils of partition. The policy was best explained by the Minister for External Affairs, Liam Cosgrave, in 1954 when he informed the Senate that 'if we work on the basis of an acceptance of the policy of conversion, of a policy of cooperation, and avail of every opportunity which is provided, either in this country or at international gatherings, to point out the injustice of partition [which] may in its own way militate against the peace of the world, we will proceed along the road towards a realisation of the aim which we all desire'.[27]

The policy had certain defects. In the first place, the international community had other things on its mind. Secondly, the task was monumental. To make a rather obvious comparison: in 1972 the British diplomatic service had over 6,000 officials and 131 accredited foreign missions,[28] whereas the Republic of Ireland had 153 officials of foreign service or equivalent grades and 31 accredited foreign missions by the mid-1970s.[29] It would be foolish to make too direct a comparison given that much of the Irish diplomatic effort was focused specifically on the Northern Ireland problem (especially in the period after 1970); by the same token it would be foolish to ignore such a discrepancy in resources.

Asymmetry asserts itself in the legacy that Britain bequeathed to independent Ireland. As early as 1881 the *Freeman's Journal* commented that if 'ever a country passed through a parliamentary apprenticeship of the fullest term, Ireland is that country'.[30] Independent Ireland inherited the concept of the nature and role of party, a civil service bearing the stamp 'made in England' and parliamentary principles such as ministerial responsibility. When de Valera came to power in 1932 he did little to change that inheritance.[31] David Harkness has drawn attention to:

> the very great extent to which British assumptions and precedents have in fact shaped both the framework and the practices of Irish constitutional and political life, even though they are to a degree transplanted to an alien environment ... Ronan Fanning has shown how deep-seated were the habits of civil servants who helped transfer power to the infant state in the 1920s and he has quoted G.P.S. Hogan's comment on the constitutions of 1922 and 1937 that they 'enshrine what have been called the "fundamental principles" of the British financial system' ... Some 98 per cent of the civil service of the Irish Free State had transferred from British employment and it has been remarked that there was 'no immediate disturbance of any kind in the daily work of the average civil servant'.[32]

It would be a mistake to assume that Ireland inherited *in toto* the Westminster model because British domination of Ireland fell short of absorption.[33] Indeed the Dáil committee that drafted the Free State's 1922 constitution departed substantially from the main British tradition. It was critical of many aspects of British political practice such as what it perceived as the artificial character of parliamentary party conflict. It sought to create a more direct and active role for the people in public affairs and tried to erect some safeguards against executive dominance. It was committed to looking after the (Protestant) minority. There were some innovations in the committee's draft including the provision for proportional representation, for the legislative referendum and initiative, and for expert 'extern' ministers in government who would be free from the constraints and uncertainties of the usual parliamentary support. As a result, the constitution had, according to Brian Farrell, 'a modern and even a continental cast'.[34]

One final comment on the Prospero complex centres on the significance of religion in Anglo-Irish relations. The point has been well made by Tom Garvin and deserves to be quoted at length when he asserts that the British government's real concern with Ireland (in the seventeenth century) was political and strategic rather than economic:

> Even the emphasis on religious issues apparent in British policy drew much of its force from a fear of Catholicism as an international political organisation actually or potentially hostile to the English post-revolutionary political settlement. It is evident that religion was central to Anglo-Irish relations, because religion was central to the basis of *English* national political integration in the seventeenth century: Catholics in seventeenth-century Britain or Ireland were politically unassimilable because the British constitution was profoundly sectarian. Ironically, this fact ensured that religion became the basis of the Irish nationalist community as well; religious passions were laid on top of an older sense of difference. The confessional basis of Irish ethnic identity was unwittingly derived from the religious basis of the English national revolution of the sixteenth and seventeenth centuries.[35]

The Reformation did not take hold in Ireland; the people did not abandon their traditional faith. It became a country 'in which the religion of the people was not the religion of the state, a situation without parallel in post-Reformation Europe; and religion was added to the grievances of the Irish against English rule'.[36] As the church of 75 per cent of the Irish population, as an instrument of cultural defence,[37] and as a body which asserted a distinctive national identity, the Catholic Church developed a certain Anglophobic ethos and a heteronomous relationship with politics. Its Anglophobia rested on its self-image as the church of the Penal Laws, the church which had withstood persecution and had given spiritual and political guidance to its flock.

In these circumstances the church was often at the forefront of the struggle for Irish freedom displaying precisely the same traits as its flock. Oliver MacDonagh, for instance, has analysed the systematic political ambivalence of the Irish church in the nineteenth century and concludes with a commonplace which is profound: 'The priests were but the populace writ large.' He traces a triple ambiguity which enabled the Catholic Church to hold an uneasy balance when the republican or revolutionary secret society was rising or dominant in Irish society. He calls the first ambiguity 'recessional' – as 'nationalistic violence receded in time so might it be the more safely sanctioned'. The second was the 'gestural' – 'the gestures which carried no dangerous consequences within themselves ... the rank-and-file clergy ... [giving] vent to their inherent anglophobia and [participating] in national posturing in complete security'. The third strand of ambiguity gave him slightly more difficulty: he described it as 'humanitarianism' – 'what one really needs is a compound embracing sympathy with suffering, the distinction between a man and his beliefs, and elemental tribal identification'.[38]

All of this added up to a 'strong sense of a shared historical fate ... acting as powerful social bonding within the Catholic community', a bonding which could be invoked 'in the mobilization of the Catholic masses for political action by Daniel O'Connell in the second quarter of the nineteenth century'.[39] O'Connell may have harnessed the Catholic Church to Irish nationalist politics in the 1820s but it was the Parnellite movement of the 1880s that cemented the relationship. The political influence of the clergy reached its peak about 1850–70 although it remained important for the rest of the nineteenth century.[40] We should be aware, too, of the constraints placed upon Catholic clerical control including a tradition of independence of clerical guidance on some major political issues, and a surprising tradition of aloofness of church and state in Ireland.[41]

One of the ironies of partition was that it 'represented a victory of sorts for the politics of community over the politics of nationality'. The result was the emergence of two confessional political entities: 'in one a disaffected minority faced an insecure and intransigent majority resulting in a deeply divided society where communal violence seemed endemic'. And in the Irish Free State the result was 'an unusual congruence of community values and symbols defined in religious terms and the legislative framework and symbols of a national state. This congruence was acceptable to the majority of the citizens, even though it was sharply at odds with the republican tradition to which the official rhetoric of the state gave regular obeisance between the twenties and the late fifties.'[42]

Religion became the badge of distinction within Northern Ireland

and between both parts of Ireland, notwithstanding the fact that the original constitution, the Government of Ireland Act (1920), explicitly outlawed religious discrimination. In an increasingly secular world religion brought communal comfort *and* added to the distance between Ireland and the outside world. Hence the Northern Ireland conflict has been perceived as a bitter communal strife based on religion and national identity: 'One has to go back to the seventeenth century to find [a war] in which both sides find their focus of cohesion and of antagonism in a version of the Christian faith.'[43] Contrast this with Britain where a religious tolerance has developed which is 'simply a reflection of the decline in religious conviction'.[44]

But there were those in Ireland who saw their faith as something more than communal comfort and, incidentally, gave some credence to fears about the internationalism of Catholicism. Prominent among them was Eamon de Valera, who in February 1933 expressed this internationalism in a broadcast from a new Radio Éireann station in Athlone when he urged his listeners to undertake the new mission 'of helping to save Western civilisation' from the scourge of materialism. Now that was a tall (and genuine) order for a tiny underdeveloped state to undertake. De Valera did not stand alone in his seeking after a 'spiritual dominion'. In a Dáil debate in 1956 the Minister for External Affairs, Liam Cosgrave, asserted that Ireland had 'throughout the world an influence far beyond any material strength or wealth', in view of the role of Irish missionaries and their contribution to education in many parts of the world.[45]

This view of religion as a mobilising agent echoes Seamus Heaney's thoughts on the state of the Irish language. It was, he said, both 'a fortification and an enrichment'.[46] Irish politicians were influenced by the 1931 papal encyclical *Quadragesimo Anno*. It fortified their own sense of community and provided them with a missionary role that enabled them to overcome other inadequacies in the world system. The *locus classicus* of this mentality may well be contained in James Hogan's introduction to his book on proportional representation: 'Progress in civilisation is at least as much a question of religious and moral and artistic values as one of material organisation or mechanical invention. Since material progress may turn to undesirable no less than to desirable ends, there can be little doubt that the most important single factor in determining the course of human affairs will always continue to be human nature itself.'[47] Human nature in independent Ireland wore the face of conservative Catholicism.

SEARCHING FOR 'TERMS OF EQUALITY'

Sometimes we underestimate the influence of symbolism on the political process. Students of Irish politics ignore this at their peril. Our history is replete with conflict centring on the question of symbols. One such conflict occurred during the Anglo-Irish Treaty negotiations when they almost broke down over the contentious issue of an oath of allegiance to the monarch. The version agreed to in the end contains the following oath: 'I . . . do solemnly swear true faith and allegiance to the Constitution of the Irish Free State as by law established and that I will be faithful to H.M. King George V, his heirs and successors by law, in virtue of the common citizenship of the group of nations forming the British Commonwealth of Nations'. This had implications for the body that was now described officially as the 'British Commonwealth of Nations' as well as the 'British Empire'. David Harkness notes that the 'treaty was an unprecedented Dominion midwife' which 'contained within itself new advances towards full Dominion sovereignty'.[48]

Ireland's entry into this Commonwealth was novel insofar as it was 'a Catholic European mother country which had arrived at its new status not by evolution but by revolution and which, by its arrival, "raised again more fundamental questions about the ordering of imperial relations and definition of dominion status" '.[49] The history of Commonwealth relations over the best part of the following three decades was one in which Ireland played its role to the full in redefining the nature of that relationship. A beginning was made with the controversy over Article 4 of the Treaty because it ended common allegiance to the Crown: 'The Irish Deputy's allegiance was to the Constitution of the Irish Free State, and to the King only in his capacity as part of that Constitution . . . Upholders of the unitary monarchy were issued with a warning.'[50]

It is not our purpose to follow the tortuous path of Commonwealth relations but it is worth while spending some moments examining the implications of these early decisions before we turn our attention to constitution-making in the Irish Free State. The Treaty removed – for the very first time in an official document – the word 'Empire'. Ireland 'had now a common citizenship instead of subjection'; and Kevin O'Higgins, a leading member of the Free State government, believed that 'the evolution of the Commonwealth 'must be towards a condition, not merely of individual freedom, but also of equality of status'.[51]

The use of the term 'equality of status' is interesting because it bears a close resemblance to a term employed by the Northern Ireland Prime Minister, Sir James Craig, when (as we saw earlier) he suggested that the purported Council of Ireland be replaced by joint meetings of the Northern and Southern cabinets, and that 'in all matters under the purview of the Council' the two governments consult each other 'on terms of equality'. His Southern counterpart, W.T. Cosgrave, feared that that would ensure a unionist veto. So, just as London was reluctant to concede equality to the Irish Free State, Dublin was not anxious to realise unionist ambitions. On yet another issue – the search for self-esteem – Belfast and Dublin had something in common. It will be asserted that Dublin has been more successful in this respect than Belfast.

The starting-point can be taken as the 1922 Constitution of the Irish Free State. The product of a negotiated treaty with the United Kingdom, it reflected two different political theories: popular sovereignty and British constitutional monarchy. The draftsmen were anxious to exclude British impositions. Harkness has noted the degree to which it departed from dominion precedent – whether it was the decision to promote the primacy of the Gaelic language, or a distinctive Irish citizenship, or an attempt to reduce the status of the Governor-General. He accepts that the 'archaic symbols' of the British constitution 'had to be introduced, but their meaninglessness for Ireland was writ large on every page. The monarchical forms paled into insignificance in the light of the enunciation.' He quotes the summation of Leo Kohn, the leading commentator on the 1922 constitution: 'a most comprehensive and, in spirit, essentially republican constitution on most advanced Continental lines'.[52]

This (constitutional) dash for freedom has to be analysed alongside constitutional evolution in Britain. In his study of the monarchy Tom Nairn describes Britain as 'an old State-nation, not an ethnic or a republican state-formation founded on popular sovereignty. Yet it has had to adapt to and assume some of the contours of the modern nation-state world … The recreation and popularization of Monarchy was a way of doing that.'[53] The 1922 constitution challenged that fundamental element and added to the distance between Britain and Ireland. The concept of popular sovereignty stood in sharp contrast to a more formally deferential political culture in Britain. Nairn, for example, cites McKenzie and Silver's study of working-class Conservatism in urban England: 'Though modern constitutions typically locate the source of sovereignty in "the people", in Britain it is the Crown in Parliament that is sovereign. Nor is that a merely technical point. The political culture of democratic Britain assigns to ordinary people the role, not of citizens, but of subjects.' Nairn adds to this that in 'its peculiar, dignified concept the People are the reliable backbone of the Nation; not the effective source of its authority, not the real makers of the state'.[54] Republican Ireland challenged 'Britain' by the very nature of its republicanism, and by its very existence as a distinct entity. Republicanism departed Britain – it 'did not pass away. Already in a seriously weakened condition, it was clubbed and then smothered to death,'[55] – in the late nineteenth century. Later manifestations were exotic and eccentric. Its resurrection in Ireland unwittingly challenged the dignity of the 'English' constitution.

Indeed it may have challenged the nature of Britishness itself. British governments were always conscious of the likely domino effect of resurgent Irish nationalism, especially in the Empire. They knew that it was the 'extraordinary external successes of the transitional English state that permitted it to survive so long': and, equally, that if 'the external secret of old England's longevity was empire, the internal secret lay . . . in the cooptive and cohesive authority of an intelligentsia much more part of the state, much closer to political life and more present in all important civil institutions than in any other bourgeois society'.[56]

That stability was being challenged by some of the very same members of the intelligentsia in Scotland and Wales towards the end of the nineteenth century. 'England' responded in Scotland by increasing the numbers of its MPs in 1863 and again in 1885, and by restoring the office of Secretary of State for Scotland (abolished in 1746 as a result of the previous year's rising) in 1885, thereby heading off the challenge of the Scottish Home Rule Association, founded in 1886. In that same year a Young Wales movement, Cymru Fydd, inspired by Young Ireland and Young Italy, was launched. The Welsh shared with the Irish a concern for land, language and religion – although with different, and sometimes opposing, emphases – but their national aspirations were more cultural and less political than the Irish.[57]

'Britain' and the 'unitary monarchy' were under some threat. The former had to be remade as a variant of 'Anglo–Britishness' with the assistance of the latter. It was to be no accident that 'the remaking of English identity and the national culture [began] in the later years of the nineteenth century. *Englishness* was to be the dominating element in *Britishness*; and (in the opinion of Matthew Arnold [1859]) "that to belong to the national life one had to belong or affiliate to certain English institutions: the Anglican Church and Oxford or Cambridge University". Arnold's definition was sufficiently flexible to accommodate John Milton, sufficiently definite to exclude the culture of the nonconformists.'[58] An earlier concept of monarchy overlays this artificial device:

The paradox of George III's 'modernization' and what followed under Victoria is therefore this: Britain couldn't do without a 'nationalism', in the sense of an ideological armour for coping with modernity. But it had to have a strongly dissembling one, a national identity simultaneously *above and beneath* all that – an undoctrinaire formula bridging directly from the popular to the transcendent, from the 'ordinary' to the supernally grand and ethical. This passage had at once to mimic political nationalism and to occlude its danger-ous side – defusing the populist threat, as it were, by awarding its *Volk* house-room in an older or 'traditional' structure. That is exactly what the country's over-obsession with Monarchy has made possible: a pseudo-nationalism fostering 'community' from above and bestow-ing a sense of 'belonging' without the damnable nuisance of ethnic and rudely democratic complaint.[59]

Irish nationalism was a vulgar and turbulent variant of republicanism, a child of its time: Britain's was more sedate, more understated, the mature outgrowth of a prosperous world system.[60]

We have lingered on only one aspect of the 1922 constitution to il-lustrate the nature of the gap that had opened up between independent Ireland and Britain. It was as much a gap about perceptions and sepa-rate cultures as it was about different political aspirations. It heralded the end of the United Kingdom of Great Britain and Ireland and it contributed to the beginning of the end of the Empire as it was un-derstood. David Harkness captures the 1922 constitution's evolu-tionary spirit when he writes that it 'aimed to provide an alkaline environment, free of the acids of British precedent and interpretation which had for so long corroded the Irish spirit. Protected by this be-nign legal structure, the Irish genius could grow to fuller expression in due course.'[61] The Irish question had a role to play on a bigger stage. And it was a role which independent Ireland was to play self-consciously and with some *élan*.

In the period between 1922 and the outbreak of World War II the Irish Free State set about removing British influence from Irish affairs. Again we are not concerned with the detail, simply the need to high-light the landmarks along the way. What deserves to be acknowledged is the very fact that independent Ireland prevailed. In his very im-pressive account of the Irish Free State's position within the Com-monwealth in the period 1921–31 Harkness demonstrates how the South had been apprehensive about the Commonwealth from the outset but 'had nevertheless recognised its potential and had set out to ensure the rapid and acceptable evolution of that anomalous British Empire towards a clearly visible association of free and equal partner-states'. The culmination of this strategy was the passing into law of the Statute of Westminster on 11 December 1931 following a series of imperial conferences. Ireland's motivation was explained at some length by the minister responsible, Patrick McGilligan, to the Dáil on 16 August 1931. He told a long and complicated story but its essence can be seen in one paragraph:

> We had one purpose in 1926 and that was that there must be up-rooted from the whole system of this State the British Government; and in substitution for that there was accepted the British Monarch. He is a King who functions entirely, so far as Irish affairs are concerned, at the will of the Irish Government and that was the summing up on the whole aim and the whole result of the conferences of 1926, 1929, and 1930.

The Irish government had done its work well and had ensured the 'legal and political stability of the State [which] was remarkable in an era of European unrest and following upon such emotional conflicts in Ireland itself'.[62]

Let us recall that the Treaty had split the country on three main issues – partition had been accepted; the Treaty was couched in the symbols of royalty and of Empire; and the Royal Navy had been given access to Irish ports. Over time these last two issues were addressed but not until a vicious civil war had been fought. When Frank Aiken (of the anti-treatyites) called for a ceasefire on 24 May 1923 he ordered that their arms be dumped rather than surrendered. The existence of an entrenched minority unhappy with an unresolved border dispute led inevitably to a crisis in authority. This has to be placed against a general background of relative economic underdevelopment, the lack of executive experience among the new leaders and a pessimistic prognosis – which made the challenge of state-building of epic proportions. And yet it endured.

Several reasons suggest themselves. We have referred already to perhaps the most fundamental reason – that 'Irish political culture was already developed into an established and sturdy parliamentary mould prior to political independence.'[63] Moreover it was a culture which inherited a sound administrative structure. After partition civil servants had the opportunity to transfer to Belfast or London but almost 99 per cent decided to remain in Dublin. The administrative class had been recruited by open competitive examination ever since 1871. Given that by 1900 'British government intervention had made Ireland the most administered part of the United Kingdom and had involved "a degree of government action and administrative penetration unknown in Britain" ',[64] the independent state was set fair for sound administration. Even with the accession to power of de Valera in 1932 there was no abrupt change in personnel although he was suspicious of the administrative machine; and as late as January 1934 '50.1 per cent of the civil service outside the industrial classes consisted of persons originally recruited under the British Government ... the proportion was considerably higher in the top ranks'.[65]

To enhance the service's reputation a Civil Service Commission was appointed to preside over the public appointments process. It has been described as 'Perhaps the major achievement of the early years, and it remains one of the most remarkable achievements in the history of the state.'[66] And to advance its democratic record the Irish Free State enfranchised all adult females in 1923, that is five years before the United Kingdom. Finally, in an effort to demonstrate its capacity for financial self-sufficiency the Cumann na nGaedhael government adopted a policy of rigorous retrenchment so that by 1926–7 the Free State was able to offer an income tax rate '6d less than in England, a historic triumph over the old enemy'.[67]

A second explanation lies in the fact that the crisis of identity – created in the disagreement about the Treaty – was translated from civil War politics to parliamentary politics through the establishment of Fianna Fáil and Fine Gael. With the end of the civil war the anti-treatyites led by Eamon de Valera contested the general election of August 1923 under the Sinn Féin label and won 44 seats in a house of 153 (against 63 for the government party). They refused to take their seats because they were opposed to the oath to the king. In anticipation of another general election a Sinn Féin ard fheis in 1926 split on the issue of the oath. De Valera resigned and established his own party, Fianna Fáil, which contested the June 1927 general election and, after some hesitation, entered the Dáil by taking the oath which de Valera described as an 'empty formality'. Fianna Fáil acted as the chief opposition until 1932, when following another general election it became the largest party and formed its first government. It has been recorded that 'as the Fianna Fáil deputies filed into the government benches, almost every man of them carried a revolver in his pocket' (and indeed in 1928 one of its future leaders, Seán Lemass, had described Fianna Fáil as a 'slightly constitutional party'[68]). That peaceful transition of government in 1932 was a credit to the Irish democratic system; and such was the success of Fianna Fáil after 1932 that Joseph Lee has described it as 'a beautifully nubile instrument of state integration'.[69]

We turn to this 'beautifully nubile instrument' to chart independent Ireland's voyage away from British suzerainty. Once Fianna Fáil came to office it indulged in a series of (constitutional) guerrilla strikes against the last vestiges of British rule. On 3 May 1933 the self-explanatory

Constitution (Removal of Oath) Act was passed and was followed by a strategy to demean the office of Governor-General. And following the abdication crisis in Britain on 10 December 1936, the government introduced two bills together with guillotine motions at an emergency meeting of the Dáil (deputies having been summoned by telegram). The first, the Constitution (Amendment No. 27) Bill, which removed all references to the Crown and Governor-General from the constitution, was passed on 11 December. The second, the Executive Authority (External Relations) Bill, which achieved the principle of external association while preserving a tenuous link with the Commonwealth, became law the following night. De Valera had achieved 'one of the most delicate manoeuvres of his quest for sovereignty' by removing the king from the constitution. He had chosen his moment well because no matter how irritated the British may have been at his initiative 'they were unlikely to relish controversy about the relationship between monarchy and dominion in the aftermath of the abdication scandal; and, as in the case of de Valera's earlier constitutional changes, they chose not to retaliate'.[70]

One of the reasons why de Valera continued with the Commonwealth link was because he wanted it to act as a bridge over which Northern unionists might cross. Similarly, his 1937 constitution was constructed in the forlorn hope of eventually wooing Northern Ireland into an all-Ireland state: 'If the Northern problem were not there', he said, 'in all probability there would be a flat, downright proclamation of a republic in this Constitution.'[71] This is not the place to rehearse the various controversies surrounding the 1937 constitution although we should acknowledge its contemporary significance in Anglo-Irish relations. Four aspects that have a bearing on relationships within and between these islands concern us here.

The first refers to 'the un-British features of rigidity of a written document containing a comprehensive bill of rights and interpreted by a judiciary with power to invalidate measures which conflict with it; this dimension of the Irish polity must be ascribed to the American example'.[72] The formal nature of a written constitution and the constraints placed upon constitutional amendment have not always been appreciated by British commentators. The second aspect is the one which plagued understanding both between the peoples of the island of Ireland and between the peoples of Ireland and Britain until very recently. It is the inclusion of the irredentist Articles 2 and 3, those that claimed jurisdiction over Northern Ireland, which were seen as offensive by unionists. Yet de Valera believed that the constitution's 'first, central and supreme purpose was to complete the national revolution and to obtain the voluntary and firm declaration from the Irish people of the independence and sovereignty of Ireland'.[73] The sovereignty inherent in the 1937 constitution was flawed; indeed it may have been a form of constitutional hypocrisy in that it marginalised the Northern population.[74]

As early as 1924 the Nationalist MP for Fermanagh and South Tyrone, Cahir Healy, wondered whether he should take his seat at Westminster in order to press the nationalist cause while the Boundary Commission sat. He was advised 'not to take his seat at present but not to do anything which would prejudice him in regard to taking his seat in the future'.[75] Thirty years later de Valera summarised his (and implicitly all Irish governments') objections to admitting Northern nationalists to Dáil Éireann: they would be talking to the converted on the partition issue; they would have representation without taxation on other issues; and their presence in the Dáil might not be in the national interest since they might take sides between the Dáil parties.[76] It was to be another thirty years before a proper Northern influence made itself felt in Dublin when the SDLP participated in the New Ireland Forum. In the intervening years Irish governments acted as proxy ombudsman for Northern nationalist grievances but could not convert concern into influence.

John Bowman has adapted the work of Joseph Frankel to describe Fianna Fáil's anti-partitionism as 'aspirational in character'. Frankel was concerned with party policies especially in the foreign policy context as being about either aspirational or operational interests. The latter category speaks for itself but the former is determined 'by political will rather than by capabilities – ideology is a strong determinant. The influence of power is ambivalent: while an ambition may be due to the people's awareness of the power of their state, it can be likewise due to their awareness of their powerlessness and their escape into day-dreams.'[77] It may be objected that Frankel's is too harsh a judgement. After all the 1937 constitution 'was hailed in some quarters as a tolerant and liberal document and proved to be a model for the constitution makers of Burma a decade later'.[78] But when we look at the third aspect that we are concerned with here, we can appreciate the extent to which the constitution was unlikely to be operational in Northern Ireland.

This refers to those articles (15, 18, 19, 40–4, 45) which imbued the constitution with a Catholic ethos. The right of divorce was forbidden; the family was recognised as a 'moral institution possessing inalienable and imprescriptible rights, antecedent and superior to all positive law'; and the Catholic Church was seen to have a 'special position'. Other religions were specifically recognised in the constitution, and it needs to be remembered that members of the Catholic hierarchy had urged that it be recognised as 'the one, true church'. Indeed, the outgoing Presbyterian Moderator, Dr F.W. O'Neill, sang its praises as 'a Constitution based on a definitely Christian attitude to life'.[79]

Perhaps the best yardstick whereby we can judge the religious ethos of the 1937 constitution is to compare it with that of 1922. John Whyte has noted that the 1922 constitution 'had been a typical liberal-democratic document which would have suited a country of any religious complexion. The only article on religion was one which briefly guaranteed religious freedom and equality.' By contrast the corresponding articles of the 1937 constitution 'were obviously marked by Catholic thought'.[80] So the 1937 constitution offended Northern unionists not only because of its irredentist claims but also because it was Catholic in ethos.

The fourth and final aspect concerns the primacy given to the Irish language in the constitution. Article 8 recognised English as no more than a second official language: in any dispute the Irish text takes precedence over the English. De Valera used the language as an ethnocentric shortcut to dignity. There was, he said, 'no use in being an imitation country'.[81] That aspect of the constitution possibly caused more dispute than the question of religion.[82]

The constitution – Bunreacht na hÉireann – was approved by the Dáil on 14 June 1937 and put to the people in a referendum on 1 July. Fifty-seven per cent approved (in a turnout of 76 per cent) and it came into force on 29 December. Henceforth the Southern state became known as Ireland, the monarch was no longer the head of state, and (in Irish law at any rate) Ireland was no longer a member of the Commonwealth). The 1937 constitution was very much the creation of Eamon de Valera. Indeed in many respects 'Irish policy' in the 1930s 'was synonymous with de Valera's policy. De Valera's personal control over the conduct of Anglo-Irish relations was such that policy-making was a more simple process on the Irish side than the British ... de Valera allowed his ministers and officials very little latitude.'[83] This personalised policy-making had a number of consequences.

It was perceived as de Valera's policy – and British politicians and officials (with the exception of the Dominions Secretary, Malcolm MacDonald) had an exaggerated opinion of de Valera's power for mischief-making. In fact he was an odd combination of Hamlet, in his scrupulous indecision, and Charles de Gaulle, in his mystical sense of destiny – he once described Ireland as being a 'nation before Augustine set foot on English soil'. He played an educative role inside his anglophobic Fianna Fáil party, a party not long removed from the shadow

of the gun and naively convinced by its own rhetoric.[84] But beneath all
that rigid rhetoric de Valera was actually a moderate, or 'a gradualist,
adopting as one writer to the Dominions Office put it "Fabian tactics"
on Partition'.[85] In fact he was resolutely opposed to force.

That was not how the British establishment perceived his accession
to power in 1932. They suffered from what Deirdre McMahon has
called a 'failure of imagination', and much of their policy was reactive
and based on contradictory advice. One example is the Irish Situation
Committee, a special committee set up inside the cabinet in March
1932 to deal with the Irish situation. Its formation coincided with the
blurring of British party lines in 1932 'whereas hitherto a clear ideological distinction existed between the various parties on the Irish
Question'. By 1932 the 'Question' was regarded as solved, and at a time
of international tension and acute economic depression, few ministers,
whatever their party, wished to resurrect such a divisive issue. It was
soon apparent that Labour and Liberal ministers regarded with distaste
de Valera and the intransigent nationalism he represented.'[86]

Clearly de Valera did not believe that the issue was settled in 1932. If
the 1937 constitution was an *affirmation* of Irish independence the conclusion of formal Anglo-Irish negotiations in April 1938 led to the *establishment* of independence.[87] The negotiations concerned a whole raft
of issues: the ending of the economic war that had dominated Anglo-
Irish trade relations in the 1930s, the question of the North and (for
Britain) the overriding need to have a secure defence policy as the
prospect of European war loomed. To the unionists de Valera offered a
federal solution and external association with the Commonwealth.
Needless to say that was not acceptable (but that is not our concern at
this stage).[88]

International defence was the issue of the moment. Britain sought a
formal defence pact with Ireland: it was offered instead a form of
benevolent neutrality. The Anglo-Irish Agreement of 1938 'so far as
defence was concerned ... amounted to a fundamental revision of the
1921 Treaty ... It marks the point at which neutrality became for
Ireland a practical state policy as well as a political value; if later
political leaders were to refer to Ireland's "traditional" policy of
neutrality it was in 1938 that this policy came to the fore.'[89] Ireland
recovered the naval facilities at Berehaven, Cobh and Lough Swilly
that had been granted to Britain under Articles 6 and 7 of the 1921
Treaty: later de Valera was to regard this as 'his greatest political
achievement ... because of its importance in the context of neutrality'.
But his ambition, in line with his policy of attrition, was greater than
that: neutrality 'was an objective at the talks, but the achievement of

sovereignty was a higher priority'.[90]

We shall see that that priority was to cost independent Ireland dear-ly, particularly in the role it pursued after World War II. Despite some attempts at blandishment Ireland remained neutral throughout the war and incurred the wrath of both Britain and the United States. An ex-ample of the latter's ire appeared in 1956. In an introduction he con-tributed to a book on Ireland that was written by William A. Carson, David Gray, United States Minister to Ireland during the war, accused de Valera of maintaining 'a neutrality which served only Hitler's ob-jectives', which was 'unjust and one-sided' and which was based on 'a specious formula devised to meet a local political situation'.[91] In fact more recent research suggests that despite Britain's refusal to formally accept Irish neutrality throughout the war it was a neutrality friendly to the Allied cause. There were not infrequent violations of Irish air space, and the Irish government secretly co-operated very closely with British security agencies, the links being maintained through the Irish army's G2 intelligence directorate and MI5.[92] The 'subtlety' of the Irish position is explained best by Salmon:

> On certain major issues touching upon the core of sovereignty, the Irish dug in their heels. On issues not so central to sovereignty, they were prepared to act and behave in 'unneutral' ways or as a 'non-belligerent' rather than as a neutral. If abstention is to be understood as offering no partial assistance to either belligerent, the Irish did not conform to this criterion, since their sympathies did spill over into partial acts.[93]

According to Ronan Fanning anti-Irish sentiment was as strong in Washington as in London at the close of World War II. A National Security Council draft statement on policy dated 17 October 1950 (NSC83/1) and concerned with the 'relationship of Ireland to the North Atlantic Treaty, and towards Irish interest in bilateral arrangements for military assistance' acknowledged Ireland's strategic location but did not consider the use of its ports and air bases essential at the time. If Ir-eland's price for joining NATO was to be a British commitment to ending partition then neither the British nor the Americans thought that the price was worth paying. A review of NSC83/1 a decade later concluded that it 'does not require updating'.[94]

Despite such hostility Ireland pursued its headlong dash towards sovereignty which culminated in the enactment of the Republic of Ireland Act 1948 and the symbolic declaration of a republic on Easter Monday 1949. Now Ireland's status as a republic was formalised and acknowledged. Ironically it was not de Valera but an inter-party government led by John A. Costello of Fine Gael which decided to break the link with the Commonwealth. This 'slapdash and amateur'[95] affair (according to Lord Rugby, the United Kingdom Representative to Ireland) highlighted the anamolous relationship – between Ireland, Britain and the Commonwealth – then in existence. The Republic of Ireland (as it was now to be called) was henceforth to be treated as a 'foreign state' even though it and members of the Commonwealth would proclaim that they did not regard themselves as foreign to each other.

In fact the Republic was to enjoy economic, social and trading relationships not normally granted to foreign states although, originally, the British cabinet had decided to treat it like any other foreign state. Following representations from Canada, New Zealand and (especially) Australia, from the Irish Minister for External Relations (Sean Mac-Bride) and Minister for Finance (Patrick McGilligan), from the Home Office (which feared formidable administrative difficulties if all Irish citizens were to be treated as aliens), and from the Foreign Secretary, Ernest Bevin (who had expressed concern that the declaration of the Republic might create an Irish vote in Britain which would be embarrassing in the conduct of foreign policy), the cabinet accepted that 'the Foreign Office should not undertake any responsibility for Irish business'.[96] Thus the Republic left the Commonwealth but was treated, for reasons of expediency rather than principle, as if it still remained within it.[97] At Westminster this was recognised in the Ireland Act 1949, which allowed Irish citizens to avail of exemptions contained in the British Nationality Act. But the downside was to be found in section 1 (2) of the 1949 Act which declared that no part of Northern Ireland would cease to be a part of the United Kingdom without the consent of the Northern Ireland parliament.

CONCLUSION

The anomalous relationship was to create its own illusions based on the simple matter of ignorance – as events after 1968 demonstrated. Problems can arise by adapting a pragmatic approach to policy-making. Regarding the making of British foreign policy in general David Vita has written:

> The consequences of the piecemeal approach to the environment and the tendency to argue from the environment to the policy, or the continual attempt to infer what policy should be from a consideration of the 'facts' or 'realities' of the 'situation' are two. Firstly, it is the external event, the act of the foreign government, for example,

which tends to dominate thinking, rather than the goal or purpose which the British Government itself wishes to pursue. The former takes on a hard, fixed quality. The latter tends to fluidity. The making of foreign policy becomes a process of adjustment, rather than one of creation. The end product of the process, the final 'policy', tends to be what is judged the most profitable or the least injurious of a number of alternatives; but the terms of the problem, and the elements of the situation which determine the range of alternatives – these are largely set by others.[98]

It is tempting to examine British policy towards independent Ireland during 1922–49 in this light. Ireland, obsessional and single-minded, made the running. Britain adapted to a policy of adjustment. The reasons are not too hard to understand.

'Dark Rosaleen' did have sex appeal. She was at the forefront of the colonial struggle. She could count on the support of those engaged in liberation struggles elsewhere, and those members of the Commonwealth intent in redefining the nature of that body. The influence of her diaspora, including her 'spiritual dominion',[99] should not be underestimated. But, equally, there were limits to her own influence in the world system. Her neutral stance during World War II may have damaged her international interests; at the very least it damaged her psychologically. When Harold Laski argued in 1951 that 'the real alternative to the House of Commons is the concentration camp'[100] it is conceivable that his meaning would have been lost on those Irish political leaders who had endured only vicariously the ravages of war. By remaining outside the hostilities 'Dark Rosaleen' placed herself in a lower division of the international order.

As a contrast consider the plight of the 'maiden aunt'. In the latter half of the twentieth century she was beginning to look haggard and preoccupied. Again it is not too difficult to find the reasons. Britain's 'world system' enforced an extremely high level of defence expenditure on it: 'In the late forties, our defence expenditure was higher as a proportion of the national income than any other western country including the United States. In Bevin's last year in office [1950] it was nine per cent of the national income. I think this figure in itself justifies the view that our immediate post-war position as one of the triumvirate of world powers was unsustainable on economic grounds.'[101]

Successive British governments in the interwar years began to realise that the Empire was a fragile and expensive system. The situation by the second half of the 1930s has been graphically described by John Gallagher:

Too few resources, too many commitments; not enough friends, too many enemies. Not since 1779 had Britain been faced with danger from three powers at once, and that was not an inspiring precedent. During the nineteen twenties Britain's imperial interests had taken second place to her domestic concerns; by the nineteen thirties they were put at risk by her European imperatives.[102]

Yet during World War II Britain reoccupied most of its former Middle East territories and was in Indonesia for the first time since 1816. All of this imposed immense strains on the system and within a few years both India and Palestine had gone their separate ways. Britain was discovering yet again that it 'is characteristic of any power that works a world system that it cannot isolate any one situation and decide it on its own individual merits'.[103] Nevertheless, although Britain had re-inherited 'Curzon's fantasy empire', Gallagher concludes that it emerged from World War II 'as much the strongest of the middle powers of the world ... still the rich man in his palace, not the poor man at the gate'.[104] But riches brought their own responsibility.

Given these circumstances, the position in Ireland, irritating and exasperating though it might be, must have seemed positively benign. The conflict with Dark Rosaleen was conducted in a civilised and diplomatic manner, and Northern Ireland appeared to be at peace with itself.

5

MUTUAL MISPERCEPTIONS

But if the focus remains on the past, the past will become the future,
and that is something no one can desire.

INTERNATIONAL BODY ON ARMS DECOMMISSIONING[1]

Britain is engrossed with an immediate problem. She assumes a
common war effort because there is a common general interest. She
sees herself as readily forgiving past transgressions, and therefore
entitled to ready pardon. But these are not pleas that can be heard
clearly by Irish ears. They are drowned or distorted by the noises of
old coercion, old condescension, old colonialism, and old battles for
parity and the rule of law.

OLIVER MacDONAGH[2]

Wrestling with political issues of identity is not in itself a sign of
abnormality though wrestling with virtually nothing else is.

NORMAN PORTER[3]

Dublin and London reacted in characteristic fashion when political
violence again became part of the political agenda in 1969. Dublin's
response was verbal republicanism combined with symbolism such as
moving field hospitals to the border with Northern Ireland. London
retaliated with the Downing Street Declaration (19 August 1969)
which affirmed 'that responsibility for affairs in Northern Ireland
is entirely a matter of domestic jurisdiction'. A lack of coordination was
to be a feature of policy-making over the next decade as both
governments, separated by their deep mistrust of each other, reacted to
the politics of the last atrocity.

In addition they were attempting to control their own clients:
Dublin had the gun-running incident and London was confronted by
the threat of a unilateral declaration of independence (UDI) led by the

Minister of Home Affairs, William Craig, who was sacked in December 1969. In short, both governments were conscious of the *intra-* as well as the *inter-*ethnic. That added to their difficulties in the search for a solution. In some ways London's problems were more profound than those of Dublin. The debate among Irish nationalists was about the merits of the means to achieve Irish unity. The quarrel between the British government and some Ulster unionists was more fundamental. Take William Craig's declaration that Northern Ireland's constitution was about 'more than a mere act of Parliament'. It represented an 'agreed settlement' – 'the settlement made when our grandfathers and fathers made their historic stand'.[4]

DUBLIN

Growth of factionalism

When the Taoiseach, Jack Lynch, addressed the United Nations on 22 October 1970, he pleaded for a reasoned way out of the Northern Ireland impasse 'through quiet diplomacy and personal conversation'.[5] Yet there was little space for reason. In the circumstances, Lynch hd to rely on the policies enunciated by his predecessor Seán Lemass. It was Lemass who had moved Dublin's policy on Northern Ireland from rhetoric to reason with an emphasis on an aspirational approach. He placed his faith in functional cooperation as an instrument of general reconciliation when he declared in the Dáil on 3 June 1959 that 'the historic task of this generation is to secure the economic foundation of independence'. His new economic thinking was meant 'to confound those Northern defenders of partition who contend that joining us in freedom would be an economic disadvantage to the north-eastern counties'.[6] That had the advantage of moving Dublin more firmly into the Anglo-American world. In signing the Anglo-Irish Free Trade Area Agreement in 1965 he brought to a close the era of protectionism. The Sinn Féin concept of economic nationalism and self-sufficiency was to be replaced by close economic ties with the United Kingdom, ultimately within the EEC.

Closer economic ties highlighted the degree of asymmetry existing between London and Dublin – 'unequal sovereigns' was the apt description of one academic.[7] The basic facts need the barest of repetition. An American analysis of the Irish economy in 1952 concluded that the country's dependence on Britain was so strong as to be incompatible with the status of political sovereignty.[8] An emigration rate of more than 500,000 between 1945 and 1961 suggested little confidence in the country's future. Yet the new economic policies appeared to be bearing fruit. In the years 1960–73 Irish productivity grew by 9.1 per cent as compared with the United Kingdom's rate of growth of only 5.5 per cent. Lemass displayed flexibility in the matter of Irish neutrality and he discouraged the use of the United Nations for anti-partitionist rhetoric. Politically, the culmination of his Northern policy was the historic meeting at Stormont with Terence O'Neill in January 1965. It symbolised the end of the cold war in Ireland but failed to give full legitimation to O'Neill.

In meeting with Terence O'Neill Lemass removed another foundation stone of the de Valera legacy: 'The policy on Northern Ireland that Seán Lemass inherited from Eamon de Valera had the merit of simplicity, and the disadvantage of failure. It was not really a policy on Northern Ireland as such but a policy on partition.'[9] While both Lemass and O'Neill appreciated the historical import of the moment, it was the former who had an astute sense of the malign influence of time. He rarely referred to history in his speeches; for example, in Belfast in October 1969 he argued that 'Ireland's outlook for the future would have to be that history did not matter – or at least that there was no problem from history that could not be resolved.'[10] Lemass enjoyed the luxury of being out of office at this stage. Perhaps he should have reflected on the experience of the all-party Committee on the Constitution, a committee he had initiated shortly before his resignation as Taoiseach in 1966 and of which he became a member shortly thereafter. The committee's 1967 report recommended a change to the wording of Article 3 of the 1937 constitution to read as follows: 'The Irish nation hereby proclaims its firm will that its territory be re-united in harmony and brotherly affection between all Irishmen.' But interfering with the orthodoxy was not appreciated by the Fianna Fáil rank and file. Many years later mention of the proposed amendment was treated dismissively by the Fianna Fáil leader, Charles Haughey: 'It was just published and left there.'[11]

Jack Lynch who had succeeded Lemass as Taoiseach late in 1966 had no option but to confront history – and with a vengeance. He followed Lemass's Northern Ireland policy by paying a visit to Terence O'Neill at Stormont on 11 December 1967. It was a civilised meeting save for a snowball-throwing reception organised by the Reverend Ian Paisley – another vignette in the politics of innocence and an early lesson in Northern intransigence for the new Taoiseach. For Jack Lynch did not know the North: 'I had little personal contact with the North, however, although Eamon de Valera did send me to a meeting in Coalisland in 1948 or '49 for a debate on unity.'[12] That was a revealing comment and speaks volumes on Southern attitudes towards Northern Ireland. It is virtually impossible to find any evidence of a real debate within the Republic prior to the late 1960s about a practical republicanism – about how to achieve Irish unity by constitutional means.

There had been the Anti-Partition League of the 1940s;[13] there had been a constitutional lawyer's public soul-searching about Southern attitudes following the resumption of IRA violence in 1956[14] – but, after that, nothing, or, at least, nothing visible to the naked eye. Even contact with the North's nationalist leaders was kept to a minimum. In 1954 the Labour Party, which had become the most republican of the three main parties, had 'supported a Bill introduced by two Independent TDs of strong republican views to allow elected representatives from the "six occupied counties of Ireland" to speak in the Oireachtas, while the two major parties [Fianna Fáil and Fine Gael] opposed it'.[15] It was not until the latter half of 1970 that proper debate began in a series of eight articles written by Senator John Kelly (a law professor and Fine Gael member) entitled 'Towards a Northern Policy' in the *Irish Times* (31 August–8 September 1970).[16] There had also been articles by other individuals in the preceding weeks, all of them frightfully aware of the southern establishment's unpreparedness for the Northern conflagration.[17]

In that respect the Taoiseach was representative of the wider electorate. Unfortunately he was also leader of Fianna Fáil, and a precarious leader at that. According to Dick Walsh, Fianna Fáil was, 'from the start, as much a movement as a party':

> Relying on tradition, emotion, a particular view of the past, it was built on simple beliefs: in the national cause which embraced unity and the restoration of Irish; in self-sufficiency, based on the land and other native resources; and in the integrity of small communities, whose borders were conveniently coterminus with those of the Catholic Church and the GAA. The beliefs were vague enough to hold a universal appeal; no-one need feel excluded.[18]

The party set out in 1926 with seven aims, none of which it managed to deliver. Nonetheless it became and remained one of the most successful parties in the European liberal democratic tradition – that is, until the outbreak of Northern violence exposed 'the gap between its rhetoric and the reality of the national question. Jack Lynch was asked to make a choice that was demanded of no other leader; and he chose the path of gradualism inherited from de Valera and Lemass.'[19]

Lynch was an incredibly popular leader, the most popular Irish politician since Daniel O'Connell, according to his Fine Gael counterpart,

Liam Cosgrave. A TD from 1948, Lynch had entered the political arena as a sporting hero, the winner of six all-Ireland medals in a row (five hurling and one football). His journey up the Fianna Fáil ladder was steady rather than spectacular, and his accession to leadership owed much to his consensual disposition. But it bode trouble. What was striking about Ireland was the political longevity of those who had participated in the events of 1916–23. Ireland 'was governed by a dominant revolutionary elite group until 1959 when de Valera left active politics. In spite of the presence of the younger men as well as the long service of Lemass who was undoubtedly a pragmatist regardless of his revolutionary service, the revolutionary ethos prevailed until the main figures of that era left active political life.'[20] Born in 1917 Lynch was the first Fianna Fáil leader not to be drawn from that revolutionary elite. That weakened his authority in a party which 'has had an almost "Stalinist" tradition of solidarity in the face of opposition pressure'.[21]

The Northern conflict spilt over into Dublin's domestic politics with the arms crisis of 1970 and challenged that solidarity mightily. Tom Garvin traces the growth of factionalism within Fianna Fáil between 1966 and 1980 and offers four explanations. The first was the 'relative lack of elite consensus and *esprit de corps* among the second generation of politicians in contrast to the sense of comradeship that had existed among the old IRA and Sinn Féin veterans of the 1918–1960 era'. The second was a change in the political culture, including a drift away from an earlier authoritarianism. The third was the effect of an electoral system that aggravated local tensions within parties. And finally there was the advent of new political issues, such as economic policy and the Northern Ireland conflict, which created differences. He describes a political system that was 'polarised around nationalist issues rather than around left–right, liberal–conservative, spend–save or even sacred–secular dimensions'.[22] Added to this was a tendency for factions to centre round personalities rather than distinctive policy positions.

One manifestation of these tendencies is reflected in the drift of the vote away from Fianna Fáil. Until the 1980s it saw itself, and was perceived, as the natural party of government. Under de Valera it expected to take between 45 and 50 per cent of the popular vote. At the local elections in June 1999 the party took only 38 per cent. The rot went back to the leadership contest in 1966 when Lynch defeated George Colley by fifty-two votes to nineteen. It was the first formal election that the party had held for the position of leader. On the only previous occasion the new leader, Seán Lemass, 'emerged' through a form of apostolic succession. The 1966 contest revealed strong internal differences centred round Lynch, Colley, Charles Haughey and Neil

Blaney. None of his rivals owed their positions to Lynch and all had been encouraged by Lemass to rule their departments as personal baronies. Imposing a corporate spirit was not going to be easy. The Northern Ireland conflict was to make it next to impossible.

Fianna Fáil's victory in the 1969 general election ended any speculation that Lynch was no more than an interim leader. The battle of the Bogside in August 1969 opened up a deep fissure in government ranks. The full title of the party was, after all, 'Fianna Fáil: The Republican Party' – but in August 1969, it seemed, they were abandoning their Northern brethren to the depradations of unionist mob rule. The call for weapons to be supplied to Northern Catholics to defend themselves and the reversion to atavisitic yearnings meant that the more militant, nationalist wing of the party was reverting to type. An axis in opposition to the leadership's more cautious approach gathered round three powerful cabinet ministers – Kevin Boland (Minister for Local Government), Neil Blaney (Minister for Agriculture) and Charles Haughey (Minister for Finance) – at least two of whom were potential leaders of the party. There was little surprise at the position adopted by Blaney and Boland – they were descendants of the 1926 strain of the party – but Haughey was noted as 'never having uttered a peep at all about the North – at party meetings or anywhere else'.[23] Despite this, 'the Bogside eruption immediately produced Haughey as the third member of a caucus which insisted this was our business, the moment of truth for the Fianna Fáil party, the time for the solution of the final problem, the time for which we . . . had been waiting so very patiently since 1957'.[24]

These three ministers became identified with the arms crisis in 1970. Haughey and Blaney were dismissed from government on 6 May on the grounds that they had failed to fully subscribe to government policy on Northern Ireland. Boland resigned in sympathy, while the Minister for Justice, Mícheál Ó Moráin, had resigned two days previously on health grounds. Three weeks later Haughey and Blaney were arrested and charged with conspiracy to import arms and ammunition. The charges against Blaney were dismissed at a preliminary hearing in July and Haughey was acquitted by a jury in October. Boland launched his own party – Aontacht Éireann (Unity of Ireland) – in September 1971 at a meeting attended by over one thousand delegates; after he had been expelled from Fianna Fáil in 1972 Blaney too set up his own party, Independent Fianna Fáil; and Haughey remained within the fold.[25] Haughey's ambition was single-minded but his presence was corrosive as he succeeded Lynch as party leader and Taoiseach in 1979. Under his leadership a small but significant faction broke away from the party to form the Progressive Democrats in December 1985. Ironically it was with the Progressive Democrats that Haughey entered the first Fianna Fáil-led coalition in the history of the state after a general election in June 1989.[26]

It is difficult to ignore the impact of the arms crisis. Richard Sinnott writes of its 'epic proportions' and the fact that no satisfactory explanation has been furnished.[27] It sent a powerful message to Northern unionists, best encapsulated in a statement from the DUP deputy leader, Peter Robinson, more than a decade later: 'Haughey is an out and out political serpent; [Garret] FitzGerald is a fairly subtle political serpent.'[28] It reminded the Southern electorate of the monster on their doorstep. Their response was to feign indifference. With the exception of the 1973 election, when it entered the list of important issues at 12 per cent, Northern Ireland never featured as an important issue among the electorate. Even in the 1981 election, which was conducted at the height of the hunger strikes and which returned two H-Block candidates (for Cavan–Monaghan and Louth) Northern Ireland was not a major issue.[29] Southern political leaders expressed alarm. They were concerned that the Republic's economic prosperity was being hampered by events in the North: 'The real barrier to unification was in the North itself, and, as long as the majority community remained hostile, there was little a government in the Republic could do ... it suggests that the political elite in the Republic perceive their role as largely responsive rather than initiatory, except in the area of economic involvement.'[30] Alarm and indifference in the south translated into consternation in the North, and much of the 1970s involved the steady trek of Northern nationalist politicians to Dublin to plead for solidarity.

We must not assume that Fine Gael and Labour were bereft of factionalism in relation to Northern Ireland. A healthy, at times reckless, debate ensued inside the Irish Labour party after 1969. The party was in bullish mood – the seventies, according to the slogan, was to be socialist – after the 1969 general election when it increased its vote and returned some significant intellectuals.[31] One of them, Dr Conor Cruise O'Brien, was appointed spokesman on foreign affairs, a position that enabled him to enunciate at great length on Northern Ireland. He could claim a greater knowledge of the North than Jack Lynch – derived through marriage and through his time as an official in the Department of External Affairs when he liaised with Northern nationalist politicians in the early 1950s.[32] It could not have been a happy posting because he maintains that as early as 1951 he had realised that propaganda about 'Ireland's right to unity' was futile.[33] His strongly held opinions and personal characteristics – 'bumptiousness, individualism'[34] – ensured that life inside the Labour Party between 1969 and 1977 (when he lost his Dáil seat) was never dull.

The kindest construction on the party's debate about Northern Ireland has been offered by Michael Gallagher when he writes: 'In a way, Labour's reaction was a more honest one than other parties', in that it reflected the confusion felt by many in the Republic.'[35] In June 1974 O'Brien, by now Minister for Posts and Telegraphs in a Fine Gael–Labour coalition government, stated that he was not personally working actively for Irish unity since he didn't see it as a practicable goal. There were those who had admired his moral courage in challenging orthodoxy but felt that he was becoming obsessional: 'The frequency and predictability of his comments – "like Radio Tirana", in the words of one member of the administration – and the generous coverage guaranteed by their stylish formulation led to a feeling that by identifying a certain viewpoint too closely with himself he might actually be reducing the support which that viewpoint would otherwise have had.'[36] O'Brien himself has drawn attention to the tensions within that government. He describes his position at cabinet meetings 'as if I was surrounded by a wall of glass, as I was clearly visible to the others, but totally inaudible'. And referring to one particular occasion he writes: 'I was acutely conscious in that moment that I was the only person in that room who was acknowledged not to be a practising Catholic.'[37]

While O'Brien serves as a good visual aid for Southern disarray generally, it is foolish to personalise because it tends to oversimplify. We have seen that Garvin identified four reasons for factionalism within Fianna Fáil. Labour mirrored that image:

> The changes initiated in the 1960s had given the party a sense of mission [but they] did not make the party's conservative rural wing disappear. When this underlying conflict was combined with close relationships between the media and the party, the scene was set for searching – and at times searing – public debates, not just about socialist economics, but about political strategy, about church–state relations and about nationalism and the Northern Ireland problem.[38]

The Northern Ireland problem simply was the one with the highest visibility.

Institutional incoherence

If the people and the parties were not prepared for the Northern conflagration neither were the defence forces or the civil service. The Naval Service was described by backbench TDs in 1965 and again in 1967 as a 'joke'. By December 1969 the Air Corps had no more than forty-eight pilots. It could do nothing to stop Royal Air Force (RAF) incursions such as an incident in 1971 when a Canberra aircraft 'flew in Irish airspace for an hour, approaching within twenty miles of Dublin and flying over crucial lines of communication around Mount Oriel'. By 1966 there was a 36.8 per cent shortfall in the number of officers and men in the Permanent Defence Force (PDF). These numbers were further depleted by contributions to UN peace-keeping operations. Though supplementary estimates in 1971 and 1972 (10 per cent and 11.5 per cent of the original estimate) were made available for additional equipment and transport, these were hardly sufficient to offset the extra costs of inflation. Nor could they prevent the eighty-eight known border incursions by the British army in the two years ending 31 March 1972. By 1971 the personnel shortfall remained at 32.9 per cent but dropped to 23.1 per cent a year later. Nevertheless there 'was a clear failure to uphold the sovereignty of the State, and more generally ... a clear inability to intervene militarily in the North'.[39] Lynch warned the Dáil on 20 October 1971 that 'if there are repeated and more serious incursions by the British Army across the border it may be necessary to seize the United Nations of this issue as a threat to international peace'.[40] Matters improved somewhat over the following decade when numbers in the PDF rose to their highest in over twenty years but the burden was such that the Irish contribution to UN peace-keeping was limited between 1974 and 1977. The task of aiding the civil power was significant. A report to the New Ireland Forum in 1983 put the total extra cost of security arising in Northern Ireland for the period 1973–82 as between 19.7 per cent and 25.6 per cent of total expenditure on security, including PDF, prisons and police.[41]

A similar picture is evident within the civil service. To take one small example, there was a need to challenge the British government's account of events in Northern Ireland following the battle of the Bogside in August 1969. Reflecting on events a quarter-century later the former director of the Government Information Bureau, Eoin Neeson, commented that the 'British attitude towards the Republic suggested we were still a kind of aberrant colony that had petulantly kicked a hole in the Commonwealth curtain after being graciously granted its protection. The official British view on the North was that what occurred there was a matter for the Stormont Parliament. Any interests our government might have simply did not exist.'[42] To counteract that mentality Neeson was offered a single information officer from one of the state bodies. In the end he got all the information and press officers in the state services, plus a few more. They were assigned to embassies and missions in London, Birmingham, Manchester, Paris, Brussels, Bonn, New York, Boston, Washington, Madrid, Rome, Canberra, Stockholm and Copenhagen. They received assistance, too, from the Department of External Affairs as it prepared for a critical United Nations debate. UN assistance was invoked on 20 August when the Minister for External Affairs, Patrick Hillery, requested, by virtue of Article 35 of the UN Charter, an urgent meeting of the Security Council in connection with the situation of the 'Six Counties in Northern Ireland' – the partitionist language was redolent of emotional times. The general demeanour of Hillery, of Con Cremin (Ireland's Permanent Representative to the UN) and of Lord Caradon (the British representative) suggested that on this occasion catharsis was what mattered – the UN as 'sacred drama'.

One of the necessary components of diplomacy is a capacity for information-gathering and political analysis. From the outset it was clear that the Dublin government lacked even the most elementary knowledge of what was happening in Northern Ireland. It was that which gave Neil Blaney the edge in the beginning. His constituency of Donegal North-East shared a border with Derry. Army intelligence was also involved. The Department of External Affairs had no officials specifically and exclusively assigned to Anglo-Irish relations at the time. Initially one official got involved in a personal capacity. Eamon Gallagher, who worked in the trade section of the department, used to return home to Donegal most weekends. He made contact with John Hume and became a channel for communication that was officially acknowledged by the Minister for External Affairs and the Taoiseach in September 1969.[43] His task was to coordinate Northern policy, and his appointment was followed by rapid recruitment to a Northern desk in the department.

There was some reluctance at the time to giving External Affairs a role in what was seen as a major domestic problem as well as a foreign policy issue. From the 1950s Dublin spent less time on Anglo-Irish relations: 'The Department of External Affairs became oriented towards the United Nations in 1955, while the shift in emphasis towards an economic foreign policy reduced the overall significance of Anglo-Irish relations in the 1960s.'[44] There was some confusion as to who was responsible for Northern Ireland affairs. At one point early in 1970 Jack Lynch set up a unit within the department of the Taoiseach to look at matters arising from the Northern Ireland situation. It was effectively a consultancy group to which specific tasks were assigned such as the

implications of a total breakdown of Northern society or the convergence of the two economies. Essentially it was a contingency planning unit rather than a policy formulation one, and it certainly did not
have executive powers. Given heightened nationalist passions and the
Irish constitution's claim to jurisdiction over all the island no Taoiseach
could publicly admit that Northern Ireland was a foreign affairs issue.
The neat, if evasive, reply to a Dáil question on 28 March 1973 by
Lynch's successor as Taoiseach, Liam Cosgrave, is revealing: 'Northern
Ireland affairs are primarily the responsibility of the Taoiseach. In so far
as those relations affect relations with Britain they are also, of course,
the concern of the Minister for Foreign Affairs.'[45]

As the conflict unfolded Foreign Affairs became more heavily committed. Until 1 January 1972 the department worked on the basis of a
series of *ad hoc* arrangements, and it was only in 1972 that administratively it became properly organised. When internment was introduced on 9 August 1971 the Irish Consul-General in Boston, Seán
Donlon, was called back the following day on a temporary basis with
the specific task of organising the collection of information on the
treatment of those interned. Soon it was obvious that the nature of the
treatment meted out justified taking a case to the European Court of
Human Rights. Donlon was to remain in the Anglo-Irish affairs division in Dublin for the next seven years until he was appointed Irish
Ambassador to the United States in September 1978. Along with Eamon Gallagher Donlon became one of the original 'travellers' to
Northern Ireland. Since his task was to gather information that eventually formed the basis of the Irish human rights case he had to move
with some discretion because, theoretically, he had no diplomatic im-
munity. Donlon's role broadened after Bloody Sunday and particularly after the imposition of direct rule two months later. Nevertheless
the hiatus of confusion and ill-preparedness had been dangerous.

LONDON AND BELFAST

It is a moot point whether London was more unprepared than Dublin
for the outbreak of violence in 1968. The steady stream of memoirs
emanating from British politicians and officials make no attempt to
hide this unpreparedness, or the sense of distaste and despair felt by the
establishment. The Secretary of State for Defence at the outbreak of the
Troubles, Denis Healey, admitted that the 'Labour Government was
seriously hampered throughout by the absence of adequate intelligence
about the illegal organisations in Northern Ireland ... and by lamen-
tably poor communications between Whitehall and Stormont. Both

of these weaknesses resulted from generations of inexcusable neglect.'[46] Cecil King records William Whitelaw as commenting that the 'Stormont ministers were inflexible in their determination to maintain the status quo without modification'.[47] James Callaghan's vivid description of the inadequacies of the General Department at the Home Office has already been mentioned.[48] What was more revealing was the anomalous position of the Foreign Office in its dealings with the Irish Republic; this too has already been mentioned.[49] Sir John Peck, British Ambassador in Dublin from April 1970, discovered that until October 1968 the embassy reported to the Commonwealth Office: 'The Foreign Office dealt with a world that is truly foreign – individual nations which might be stronger or weaker than Britain, friendly or hostile, but which were in any case wholly detached. The Commonwealth Office dealt with former British colonies ... where, as befits a member of the family, a good deal could be taken for granted.' Even after a separate Republic of Ireland department was formed within the Foreign Office it reported to an under-secretary whose principal concern was liaison between the Foreign Office, the Ministry of Defence and the service departments: 'This inevitably introduced the danger that departmental advice reaching the Foreign Secretary about policy towards the Republic would be related primarily to our military policy and interests in the domestic law and order situation in the north'.[50] Initially, then, London received inadequate advice from Belfast and Dublin, and responded by appointing Oliver Wright 'Representative of the United Kingdom Government in Northern Ireland' in August 1969. Wright had been Private Secretary at No. 10 from 1964 to 1966 and Ambassador to Denmark since then. He was Ambassador to West Germany from 1975 to 1981 and Ambassador to the US from 1982 to 1986. The appointment of such a senior diplomat was indicative, firstly, of the growing alarm in Whitehall, and secondly, of the anomalies of the Belfast–London relationship. When this hardened into direct rule unionists were frequently to complain of a 'colonial' style of government.

The unionist community presented great problems for London. It lacked political sophistication and leadership and placed an almost total reliance on a security response. Fifty years of devolution had created its own form of insularity. In 1963 the Northern Ireland government produced a myopic account of its stewardship. It concluded:

> Linked directly to the heart of the Motherland, Ulster has shared richly in that high seriousness and idealism which lie at the heart of the British constitution and are the foundation of the British way of

life. In a world of stress and uncertainty, the Ulster community today looks into the future with the confidence that springs from three and a half centuries of trial and achievement, from forty years of its present form of government and from a vivid sense of high purpose.[51]

When it was confronted with political violence that purpose was severely tested. The collapse of the old order was visible to see. As already mentioned, between April 1969 and March 1972 no less than three Unionist prime ministers were replaced. The first to go was Terence O'Neill.

Like Lynch he had some powerful rivals who vied for his position. He did not enjoy the endorsement of his predecessor (Lord Brookeborough); he had had to rely on a 'kingmaker' (the Chief Whip, William Craig); and he had to work closely with a powerful and embittered rival (Brian Faulkner). His style and his policy were in sharp contrast to those of his predecessor. He considered that the cabinet should work full-time and he drew up a code of conduct. This was not universally popular with men grown used to the 'graceful' ways of Brookeborough; in fact, O'Neill used the code to sack his Minister of Agriculture, Harry West, in 1967. He had also removed the Leader of the House in 1965 and demoted William Craig in 1966, moving him from Development to Home Affairs. He gave the impression of being remote and aloof, traits that were not admired in a small place like Northern Ireland. He felt the need to seek a vote of confidence in April 1965; and in 1966 and again in 1967 there were revolts inside the Unionist Party, both of which ended in a vote of confidence of specious unanimity.

His premiership has been noted for two interdependent themes which upset the *status quo*: improving community relations and broadening the economic base. The latter was a recent phenomenon. It entailed central planning and a challenge to the authority of local politicians, many of whom resented interference from Stormont. The modernising O'Neill was building up problems for himself. The former angered traditionalists who considered Catholics to be essentially disloyal. This brought Ian Paisley's Protestant Unionist Party into existence.[52] It contested four local government seats in Belfast in 1964; and in a bid to broaden its appeal it became the Democratic Unionist Party in 1971. Paisley personified and enlarged Protestant fears in a period of great political uncertainty. A survey conducted in 1966–7 by Richard Rose found that 52 per cent of Protestants endorsed the use of violence to keep Northern Ireland Protestant: 'The reasons given are few, simple and unambiguous: defence of Protestantism and the British

connection, and opposition to Catholicism and the Republic. Few
Protestants refer to economic or conventional "good government"
justifications for taking up arms.'[53]

In demanding 'British' rights the civil rights movement discommoded unionist certitude. As his autobiography demonstrates,
O'Neill conceded the justice of many of the civil rights demands; and
in a televised broadcast on 9 December 1968 he laid out the alternatives:
'What kind of Ulster do you want? A happy and respected Province in
good standing with the rest of the United Kingdom? Or a place con-
tinually torn apart by riots and demonstrations, and regarded by the
rest of Britain as a political outcast? As always in a democracy, the
choice is yours.'[54] Those words, and that challenge, resonate more than
three decades later with two addenda. Firstly, O'Neill did not foresee
the intensity and the barbarity of the violence that was to come. Secondly, the world has grown smaller: it is not simply relations with
Britain that matter any longer – Northern Ireland has joined that small
league of conflicts engaged in conflict transformation in which it will
serve as an exemplar or become a pariah. What was becoming evident
was that unionism was factionalising and was becoming more insular.

The first manifestation of factionalism can be found in the Northern
Ireland general election called by Terence O'Neill in February 1969 to
bolster his position. In response to growing Catholic agitation O'Neill
announced the establishment of the Cameron Commission to inquire
into the reasons for the civil disturbances. This displeased his Deputy
Prime Minister (and Minister of Commerce), Brian Faulkner who
resigned on 23 January. Two days later another minister, William
Morgan, Minister of Health and Social Services, followed Faulkner's
example. Finally thirteen Unionist backbenchers met in Portadown to
publicise their grievances against O'Neill. He responded by calling a
general election for 24 February. Of the forty-five contested seats thirty-nine O'Neill Unionists were opposed by seventeen anti-O'Neillites
(eleven of whom secured seats) and five Protestant Unionists (none of
whom were successful, although two were to win by-elections in
1970). It was the worst performance by the Unionist Party since
Northern Ireland had been created.[55] It was to be the beginning of
political decline and incoherence. O'Neill resigned as Prime Minister
on 28 April 1969. His successor, James Chichester-Clark, was essentially a stopgap concerned with halting the erosion of the unionist
heartland. He resigned after two years in office. His successor, Brian
Faulkner, was undoubtedly one of the most talented and astute politicians in the history of Ulster unionism. He possessed enough acuity to
realise that unionism could no longer resist the sovereign parliament,

and he demonstrated sufficient moral and political courage to lead unionism into a new dispensation.[56] His rejection of direct rule in 1972 cost him the premiership (after only a year in office) and his acceptance of power-sharing in 1974 his political inheritance. It wasn't until David Trimble became leader in 1995 that Ulster unionism displayed a similar vision and a willingness to take risks.

It is not our intention to explore the ramifications of unionist factionalism but simply to explain why it followed the course it did. One reason lies in the history of devolution and in the benign, if not soporific, Belfast–London relationship. We have examined the latter in chapter 1. Before the civil rights movement challenged the *status quo* the one period of concern for unionism was the return of a Labour government in 1945. The diary of Sir Basil Brooke, Prime Minister from 1943, conveys a real worry that radical change might be in the wind.[57] Had he known the innermost thoughts of the Home Secretary, James Chuter Ede – he had characterised the Northern Ireland cabinet as being 'remnants of the ascendancy class, very frightened of the Catholics and the general world trend to the left', and he stated in 1949 that 'he did not like and would be unable to defend the electoral methods of the Northern Ireland government' – Brooke might have had real cause to worry. As against that, Northern Ireland's wartime record and Ireland's neutrality and withdrawal from the Commonwealth ensured that Northern Ireland's position within the United Kingdom was secure. But the underlying reason for non-intervention lay in procrastination. It was put in a letter to the Foreign Secretary, Ernest Bevin, by one who was actually encouraging intervention: 'Because this is such a troublesome political question in Britain, and because you have all so much to do there is a natural tendency to shelve it.'[58]

That had suited unionist purposes adequately. The shock of the new in terms of much closer scrutiny after 1969 (and direct rule after 1972) led the unionist community to turn inwards. It was stated most starkly in a Vanguard Unionist pamphlet produced after the imposition of direct rule. It asserted that 'Ulster loyalists' are 'an old and historic community' for whom union with Britain had never been 'an end in itself' but 'was always a means of preserving Ulster's British tradition and the identity of her loyalist people'. British politicians, by 'dismantling Ulster's capacity for resistance to *friend* or foe', had 'unwittingly forged a nation that cannot entrust to them its security or national destiny'.[59] Here were a people who had failed to follow E.M. Forster's aphorism, 'Only connect'. They stretched the concept of devolution and autonomy to the point where independence seemed the logical outcome for those who had not connected. In any case they had a proud tradition of procrastination from the 1880s onwards. It was the British government who came to heel, as the failure of the Home Rule bills had demonstrated – and as the fall of the power-sharing executive was yet to show. So batten down the hatches, indulge in navel-gazing, reinforce 'Ulster' as the Albania of the western world hermetically sealed from the outside and return to the search for identity. It had worked in the past – why not again?

There was then in a certain unionist mindset a curious mixture of insecurity and complacency. Insecurity was illustrated by the rise of loyalist paramilitaries and the verbal pyrotechnics of some of the more 'respectable' leaders. Complacency grew after February 1974 when the United Ulster Unionist Council (UUUC) contested the general election and won eleven of the twelve Northern Ireland seats. United in opposition to the power-sharing executive which had been installed in January, the UUUC was composed of the rump of the UUP led by Harry West, Ian Paisley's DUP and William Craig's VUUP. Their success was compounded by the fall of the executive in May. They had some worries that the paramilitaries might have political ambitions so they worked out a pact for the May 1975 elections for a Northern Ireland Constitutional Convention. Having seen off that challenge the parties returned to their internecine battles, and in May 1977 the UUP stood in local government elections without UUUC endorsement. By June the UUUC was dead. No matter: there was no evidence that British governments had the stomach to take on the IRA *and* the unionist community as well.

Another sign of complacency was a reluctance to seek advice and assistance from outside. Terence O'Neill had suggested Arnold Goodman as a mediator in 1974.[60] During the Northern Ireland Constitutional Convention period the SDLP called on the services of two senior counsels from Dublin, Donal Barrington and Rory O'Hanlon. According to Maurice Hayes, who was senior adviser to the convention chairman, the UUUC 'tried to employ a Colonel Hezlet, who had written a history of the B Specials, to write a paper on security. This we disallowed because security did not fall within the purview of the convention and also because of Hezlet's lack of academic (and indeed current military) standing.'[61] Instead they employed the distinguished political scientist Bernard Crick at the behest of William Craig who had been reading Crick's *In Defence of Politics*. At the end of the process Craig was happy to consider a form of voluntary coalition which would include the SDLP but he could not bring the bulk of his UUUC colleagues with him. In effect that was to be political suicide for him: he lost his Westminster seat in 1979 and never recovered. By this stage the

UUUC had broken into its disparate parts (and low-level conflict). The Ulster Unionists were being led by James Molyneaux, a House of Commons man *par excellence*.[62] Never a man to go in for (to borrow one of his most oft-quoted phrases) 'high-wire acts' Molyneaux didn't feel the need to move the action beyond Westminster and Stormont. He gave the impression that he had done all the travelling he intended to do during his wartime service with the RAF. Admittedly he was to make one parliamentary visit to the United States and one fraternal visit to Australia but he appeared most at ease in the Palace of Westminster or among the loyal orders in Northern Ireland. He took the long view. Unionism had faced crises in the past but had always triumphed. The downfall of the power-sharing executive was a case in point. A combination of battening down the hatches and organised protest seemed to do the trick. There were merits in procrastination. In any case much of his time was spent in ensuring that the DUP never again overtook the UUP as the largest party as it had (for a short period) in 1981.

So the unionist position throughout much of the 1970s and 1980s was one of insularity. Some of the more dynamic unionist politicians recognised as much. A task-force comprising the UUP's Harold McCusker MP and Frank Millar and the DUP's Peter Robinson MP was mandated to report on the state of unionist opinion in the aftermath of the November 1985 Anglo-Irish Agreement. Their report, entitled 'An End to Drift' and presented to the two party leaders in July 1987, recognised 'the inadequacies of the existing protest campaign' against the agreement and the 'limits of Unionism's negotiating strength'.[63] That realism was not recognised by Molyneaux and Paisley, and the report was not published in full. But when Peter Brooke became Secretary of State for Northern Ireland in July 1989 he attempted to rescue unionism from its 'internal exile', a phrase he used in a speech to Bangor Chamber of Commerce on 9 January 1990. That was to be the beginning of a new initiative involving the two governments and all the constitutional parties in Northern Ireland to consider the three-stranded relationship: (1) relations internal to Northern Ireland; (2) North–South relations; and (3) east–west relations. It is not our purpose to examine these negotiations at this stage but simply to comment on the fact that Strand 2 was to be chaired by an independent chairman. Finding one involved elements of farce. Once the Irish Minister for Foreign Affairs and the Northern Secretary were ruled out Lord Carrington became the British government's choice. That scandalised unionist leaders who issued a statement on 29 May describing his record on Northern Ireland as 'deplorable' and adding that his remarks about unionists 'have been disparaging and offensive'.[64] After scouring the globe and considering about thirty names the various parties to the talks agreed on the former Governor-General of Australia, Sir Ninian Stephen, as chairman. It was another little example of the politics of navel contemplation.[65]

That type of politics had flourished in the devolution years. Stormont had been 'an ego-trip for Unionists; and it bolstered a self-confident and highly provincial political culture. The removal of Stormont in 1972 damaged this self-regarding Unionist provincialism and flagged the beginning of the party's retreat from its local ascendancy.' Equally the collapse of the power-sharing arrangement two years later, while a short-term boost 'to militant, majoritarian Unionism', was disastrous for the unionist tradition: 'For the Ulster Unionist Party had been taught that popular loyalist mobilization could serve as a substitute for difficult or dangerous concessions; and its leaders had been taught that the articulation of a simple Unionist faith was an easier and – in the short term – a more popular strategy than complicated and potentially disastrous cross-party dialogue.'[66] Where evasion and complicity and insularity ran together there was little room for vision.

CONCLUSION

We need not detain ourselves overmuch in examining Belfast–London relations after 1968. We have noted already the exasperation expressed by William Whitelaw and Lord Carrington – or, at least, Cecil King's version of that exasperation. It can be found, too, in the Crossman diaries and in the reform programme initiated by the Wilson government. It was given physical expression by the presence of Oliver Wright and his colleagues. Even a more sympathetic Conservative government was to lose patience. When Brian Faulkner became Prime Minister Edward Heath 'responded immediately to his energy, decisiveness and professionalism', that is until internment was introduced in August 1971: 'Heath was anxious about the decision. He was right to be. He should have put his foot down and disallowed it. But he was impressed by Faulkner. He wanted to support him, and he wanted to smash the IRA if it could be done.'[67] In fact internment was a tremendous boost for the IRA. It began on 9 August 1971 when over 300 men were detained and lasted until 5 December 1975 by which time 2,158 'graduates' had passed through the internment camps. It led to huge resentment and failed to control the violence: of the 174 people who died violently in 1971 only 28 were killed before internment was introduced. The bulk of IRA activists escaped the security sweep and many of those detained initially had not been involved in the post-1969 violence. Catholics saw it as yet another indiscriminate attack on their community.

Direct rule was imposed simply because governments (in Belfast and London)

> were unable to perform the classic function of government, the provision of public order, which was essential if the United Kingdom state was to become an object of allegiance on the part of ghetto Catholics ... Whereas in 1969 Stormont had lost this monopoly in Catholic territory largely because it lacked agencies of physical force capable of treating Catholics as citizens rather than as enemies, the events of 1969–72 demonstrated that even when ethnically neutral forces were placed at its disposal the regime was incapable of devising policies which would transform mere force into effective authority.[68]

In short, the policy of rule by proxy had failed. Westminster could neither rule nor properly control events at a distance. The fiasco of internment had proved that; and allegations of army brutality in its aftermath compounded the need to take drastic action. As a consequence of these allegations, and following widespread public criticism of a previous inquiry under Sir Edmund Compton, the Home Secretary, Reginald Maudling, set up a three-man inquiry to review interrogation procedures under Lord Parker. Its report in March 1972 carried a minority rider from the former Lord Chancellor, Lord Gardiner, who 'strongly condemned' the methods used in interrogating detainees as 'secret, illegal, not morally justifiable and alien to the traditions' of British democracy. Heath accepted Gardiner's minority report and promised that the use of 'intensive techniques' would cease.[69]

The Parker report was delivered on 2 March 1972 and direct rule was imposed before the month was out. Most commentators assert that it was Bloody Sunday that made direct rule inevitable. We have noted already in chapter 3 the impact of the Hume case and the alacrity of the government in giving retrospective validity on any actions taken by the armed forces under the Special Powers Act. The government's legislative speed owed much to concerns about international opinion. With troop levels rising from seven thousand in 1970 to twenty-one thousand in 1972, the government's desire to have absolute power was understandable. Add to that the wide array of powers the security forces possessed to deal with the emergency, and the series of reports chaired by members of the judiciary examining areas of security force activity – Cameron, Scarman, Hunt, Compton, Parker – and the need for a direct line of authority becomes obvious. The Northern Ireland conflict was polluting British democracy: something had to be done. Direct rule was to be the panacea.

SPECIAL RELATIONSHIPS

... the history of theorizing about nationalism displays two dramatic
faults. One is a tendency to treat the subject in a one-nation or one-
state frame of reference: so that each nationalism has to be
understood, in effect, mainly with reference to 'its own' ethnic,
economic, or other basis – rather than by comparison with the
'general historical process'. The second (and obviously related)
tendency is to take nationalist ideology far too literally and seriously.

TOM NAIRN[1]

The relationship between Britain, Ireland and Northern Ireland
is more like that of a disputed nationality zone with
dependency upon two powers.

FRANK WRIGHT[2]

When the Anglo-Irish Agreement was signed in November 1985
commentators were struck by its innovatory nature. One went so far as
to refer to it as 'a unique experiment [which] may itself serve as a future
precedent for the protection of cross-border minorities and neighbouring States' co-operation including the field of security'. He reinforced the point by quoting an Irish academic lawyer's opinion that
'it will be seen by international lawyers as an important new legal
model for consideration, adaptation and possible application in other
similar international situations of disputed sovereignty over territory'.[3]

The thrust of this chapter is not concerned with the minutiae of the
Anglo-Irish Agreement but with the political and intellectual climate
which enabled this 'unique experiment' to be undertaken. In that
respect we shall be concerned with what Nairn calls the 'general historical process' as it impinged on the conflicting claims of Britain and
Ireland in relation to Northern Ireland. Such a broad-brush approach

permits us to comment upon the eclipse of Empire, the diminution of the Anglo-American relationship, the growing significance of the European dimension, the variety of contradictory tendencies to be found in international relations, and the redundancy of certain modes of political discourse. It enables us to contrast the global pretensions imposed upon a once mighty imperial power and the more modest ambitions of a small independent state. Additionally, it removes us from the claustrophobic bilateralism of an ancient quarrel. What all these themes have in common is that they challenge that type of nationalism ('British' and Irish) which operates in a one-nation or one-state frame of reference.

We are suggesting that at the very least the old political vocabulary may have to be modified to recognise the interdependence of the modern world; and that because the British–Irish conflict has been so complex and (in recent years) so intense it has been (unwittingly) to the forefront of the debate about a new vocabulary. In short we are proclaiming the obsolescence 'of "the Woodrow Wilson model" of a world divided into nation-states, each one sovereign within its area and independent of the rest'.[4]

THE ANGLO-AMERICAN RELATIONSHIP

When the Taoiseach, Charles Haughey, attended a Washington luncheon hosted by the Speaker of the House of Representatives, Jim Wright, on St Patrick's Day 1987 he indulged in a little bit of rhetoric when he said that there 'are no two countries anywhere in the world which have such a special relationship as ours'. It may have been unconscious irony; or it may be that Haughey actually believed it.

He had some grounds for his optimism. The United States administration had played a significant role in the signing of the Anglo-Irish Agreement and was contributing directly to the workings of that agreement through its contribution to the International Fund for Ireland. No one could be unaware of the Irish contribution to the development of the United States. No less an authority than the distinguished American historian, Arthur S. Link, has commented that during the past three centuries the tiny island of Ireland has made 'a greater contribution to the character and development of the American people than any other territory of comparable size and population on the face of the earth'.[5] Indeed in 1980 – in the first census which enabled Americans to identify their ethnic origin or heritage group – more than forty-three million Americans (19 per cent of the total population) identified themselves as Irish. It is not surprising then that a myth has arisen about the political clout of Irish-America. But the figures need to be treated with some caution. No distinction is made, for example, between Irish-Americans of Catholic or Protestant origin. That is an important distinction, a fact acknowledged by Senator Daniel Moynihan of New York when he described that first huge wave of Catholic Irish emigrants – over 3,800,000 of them emigrated to the United States between 1820 and 1900 – as 'our first foreigners, the first perceived *internal* threat to the American way of life . . . Nothing before had so threatened the essential *Englishness* of our society. And the heart of it was religion, which Americans then considered the foundation of our political institutions.'[6]

Their Protestant counterparts – the 'Ulster-Scots' or 'Scotch-Irish' – posed no such threat. For the most part they had arrived in the eighteenth century – 200,000 or more Ulster Presbyterians emigrated to America in the period 1700–76 – and helped to shape modern America through the Revolution. It has been calculated that by 1790 perhaps 50 per cent or more of the settlers on the trans-Appalachian frontier were of Ulster lineage and that by the end of the eighteenth century one-sixth of the total European population of the United States claimed Scotch-Irish descent. By then they were integral parts of the American nation; thereafter 'if any man left his impress on American life, he did it as the individual he was, not as a member of the Scotch-Irish community'. With few exceptions they seem to have lost 'the kind of distinctive identity maintained by the Irish-American community'.[7] So the Scotch-Irish passed President Woodrow Wilson's 'infallibility test' for the hyphenated American – that, while he might retain 'ancient affections', nonetheless 'when he votes or when he acts or when he fights his heart and thought are centred nowhere but in the emotions and the purposes and policies of the United States'.[8]

(Catholic) Irish-America made the mistake of assuming that numbers (and organised pressure) could be converted into influence. They worked on the assumption that the United States was a key player in removing the British presence from Ireland. Like all myths it contained an element of truth. During World War I, for instance, the 'Irish Question was transformed from an essentially domestic problem into one occupying the stage of international politics. This arose from two main issues: Ireland's possible effect on the European balance of power up to August 1914 and, subsequently, her growing role in Anglo-American relations.'[9] The latter was not lost on British politicians: during the passage of the Third Home Rule Bill in 1914 the Prime Minister, Herbert Asquith, stressed the cabinet's concern about the probable effects of postponement of Home Rule on Irishmen at home and 'in that great kindred country of the United States'.[10]

While the Irish question plagued Anglo-American relations until the signing of the Anglo-Irish Treaty in December 1921, Irish-American pressure had its downside to the extent that President Wilson complained during the Paris Peace Conference in 1919 that Irish-Americans 'can see nothing except their own small interest',[11] a narrowness of vision which worried the Irish revolutionary leader Eamon de Valera. He had insisted on a bipartisan approach towards Republicans and Democrats whereas in the 1920 presidential election militant Irish-America supported a fundamentally isolationist Republican candidate. De Valera recognised this as a dangerous cul-de-sac: 'In opposing their machinations de Valera was rescuing the cause of Ireland in America from the embrace of essentially xenophobic anti-British forces which once in power would have closed the door on any diplomatic leverage on Ireland's behalf.'[12] That divide in Irish-America remained until recent times but what concerns us at this juncture is that no US administration could afford to ignore the interests of its major ally. Xenophobic anti-Britishness was counterproductive. A cursory survey of relations between Ireland and the United States from the 1920s to the 1970s illustrates the very limited impact of the Irish question on American domestic or foreign policy. Ireland's policy of neutrality may have antagonised later US administrations just as it did those in the 1940s and 1950s, as we saw in chapter 4.

The reason for the Anglo-American entente was obvious. They enjoyed a 'special relationship' – based on a common sense of history and of language in addition to kinship – which can be traced back to the 1890s. Its special nature can be isolated in three features: similar interests reinforced by similar ideology enclosed within a network of close personal contacts and friendships. In the world after 1945 interest was based on maintaining the independence of Western Europe and protecting their respective stakes in Asia and the Middle East. The ideological bond resided in a shared Anglo-American democracy with a common belief in the rule of law and an abhorrence of totalitarianism. In these circumstances American foreign policy was pro-British, and Ireland was considered to be within the British sphere of influence.[13]

A case study of Irish-American impotence presented itself in 1951. An anti-partition resolution seeking a congressional hearing had been favourably reported by the House Foreign Affairs Committee and was debated in the House of Representatives on 27 September. Despite intense Irish-American pressure the motion was beaten decisively by a vote of 206 to 139. In a confidential memo from the British embassy in Washington dated 6 October to the American department at the

Foreign Office three arguments against the motion were noted: (i) the principle of self-determination should be extended to Northern Ireland rather than be taken solely on an all-Ireland basis; (ii) the motion was an unwarranted interference in the affairs of the United Kingdom; and (iii) Ireland's neutrality in World War II and non-membership of NATO. The author suggested that the wider reasons for the defeat of the motion could be traced to a loss of support for the Irish cause in America due to Ireland's neutrality and wartime stances; a reaction against an organised ethnic group using the national legislature for 'purposes which bear little relationship to the foreign policy interests of the United States'; and a wave of anti-Catholicism because of renewed Catholic pressure on the parochial schools issue. Despite this setback it would be foolish to totally discount Irish-American influence – as events from the mid-1970s were to demonstrate. The Irish embassy in Washington, for example, saw little merit in challenging the State Department–Foreign Office hegemony. Instead their lobbying concentrated on the legislators on Capitol Hill and on the editorial writers throughout the nation. This tactic proved to be a very sound investment.

Neither should we make too much of the Anglo-American special relationship because its underlying basis has always been interest and, not in the first place, emotion.[14] Perhaps the most colourful definition of the relationship comes from President Lyndon Johnson in what David Watt describes as 'a characteristic metaphor and a wealth of expressive gesture': 'Britain', Johnson said, 'may dicker around in the night clubs and dance with a few of the girls but in the end you'll always come home to bed with the same old girl.'[15] The evidence does suggest that Britain was the ardent suitor with some of its spokesmen losing all sense of perspective. In a realistic survey of the postwar literature on the topic David Reynolds quotes an authority who wondered in 1952 whether 'the deed of 1776 might in some sense be undone'; Reynolds himself concludes that in some aspects (such as intelligence and nuclear matters) 'the relationship remains special in quality . . . Yet it is no longer special in importance, either to America or to the world at large. That is the difference between the 1980s and the 1940s.'[16]

A swift tour of a range of issues in which the United Kingdom was bypassed by the United States between the 1940s and the 1980s is indicative of its diminishing influence: the abrupt end of Lend Lease; the insistence on sterling convertibility; the refusal to share nuclear technology; the exclusion of the UK from the ANZUS pact; failure to join the Baghdad pact; Suez and much of Middle East policy generally;

cancellation of the Skybolt weapons system in 1962; the decision to deploy neutron bombs in Western Europe in 1978; the hostage rescue mission to Iran in April 1980; the pressure to cancel the Soviet gas pipeline from Siberia to Western Europe in 1982; the launching of the Strategic Defence Initiative in 1983; the Grenada affair in 1983; Afghanistan, Central America and Angola; suggestions in 1985 that the limits of the SALT 2 Treaty would be exceeded; difficulties with the sale of Plessey's Ptarmigan system to the American army late in 1985; the air raids on Libya in 1986 (the decision to attack, that is, rather than the use of British air bases); and the Reykjavik summit in 1986.[17]

The ledger is by no means exhausted but it does illustrate the changing nature of geopolitical relationships and Britain's place in the world order. The Grenada affair in 1983, for example, illustrates a deficiency in another of Britain's special relationships – that with the Commonwealth. One reason for its decreasing influence is demographic. In 1800 around 20 per cent of the world's population lived in Western Europe; today that stands at 8 per cent and will be under 5 per cent by the end of this century: 'The loss of empire . . . was *au fond* the entirely to be expected contraction of the all-to-overstretched dominion of a none-too-large and very distant island brought about . . . by the nemesis of normalcy.'[18] When we consider that by 1990 the Commonwealth had fifty members from all corners of the globe encompassing a quarter of the world's population and a third of its nation-states – 'Upon any calculation they now compose a large international aggregation, which has no real counterpart'[19] – Britain's diminishing role becomes evident. In that respect 'not only has England markedly contracted, "England" as part of the historiography of its former colonial territories has steadily contracted too'.[20]

The Irish viewed that contraction through a narrow nationalist lens. Much more interesting is to look at the larger picture for what it tells us about the 'general historical process' and the changing world system. We see this in the case of the shift from Empire to Commonwealth, with Britain's benign acquiescence in accepting India, Pakistan, Ceylon, Ghana, Malaya and Nigeria into 'the hitherto white man's club' being an 'eloquent testimony to Britain's ardent concern to continue to perform a role on the world's stage analogous to the one it had previously played'. The result was not altogether to Britain's liking: 'there ran a strain of deep disappointment in the UK with the Commonwealth for having totally failed to be the central underpinning of Britain's continuing greatness in its post-imperial era which it was supposed to be'. The Commonwealth's principal mechanisms slipped from Britain's grasp, and by 1965 a separate Commonwealth secretary-general was in control rather than the cabinet secretary and the Commonwealth Relations Office. As a result the Commonwealth 'turned out to be instead a new, unplanned and quite major arena in which Britain actually found itself pilloried'.[21]

Besides criticism of British policy in southern Africa another bone of contention in the Commonwealth was the UK's application to join the EEC. Australia and New Zealand wanted to protect their overseas market in the UK – in 1939 over 40 per cent of Australia's trade was with the UK; by 1990 it was less than 4 per cent. Part of the reason for British hesitation in seeking EEC membership was the delusion about its role in the Commonwealth. That delusion was shattered as the new Commonwealth began to find its own expression. In its place a new myth had to be invented: Britain's unique position between Atlanticism and Europeanism. The cost of maintaining global pretensions was not to be underestimated.

Given its diminutive size and humble position in world affairs independent Ireland worked on more modest scales. Until 1939 the authorities were obsessed with establishing Irish sovereignty (especially in relation to Britain), but that 'was undermined by the lack of adequate unilateral defence and economic self-sufficiency, and by the enormous continuing dependence upon British trade'. These inadequacies were exposed during the course of World War II. The postwar period seemed to confirm that the Irish 'had managed to maintain a basic freedom of decision and action' by staying out of, for example, NATO; but according to Trevor Salmon 'to some extent the Irish were again allowed this freedom because neither the United States nor Britain considered Irish participation in the new defence arrangements to be crucial'. Similarly Ireland's decision to seek entry into the EEC in the 1960s and again early in the 1970s may not have been the action of an independent actor but the result of a stark choice between the perils of autarky and the opportunity to make economic progress.[22]

THE EUROPEAN DIMENSION

On 9 May 1973, in his first major policy speech to the Dáil as Minister for Foreign Affairs, Dr Garret FitzGerald announced that it was time to formulate new general guidelines for future foreign policy because of the movement 'towards greater interdependence' in the world economy, 'the evolving situation in Northern Ireland' and 'the accession to membership of the European Communities'.[23] The key word was 'interdependence'. The Irish were very conscious of their humble position in the world economy and of the need to find new markets. Of the three countries that joined the EEC in 1973 (Ireland, the UK and Denmark) only in Ireland was public opinion strongly in favour of membership; this support was based on the belief that the country would benefit from the Common Agricultural Policy and from European regional development funds. Hence in a turnout of 71 per cent in a referendum held on 10 May 1972 some 83 per cent of Irish voters endorsed the decision to join.

That was in sharp contrast to the situation in the UK: 'the British entered the Community in an unemotional frame of mind'.[24] This was not surprising given their history and culture of mistrust about 'the continent', a mistrust compounded by their sense of superiority in relation to the French and Germans in the postwar period. Hence the British refused to get involved (even against the advice of the US Secretary of State, Dean Acheson) in the original proposal for a European Coal and Steel Community in 1950 because, to quote Lord Plowden, 'We'd won the war and we weren't ready to form any special links with the continent.'[25] A decade later Britain saw the economic advantages of being a member. By spring 1961 the country was in a serious balance of payments crisis. 'While exports to the Commonwealth accounted for slightly over half of total British exports in 1951, they had fallen by 1961 to only a little over 33 per cent. On the other hand [the European Free Trade Association] was only a moderate success as a trading group and Britain registered the lowest percentage of total exports going to EFTA partners, namely, 12 per cent in 1962.'[26] Thus, along with Denmark, Norway and Ireland, Britain made an application to join the EEC in 1962 – an application which was vetoed by President Charles de Gaulle on 14 January 1963 because 'in his view, Britain would constitute a Trojan horse for the United States, on the one hand impeding Western Europe's emergence as a unified entity under French leadership and, on the other, leading ultimately to an Atlantic Community under American "hegemony" '.[27]

Hence Britain was hoist on its own petard. Its (largely psychological) Atlanticism was viewed with suspicion by its putative European partners and in the meantime its economic prospects were being undermined because it was outside 'Europe'. When Britain did enter on 1 January 1973 global economic conditions had deteriorated: '. . . the first stage of the Community's development coincided with the optimism and burgeoning prosperity of the 1960s. Britain's accession, by contrast, came just as that boom was about to end with the first oil shock, and its first years of membership coincided with the worst recession since the 1930s.'[28] Nor was Britain to find the obligations of membership altogether to its liking. Britain's problem was that it was not in control. It has to be remembered that – borrowing an expression used by the Foreign Secretary, Tony Crosland, when he addressed the European Parliament in 1977 – the Community represented Britain's first permanent peacetime engagement on the continent of Europe since the Reformation.[29] Unlike its other alliances the Community was the only international organisation of which Britain was not a founder member. Nor was Britain tuned into the wave of idealism that created the Franco-German *rapprochement* which in turn launched the EEC. Tugendhat describes its dilemma succinctly: 'In a nutshell Britain was turning away from a set of assumptions and policies that had failed, towards an experiment that seemed to be succeeding, in the hope that it would yield political influence and economic growth that could not be obtained by other means.'[30]

In short, Britain's external support system was collapsing and that, in turn, was undermining some of its more cherished illusions. It was for that reason that a (very unBritish) referendum was held on 5 June 1975 to decide on Britain's continuing membership of the Community. The immediate cause centred on a dispute within the Labour government about the costs and benefits of membership: 'dispute' indeed is much too mild – the European debate highlighted the fundamental Anglo-Saxon/European faultline which cut across the main British political parties.[31] With a deeply divided party Harold Wilson's solution was to launch a largely phoney renegotiation of the original terms of accession to the EEC and put it to a referendum. His cabinet was split sixteen to seven between pro- and anti-Europeans but 'the "Yes" side had a clear propaganda advantage in the support of most business firms, who did not hesitate to use their money, their advertising power and their communications with their workers, and of the great majority of the national and regional press'.[32] In all of those circumstances the outcome of the referendum – a two to one majority in favour of continued membership – was a foregone conclusion.[33]

Nevertheless Britain continued to be an awkward partner inside the Community. Under Labour Britain 'had been a conspicuously difficult and unhelpful partner over a whole range of Community activities, and two of the Government's most prominent members, John Silkin and Tony Benn, had continued their anti-EEC campaign while participating in the work of the Council of Ministers; something many on the Continent found shocking'.[34] Much of the same anti-EEC strategy was to continue, of course, under Margaret Thatcher.

The anti-European animus was fuelled by a vaunted British conception of sovereignty. Just as the Statute of Westminster had finally transferred sovereignty to the dominions in 1931, the European

Communities Act of 1972 achieved the same purpose by transferring a large and increasing measure of British sovereignty to the EEC.[35] That fact seemed to escape the notice of many in the British political establishment who continued to indulge in an ersatz debate about the nature of sovereignty. In fact even before Britain joined the EEC the die may have been cast. In 1963–4 the Court of Justice of the European Communities delivered a series of decisions which ensured that the EEC underwent, in the phrase of Joseph Weiler, 'a real *legal revolution*'. The first decision enunciated the doctrine of direct effect, which 'meant that each time a member state introduced a law (or failed to introduce a law) which had the effect of disturbing the operation of the Common Market, individuals could go to court and seek the disapplication of the offending measure ... By one judicial stroke the centrepiece of the European legal-political structure received a status unknown on a similar scale in any other international organisation, and individuals became the real *de facto* vigilantes of the Community order.'

The second decision introduced a supremacy clause, the sort which can be found in many federal state constitutions but was not to be found in the Treaty of Rome: 'Community law, *per* the court, whether the treaty itself or every regulation, decision and directive of the most menial character, was to be held by national courts as supreme and overriding *any* conflicting national law, whether a ministerial decree or a fully-fledged parliamentary enactment.' What Weiler found particularly surprising was not that the Court of Justice had made such a pronouncement but that the doctrine was accepted by the overwhelming majority of supreme courts in the member states: 'The only exception is the delicate problem of Britain which has no written constitution.'[36] Weiler's conclusion on the overall effects of this legal revolution deserves comment. He believed that it has 'to a large extent *nationalised* Community obligations and has introduced on the Community level the *habit of obedience* and the respect for the rule of law which traditionally is not associated with international obligations'.[37] In other words Britain and Ireland entered a community that already possessed a strong legal culture which challenged some of the more dogmatic beliefs about sovereignty.

THE SOVEREIGNTY ISSUE

In the second edition of his book *Sovereignty* (published in 1986) F.H. Hinsley turned very briefly to the evolution of the European Communities and pronounced magisterially that if that body had replaced 'the several separate states by a United States of Western Europe

– by a single sovereign body-politic – as its designers and some of its supporters intended, it would be of immense interest to the student of the origin of new states and of the transfer of sovereignty'. But since it hadn't it 'had to bow to the fact that the established territorial body-politic is highly resilient as the most appropriate frame for the conduct of political life'.[38] This section will challenge the inherent complacency buried in that statement by suggesting that the universal recognition of territorial sovereignty as the differentiating principle in the international arena has come under some scrutiny in recent years.

In a series of articles William Wallace has delineated a new British disease: its obsession with sovereignty. He bemoans the fact that 'this preoccupation ... – in particular, with the nature of the formal European commitment – has distracted attention from the progressive informal encroachment of international linkages on British autonomy'.[39] In what may be one of history's little ironies that message may have been absorbed by the Irish when Ireland entered the EEC. In a White Paper of January 1972, *The Accession of Ireland to the European Communities*, the Department of Foreign Affairs drew the distinction between independence and sovereignty. The latter was defined as 'the freedom to take autonomous decisions and actions in domestic and foreign affairs'. It acknowledged that 'as a very small country independent but with little or no capacity to influence events abroad that significantly affect us' Ireland enjoyed very little effective economic sovereignty, and stated:

> For most countries other than the major powers, the real freedom, as distinct from the nominal right, to take national action and pursue policies in the economic and trading sectors is circumscribed to a very great extent by the complex nature of international, economic and trading relationships ... our vital interests may be affected by the policies and actions of other larger countries or groups of countries. This gravely restricts our capacity to exercise the right of freedom of action and thus represents a very real limitation on our national sovereignty.[40]

That was a lesson that had been hard learnt in the course of Anglo-Irish relations throughout the twentieth century and also in the attempts to woo American official opinion around to an anti-partitionist stance. The stark lesson was that, in the words of Joseph Lee, 'the national interest was the only valid criterion in policy formulation. Everything else, even sovereignty, which was merely a means towards serving the national interest, must be subordinated to that decisive consideration.'[41] As the White Paper poined out, the other member states of the EEC had already 'accepted the limitations involved on their own national freedom of action because they consider that their national interests are best being served by membership'.[42]

Britain, of course, was not a member state at the time of the Irish White Paper; if it had been, the suggestion that *all* member states accepted the limitations of membership would have required qualification. Wallace, for example, finds British foreign policy to be more ideological than pragmatic; and since 'foreign policy is about national identity itself: about the sources of national pride, the characteristics which distinguish a country from its neighbours, the core element of sovereignty it seeks to defend, the values it stands for and seeks to promote abroad',[43] British foreign policy has been antithetical to the 'European concept'. Wallace detects a British national identity which was 'essentially Protestant and liberal', thereby dividing Britain from France and the Catholic and corporate states of southern Europe. And he writes: 'historical definition of Britain's external sovereignty in terms of independence from continental Europe reinforced the sense of British identity as Anglo–Saxon and Atlantic'.[44] In that sense accession to the EEC was not widely recognised in Britain as a bonus: rather it was something wished upon a reluctant suitor – with the inevitable negative consequences: 'The doctrine of parliamentary sovereignty *is* incompatible with Britain's European entanglements, even in some ways with the whole network of rule-based interdependence within which British governments now work.'[45]

Hence many of the contemporary divisions in British society centre around the European debate, and their causes lie deep in British history. More specifically that debate was concerned with the perennial debate about parliamentary sovereignty within the United Kingdom. According to Bernard Crick, 'Historically the very formula "United Kingdom" was developed to stress the primacy, first of the crown, then of parliament, in the practical business of holding together the different historical communities of England, Wales, Scotland and Ireland.' In that respect parliamentary sovereignty 'was the ideology of an imperially minded governing class, not a universal truth about or necessity of British politics (or of any other, for that matter)'.[46] In fact, as Crick demonstrates, the United Kingdom operated under the pretence of being a strong centralised state when in reality it allowed a kind of informal federalism. The virtual autonomy conceded to Northern Ireland after partition stands as a monument to just such an informal arrangement.

While it might be asserted that Britain's handling of the Northern Ireland problem after 1968 demonstrated that British sovereignty within the North remained intact, we are on much more dubious ground when we analyse the debate about Europe because here we are involved in making distinctions between sovereignty, autonomy, interdependence and integration. We should acknowledge the comments of Richard Cooper who has traced that particular route:

> The illusion of national autonomy is still widespread and is widely confused with national sovereignty. The latter concerns the formal ability of a nation to act on its own rather than under the instruction of another nation. That remains undiminished. National autonomy, in contrast, is the ability of a nation to attain its objectives through unilateral action. That is heavily constrained . . . in an environment of high interdependence.[47]

The British authorities may have been loath to recognise the obligations of interdependence. Membership of the EEC signalled the degree to which the western world was becoming more interdependent, an interdependence in which there is 'the tendency towards erosion of the exclusivity associated with the traditional notion of territoriality'.[48] Friedrich Kratochwil detects a 'variety of contradictory tendencies . . . in present international life'. The first is the universal recognition of territorial sovereignty, while the second is the erosion of boundaries through the growth of interdependencies: 'while political systems are boundary-maintaining systems, markets – although dependent for their creation upon political power and economic networks – are not. . . . A *third* identifiable trait is the result of the power differentials among nations, and the tensions between bounded political systems and unbounded exchanges such as economic, ideological or informational transactions.'[49]

Translated into concrete terms we are suggesting that when Britain entered the EEC it moved out of the more comfortable existence of exclusive territorial sovereignty into the uncertain world where such boundaries were eroded *and* became more aware of its vulnerability in the international system. Of course, Britain had been part of an interdependent world long before 1973. Its membership of the United Nations and before that the League of Nations dated back to 1919. But, as we noted earlier, the EEC was the first international organisation to which Britain belonged which it had not helped to form. Conscious that its relationship with some of the larger partners inside that organisation was asymmetrical, Britain reverted to a (subconscious) incantation of sovereignty.

Contrast Britain's attitude to joining the EEC with that of Ireland. The latter had high expectations. We have noted the material advantages such as the agricultural and regional development grants

Ireland hoped to gain. An important psychological boost was that Ireland would enter the EEC as a coordinate member with Britain, thereby laying to one side the country's depressing historical sub-ordination. We have noted, too, that in 1973 Irish foreign policy was being re-evaluated to take account of new conditions. One of the early important results of this re-evaluation was the decision to establish diplomatic relations with the Soviet Union in September 1973 and to sign a trade agreement with that country in 1974. We should not underestimate the symbolism of these steps because Ireland had always been antipathetic to and suspicious of the Soviet Union for political and religious reasons. The new realism signified a major change in Irish foreign policy making:

> This involved elevating the economic dimension in Irish foreign policy and demoting the principle of nationalism, self-identity, the right to self-determination, anti-imperialism and religious liberty that had guided de Valera, Frank Aiken and other members of the revolutionary elite in their conduct of Irish foreign policy. It was achieved by divorcing trade policy from other aspects of foreign policy, and the new approach seems to have been approved by all the major political parties.[50]

It reflected Ireland's enhanced international role. It was as if Ireland found itself in a period of expansion while Britain's self-perception was one of diminution.

THE 'AGREEABLY WIDER EMBRACE'

Ireland no longer falls exclusively within Britain's 'sphere of responsi-bility'. The very phrase is redolent of colonialism, the Cold War and big power rivalry. Common membership of the European Commu-nities has removed much of the claustrophobic bilateralism of the an-cient quarrel. The European context has reinforced Anglo-Irish contacts through frequent meetings of the respective foreign ministers (and of prime ministers on the margins) as well as, of course, officials. An Irish offical on the staff of the European Commission has com-mented that 'the effects of common United Kingdom and Irish mem-bership of the Community and particularly their attitudes to the emerging Community are so great that Anglo-Irish relations can hardly usefully be discussed except in that context. This, in my view, is healthy for both partners as it substitutes an agreeably wider embrace for what has been an excessive intimacy.'[51]

When the Northern Ireland problem re-emerged in the late 1960s it coincided with changes in the international system: the gradual diminution of the Anglo-American special relationship; a more assertive Commonwealth unwilling to accept unilateral British decisions; an acknowledgement that the world had grown more interdependent, which was manifested in the entry of Britain and Ireland to the EEC a few years later. That last had an impact on the Northern Ireland question: 'Since 1972 Britain has never made the defence of the union between Britain and Northern Ireland a touchstone of national strength in a way, for example, that it elevated the Falklands–Malvinas in 1982 . . . in the last analysis Britain has behaved towards the Irish Republic as another member of the EEC to which it might accord a recognition of the kind it expects itself.'[52]

In response to changes in the international system three types of management devices have evolved. We are most familiar with the first, *spheres of responsibility*. It has played a role since the Congress of Vienna in 1814–15 by designating 'powers with system-wide interests – those that were to have a say in matters pertaining to the management of the system'. As a world power Britain clearly had a role to play, and Ireland was within its sphere of responsibility. The second, *spheres of abstention*, is a form of 'preventive diplomacy' which allows for a 'tacit understanding among the superpowers to leave most of the developing world to its own devices'. Its negative quality raises questions about its utility and, in any case, it has little relevance to the Northern Ireland problem save the international goodwill generated in the aftermath of the 1985 and 1998 agreements.

The third, *functional regimes*, may be of much greater interest. Basically, they 'unbundle' the 'package of rights inherent in territorial sovereignty . . . Functional regimes, it was hoped, would not only downgrade the importance of national boundaries, but could, through the expansion of transboundary co-operative networks, lead to "peace in parts".'[53] Later we shall see the significance of such a device in attempting to arrive at a solution to the Northern Ireland problem. For the moment suffice it to say that the mechanism of the two Agreements, reliant as they are on international goodwill, may serve as an example of a functional regime. But if functional regimes are to work they presuppose a political vocabulary attuned to changes in the international system.

In the meantime we should recognise the arrival of another 'special relationship'. It received the imprimatur of the Secretary of State for Northern Ireland, Humphrey Atkins, in a parliamentary debate in 1980: 'The geographical and historical facts of life oblige us to recognise the special relationship that exists between the component parts of the

British Isles ... we do improve our chances of success by recognising that the Republic is deeply interested in what happens in Northern Ireland.'[54] That was the theme which was to dominate from the 1980s onwards.

7

'OUR GREATER IRELAND BEYOND THE SEAS'*

Northern Ireland illustrates the extent to which developments in socially differentiated societies are drawn from surrounding and more powerful 'histories'. There is no logic within a particular society that creates basic linguistic, religious, cultural, or national cleavages. Almost invariably they draw their sentiment and symbolism from conflicts that transcend the particular society.

STANLEY B. GREENBERG[1]

In addition to our fierce Irish pride, there was our American heritage as well. Kids in other cities were playing cops and robbers, or cowboys and indians, but with us it was patriots and redcoats.

THOMAS P. ('TIP') O'NEILL[2]

music-hall diplomacy

TIMES[3]

E.H. Carr, the distinguished historian of Soviet Russia, once advised that it could be revealing to look for the date of publication as well as to the author's name. It was sage advice. Attitudes change over time and the annalist has a duty to record these changes. In the manner of an indolent scholar it can be worth while, too, to go first to the index of a publication. That can impose its own realism and perspective. Take the case of Donald Regan, a former chief of staff to President Ronald Reagan. In the index to his memoirs astrology makes several appearances but there is no mention of Anglo–American or Anglo-Irish or Irish–American relations.[4] Given the flurry of books which have appeared in recent years and which appear to put the Anglo-Irish peace process at the front of American foreign policy, we do well to keep this in mind.[5] Yet two footnotes from recent times illustrate how the conflict in Ireland has become part of the American political architecture.

The first was a blistering attack on President Bill Clinton' s conduct of American foreign policy. It came from the former Secretary of State, James Baker, who had served under President George Bush. The location was the Republican convention in San Diego during the 1996 presidential campaign: 'We have seen a representative of the IRA hosted in the White House just prior to its resumption of terrorist bombings in London. The result has been the worst relationship with our closest ally, Britain, since the Boston Tea Party in 1773.'[6] He was referring, of course, to Clinton's decision to give Sinn Féin's president, Gerry Adams, a visa to visit the United States and to persist in supporting the peace process even after the bomb at London's Canary Wharf had marked the end of the first IRA ceasefire in February 1996. Baker's reaction may have belonged to convention rhetoric, and, in the greater scheme of things, its impact was way down in the political Richter scale. Be that as it may, Baker's comments pointed once again to the Anglo-American 'special relationship' and in particular to the close working relationship between senior Republicans and British Conservatives.[7] Another former Secretary of State, Henry Kissinger, who had also served a Republican President, had a more sanguine view when he placed that relationship in its historic context:

> When Britain emerged from the Second World War too enfeebled to insist on its views, it wasted no time in mourning an irretrievable past. British leaders instead tenaciously elaborated the 'special relationship' with us . . . in effect, a pattern of consultation so matter-of-factly intimate that it became psychologically impossible to ignore British views . . . an extraordinary relationship because it rested on no legal claims; it was formalised by no document; it was carried forward by succeeding British governments as if no alternative was conceivable.[8]

The second came in the wake of the signing of the Belfast Agreement in April 1998 in the midst of the Monica Lewinsky affair. It was a press release from the chairman of the Republican National Committee, Jim Nicholson, which congratulated 'George Mitchell and the party leaders in Ireland who came to the table with peace in their hearts to end the centuries of sectarian violence.' Nicholson was sufficiently *au fait* with Irish-American politics – he had been cited as one of the top 100 Irish-Americans of 1998 a month earlier – to know that 'George Mitchell' would be read as meaning 'Bill Clinton'. As a fierce antagonist Nicholson had had no difficulty in calling the President a liar and a hypocrite during the Lewinsky affair, so the turnaround was remarkable. It was President Clinton who had appointed Senator George Mitchell as special economic envoy to Northern Ireland on 1 December, 1994 – an idea which had been floating around in Irish-American circles ever since President Reagan had appointed Philip Habib to the Middle East in 1983. Mitchell's appointment reinforced the extent to which US involvement in seeking a solution to the Northern Ireland conflict had increased incrementally over the previous decade or more. His subsequent heading of the decommissioning body and of the multi-party talks that led to the Belfast Agreement suggests that that American influence had changed in quality as well as in quantity. More remarkable was the fact that Clinton had persuaded Ulster unionists that he was even-handed. The UUP's American representative, Ann Smith, said that 'His word has been good'; and a prominent unionist ally residing in Virginia stated: 'The President has played it very straight and very fair.'9

This chapter takes as its starting-point the major shifts in official American attitudes towards the Northern Ireland conflict as personified by Bill Clinton in contrast to 'the traditional policy of cautious impartiality' adopted by the previous Democratic incumbent at the White House, Jimmy Carter.10 But rather than concentrate on the significance of particular individuals we shall pay more attention to broader, contextual factors, 'to the United States' more active "managerial role" in the New World Order [which makes] its involvement in internal or regional disputes more likely'. The incremental increase in US involvement in the Northern question made interventions more likely. The 'more active intervention during Clinton's tenure' may be explained 'by the power of Irish Americans in terms of Congress, corporate America and the electorate'.11 All of these factors came into play in the battle to secure a visa for Gerry Adams to enter the United States in 1994. In short we are concerned in this chapter with the more rounded view implicit in the Greenberg epigraph with which we opened.

But we need, too, to be especially aware of the relationship between domestic and foreign policy in the post-1970 period:

> To many Americans what appeared to threaten their way of life was not Soviet 'expansionism' but rather the more tangible problems of high oil prices, Japanese imports, the export of capital and, with it, jobs. Domestic prosperity seemed to be being undermined by the growth of new centres of economic power, in Europe and Japan, as well as new forms of economic power, such as multi-national corporations, which were engaged in a considerable redistribution of investment to Latin America and the Pacific region.

In these circumstances foreign policy became 'domesticated'. Policy-makers 'began to talk about "intermestic" affairs: those issues (such as trade, finance, pollution, energy, terrorism, human rights etc.) which overlapped the foreign and domestic policy boundaries'.[12] From the outbreak of the Troubles prominent Irish-American activists had tried – and failed – to make the Northern Ireland conflict a concern of domestic politics. Our concern in this chapter is to explain how they managed to turn that failure around by putting it in the context of ethnic politics.

In the first edition of their highly influential study of ethnic politics in New York City, *Beyond the Melting Pot* (1963), Glazer and Moynihan maintained that the immigration process could be considered 'the single most important determinant of American foreign policy'.[13] They asserted at the outset that the 'notion that the intense and unprecedented mixture of ethnic and religious groups in American life was soon to blend into a homogenous end product has outlived its usefulness, and also its credibility'.[14] In the conclusion to their 1970 edition they stated: 'Ethnicity is more than an influence on events; it is commonly the source of events. Social and political institutions do not merely respond to ethnic interests; a great number of institutions exist for the specific purpose of serving ethnic interests. This in turn tend to perpetuate them.'[15] It was in this milieu that Irish-Americans thrived, especially with the expansion of 'intermestic' affairs. Herein lies a paradox. As Speaker of the House of Representatives in the late 1970s an early 80s Thomas P. ('Tip') O'Neill bewailed the 'egocentric single-issue candidate', saying, 'I really hope that the Eighties relieve us of that single-issue emotionalised approach, the candidates with the simple solutions. They have just ripped at the very foundations of our two-party system.'[16] As an Irish-American politician he was open to the charge that he too engaged in single-issue politics – although it has to be said that he recognised the complexity of the problem and that he expended much energy in challenging the certitude of other Irish-American groups who relied on simple solutions.

'A LEGITIMATE AND SERIOUS ISSUE'?

'The Irish issue has become a legitimate and serious issue in the Atlantic relationship between London and Washington.'[17] That statement by John Hume may have seemed both foolhardy and premature in 1979. After all, as Hume acknowledged, since the great waves of Irish emigration to America in the nineteenth century, the Irish in America tried without success to interest Washington administrations in the Irish question. This chapter will seek to probe Hume's optimism by following events since the late 1970s with particular emphasis on human rights and security issues.

To begin we return to the 1980 US census which showed that 43.7 million Americans (19 per cent of the total population) identified themselves as Irish.[18] As was mentioned in the previous chapter, this figure needs to be treated with some caution because it does not differentiate between Irish-Americans of Catholic or Protestant origin. We noted that their separate experiences of immigration led to a loss of visibility on the part of the Ulster-Scots and an exaggerated sense of political importance among those of a Catholic background.[19] It was as if Ulster Protestants had been written out of the script – and that might explain why unionist politicians were so wary for so long in engaging with American politicians. Most unionists were slow to recognise the opportunities that America presented. By the end of 1989 the *Boston Irish News* was bemoaning the fact that 'for too long Unionists have been content to complain about their negative image. In America, they have ceded the field to Nationalists while relying on the less than enthusiastic efforts of British diplomats to make their case.'[20] The DUP and UUP had sent a joint delegation in 1982 when they presented a booklet entitled *Ulster – The Facts*, and individual unionists had made the trek on several occasions. But generally they ceded the ground to John Hume and admired from afar the very effective lobbying done by a tiny group of Irish diplomats in Washington, New York, Boston, Chicago and San Francisco.[21] The UUP did not appoint a lobbyist to look after their interests in Washington until 1995 (and even then that person, Ann Smith, was employed on a part-time basis only). In contrast loyalists had begun to revise their opinions about the efficacy of American support much earlier. In early 1978 the supreme commander of the UDA, Andy Tyrie, welcomed the idea of a peace forum in the United States and suggested that Ted Kennedy would make a good mediator because of his 'integrity and credibility'.[22]

A second point about the statistics is that they cannot begin to differentiate between the ethnically *aware* and the ethnically *conscious* – that is they cannot quantify who are the *active* members of the Irish diaspora. For most Irish-Americans the annual celebration of St Patrick's Day may be enough. They have a sentimental awareness of who they are (or were). But our concerns are with the *mobilised* groups, those who sought to bring pressure on several administrations to do something about Ireland. In that respect it is an examination (initially) of intraethnic conflict which culminated in a closing of ranks during the Clinton years. Despite the divisions among Irish-Americans their profile was remarkably high from the late 1970s onwards. If we accept that US policy 'is the product of political interaction and bargaining between Congress, organised interests and the bureaucracy'; and if we accept that the 'new "intermestic" issues . . . straddle the domestic and foreign sectors [and] are symptomatic of an increasing interdependence between America and the outside world'; and if we accept that, although 'the role of organised interest groups in the foreign policy process has never been as extensive as that in purely domestic matters, the growth of intermestic issues and problems has brought them increasingly into the policy arena'[23] – then we can analyse Irish-American lobbying as a classic case study. We will do this at two levels: the 'high' politics of transatlantic diplomacy and the more quotidian activities of the lobbying groups.

But we need to make a further distinction between what we might call the 'treetops' and the 'grassroots', between those who identified firmly with constitutional nationalism and those who appeared more ambiguous about the use of Irish political violence. The 'treetops' are so called because they occupied the higher slopes of the political terrain: Speaker Tip O'Neill, Senators Edward (Ted) Kennedy and Daniel Patrick Moynihan and Governor Hugh Carey of New York. The Speaker is the third most senior politician in the United States system; O'Neill (who was Speaker from 1977 to 1987) had a particularly crucial role to play during the Carter years and Reagan's first term (and his successors, Jim Wright and Tom Foley in the later Reagan and the Bush years, followed a similarly sympathetic line on the conflict in Ireland). Ted Kennedy, of course, was a brother of the fallen President and a candidate himself for the Democratic presidential nomination in 1980: his was the line of continuity which stretched from the Nixon presidency all the way through to the Clinton administration and the signing of the Belfast Agreement. O'Neill, Kennedy, Moynihan and Carey were dubbed the 'Four Horsemen' but they had the wit to realise that no sustained campaign could be undertaken by four individuals, no matter how powerful they were. Theirs was a campaign of challenging the orthodoxy of the special relationship while simultaneously broadening their base. Their consistent position of being opposed to violence was to prove a tremendous bonus in the longer run.

The 'grassroots' contained their share of congressional heavyweights but differed from the Horsemen in that they identified more closely with the Irish republican tradition. In turn that gave them greater access to traditional Irish-American blue-collar districts in New York, Boston and further afield. One of the characteristics of the competition between grassroots and treetops was its ability to transfer the intense animosities within the Catholic ghettoes of Northern Ireland on to the American political scene and a corresponding inability to anticipate when and where they shared a common interest. Although there were several congressional representatives who belonged to both the grass-roots and the treetops – their natural propensity was to cover all points on the ethnic jigsaw – it might be said that their major point of commonality was what Conor Cruise O'Brien called 'attentuated anti-Britishness' (see the quotation from Tip O'Neill at the opening of this chapter) and a more recent perception of being patronised by British politicians and diplomats. In addition there were further divisions inside the grassroots.

The first on the scene was the Irish Northern Aid Committee (better known as NORAID) which was founded in 1970 by Michael Flannery, a former IRA man who had emigrated in 1927. It was formed in response to a plea from the Provisional IRA for assistance for beleaguered Catholics and republicans in Northern Ireland. NORAID affirmed that it was in the business of raising funds for prisoners' families. It came under the scrutiny of the Justice and State Departments, and eventually, in 1984, it had to register under the Foreign Agents Registration Act as an agent of a 'foreign principal' (namely the IRA). NORAID's activities were a source of embarrassment for other grassroots organisations.

The Irish National Caucus (INC) and the Congressional Ad Hoc Committee on Irish Affairs shared NORAID's goals but had problems with the image it conveyed. The INC was founded in September 1974 and was charged with the task of improving the image of the NORAID cause: it was endorsed by thirty different Irish-American groups. The Ad Hoc Committee was established three years later. Both worked in tandem if on different planes. The INC sought to be the sole lobby group speaking for the republican interpretation of the Northern Ireland problem in the US whereas the Ad Hoc Committee worked in, and drew all of its members from, Congress. At one stage it could boast that it had 130 signed-up members working to revise existing State Department policies on Northern Ireland and to influence the development of foreign policy in relation to Ireland. All three groups were opposed, to a greater or lesser degree, by the Irish government, by constitutional nationalists in Northern Ireland and by the Horsemen.

John Hume's optimism in 1979 owed much to his capacity as a conceptual thinker, a trait he exhibited more than any other practising politician in Northern Ireland. A historian by profession he applied his analytical skills to the conflict. Following the collapse of the power-sharing arrangements in 1974 he concluded that a purely internal solution would not succeed and that in an intimidatory culture constitutional nationalism was not strong enough in its own right to win its case through reason. There was a need to woo a wider constituency by strengthening relations with other constitutional nationalist parties in Ireland and by appealing to the Irish diaspora. In that latter respect he paid particularly close attention to developments in the United States.[24] His influence was unparalleled because his was the one consistent voice that spoke out against violence and offered an alternative strategy. His message was carried by the Horsemen all the way to the White House and his imprint can be found on every major statement of American policy on Ireland from the late 1970s onwards. That is not to diminish the role played by individual taoisigh but since their time in office was limited, so too was their influence. We shall see that Hume's approach generated considerable resentment among spokesmen for the grassroots. Nevertheless they acknowledged that he was the gatekeeper who controlled access to ultimate power in Washington.

The first fruits of that strategy appeared in three statements during 1977. In the first of what would become an annual event the Four Horsemen issued a St Patrick's Day message in which they appealed to 'all those organisations engaged in violence to renounce their campaigns of death and destruction' as well as to 'our fellow Americans to embrace this goal of peace and to renounce any action that promotes the current violence or provides support or encouragement to organizations engaged in violence'.[25] It would be foolish to underestimate the importance of this message. It showed a highly influential element of Irish-America to be unambiguous about political violence at a time when emotions were running high in Irish-American circles – but laid them open to the charge of being negative and being soft on the 'Brits'. However this negative could be turned into a positive. For one thing, enlisting the support of Americans in a campaign against political violence in the North was one way of engaging the administration. It also enabled Irish diplomats to present a more attractive side of Ireland and to capture the attention of influential opinion-formers such as journalists Mary McGrory, Michael Killian and Marty Nolan. This allowed a tiny diplomatic corps to play a role out of all proportion to its numbers in Washington.[26] The second statement, delivered in the Senate in August, was a paean by Edward Kennedy on behalf of the contribution of the Scots-Irish to the development of the United States.[27] Just as important as the statement itself was the source from which it emanated. Kennedy had been a bête noir of loyalism; this was the first step towards rapproachement with that vital constituency. The third was a statement from President Jimmy Carter on 30 August promising US investment in Northern Ireland if violence were to cease. It was the first positive statement from a US President which probed the nature of the Anglo-American relationship. It was noteworthy, too, that the Carter statement *seemed* to sink without trace – emphasis on the tentative because we are suggesting that the statement was a potent landmark on the road to Good Friday 1998. One short-term explanation for its low visibility lies in the fact that historically Irish-Americans had not spoken with one voice.

While the reaction to these statements was fairly low key, they constituted a landmark in evolving American policy towards Ireland and, just as significantly, in Irish-America's growing self-confidence. Wilson notes that they 'marked the culmination of a process that had many detrimental consequences for *militant* Irish-American nationalism'.[28] He quotes from a former US Ambassador to Ireland, William Shannon, who pointed to a shift from blind Irish-American support for the republican cause at the outset of the Troubles to an acknowledgement of the realities of continuing violence. 'But as the guerrilla war dragged on', Shannon wrote in September 1977, 'people have become more conversant with the realities and complexities of the situation. Now Irish Americans realize that if the British withdraw it would be nothing like the withdrawal from Dublin in 1922. On the contrary, if Britain were to withdraw now there would be more violence.' In the eyes of a contemporary political analyst, this shift from a traditional republican position to a constitutional nationalist analysis of the problem represented 'a shift in ethnic political thinking about as momentous as any that has happened in recent memory'.[29]

It is important to recognise the sequence, the *realpolitik* and the cumulative effect of these three statements. The St Patrick's Day pronouncement established the pacific credentials of the Irish-American political establishment and returned the initiative to the constitutionalists. But a prize had to be secured to demonstrate that the Horsemen had not indulged solely in negative politics. The reward came in the Carter statement because it moved the Irish issue nearer to the centre of power and it discommoded those who were perceived as being closer to violent republicanism. Paul O'Dwyer, for example, first-generation Irish-American and a champion of ethnic minorities throughout the United States, described the statement as a 'non-initiative' because the President 'didn't commit the United States Government, but industrialists, people over whom he has no control'. Further he was critical of the Horsemen, whom he said 'sometimes irritate Irish-Americans . . . [who] feel they are being singled out as the people who are keeping the violence going, as if the accusing finger is being pointed at them, while no mention is made of Britain and her share of the responsibility'.[30] That latter point is crucial in the psyche of Irish republicans and their American supporters (as the hunger strikes were to underline). They needed to be removed from the charge of criminality. O'Dwyer's statement reflected the underlying tensions within Irish-America. But he was premature. Certainly British diplomats had greeted the Horsemen's 1977 statement with some satisfaction, and had said so. What they were not prepared for was the 1978 St Patrick's Day statement which was critical of British efforts in Northern Ireland and which was followed by demands for real political progress there. In that respect a second reward was the capacity to turn the spotlight on British efforts. Such was the increasing interest that the British Ambassador in Washington, Peter Jay, reported that up to 10 per cent of his time was being taken up with 'the Irish question'. Moreover he felt that 'there has been a tremendous turnaround in attitudes because of the turnaround in the understanding of the facts ... there is now a constructive spirit of genuine concern and sympathy for what the London and Dublin Governments are trying to do about the problem of terrorism'.[31] The significance of the Kennedy statement was that at this early stage he was seeking a more inclusive approach.

But the *realpolitik* centred on relations inside the Democratic Party. Tip O'Neill was a strong Speaker of the House in contrast to the relative weakness of Jimmy Carter. Despite the fact that 130 Congressmen, one-third of the House of Representatives, had requested congressional hearings on Northern Ireland, O'Neill used his power to block the move because he thought it would give too much publicity to the Provisional IRA. Along with Senator Kennedy he was considered 'among the top half-dozen most important political figures in the US'.[32] And while the President's relations with Ted Kennedy were never good, he was shrewd enough to realise that Kennedy could be an opponent in the 1980 presidential race.[33] With the publication of the Carter statement the Irish conflict was placed on the administration's agenda. President Carter raised it when he met Margaret Thatcher at an international energy summit in Tokyo in 1979; this 'was perhaps the first time in decades that an American President and a British Prime Minister have spoken about the Northern Ireland problem'. A Washington insider put the meeting in context: 'Carter quietly expressed his interest, that's all ... If you like, it's putting down a marker on the problem so that when Thatcher has been in office for a time he might bring it up again, maybe ask what progress has been made. That's exactly what happened: Now don't exaggerate it.'[34] Nevertheless the marker had been put down. Mario Biaggi, leader of the Congressional Ad Hoc Committee on Irish Affairs, told a journalist about a conversation he had had with President Carter on a train going to a Democratic convention in Baltimore in the summer of 1979: 'They talked about Northern Ireland: Carter made no commitments of any kind to Biaggi, and declined to identify himself with the peace forum, but it was an illustration of the interest that even Presidents these days have to take in Irish affairs.'[35] And it was to become even more pronounced during the Reagan presidency.

Before we leave the Carter presidency we should note his emphasis on human rights issues. In his inaugural speech he had stated 'Because we are free, we can never be indifferent to the fate of freedom else-where.'[36] This agenda created a space for more militant Irish-Americans to lobby against security policy in Northern Ireland – and often, the propaganda was fairly crude. In 1977, for example, the National Council of Irish Americans described Roy Mason, the Secretary of State for Northern Ireland, as 'a military commissar', and the RUC as 'the private police force of the three fragmented Unionist parties, le-galised in Whitehall and financed with US taxpayers' dollars through the International Monetary Fund'.[37] The accuracy, or otherwise, of such propaganda was not the vital element. What mattered was the climate it produced. Already there was a prima facie case against the British security response in Northern Ireland. In 1978 Amnesty Inter-national produced a report which 'provided strong evidence of se-venty-eight cases in which suspects suffered serious physical injury while being held at the RUC interrogation centre at Castlereagh'.[38] The British government established an independent inquiry under a Crown Court judge, Harry Bennett, which confirmed that RUC detectives physically mistreated suspects during questioning. The Horsemen's anger manifested itself in their 1979 St Patrick's Day statement when they accused the British government of 'negligence' and 'acquiescence' in the face of 'gross violations of human rights'.[39] One of their de-mands was for a fresh political initiative in Northern Ireland.

To encourage such an initiative Tip O'Neill led a fourteen-person congressional delegation to Britain and Ireland in April 1979 to coin-cide with the British general election campaign. On 20 April he issued his strongest attack on British policy: 'we insist that Britain bears a heavy responsibility for the failure of recent years on the political front. We have been concerned that the problem has been treated as a political football in London ... We insist on an early, realistic and fresh initiative on the part of the incoming British government, so as to get negotiations moving quickly.'[40] This was breathtaking stuff, inconceivable only a few years before, and calculated to produce the high moral tone from Fleet Street and the recesses of the Palace of

Westminster. It was followed in August with the State Department announcing the suspension of its licence for arms sales to the RUC, a move which had been initiated by Mario Biaggi and supported by Tip O'Neill.[41] O'Neill's support was as much an expression of exaspera- tion with British procrastination as anything else: 'In fact O'Neill only wanted, to coin a phrase, to fire a shot across the bows of the British, and was taken aback by the amount of publicity it received here ... some of the big four acknowledge it as something of a setback, for it has made them look anti-RUC.'[42] Nevertheless it demonstrated once again the pivotal position he occupied. It was by no means certain that the State Department (which was perceived as being very pro-British) would have revoked the licence at the behest of Biaggi. It was one of the few occasions on which O'Neill was seen to cooperate with more militant tendencies, and in that respect was a precursor of the type of cooperation which was to be established in the 1990s.

Another campaign of this time also served as a precursor of later events. Mario Biaggi's attempt to establish a 'peace forum' in 1978 had an underlying agenda – getting visas for republican leaders, in parti- cular the Sinn Féin leader, Ruairí Ó Brádaigh. The fact that leading republicans are usually denied access to the United States was im- portant to some: 'The US let in Joshua Nkomo; they let in Yasser Ara- fat; they let in the UDA. Jesus, they even let in Sid Vicious – so why won't they let in Ruairí Ó Brádaigh?'[43] The peace forum was to con- vene in Washington on 14 May. But Biaggi failed to raise the funds from corporate America and none of the constitutional parties in Ireland would support it, so it never took place.[44] It should be pointed out that at a later date the State Department revoked the visa of the Reverend Ian Paisley, leader of the DUP, because his presence would be 'contrary to American foreign policy interests'.[45] Here again was a rehearsal for a later debate.

THE CHANGING OF THE GUARD

The political landscape in Britain and the United States began to change in 1979. In May Margaret Thatcher became Prime Minister at the head of a Conservative government. References to Northern Ireland in the Conservative election manifesto were minimalist, with the emphasis on a stronger law and order policy and on integrating Northern Ireland more fully into the British political system. Thatcher was perceived as a strong unionist. Nonetheless she did a U-turn on Northern Ireland. In her first major interview with a foreign journalist she told Johnny Apple of the *New York Times* (12 November 1979) that she would not permit 'the squabbling political parties' in Northern Ireland to block her (then limited) political initiative of restoring a devolved administration; and in little over a year she was to enter into an Anglo-Irish process which resulted in the Anglo-Irish Agreement of November 1985, itself a precursor of the Belfast Agreement of Good Friday 1998.

This radical revision in policy produced its own cottage industry in paranoia. We saw in chapter 3 how Northern Ireland has been described as a 'paranocracy' in which the basis of power 'was the successful appeal to paranoid fears in the Protestant electorate about the political, social, philosophical and military potential of their Catholic neighbours'.[46] The imposition of direct rule in 1972 did not remove these fears. In fact, with the failure of successive internal solutions, the paranoia intensified and may even have become contagious with the burgeoning Anglo-Irish relationship. The high priest of paranocracy was Enoch Powell, a former Conservative cabinet minister and the Ulster Unionist MP for South Down from 1974 to 1987. In an article in the *Spectator* in 1983 he outlined the principles which, he alleged, guided the Irish Republic, Britain and the US to tease out a solution to the Northern question based on Irish unity. He asserted that the strategy was based on the following: (i) the Republic cannot take Northern Ireland by force; (ii) to end partition there needs to be an autonomous Ulster with 'guarantees' in a federal Ireland, possibly in some loose relationship with Britain; (iii) United Kingdom pressure is necessary to accomplish this; but (iv) that will be exerted only when Irish unity is strategically necessary to Britain. The key, therefore, lies in the 'defence of the West' with the United States playing the leading role.[47]

Within eighteen months of her accession to power Margaret Thatcher was joined on the world stage by Ronald Reagan who was elected President of the United States in November 1980. Here began one of the great political romances, a twentieth-century version of Antony and Cleopatra.[48] They were ideological soul mates. She described him as 'a buoyant, self-confident, good-natured American who had risen from poverty to the White House – the American dream in action – and who was not shy about using American power or exercising American leadership in the Atlantic alliance'. The contrast with his predecessor, Jimmy Carter, could not have been more striking. She found it impossible not to like Carter, with his 'marked intellectual capability, rare among politicians, of science and the scientific method'. But there the praise ended. He 'had an unsure handle on economics . . . in general he had no large vision of America's future . . . [and] he was in some ways personally ill-suited to the presidency, agonizing over big decisions and too concerned with detail'. Reagan did not suffer from an over-concern with detail, but that may have been one of the reasons why they made such a 'good team': 'although we shared the same analysis of the way the world worked, we were very different people. He had an accurate grasp of the strategic detail but left the tactical detail to others. I was conscious that we must manage our relations with the communists on a day-to-day basis in such a way that events never got out of control.' She considered that one of her tasks inside this partnership was to be 'perhaps his principal cheerleader in NATO'.[49]

Several points need to be made about the Reagan–Thatcher partnership. One is that it was based on personal friendship. Each defended the other as a person 'of integrity' – he when she was under severe domestic criticism for her role in the Westland affair; she when the Irangate affair engulfed him.[50] Secondly, they were on the same ideological wavelength. Donald Regan recalls Thatcher welcoming Reagan enthusiastically into the G7 summit 'at least in part because he shared her political views. In my opinion, the close friendship between the two owes much to the early battles that they fought side by side against such voluble socialists and social democrats as [Pierre] Trudeau [of Canada], Mitterrand of France, and Helmut Schmidt of West Germany.'[51]

Thirdly, they were conscious of working on a world stage with the forces of history behind them. Thatcher noted foreign policy humiliations under the Carter presidency such as the failure to rescue United States hostages in Iran but felt that '1981 was the last year of the West's retreat before the axis of convenience between the Soviet Union and the Third World . . . The election of Ronald Reagan as President of the United States in November 1980 was as much of a watershed in American affairs as my own election victory in May 1979 was in those of the United Kingdom, and, of course, a greater one in world politics.'[52] That sense of history is captured in Reagan's farewell address to the Republican Party when he concluded: 'We did all that could be done. Never less.' These words echoed the speech that had launched his political career in 1964 during Barry Goldwater's presidential bid: 'You and I have a rendezvous with destiny. We can preserve for our children this, the last best hope of man on earth, or we can sentence them to take the first step into a thousand years of darkness. If we fail, at least let our children say of us . . . We did all that could be done.' Here was a man with what George Bush called the 'vision thing'. Unpalatable facts were not to intervene. In that respect one aspect of his personality is encapsulated by the comments of Jay Rosen that 'Reagan *believes in belief*, while even his strongest supporters feel the need to modify their views when reality closes in. The heart of the Reagan legacy resides here: in a conception of the president as a man who is in history but exempt from it.'[53] Margaret Thatcher's *conviction politics*, her concerns about 'an empire of evil' and her support for the Strategic Defence Initiative mirrored that personality.

Finally, no matter how close the relationship was perceived to be, it fitted into the classic Anglo-American asymmetric relationship. This can be seen in the American invasion of Grenada, a Commonwealth country, in which in Thatcher's words 'at best, the British Government had been made to look impotent; at worst we looked deceitful'. Despite that, she reached the conclusion that 'Britain's friendship with the United States must on no account be jeopardised', a theme which was to run through the relationship.[54] It appears in the American bombing of the Libyan capital, Tripoli, the outcome of which led Thatcher to comment that she 'was depicted as cringing towards the US but callous towards their victims'.[55] That mentality of being the ardent suitor was there from the outset. Thatcher was the first foreign head of government invited to meet the new President in February 1981. She was accompanied by her Foreign Secretary, Lord Carrington, who wanted her to raise the issue of South African withdrawal from Namibia. But she did not see the point. Her rationale was highly revealing: 'there is no point in engaging in conflict with a friend when you are not going to win and the cost of losing may be the end of the friendship'.[56]

That axiom might serve in her handling of the Northern Ireland conflict. She had seen one of her closest confidants, Airey Neave, murdered by Irish republicans and was to come close to death herself (along with most of her cabinet) in the IRA's Brighton bomb in 1984; she was the one who had stood out most against the hunger strikers' demands in 1980–1 – 'murder is murder'; she it was who considered Northern Ireland to be as British as Finchley; yet it was her government which developed a burgeoning relationship with Irish governments from 1980 onwards culminating in the signing of the Anglo-Irish Agreement on 15 November 1985, an agreement which challenged rigid concepts of sovereignty and for the first time gave the Irish government a voice in the affairs of Northern Ireland. Left to her own devices it is unlikely that she would have pursued that path. There can be little doubt that she was influenced in her Irish policy by the White House.

But why should a Reagan presidency have shown any interest in Ireland? In the context of the world stage that we have just discussed, Ireland was small beer. If we leave to one side the views of the peddlers in 'paranocracy', we can produce sentimental, political and ideological

reasons for the President's interests. Ronald Reagan was not a sophisticated man. His authorised biographer, Edmund Morris, recalled that
after 'three or four meetings, I realised that culturally he was a yahoo
and extremely unresponsive in conversation'.[57] He was known to
conduct meetings speaking from notes on cards.[58] Others have commented on his lack of focus. Heldrick Smith records: 'Republican senators, coming away from the Oval Office, told me of their shock at
his weak grasp of important issues. Most Reagan aides loyally defended him, but some admitted embarrassment at his gaps or his mental laziness. Others reported having to step in and handle conversations
for Reagan so that he did not look stupid.'[59] His own upbringing had
induced a sense of rootlessness. In the opening pages of his authorised
biography his biographer notes: 'Most public yet most private of men,
he does not welcome undue familiarity with his past.'[60] Nevertheless
he was delighted to be told at his first meeting with the Irish Ambassador, Seán Donlon, in Washington that his genealogy would be presented to him. On the back of this one of his annual social events was
the St Patrick's Day lunch at the Irish embassy. There was an Irish-
American strain, too, among his closest advisers, chief amongst whom
was William P. Clark. He came into the Reagan administration as
Under-Secretary of State and then went on to the National Security
Council before becoming Secretary of the Interior, a post he resigned
from in 1985. Nevertheless he continued to maintain a very close
relationship with the President.

Clark is significant for several reasons. A career diplomat considered
him to be a 'naïve but decent man [whose] grasp of world events beyond Sacramento and San Luis Obispo was not renowned'. Despite
that he was 'Reagan's closest friend and ally in the entire administration', the man who had hired two of the so-called Troika which controlled the direction of policy in the early years of the administration.[61]
Proximity to the President gave him particular influence: 'The senior
White House staff . . . live with the President . . . They know his views,
feel his triumphs, share his frustrations, read his moods, sense when to
make his pitch and when to leave him alone. They are like family or
like courtiers in royal households, contesting the power of cabinet
barons.'[62] Within a few months, after taking over as National Security
Adviser in January 1982, Clark 'became the most influential foreign
policy figure in Reagan's entourage . . . He pushed Reagan to center
stage on foreign policy and encouraged Reagan's hard line. As an old
Reagan crony (chief of staff in Sacramento), Clark had enough clout to
muscle the cabinet barons.'[63] Hence his bailiwick roamed over such
spheres as southern Africa, Central America, the Middle East and arms

negotiations to name but a few. Less well known was his attachment to the cause of Irish unity, a view he expressed in 1981 when, while Deputy Secretary of State, he declared that 'the hope and prayer of all Americans' is the unification of Ireland.[64]

A second reason why the President paid any attention to Ireland lay in the congressional arithmetic and the status enjoyed by Speaker Tip O'Neill. Following the loss of the presidency by the Democrats the Irish-American treetops broadened their base by expanding beyond the Horsemen into the Friends of Ireland, launched on St Patrick's Day 1981. Crucially, this formal group in Congress – composed of twenty-four of the most influential senators, congressmen and governors – was bipartisan. When O'Neill visited Britain and Ireland in April 1979 his entourage was made up of both Republicans and Democrats. As Speaker he had to work reasonably closely with the White House but relations with the new President were not good: 'Only Tip O'Neill seemed immune to Reagan's gift for conciliation ... the reality was that they were hammer and anvil. O'Neill seemed determined to dislike Reagan and disagree with him, and sparks flew as a result.'[65] He had a basic contempt for Reagonomics and 'began to treat the President like a fiscal retard'.[66] Yet, on the matter of Ireland the President and the Speaker worked in harmony.

The third reason centred on ideological congruence. President Reagan made much of his desire to defeat the 'international network of terrorism'. At his first ever St Patrick's Day lunch in the Irish embassy in 1981 he condemned 'all acts of terrorism and violence, for these cannot solve Ireland's problems' and he called on all Americans not to offer any financial contribution or other aid to groups which perpetuated violence.[67] Interestingly, Thatcher recalled that at one of her earlier meetings with Reagan (in Ottawa for the G7 summit in July 1981) perhaps her most useful discussion was a private meeting where she took the opportunity 'to thank him warmly for his tough stand against Irish terrorism and its NORAID supporters. It was good to know that however powerful the Irish republican lobby in the USA might be, the Republican Administration would not buckle before it.'[68] It is not clear how aware she was that the groundwork in this respect had been prepared by the Horsemen in their statement of St Patrick's Day 1977. In any case she was working on a larger stage – on the threat from terrorism wherever it arose – and she had the enthusiastic support of the Reagan administration. Reagan's Secretary of State, George Shultz, recalls a G7 summit in London in June 1984 where he worked hard to get a strong statement on terrorism signed by the leaders of the seven largest industrial democracies: 'Margaret Thatcher's voice was powerful and determined.'[69] Despite that, we shall see that their joint efforts on the Irish conflict were mixed.

THE ISSUES

On the surface President Reagan's record on the Northern Ireland conflict was mixed. During his presidency the hunger strikes came and went; the IRA attempted to assassinate Margaret Thatcher and most of her cabinet; the New Ireland Forum was established and reported; and Anglo-Irish relations moved into a higher gear to confront all of these but also to be more proactive – hence the signing of the Anglo-Irish Agreement in November 1985. It would be foolish to assume that presidential politics were dominated by any of these issues – indeed the President declined Irish imprecations to get involved in the hunger strikes, and had little comment to make on the New Ireland Forum Report in May 1984 – but in the context of intermestic politics the first half of the 1980s were fruitful years for Irish-American activists. They engaged in a number of campaigns that brought them into the heart of the American political process, while simultaneously removing them from the charge that they were a front for the IRA. They continued this activity during the Bush presidency with a particular emphasis on immigration issues.

All these campaigns had one thing in common: a concern for human rights. It was something that struck a chord in the United States, as Thatcher was to find to her cost. In 1988 she introduced a media ban on interviews with supporters and members of the IRA and loyalist para-militaries, and also attempted to abolish the right of suspected criminals to keep silent. A *Newsday* editorial commented that 'Britain hasn't yet torn up the Magna Carta but it's sending some of the country's most revered civil liberties to the shredder.'[70] Interestingly with regard to the media ban the British government was doing no more than following Irish government practice; as early as November 1971 the Irish government had issued a directive to the state broadcasting company, RTÉ, 'to refrain from broadcasting any matter that could be calculated to promote the aims and activities of any organisation which engages in, encourages or advocates the attaining of any particular objective by violent means'. The directive was reinforced in October 1976.[71] Yet American media fire was directed solely at the Thatcher government. In an article by H.D.S. Greenway, the *Journal of Commerce* proclaimed 'Britons' civil rights at risk' (28 October 1988). *Newsweek* (31 October) announced 'A Loss of Liberties' and commented that the policy 'could backfire by bolstering IRA claims that above-ground politics won't solve the Ulster problem'. An editorial in the *Salt Lake Tribune* of 22 October was titled 'Mistaken Censorship'; and the *Tribune* in Oakland, California, opened its editorial of 25 October with the words 'Power breeds arrogance' and suggested that the policy was a victory for the IRA. Finally, on the following day, the *Arizona Republic*'s editorial stated simply 'Mrs Thatcher Unhinged'. The same sentiments could be found in papers such as the *Washington Post* which carried great weight in the Capitol.

We have used this example of censorship and the trawl of the print media for two complementary reasons: first, to reinforce the point that the Anglo-American relationship was vulnerable and that British politicians and diplomats were not very impressive in handling human rights issues; and second, to point up an important contrast – 'the effectiveness with which Irish-Americans have used the language of American public life to state their case – equal opportunities, civil rights, freedom of expression, pluralism – and mobilised multiethnic coalitions to advance their programmes'.[72] We now turn to some of these issues.

Chief among these was a campaign aimed at discouraging American investment in those companies which were perceived as practising employment discrimination against Catholics in their Northern Ireland plants. The aim was to make US investment in the North conditional on the adoption of a set of fair employment principles known as the MacBride Principles. Here was a human rights issue of huge potential. Launched in 1984,[73] the campaign was conducted in state legislatures and city halls across the country; by 1989 a dozen cities and ten states had accepted the principles and they were being debated in Maryland, New Hampshire, Vermont, Texas, Oklahoma, Missouri, Nebraska, Utah, Indiana and California. The geographical range is noteworthy, and the lobbying effort was enormous. In essence it was an appeal to small investors and to the hearts of middle America. It ensured maximum inconvenience for the British who were forced to attend all the hearings to defend their record of fair employment, and maximum publicity for its sponsors, the INC, led by Fr Seán McManus.[74] The choice of Sean MacBride as the person whose name would be given to the principles was shrewd. Besides being a former chief of staff of the IRA (in the 1930s) and an Irish government minister (1948–51) he was a recipient of the Nobel and Lenin peace prizes and the first non-US citizen to be awarded the American Medal for Justice. His reason for getting involved added to the allure of the campaign: 'I first of all came into direct contact with the Rev. Leon Sullivan, a black clergyman who drafted the Sullivan Principles in regard to employment by American corporations in South Africa, to get rid of apartheid, and naturally I thought we should try to apply the same principles in regard to American money invested in Northern Ireland.'[75]

All the right buttons on the human rights agenda were being pushed, and McManus went to considerable lengths to argue that the 'Irish National Caucus believes that human rights for Ireland is AN AMERICAN ISSUE'.[76] That was not to say that Irish-America was at one on the issue;[77], nor for that matter were Irish nationalists – as of 1 June 1987 the INC claimed that among its supporters were the Taoiseach, Charles Haughey, and the British Labour Party but opposition had come consistently from John Hume who feared an even greater lack of investment in Northern Ireland.[78] Nevertheless, the campaign acted as a tremendous fillip to the more militant wing of Irish-America. In a bullish interview in 1986 McManus claimed that Irish-America 'has come of age … [This is] the first time ever that the two major issues were initiated and campaigned upon and conducted by Irish-America here in Washington. It's engaging the British government at the very top level and the State Department and national legislatures around the country. The ironic thing is that the British handed us this on a silver plate. For years we have struggled to get hearings and the British and Irish governments successfully blocked us.'[79]

The second issue to which McManus alluded was extradition – or, to be more precise, a Supplementary Extradition Treaty drafted by the British and American governments to enable the latter to return suspected IRA members to British jurisdiction for trial. This was a highly emotive issue. In an address to both Houses of Congress on 20 February 1985 Margaret Thatcher linked the Irish question to the campaign against 'international terrorism'; and in a newspaper interview over a year later she asked rhetorically, 'What is the point in the United States taking a foremost role against terrorism and then do nothing against Irish terrorism, which is afflicting one of her allies?'[80] The gap in time between these two statements is interesting in itself. The treaty had been agreed on 25 June 1985 and was submitted to the Senate on 17 July, where speedy ratification was expected – this at a time when President Reagan had 'drifted slowly into *impotentia Carteris*, power paralyzed by Christian conscience'. The paralysis had been induced by an Arab highjacking of TWA Flight 847 out of Athens on 14 June in which a US Navy petty officer was murdered and another thirty-nine Americans were held hostage over a two-week period in return for the release by Israel of over 700 Shiite political prisoners. During the same period 'other terrorist groups murdered Marines in El Salvador, blew up an Air India flight with 329 aboard, and bloodily bombed Frankfurt and Tokyo airports'. Pressure was on the President to appeal to Israel to release the Shiites. In these circumstances President Reagan recorded in his diary on 17 June: 'This of course means that we – not they – would be violating our policy of not negotiating with terrorists.'[81] Defeating the 'international network of terrorism' was something that was close to the President's heart and something that affected most Americans at that time.

Nonetheless the treaty was held up for almost a year while Britain's role in Ireland was scrutinised. It was yet another issue that fitted into the INC agenda. The INC's motto, 'Human rights, freedom and peace for Ireland is an American issue', spoke for itself. It enabled McManus to pursue a policy of distancing the INC from any faction or party in Ireland – this after a sustained period when Irish governments had been criticising republican fronts in the United States. 'Never mind that the Dublin government doesn't really have a policy', he said quite forcefully in his 1986 interview. 'Our entire thrust is to see that Irish-America [plays] a positive role and positively sets out to change American policy.'[82] And he did so quite brilliantly by calling on the imagery of the American Revolution and on the United States' tradition as a home for political refugees: 'Let's send the British packing as George Washington once did' was the none-too-subtle message from an INC press release on 9 May 1986. This was coupled with a campaign slogan, 'The British are Coming! The British are Coming! (. . . this time right into the US Senate)'.[83]

It was a highly contentious issue. At hearings before the Senate Foreign Relations Committee on 1 August 1985 the Democratic Senator Joe Biden contended that the Supplementary Extradition Treaty was 'an opportunity to do what we have been unable to do so far. There is an incredible reluctance on the part of this Government to criticise one of our closest allies for what I believe to be an absolutely outrageous position which they have continued to maintain with regard to Northern Ireland.'[84] Biden's views were important because he was not perceived as one of the more militant representatives of Irish-America and because he was indicating that this was a battle which would be fought to the end. On the other hand, Thomas O. Melia, a former aide to Senator Daniel Patrick Moynihan, wrote passionately about the procrastination of the treaty's opponents, and of 'the cuckoo reasoning' which some of them employed: 'The Irish Republic extradites murderers to Northern Ireland for punishment. The US should do as much.'[85] Before 1986 was out the administration succeeded in having the treaty accepted. But that was not the end of the matter because Irish-America turned it into an exercise in martyrology.

The 'martyr' was Joe Doherty. In May 1980 Doherty had killed a British army captain in an IRA ambush in Belfast. In June 1981 he escaped from Crumlin Road jail in Belfast and turned up in New York in February 1982. He was arrested by federal agents in June 1983 and began a long campaign against extradition to the UK. The provisions of the 1986 extradition treaty were applied retroactively to include Doherty. He was already a *cause célèbre*. The British consulate-general in New York was being picketed nightly by his supporters.[86] Doherty was eventually extradited in 1992 but his incarceration became a rallying cry for Irish-Americans. One of their most prominent leaders, Brian O'Dwyer, considered it a 'miscalculation' by the British. Doherty had become a symbol of latent anti-Irishness amongst the British and their republican allies in Congress: 'I travelled the country for Clinton almost as soon as he [Doherty] lost his battle for extradition. The most emotional issue was "Can you face yourself on the day after the election that Joe Doherty is in jail in Belfast and we have George Bush for President for the next four years?" '[87]

O'Dwyer was a member of a group known as Americans for a New Irish Agenda, in effect supporters of the Clinton–Gore bid for the White House in 1992. The group travelled to Little Rock, Arkansas, in January 1993 in an effort to influence the new administration's policy on Ireland. Besides O'Dwyer and his father Paul, others present were Ray Flynn (former Democratic mayor of Boston), John Dearie (a New York State assemblyman serving the Bronx), Joe Jamison (of the Irish American Labor Coalition), Niall O'Dowd (publisher of the *Irish Voice*), Bob Linnon (of the Irish American Unity Conference), Chuck Feeney (a billionaire businessman) and Mike Quinlin (an adviser to Ray Flynn). One leading member of the group was unavoidably absent – Bruce Morrison, a Democrat who had given up his congressional seat to run for the post of Governor of Connecticut, and a former classmate of Bill Clinton's at Yale Law School. It might be argued that only two of those present – Paul O'Dwyer and Ray Flynn – had had a high visibility in Irish-American affairs over the previous two decades. But the very diversity of the group was interesting in itself as an example of the convergence taking place in Irish-America.

Two reasons can be offered for this convergence. One concerns the easing of tension between Sinn Féin and the SDLP back in Northern Ireland. It was easier, as Brian O'Dwyer put it, 'to find common ground when Hume and Adams weren't sniping at each other'.[88] That common ground had been explored in talks between the SDLP and Sinn Féin during 1988, and was furthered in direct talks between John Hume and Gerry Adams which began some time after 1990. Their search for commonality played well in the United States and assisted the process of speaking with one (ethnic) voice. The second reason was that the new activists learnt the advantages of coalition-building during a campaign for the reform of American immigration laws. In an interview with *Newsweek* in late September 1987 the Irish Minister for Foreign Affairs, Brian Lenihan, was asked about the large influx of Irish immigrants into the United States. He replied that 'we shouldn't be defeatist or pessimistic about it. We should be proud of it. After all, we can't all live in a small island.' That last throwaway comment caused great hurt among Irish immigrants living illegally in the US. Calculations of their numbers varied widely – anywhere between 100,000 and 200,000. Brian Donnelly, a Democratic Congressman and (later) chair of the Friends of Ireland, championed the cause of the illegal Irish immigrants in what became known as the 'Donnelly Visas' programme. Earlier amnesty provisions did not really benefit the Irish because they only applied to those who had entered the US illegally prior to 1 January 1982. Most of the Irish had arrived after that date, and consequently 'no more than a few hundred secured green cards by the amnesty route'.[89] The Donnelly programme, which ran for four years up until 1990, secured over 16,000 (or just over 40 per cent) of the next allocation of visas for Irish citizens, over a third of whom were already in the US working as illegals.

The trend was continued through the Family Unity and Employment Opportunity Immigration Act of 1990. The details need not detain us here.[90] What is important is that the campaign that led to this Act highlighted the significance of ethnic coalition-building because the fruits of the measure were to be distributed among thirty-six disadvantaged countries. The Irish had had to break out of the 'us and them' attitude. Its author and sponsor, Congressman Bruce Morrison, realised the shortfalls in ethnocentric politics in discussions he had with the Irish Immigration Reform Movement (IIRM): 'I told the IIRM that their presentation had a racial tone, that it was strategically flawed. There were enough anti-immigration advocates against everybody and the IIRM needed support from pro-immigration groups . . . In the end, there was greater cooperation between the Irish and both Asian and Hispanic groups.'[91]

The MacBride Principles and extradition campaigns fitted into the normal parameters of Irish-American politics in that they could be presented as fitting within 'accentuated anti-Britishness', albeit couched in a human rights package familiar to American political discourse. The immigration issue belongs to another realm. It was about the melting-pot tradition of American politics. It was an 'intermestic' issue that taught a valuable lesson to Irish-Americans in the arts of coalition-building. It moved them out of the ghettoes and pricked the consciences of some of the older, more settled, generation. Ray O'Hanlon's account of the struggle is entitled *The New Irish Americans* but that tells only part of the story.

THE ADAMS VISA AND THE POLITICS OF INCLUSION

It is tempting to read all of the above as the 'pre-play' to the granting of a visa to Gerry Adams to enter the US in January 1994. It is difficult to ignore the immense role played by President Clinton himself in this momentous decision. One commentator has pointed out that 'the real authority of the modern American President can be summed up in the three "Vs": voice, vanguard and veto'. The first and the third are self-explanatory: 'The sheer media profile of the chief executive is such that whatever he says is always news and others are obliged to react'; whereas if the President's authority is extremely modest 'he can usually veto the ambitions of other actors'. The part played by the 'vanguard' is pertinent in this context: 'The President might not really be able to impose himself on Congress or foreign nations, but he can surround himself with a vanguard of appointed acolytes so that his disappointment is at least a shared experience.'[92] In this context the vanguard was extremely selective – and therefore vulnerable.

Bill Clinton became President after a rather static period in relations between the US and Ireland. The Reagan years had seen much activity. He had endorsed the 1985 Anglo-Irish Agreement. During his presidency Margaret Thatcher addressed both Houses of Congress and talked to them directly about how she was cooperating with her friend the Taoiseach, Dr Garret FitzGerald, to find a solution. And after she had rejected the conclusions of the New Ireland Forum in 1984, she visited the United States to be told by President Reagan of his interest in 'the Forum initiative and of his support for a concentrated attack on terrorism ... By the time Mrs Thatcher returned to Washington in late February 1985, serious Anglo-Irish talks were under way, buttressed by American willingness to underwrite such negotiations with an offer on extradition.'[93] It has been calculated that Reagan spoke 'publicly about Northern Ireland on at least fifteen occasions and frequently [raised] Anglo-Irish relations in conversations with Mrs Thatcher. He lent strong support to Dublin's effort to persuade the British government to enter into the Anglo-Irish Agreement of 1985.'[94]

Reagan had appointed the energetic and experienced Margaret Heckler as US Ambassador to Ireland after the signing of that agreement. She came into post on the back of managing one of the largest departments – Health and Human Services – in the administration. On the other hand, during his tenure in the White House George Bush nominated two septuagenarians to the embassy in Dublin. That properly summed up his interest in Irish matters; he operated on a much larger screen. He owed no favours in Congress and he had no obvious Irish background. Consequently, Bush's presidency was, as mentioned, a rather static period in Irish–American relations. Much has been made of the fact that one motivation for President Clinton's closer relations with Ireland was revenge because he was angered by the fact that Conservative Central Office in London had assisted Bush's presidential campaign in 1992. That would be to exaggerate. John Major's assessment is probably correct: 'It was a staffers' feud and never an issue between the two of us.'[95]

The early months of the Clinton administration proved a disappointment for the Irish republican lobby in Washington. A request for a visa for Gerry Adams to engage in a book launch publicity campaign in summer 1993 was rejected. The time was not considered to be right. In the view of one who while being close to the President had also been pressing strongly on the visa issue, strong resistance came from within the National Security Council (NSC). Tony Lake, Clinton's National Security Adviser, was dismissive and considered Ireland to be a second-rate issue – 'This was *not* the Middle East', was allegedly his position. There were, too, lingering animosities. Lake's assistant, Nancy Soderberg, came with what one source called 'her Kennedy baggage' – that is, she had worked previously for Senator Ted Kennedy and was, *ipso facto*, anti-republican.[96]

Less than six months later, a sea change occurred and it involved many of the forces to which we have referred. The trigger was the Joint Declaration signed by the Taoiseach, Albert Reynolds, and the Prime Minister, John Major, at Downing Street on 15 December 1993 and known as the Downing Street Declaration. The declaration was a classic exercise in obfuscation – indeed it won first prize for the worst piece of official English for 1993. Its tortuous syntax was deliberate. One of the more astute observers commented on its skilful drafting and abundant use of coded language. He described it as a 'minor diplomatic masterpiece . . . [which] is not a formal agreement or treaty setting the framework for a comprehensive constitutional settlement; it is a political statement of attitude and intent directed primarily at the IRA. The two heads of government have carefully shelved all the difficult longer term issues . . . in order to make a bid for an IRA ceasefire.'[97] 'Fudge' and incrementalism were becoming part of the process.

One of the first signs was a one-page advertisement placed in the *New York Times*. It was done 'intuitively' in the aftermath of the Joint Declaration. The response was so positive that it was followed by a second. This was 'Irish-American corporate people' taking the 'issue out of the bars and into the boardrooms'.[98] The vehicle that delivered the boardrooms was *Irish America*'s 'Top 100'.[99] The 'Top 100' compilation had become an unofficial showcase of Irish-American life, a vanity listing with a purpose; eventually there were two categories – one list drawn from all walks of life in the United States and a second list, introduced in 1994, drawn solely from the business community. In her introduction to the 1996 Business 100 the editor-in-chief of *Irish America* – commented that never 'before have we had a more educated, monied, powerful group'. She noted their sense of compassion and their need to relate to new Irish immigrants. She closed with an appeal: 'Let not our success buy us so much distance from our past that we mortgage the future of this great country. Let's keep the dream alive.'[100]

That powerful appeal conveyed a significant message. It was that the 'new' Irish-Americans consisted of many who had their roots deep in United States politics, commerce and culture. Some such as those behind the Ireland Funds had eschewed politics in order 'to promote peace, culture and charity in all of Ireland'. The brainchild of Dr Tony O'Reilly and Dan Rooney, the Ireland Funds had been founded in the United States in 1976 and had spread its wings to Canada, France, Australia, Great Britain, Mexico, Monaco, Japan, New Zealand and South Africa. Its mandate was broad enough to allow it to play a discreet, but significant, role in the peace process as it unfolded in the 1990s. Other very wealthy individuals such as Bill Flynn, Tom Moran and Chuck Feeney, generally first- or second-generation Irish-Americans, were totally committed to the peace process. It was Bill Flynn who extended an invitation to Gerry Adams to attend a one-day conference organised by the National Committee on American Foreign Policy in New York in January 1994, thus paving the way for Adams' first visa. It was people like Brian O'Dwyer, Bruce Morrison and Niall O'Dowd who worked through Senators Ted Kennedy and Chris Dodd to persuade the Clinton administration of the republican movement's *bona fides*. Some of these people had visited Ireland in September 1993 when the IRA carefully manufactured a temporary ceasefire as an indication of the direction in which the movement hoped to proceed. It was as if the 'tree-tops' had become more inclusive and fulfilled a judgement made a decade earlier: 'it cannot be said that the Irish lobby today represents a disruptive influence in American foreign policy or a threat to the national interest. Among other reasons for this salutary state of affairs, the restraint and responsibility of Irish-American political leaders, who could probably exploit the issue to their advantage if they chose, is critical, and also exemplary.'[101] In that respect, Irish-America had finally passed President Woodrow Wilson's 'infallibility test' for the proper hyphenated American.

The manner in which the process was moved forward is also revealing. Irish-Americans realised that securing a visa for Adams 'was the key. We knew that. The pitch always was to the White House and to Bill Clinton. It wasn't that you had to convince Bill Clinton but to convince him to ignore the State Department.'[102] That was not going to be easy because it could involve a turf war between the NSC and the State Department.[103] The NSC had been established in 1947 as the President's cabinet-level advisory group whose job was to integrate policy, to help other foreign policy agencies and departments to co-operate more effectively and to advise the President. Initially it was a high-level administrative unit rather than a policy-maker. Down the years it gained more power by becoming a policy-making body. The trend probably began in the Kennedy presidency under McGeorge Bundy. President Reagan attached great importance to the NSC; it met about 150 times during his first administration, as opposed to 45 in Jimmy Carter's time.[104] NSC staffers had the advantage that they worked very closely with the President; and in the game of bureaucratic warfare they enjoyed the further advantage that part of their job was to write memos critiquing other agencies. In more recent times the White House (where the NSC is located) gained the technical capability to bypass the State and Defence departments electronically. And the NSC had a different outlook from the State Department, whose stress was on patient diplomacy, accommodation and the pursuit of long-term interests (of which Anglo-American relations were probably the longest).[105] NSC staff, on the other hand, were more likely to think in terms of the domestic pay-off particularly in an era when the presidency is more prone to engage in personal diplomacy.

The stage was set for a serious confrontation. The Major government, the US embassy in London, the Federal Bureau of Investigation and above all, the State and Justice departments were totally opposed to granting a visa to Adams for the foreign policy conference in New York. One insider has explained the NSC predicament: 'We were not involved in the New York conference. That was clever of them [the organisers]. They knew enough to know that the visa was under review. We were looking at other options than a visa but that was not enough to help Adams. We had to take some hits for being soft on terrorism and knew that we would bring down State and Justice on top of us.' Further, 'the British issue was not insignificant. It was the first time in history that the United States had stood against Britain on Northern Ireland. We needed them on Bosnia, Russia and elsewhere and we knew that their interests and ours coincided on these issues.' On the other hand 'Adams was not a security threat if he came here. His coming for a conference on peace was not a victory for terrorism.' In the end the decision was the President's acting on the advice of the NSC. The latter perceived itself as standing 'above the bureaucracy. We had to make sure that the bureaucracies got the opportunity to make their case to the President.'[106]

And the bureaucracies were quick to present their opposition. The Secretary of State, Warren Christopher, 'had an angry 30-minute conversation which left Clinton in no doubt where the Secretary of State stood. Also opposed to the visa and his general Irish involvement were Attorney General Janet Freno and FBI chief Louis Freeh.'[107] Niall O'Dowd comments that normally 'such a phalanx of opposition would daunt any president'.[108] When the President refused to bend he demonstrated his capacity to make use of all three 'Vs'. This was the first occasion in Anglo–American relations when 'voice' and 'veto' were used so powerfully. The Carter statement of 1977 and President Reagan's support for the 1985 Agreement had been endorsed by the political establishments in Dublin, London and Washington. The visa decision was one where the 'vanguard' was small and it was vulnerable. But it endured; and Clinton's decision to grant a visa to Adams gave the process the momentum to establish conditions for peace. Besides listening to Tony Lake and Nancy Soderberg of the NSC the President had consulted closely with Senators Kennedy and Dodd, both of whom had been influenced by the American Ambassador in Dublin, Jean Kennedy Smith, and by John Hume.[109] Ultimately the granting of the visa was a victory for the politics of convergence and of inclusion. Only those who were completely out of touch – or, more appropriately, at the rear end of the pantomime horse – could describe it as 'music-hall diplomacy'.

THE ENDOGENOUS AND
THE EXOGENOUS

> I waited outside the gate-lodge,
> waited like a dog
> in my own province
> till a policeman brought me
> a signed paper.
>
> TOM PAULIN[1]

Its return to government in 1974 exposed the myth that British Labour is an anti-partitionist party. True, its 1981 policy document stated that the party had 'a long and deeply held belief . . . that Ireland should, by peaceful means, and on the basis of consent, be united'.[2] Yet nothing in the previous decade warranted such a conclusion. We shall see that the policies pursued by the two Labour Secretaries of State for Northern Ireland, Merlyn Rees and Roy Mason, between 1974 and 1979 gave no grounds for thinking that the Labour government favoured Irish unity. It was Labour that conceded extra parliamentary representation to Northern Ireland in 1977, a move which was perceived at the time as being integrationist and in line with Enoch Powell's strategy. Even James Callaghan's senior policy adviser, Bernard Donoghue, described it as being wrong tactically, politically and 'in principle as far as the long-term future of Britain and Ireland is concerned, because it misled the Unionists into believing that their long-term future rested on the direct link to London'.[3] In fact, Labour and the Conservative Party pursued a bipartisan policy whose roots go back to the 1920s.[4] The 1981 statement belonged to Labour in opposition and to the dominance of the left wing of the party. This chapter seeks to explain how successive British governments moved from creeping integrationism to a much bolder Anglo-Irish approach, from an obsession with security – 'the Cabinet Committee in Downing Street never after 1974 actually discussed Northern Ireland *policy*: it only discussed law and order'[5] – to constitutional innovation. Again we will examine this from the vantage points of Belfast, Dublin and London in the period from 1974 to the early 1980s, and specifically through the eyes of those in government at the time.

The statistics on violence explain why there was such a concentration on security. Figures for deaths, injuries and explosions suggest that the period 1971–5 was particularly frenetic but that the 'years 1976–7 were turning points in the scale of all violence – not simply deaths – for three main reasons'. The first was improvements in security capability (including intelligence) with a consequential reduction in republican paramilitary activity. Secondly, loyalist paramilitary activity diminished because loyalists had grown more self-confident after the success of the Ulster Workers' Council strike in 1974, and because increased residential segregation meant that fewer easy targets were available. Finally, IRA reorganisation in 1976–7 around a new cell structure led to a reduction in the scale of their activities.[6]

It would be a mistake, however, to assume that the security issue was singularly predominant. Between the imposition of direct rule in 1972 and the emergence of a broader Anglo-Irish approach in the early 1980s there were four attempts at *internal* settlement: the power-sharing arrangement that lasted less than five months in 1974; the Northern Ireland Constitutional Convention which was established in 1975 to consider what 'provision for the government of Northern Ireland is likely to command the most widespread acceptance throughout the community there';[7] the Constitutional Conference convened by the Secretary of State for Northern Ireland, Humphrey Atkins, during 1980;[8] and an ingenuous scheme for 'rolling devolution' devised by his successor, James Prior, which created the Northern Ireland Assembly (1982–6).[9] All of these initiatives are now matters of history. All of them failed, and all of them were based on certain assumptions: the *status quo ante* was void; direct rule was to be temporary; the long-term solution would be based on endogenous, rather than exogenous, factors; and a form of devolution which accepted power-sharing and the recognition of an Irish dimension was the most desirable (British government) option. In that respect successive British governments were not prepared to countenance the discussion of issues such as Irish unity, confederation or negotiated independence. In this chapter we shall follow the debate about the merits of the endogenous and the exogenous which eventually led to a more focussed Anglo–Irish approach in the early 1980s.

LABOUR AND IRELAND

... for Labour the Irish cause was never an end in itself but
always a matter of British domestic politics, a factor to be used
or avoided, especially in its challenge to the Liberal Party ...
its attitude towards Ireland and its determination to present
itself as a party of the Irish in Britain was primarily a function
of its own political development.

BILLY McCARRICK[10]

During the 1960s the Northern Ireland Labour Party was ploughing a rich and fallow furrow in an attempt to have 'class politics' replace the politics of creed and constitution. The NILP edged matters on by turning Westminster's attention to the lack of civil rights in the North. Even before the 1964 general election Harold Wilson had committed Labour to reform in Northern Ireland.[11] That policy opened up a can of worms which destroyed the NILP and led to the outbreak of political violence. As Home Secretary, James Callaghan met the immediate challenge with energy and sensitivity. And why wouldn't he? Here was what appeared to be pristine Labour territory – the poorest region of the United Kingdom, with the highest cost of living, highest unemployment and lowest life expectancy: Scotland across the water.[12]

But even Scotland's 'advantages' were missing. The NILP never won more than four of Stormont's fifty-two seats at any general election, was poorly organised outside Belfast and only once returned a Westminster MP. Nor could it rely on a strong trade union base. The 'contracting in' clause (whereby workers had to sign an agreement to pay rather than abstain from paying a levy to the NILP) was not repealed in Northern Ireland until 1968, almost forty years after Britain. Additionally the trade union movement was part of the partition game since their headquarters were to be found in Belfast, Dublin and London. Callaghan discovered in the NILP a party in poor organisational shape but he was not there as an emissary of Labour. He was there as a government minister concerned with the disintegration of part of the kingdom. Essentially the North was a sideshow; there were few pickings for Labour in Northern Ireland, so the general tendency was to ignore it. There were exceptions. During the time of Attlee's postwar government about thirty back-benchers formed the 'Friends of Ireland' group to work for the establishment of 'democratic Labour governments in Ireland both north and south with a view to attaining a united Ireland by common consent at the earliest possible moment'.[13] Following Labour's electoral victory in 1964, the Campaign for Democracy in Ulster concerned itself with human rights issues. However, neither group made any real impact.

The reality was that Northern Ireland presented Labour with a major psychological problem. The North did not fit into the wider scheme of things, into the overwhelmingly centralist spirit of the British political and administrative system. In electoral terms three of the five Labour victories in general elections between 1950 and 1979 had depended on the seats won in Scotland and Wales. Northern Ireland did not count unless, that is, one recognised its domino effect during the devolution debate of the 1970s. Labour saw this debate as an unnecessary diversion from its egalitarian mission which was best pursued in a centralised United Kingdom. To make too many concessions to Irish nationalism could have a triggering effect on nationalist sentiment in Wales and Scotland. In fact, to remain in office after 1977 the Callaghan government bought unionist acquiescence by increasing the number of Northern Ireland seats at Westminster. So, what to do about Ireland? As Home Secretary, James Callaghan worked on a policy of political incorporation – if the Catholic minority demanded British standards then they should have them. But as the beleaguered Prime Minister he was prepared to contemplate creeping integration. And in the post-Callaghan days of socialist contrition the party's National Executive Committee (NEC) adopted its aspirational Irish unity document. To interpret Labour policy on Ireland we have to veer between the expediency of Callaghan and the lofty rhetoric of the NEC. One is left with confusion and ambiguity.[14]

That might serve as an apt description of Labour's first Secretary of State for Northern Ireland, Merlyn Rees, who held the post between March 1974 and September 1976.[15] He had 'shadowed' the post from October 1971 with enthusiasm and concern. And yet his sojourn in Northern Ireland sadly suggests that he was temperamentally and ideologically unsuited for the task. He came to the office in the aftermath of a period of constitutional innovation instituted by the Conservatives. He did not believe that their plans for power-sharing would work, recording in his diary on 27 September 1973: 'We would have to face up to the fact that the new constitution could not work.'[16] He was to describe the Sunningdale talks which led to the power-sharing executive as something which had 'been pushed down the throats of the loyalists', and as 'a London/Dublin solution that had ignored the reality of the situation in the North of Ireland and especially the lack of support there for the Faulkner Unionists'.[17] The simple fact was that Sunningdale was a Conservative show. Labour would go about things differently. Rees's deputy, Stan Orme, had already established his credentials with the civil rights movement and the SDLP. Naturally that created problems with the unionist community but Orme hoped to overcome that through the myth of fraternity – Labour, and Labour alone, was at one with the working class. Orme, we are told, 'fully understood Protestant working-class feelings'.[18]

It is as if Divine Right had been imposed upon the Labour Party. Perhaps it was this Divine Right that excused Harold Wilson's inept and insensitive broadcast towards the end of the UWC strike on 25 May 1974 when he complained about Ulster people 'who spend their lives sponging on Westminster and on British democracy'.[19] Perhaps, it excused, too, the forlorn hope that the Trades Union Congress could persuade the striking workers back to the shop floor. And perhaps it was Divine Right that enabled Rees – on one of the rare occasions when wrestling with his conscience allowed him to be decisive and produced a result – to place the blame on others. The Dublin government suffered from 'the usual lack of understanding of the Protestant working class in the North'; too many members of the power-sharing executive did not behave sensibly; and the RUC 'was not organized in a way that would have enabled it to respond quickly in the first days of the strike'.[20] He does allow that there may have been 'marginal mistakes' in the handling of the strike but saw no way of putting down an 'industrial/political dispute supported by a majority in the community'.[21] That begs too many questions. The dispute was industrial only in the sense that the strikers used the withdrawal of their labour from key industries as their most potent weapon. Nor should we ignore the violence – and the threat of violence – which was at the heart of the strategy in the early days of the strike. Rees's analysis ignores the whole field of intelligence gathering and of contingency planning which we are led to believe is at the heart of state strategy. Fundamentally, it ignores the role of the army.

With the failure of power-sharing successfully behind him, Rees moved on to other matters. First there was the Constitutional Convention with its fail-safe device: 'If the Northern Ireland politicians failed to find a way through, it would at least show the world, and give a message to the South of Ireland, that the blame did not all lie with the British.'[23] Needless to say it did not come within a donkey's roar of unanimity – and there were those who had their doubts whether that outcome was even intended: 'I was never sure whether this was intended to be a constructive contribution to a solution or a process of *reductio ad absurdum* which would legitimise direct rule, or just another hurdle placed there in the hope and belief that Northern Ireland politicians failed to clear it.'[23] The Constitutional Convention issued a report in 1975 that Rees (rightly) decided did not command 'sufficiently widespread acceptance throughout the community ... to provide stable and effective government'.[24] It was reconvened briefly in 1976. Perhaps its real merit was that it dissipated loyalists' euphoria and their uncompromising demand for a return to direct rule. Thus ended his one foray into constitutional tinkering. He was to devote most of his time to the security question where he achieved his greatest triumphs – or so his *memoirs* suggest.

The 'primacy of the police' was to be Rees's long-term aim through what became known as 'Ulsterisation' and its corollary, 'criminalisation'. Essentially what these policies entailed was placing the police in the front line, and criminalising the paramilitaries by removing their political status inside the prisons. Rees was convinced that by adopting the line he drove a substantial wedge between the IRA and the minority population as a whole – a claim that was to be sorely tested by the hunger strikes. Simultaneously an attempt was made to restore the status and credibility of the RUC based on a document, *The Way Ahead*, produced by a committee of senior army, police and intelligence officers in 1975. It was a tentative effort to re-establish a degree of trust between the Catholic community and the police. In the years of most sustained violence, 1970–6, the police had maintained a lower profile as they set about implementing a reform programme after the Hunt Report. The army had borne the brunt of nationalist wrath. In the meantime a greater awareness of 'professionalism' and public relations had been inculcated inside the RUC. Finally, the police were to demonstrate their ability to deal evenhandedly with political thuggery in May 1977 in the so-called 'constitutional stoppage' led by the DUP and UDA. Decisive political and security leadership defeated this attempt to commit the government to a tougher security policy and to oppose the continuation of direct rule. The stoppage failed because it did not get the support of the UUP or VUPP and, unlike 1974, the power workers refused to support it. In addition the British government stood firm against it.

This twin-pronged approach – Ulsterisation and criminalisation – had certain advantages for the authorities: the use of locally recruited security forces allowed the problem to be presented to international observers as an internal one between conflicting Irish groups, and hence downplayed the role of Britain and the army as part of the equation. It was reinforced by the use of the legal process rather than detention; this emphasised the 'criminal' nature of the violence rather than its political element. But it was a policy that entailed high risks because, essentially, it was concerned with managing, rather than resolving, conflict. One area in which the high risks were evident was relations with the republican movement. A ceasefire negotiated between the IRA and the NIO lasted from February to November 1975; yet, despite the ceasefire, more people died from conflict-related incidents in 1975 than in the previous year. To ensure that the ceasefire would hold, a number of 'incident centres' (staffed by civil servants on a twenty-four-hour basis) were established throughout the North, and talks were held with Sinn Féin. The incident centres gave Sinn Féin (and the IRA) spurious legitimacy. This arrangement with Sinn Féin appeared to make the SDLP redundant, and added to that party's unhappiness with Rees over his handling of the UWC strike. Relations between the government and the SDLP (and between the British and Irish governments) were not good.[25]

In September 1976 Rees returned to London as the new Home Secretary. His reputation had been shaped by his handling of the 1974 strike and his approach to security policy. They complemented each other. Looking back, the Prime Minister's senior policy adviser at the time, Bernard Donoghue, reflected that 'when I later discussed the Protestant strike with senior military officers from Northern Ireland they expressed surprise at our precipitate surrender and said that the strike could have been resisted had central government shown the necessary will'.[26] That viewpoint was shared by John Hume, who, along with Brian Faulkner, was the real success story of the executive: 'The greatest factor of all, of course, was the lack of will on the part of the British Government, particularly its Prime Minister, to face up to the Loyalists and instead to adopt a policy of inaction and delay which could only lead to the collapse of the Executive, while absolving itself of any apparent responsibility.'[27] We should not underestimate the significance of this opinion. Hume was the real strategist of the SDLP and, following the failure of the Constitutional Convention, his party moved towards what its opponents (internal and external) dubbed the 'greening' of party policy; this became evident with the publication of the policy document *Facing Reality* at its 1977 annual conference in which the Irish dimension was upgraded.[28] It was yet another indication that nationalists had lost patience with the endogenous approach. Outside the republican movement, it is difficult to find any winners from the 1974 debacle. It destroyed Brian Faulkner. It exposed loyalist paramilitaries' limited room for political manoeuvre and heightened their sense of betrayal.[29] It deluded the wilder shores of unionism into believing that they were in control: the failure of the 1977 'constitutional stoppage' had a sobering effect on some of them, whereas others had to wait until the collapse of the campaign against the 1985 Anglo-Irish Agreement before they realised that they were no longer in control.

Rees's successor was Roy Mason, who as Secretary of State for Defence had famously infuriated Rees when he hinted at the withdrawal of troops from Northern Ireland in April 1974.[30] It is known that late in the UWC strike he had 'counselled against any serious Army involvement in strike-breaking'.[31] Mason came to Northern Ireland with two priorities: security and employment – 'I wanted the whole issue of constitutional change put on the back burner.'[32] He inherited a 'solid' ministerial team with the exception of Lord Melchett: 'young, naïve and – in the environmental sense of the word – very green, not the type I'd personally have chosen to face the terrorists'.[33] Mason himself was small in stature, brusque, opinionated and driven. Bernard Donoghue, who worked closely with him, goes to the essence of the man:

> he was more military than the military and appeared to carry their confidence. The problem was that he also seemed more 'Protestant' than the 'Prods' and but for his accent might have been taken for a classic Ulsterman. He had little time for fools or romantics – and clearly many of the Catholic Irish, whom he called 'greens', came into this category. He ran his department well and was an appropriate Minister to conduct a 'status quo' policy of restoring law and order under direct rule.[34]

Such a personality had its advantages, as he proved in putting down the 1977 loyalist stoppage – no wrestling with his conscience for this man. In fact he recalls singing 'Don't cry for me, Ballymena' as he flew over the blockaded town on 10 May 1977.[35]

Mason lived up to his word on constitutional change. Initially he made some attempts at a form of interim devolution through a series of desultory talks with the local politicians. More importantly when the Prime Minister made a firm commitment in March 1977 to increase the number of Northern Ireland seats at Westminster by about five,[36] his Secretary of State was perceived by the SDLP and the Irish government as having taken sides. The damage was compounded early the following year when Mason announced in the House of Commons that he had

> never used the expression 'power-sharing'. I have always insisted that it should be a case of partnership and participation in the

administration in Northern Ireland. The House will remember that my predecessor, more than fifteen months ago, had also dropped the use of that emotive term. It is right to inform the House that the term 'power-sharing' tends to be taken in Northern Ireland as meaning the system laid down in the 1973 Act. The Government are in no way committed to this system or, indeed, to any other system.[37]

Finally when he described the SDLP as extremists and the Ulster Unionists as moderates in February 1979 the die was cast.[38] When Margaret Thatcher introduced a motion of no confidence in the government the following month Labour lost by 311 to 310. Gerry Fitt voted against the government and Frank Maguire (independent nationalist) abstained. Either could have saved the government.[39]

Fitt's vote was not an act of pique. Although he was not to remain much longer as leader of the SDLP he was reflecting a real concern at Labour policy on Ireland – not simply the government's desire to keep the Ulster Unionists on side but the whole thrust of security policy. Undoubtedly Roy Mason's demeanour was a problem.[40] But it went beyond that. From the outset he had stuck to his declared priorities – his tenure was going to be about security and jobs. His preoccupation with security may have come from his previous incarnation as Defence Secretary, a position he had 'shadowed' in opposition. He was to enjoy a good relationship with Lt.-Gen. Timothy Creasey, the General Officer Commanding, and Maj.-Gen. Dick Trant, Commander Land Forces, both appointed to their Northern Ireland postings in 1977. They believed in intensifying undercover operations and in increasing the success rate of court prosecutions by obtaining more detailed intelligence about suspects. Hence the SAS were responsible for ten deaths between 1976 and 1978: seven were of IRA members but three were innocent civilians. The ambushes stopped in December 1978 (and the SAS did not kill anyone again until December 1983).[41] After a highly critical Amnesty International report in 1978 about police interrogation procedures, the government asked Harry Bennett QC to investigate these allegations. His report was critical of certain aspects of interrogation methods, and noted that the government had shown little determination to punish the perpetrators of past offences.[42] Plainclothes interrogation teams had become an essential plank of security policy: '90 per cent of cases coming before the special non-jury Diplock courts result in conviction and 80 per cent of these convictions rest solely on confessions of guilt made during police interrogation'.[43] Besides the SAS controversy and the Bennett investigation, Mason also found himself embroiled in allegations of attempting to censor the BBC, for which he remained unapologetic.[44]

On the day he effectively left office (30 April 1979) Mason announced that a contract had been signed with the Hyster company to build a £30 million factory to manufacture fork-lift trucks. This was the seventh such US investment deal negotiated in an eighteen-month period, bringing total American investment in the North to £550 million. All of this was very welcome news after a sustained period of failure to attract inward investment; yet it could not hide the fact that the policy of economic regeneration had not succeeded. Mason had managed to wheedle extra cash out of the Treasury, but this was spent on 'propping up the economy rather than strengthening its base'.[45] The one enterprise for which Roy Mason will be remembered was the DeLorean project, involving a deal to construct a purpose-built factory on a greenfield site in west Belfast to manufacture a revolutionary sports car. Negotiations were rushed through in a frantic forty-eight days before the deal was announced in Belfast in August 1978. It was an extraordinarily high-risk investment in which the taxpayer paid £23,000 for each job created. Despite warnings from bodies such as the US Securities and Exchange Commission, which had noted seventeen high-risk factors in the project, the contract was signed, and the company prospered for two years. But a collapse in the US market, and a more hard-headed approach by the incoming Conservative government, saw the end of the DeLorean gamble and the return of pessimism to west Belfast. DeLorean was to be another mirage that had held out hope only in the short term.[46]

TORY RADICALISM?

When the Conservatives won the 1979 general election there was little indication that a radical initiative would be undertaken. Their manifesto had barely touched on the problems of Northern Ireland, save to stress the policy of defeating terrorism and of maintaining the Union 'in accordance with the wish of the majority in the Province'. A cryptic reference to future government stated that 'in the absence of devolved government, we will seek to establish one or more elected regional councils with a wide range of powers over local services'. This policy bore the imprimatur of Airey Neave, the party's spokesperson on Northern Ireland since 1975 and a close confidant of Margaret Thatcher. His assassination by the Irish National Liberation Army at Westminster on 30 March 1979 robbed the Prime Minister of a Secretary of State for Northern Ireland but not, it seemed, a policy. Moreover, the Tories had a comfortable majority in the Commons and could rely on the enthusiastic support of James Molyneaux's Ulster

Unionists. The appointment as Secretary of State of Humphrey Atkins – a man without previous cabinet experience or any knowledge of Northern Ireland – seemed to confirm that a period of consolidation was under way.[47]

The Tories did not worry unduly about the economic situation. However, security was another matter. It came to a head on 27 August 1979 when eighteen soldiers were killed in a carefully constructed IRA ambush near the border. On the same day Earl Mountbatten, a member of the royal family, and three companions were killed by a bomb concealed in their pleasure boat in the Republic. These two incidents 'brought to a head a crisis which had been brewing between the police and the army'.[48] Thatcher was confronted with the army's desire to roll back police primacy and with the police's concern about the effect of offensive operations by army special forces. Her solution on 2 October was to appoint the former head of MI6, Sir Maurice Oldfield, as security coordinator and to expand the RUC by 1,000. Oldfield's appointment coincided with the planned departure of the two senior security officers, the Chief Constable of the RUC, Sir Kenneth Newman, and the General Officer Commanding, Lt.-Gen. Timothy Creasey. Their successors, Jack Hermon and Lt.-Gen. Richard Lawson, established a closer rapport and left operational matters to their respective deputies.

For a while it seemed that the security response was yet again dominant. But the Prime Minister found herself moving on the political front as well after the intervention of Speaker Tip O'Neill during the British general election (as we saw in the previous chapter). In November a consultative document that sought no more than the 'highest level of agreement ... which will best meet the immediate needs of Northern Ireland' was published.[49] Atkins announced that he was inviting the four main parties in Northern Ireland – UUP, SDLP, DUP and Alliance – to a conference to discuss a possible political settlement. The areas for discussion were narrowly circumscribed: debate on Irish unity, confederation, independence or the constitutional status of Northern Ireland was ruled out of order. In addition, Thatcher appointed a high-powered cabinet committee to oversee the process: besides the Secretary of State for Northern Ireland, it included his two Conservative predecessors (Francis Pym and William Whitelaw), the Lord Chancellor (Lord Hailsham) and the deputy Foreign Secretary (Ian Gilmour). Clearly the Prime Minister had invested considerable prestige in the exercise, with some commentators comparing it to the negotiations on Rhodesian Independence then going on at Lancaster House.

But that is to exaggerate. It was to be another fifteen years before *all* the parties had an opportunity to get round the table. Indeed only the Alliance Party endorsed the notion of a conference. The Ulster Unionists considered it a dereliction of the Conservative manifesto and refused to participate. Initially the DUP reserved its judgement before it became an enthusiastic participant – partially, it should be said, as a means to upstage the Molyneaux Unionists. The DUP had been doing well electorally out of direct rule. It had made substantial gains in the 1977 local government elections (despite its role in the constitutional stoppage), and in the 1979 general election it had increased its Westminster representation from one to three. That result was compounded by Ian Paisley's massive personal vote at the direct elections for the European Parliament in 1979, when he topped the poll and John Taylor of the Ulster Unionists came in a humiliating third.

The idea of a conference produced problems for the SDLP. Initially Gerry Fitt welcomed the document but his party balked at the omission of an Irish dimension and refused to participate. Fitt resigned as party leader and was succeeded by John Hume. He had two meetings with Atkins on 10 and 15 December when the Northern Secretary agreed that he would 'be willing on request, and quite apart from the conference, to have separate meeting with the parties represented at the conference on wider issues'.[50] They agreed, too, that the conference was 'not an end in itself'. So the ideas of politics as process and of parallel talks were established, enabling the SDLP to invoke the Irish dimension and to enter the talks. The conference did not succeed. It opened on 7 January 1980 and adjourned on 24 March. In the meantime the government prepared proposals for further discussion in the form of another paper.[51] During the Commons debate on that paper in July Atkins spoke of the 'geographical and historical facts of life' obliging 'us to recognise the special relationship that exists between the component parts of the British Isles ... we do improve our chances of success by recognising that the Republic is deeply interested in what happens in Northern Ireland ... there will continue to be a practical "Irish dimension" '.[52] That statement was in keeping with the beginning of a new phase in Anglo-Irish relations.

Other matters were exercising the mind of the British government. The most urgent was the prison issue. On 27 October 1980 republican prisoners in the Maze went on hunger strike in protest at their conditions and status. Republicans resented criminalisation. Writing some years later, Gerry Adams cited the Glover report on *Future Terrorist Trends*[53] and a study by lawyers of defendants appearing before

Diplock courts on 'scheduled' offences to justify the claim that republican prisoners 'do not fit the stereotypes of criminality which the authorities have from time to time attempted to attach to them'. He insisted that it 'has nothing to do with any contempt for the "ordinary criminals", who are so often the victims of social inequality and injustice. From Thomas Ashe to Bobby Sands the concern has always been to assert the political nature of the struggle in which the IRA has always been engaged.'[54] Generally, the wider nationalist community shared Adams's belief that the profile of the prisoners was not that of a criminal class.[55] And they were aware of a tradition of hunger striking that had already claimed twelve republican lives earlier in the twentieth century. This was to be the culmination of the campaign against criminalisation.

The first hunger strike was called off on 18 December, but a second began on 1 March 1981. The IRA's leader in the Maze, Bobby Sands, was the first to volunteer. If the prisoners' demands were not met it was likely that he would be dead by Easter – a secular celebration of destruction and renewal as well as a holy beginning. In fact his hunger strike lasted sixty-days and he died on 5 May. While 4,000 people had marched in support of his decision to go on hunger strike, 70,000 turned out for his funeral. By 20 August another nine republican prisoners had died on hunger strike, and the remainder ended their protest on 3 October. The whole business created deep emotional scars and polarised the community as never before. It threatened to make constitutional nationalism redundant inside Northern Ireland; it caused tremendous tension between the British and Irish governments; and it aroused an inordinate amount of international attention, much of it embarrassing to the Thatcher government. In short it was a disaster.

That is not to say that lessons were not learned. In the name of 'the people' and the 'dead generations' the IRA sought the moral high ground: 'In 1976 the British government tried to criminalise the republican prisoners. In 1981 the republican prisoners criminalised the British government.'[56] Republicanism underwent a transformation, with the fusion of military and political tactics being underlined by a certain degree of cynicism: 'the essence of republican struggle must be in armed resistance coupled with popular opposition to the British presence. So while not everyone can plant a bomb, everyone can plant a vote.'[57] While on hunger strike Sands had been elected MP for Fermanagh-South Tyrone in a by-election on 9 April under the highly effective slogan of 'Your vote can save this man's life.' It didn't, and his election agent, Owen Carron, succeeded him at a further by-election on 20 August. Meanwhile nine prisoners contested a general election in the South in June, and two were elected. That was enough to deprive Charles Haughey's Fianna Fáil party of power. Contesting elections became addictive and, according to Gerry Adams, was playing 'a major role in changing the nature of Sinn Féin'.[58] Adams himself was elected MP for West Belfast at the 1983 general election. Sinn Féin had become the largest nationalist party in Belfast, where it held more seats on Belfast City Council, and was narrowing the electoral gap with the SDLP throughout the North.

That sequence of events ran counter to the Prime Minister's own conception of how the IRA could be beaten. Her strategy relied on three conditions. First, the IRA would have to be rejected by the nationalist minority. Second, they would have to be deprived of international support, which would require 'constant attention to foreign policy'. Third, 'and linked to the other two, relations between Britain and the Republic of Ireland [would] have to be carefully managed'.[59] It could be said that all three conditions were not met. We will examine these more closely when we look at the burgeoning Anglo-Irish relationship in the 1980s and 1990s. But this failure points to a paradox at the heart of Thatcher's Irish policy. Here was someone who had been prepared to contemplate constitutional innovation but who was ultimately ruled by security considerations. The simplest explanation comes from the former Tánaiste (deputy Prime Minister) and leader of the Irish Labour Party, Dick Spring: 'Margaret Thatcher knew everything, and above all, she knew that it wasn't necessary to listen … She was always baffled at the reluctance of Irish ministers to talk about issues like extradition *in isolation from political development*'.[60] It may be, too, that she suffered in her choice of Northern secretaries of state.

Humphrey Atkins was replaced in September 1981 when he became Deputy Foreign Secretary. He left as he arrived: bewildered. His successor, James Prior, was a real political heavyweight in the mould of a William Whitelaw. Unfortunately, his appointment had more to do with the incipient civil war inside the Conservative Party than with the interests of Northern Ireland. The Prime Minister wanted to see the back of a putative rival. In an earlier age he would have been sent to somewhere like New South Wales as a Governor-General. He had been very reluctant to vacate his post as Employment Secretary and took the Northern Ireland job only after he had wrung some concessions from Thatcher: he was allowed to remain on the Cabinet Economic Committee and to install three of his close political friends in the Northern Ireland Office – Lord Gowrie, Nicholas Scott and John

Patten. Crucially he did not have the Prime Minister's support.[61] He was beset with problems the moment he arrived: bringing the hunger strike to an end; the DeLorean fiasco and another high-risk venture in the Lear Fan executive jet project; and the murder in November of the Reverend Robert Bradford, Ulster Unionist MP for South Belfast, the first MP to be murdered in the IRA campaign. At Bradford's funeral the Northern Secretary had to endure verbal and physical abuse from a section of the congregation.

Prior decided to make his mark in Northern Ireland by attempting yet again to arrive at an internal settlement. In April 1982 he launched his blueprint, a minimalist plan for devolution based on 'acceptance' rather than 'reconciliation'.[62] It had the merit of flexibility and could progress only as 'cross-community agreement' was arrived at. In keeping with his previous incarnation as Employment Secretary, his initiative was managerial in style − as opposed to the imposition of Sunningdale and the exhortation of the Constitutional Convention and the Atkins initiative. The first stage was to be the election of a Northern Ireland Assembly in October. The Assembly was to be in-vested with a scrutiny and consultative role to make direct rule more accountable.

Immediately his 'rolling devolution' plan ran into serious difficulties.[63] The Northern Ireland Bill was fought line by line by the UUP in the committee stage with the support of about thirty Tory back-benchers. The first amendment, in Enoch Powell's name, took some twenty hours before a closure motion was successful; eventually it had to be guillotined.[64] With the passing of the bill the Ulster Unionist leadership took the view that the price of making the Assembly work − power-sharing − was a price they were not prepared to pay. They need not have worried. While the SDLP and Sinn Féin had contested the Assembly elections, neither party took its seats. The only time that the SDLP seriously contemplated participating was when James Prior threw out the idea of an American-style executive.[65] That was unacceptable to the other parties, and the idea died. The Assembly functioned in its own fashion, but long before it was wound up Prior had departed Northern Ireland.

One of the most astute commentators on Anglo-Irish relations asserted at the outset of the experiment: 'If it fails, public opinion in Britain may finally accept what the Northern Ireland Catholics have argued all along − that a purely internal settlement cannot work. The only alternative to continuing stalemate, violence and economic decline appears to be an enlarged role for Dublin in finding new arrangements. The Loyalists have been warned.'[66] Both major parties in the Republic had expressed their reservations about the Prior initiative, and when he persisted with the plan they turned their attention to the SDLP's proposal (contained in the party's 1983 election manifesto) of 'A Council for a New Ireland'. A parallel process to the Northern Ireland Assembly was created and the 'New Ireland Forum' was born.

IRISH CONFUSION

... in the 25 years between 1948 and 1973 there were only six changes of government [in the South]; while in the 25 years between 1973 and 1998 there have been 12 such changes (including major reconstructions that have involved a new Taoiseach or the acceptance of coalition partners by the governing party).

ALVIN JACKSON[67]

The rapid rotation of governments in the Republic of Ireland – particularly in the early 1980s – was indicative of a society in transition. We can identify several factors to explain it. The continuing crisis in Northern Ireland placed huge strains on Southern society. Accession to the EEC added to the complexity of domestic and foreign policy. Economic turmoil was yet another. The impact of the Yom Kippur war in 1973 reduced 'economic growth and led to massive inflation and unemployment throughout the Western world, and had a particularly strong impact on the Irish Republic, which was almost entirely dependent on imported energy sources'.[68] But not all of the economic problems could be put down to exogenous factors. For the first time since the foundation of the state, the 1972 budget deviated from the principle of balancing the books. The chief culprits seem to have been George Colley, the Fianna Fáil Minister for Finance in 1972, and Richard Ryan his Fine Gael counterpart from 1973. This profligate tendency culminated in the 1977 general election, in which 'the politics of the auction house reigned supreme'.[69] Another feature of the times was greater concern with moral legislation, and this caused strains both between and within parties. And finally there was a clash of personalities, particularly that between Charles Haughey and Dr Garret Fitz-Gerald.

A general election in February 1973 brought a Fine Gael–Labour coalition government into office. The Fianna Fáil leader, Jack Lynch, had fought the election on the issues of security, Northern Ireland and his own huge popularity throughout the country. Fianna Fáil increased its overall vote by just over half a percentage point but lost the election. The new Taoiseach, Liam Cosgrave, was the son of the first leader of independent Ireland, W.T. Cosgrave. Like his father, he was strong on law and order and deeply conservative – as he demonstrated when he voted against his own government on a bill to liberalise the law on contraception in July 1974.[70] His background ensured that he was 'adamantly opposed, for reasons which have to do with his family political history, to the IRA and unlikely to be swayed from his convictions by any movement of public opinion'.[71] He had appointed as his Minister for Foreign Affairs Dr Garret FitzGerald, whose father, Desmond, had held the same portfolio in W.T. Cosgrave's government between 1922 and 1927. In relation to Northern Ireland, the relationship between the Taoiseach and the Minister for Foreign Affairs was crucial.[72] Despite earlier tensions between them, Cosgrave and FitzGerald worked well on this sensitive topic. The same could not be said of the relationship between FitzGerald and the Minister for Posts and Telegraphs in the new coalition, Dr Conor Cruise O'Brien. The latter had coveted the Foreign Affairs portfolio; as a member of the junior coalition party, he was unable to secure that position, but he retained his position as spokesperson for the Labour Party on foreign affairs and Northern Ireland. Inevitably there were clashes – not just between O'Brien and FitzGerald but between O'Brien and the whole of the cabinet.[73]

The election of the Cosgrave government coincided with Ireland's accession to the EEC. That led to an expansion in the Department of Foreign Affairs, with the appointment of twenty-nine new third secretaries in 1974 and the opening of new embassies. It has to be remembered just how small is the Irish foreign service. By 1996 it had no more than 246 diplomatic staff, of whom about half worked from headquarters; it had forty-seven overseas resident missions unevenly spread across the globe: 'In relative terms, the Irish foreign service is of a very modest size', with the numbers of diplomats remaining fairly static over the previous decade.[74] We need to be careful about the precise relationship between the department and Northern Ireland matters. FitzGerald explains that 'the practice has been that the primary responsibility for matters relating to Northern Ireland rests with the Taoiseach rather than a departmental Minister. The role of the Minister for Foreign Affairs is a supporting one; he and his department provide advice to the Taoiseach and implement policy under his general direction.'[75] We are concentrating on the Department of Foreign Affairs for several reasons. Firstly, its personnel were primarily responsible for information-gathering on Northern Ireland. Secondly, Ireland's membership of the EEC gave Foreign Affairs officials frequent access to their British counterparts, and much Anglo-Irish business was conducted on the margins of European meetings. Thirdly, Dublin placed great weight on using its leverage on the international stage, especially the United States. Fourthly, smallness can have its advantages in that several key personnel gained invaluable experience on Anglo-Irish matters. On the key question of Northern Ireland there was a much stronger sense of continuity in the Irish civil service than the British.

None of that is to deny that there was a sense of frustration in Dublin in dealing with British ministers. FitzGerald records that after a meeting on 1 November 1974 it 'was a depressed and frankly furious Irish party that left Downing Street that day'; and that he was convinced of 'Merlyn Rees's determination to avoid any contact with us'.[76] In a review of his time as Northern Secretary Rees mentioned favourably some aspects of security cooperation with the Republic but added: 'What was lacking was day-to-day co-operation due to the traditional anti-British feeling which still existed widely in the South. I repeated how angry I felt about the pursuit of the Irish state case against us with the European Commission of Human Rights.'[77] It was interesting that he singled out security cooperation because, as we have seen, it was a matter of particular interest to Margaret Thatcher. Shortly after becoming Prime Minister she had to do business with Charles Haughey, who succeeded Jack Lynch as leader of Fianna Fáil and Taoiseach in December 1979. There was some apprehension in London that Haughey might be soft on the IRA. In fact he demonstrated his anti-terrorism credentials, and political cooperation followed security cooperation with an Anglo-Irish summit meeting in London on 21 May 1980. In the joint communiqué the two leaders referred to the 'unique relationship' between Britain and Ireland and promised to engage in much closer functional cooperation.

A second summit was held in Dublin on 8 December 1980 when it was agreed that substantial progress had been made since May in matters of energy, transport, communications, cross-border economic developments and security. Additionally senior officials agreed to undertake joint studies covering possible new institutional structures, citizenship rights, security matters, economic cooperation and measures to encourage mutual understanding. At a third summit in November 1981 (this one involving Thatcher and FitzGerald) an Anglo-Irish Integovernmental Council was established. During 1982 it met seven times but the relationship had been harmed in the meantime.

Three factors undermined the process. The first concerned different perceptions of the hunger-strike campaign. The Irish sought compromise on humanitarian grounds (if only to avoid polarisation within Northern Ireland), whereas the Prime Minister conducted the debate in terms of a battle between good and evil. Secondly, Ireland's unilateral stance during the 1982 Falklands/Malvinas war (after the sinking of the *Belgrano*) had a catastrophic effect on Anglo-Irish relations during a period when jingoistic feelings were running high in Britain.[78] And finally, as we have seen above, further attempts at an internal settlement were also damaging Anglo-Irish relations.

By 1982, then, both the endogenous and the exogenous were in conflict. The next chapter will look more closely at how both governments managed to overcome this hurdle through two distinctive exercises – the New Ireland Forum and the Anglo-Irish Agreement.

9

THE POLITICS OF TRANSCENDENCE

In politics, personalities are just as significant as policies and events.

JAMES PRIOR[1]

Transcenders are many things – people, actions, events,
gestures, dreams, and visions . . . The form is not important. It is the
task they accomplish that is significant; they connect what
violence has severed.

BYRON BLAND[2]

. . . the two governments have set in motion a process of change.
The way ahead for this kind of intergovernmental co-operation
is uncharted. It may be the end of the century before it finally
becomes clear how far Northern Ireland has drifted from its
old habits of conflict.

WILLIAM SHANNON[3]

James Prior's maxim points to an important distinction: that between
political personalities and political leadership. Tolstoy recognised as
much: 'If we assume, as historians do, that great men lead humanity
towards the attainment of certain ends . . . it becomes impossible to
explain the phenomena of history without intruding the concepts of
chance and *genius*.'[4] We need to marry this insight to one of the more
fashionable nostrums peddled by Whitehall since the 1970s –
consociationalism, or power-sharing as the basis for peace. It was the
foundation of the 1973 Sunningdale Agreement, and variants have
appeared on the scene ever since. It is at one with Tolstoy on the
role of leadership, but it leaves a lot less to *chance*. And like much

contemporary political science it wallows in obfuscation – Tolstoy would not have been amused. Its architect, the Dutch political scientist Arend Lijphart, acknowledges that the model is frankly elitist: 'Elite cooperation is the primary distinguishing feature of consociational democracy'; and again, 'consociational democracy requires an exceptionally able and prudent leadership'.[5] In that respect 'the essence of the theory is to assert that political leaders have an autonomous influence upon events and to deny that they are merely passive instruments of "social forces" or "political cleavages"'.[6] This approach is by no means a novel phenomenon in political theory and is increasingly plagued by criticism, one of the more obvious being the appeal to common sense; as Karl Popper wrote long before the term consociationalism was invented: 'It appears to me madness to base all our political efforts upon the faint hope that we shall be successful in obtaining excellent, or even competent, rulers.'[7]

This chapter will examine the role of leadership in an Anglo-Irish context since the 1970s. It will expose the strains created by the Northern Ireland conflict on British–Irish relations; on fractious relations among the main parties in the Republic and their relationships with the North; and on faltering attempts to repair all these relationships. It will concentrate on two parallel processes: the New Ireland Forum exercise of 1983–4, and the process that culminated in the signing of the Anglo-Irish Agreement on 15 November 1985. It will be concerned with the synthesis arising out of the conjuncture of the endogenous and exogenous. In that respect it will return to the 1920 settlement in that, it might be said, 1920 produced the Northern Ireland problem: before then there had been an Anglo-Irish problem. Nineteen twenty quarantined Irish affairs from domestic British politics; it re-created a sense of contested space in the 'narrow ground'; it reinforced the defensive psychology of conditional loyalism; it placed the emphasis on exclusion and on internalising differences. The thrust of the 1980s was to move towards wider dimensions and to recognise the interaction of the three discrete political entities – the three solitudes of chapter 1 – and their place in the wider world. It was the beginning of wisdom, of *inclusion* and of *process*. But before inclusion there had to be introspection.

Throughout the 1980s Anglo-Irish relations were dominated by four individuals: John Hume, Margaret Thatcher, Garret FitzGerald and Charles Haughey. Their fingerprints can be found on virtually every political proposal from that decade. But our enquiry will stretch beyond those particular individuals. We cannot, for example, ignore the role of the bureaucratic machine or of key players within it. In terms of Anglo-Irish relations Sir Robert Armstrong in London and Dermot Nally in Dublin were two such actors. Armstrong had been Edward Heath's principal private secretary at the time of Sunningdale, at which he had been present. When Margaret Thatcher became Prime Minister he rose to the rank of Cabinet Secretary and acquired a greater concentration of power than any of his predecessors. In addition he was the first Cabinet Secretary to serve only one Prime Minister. His influence on Thatcher was striking and she placed great trust in him: 'She trusts Robert's judgement, trusts him to get a solution, to smooth out problems. She listens to him a good deal about what is going on in Whitehall and about summitry.'[8] His role was crucial in the run-up to the signing of the Anglo-Irish Agreement in November 1985. His Irish counterpart, Dermot Nally, was Secretary to the Government between 1980 and 1992. Nally was once described as '*the* perfect civil servant'; he attended every single European summit between 1973 and 1992 and was the 'only civil servant present at the tête-á-tête meetings between heads of government since 1980'.[9] He enjoyed a close working relationship with Robert Armstrong and was said to have the confidence of Margaret Thatcher – needless to say he had the absolute confidence of successive Irish governments. Armstrong and Nally were central to developments in Anglo-Irish relations and personified incrementalism and the repository of bureaucratic wisdom.

THE NORTHERN IMPACT ON SOUTHERN POLITICS 1972–83

With the ongoing campaign of violence the Northern problem began to impinge on Southern politics in a period when there were signs that Ireland's economic dependence on the United Kingdom was diminishing.[10] Bipartisanship had begun to break down after 1973. One commentator lays the blame on the 1973–7 coalition. He attributes this to the coalition's belief that 'they could use the unhealed wounds of Fianna Fáil to their advantage'. The Fine Gael–Labour coalition reasoned that Fianna Fáil had not recovered from the arms trial and that a period in opposition would see the split in the party widen. While they developed a respect for Lynch, they 'did not wish to concede him a share in the electoral benefits of their moderation on the North – so appealing to the middle classes, increasingly alienated from any interest in the subject by the continuing violence – or their vaunted successes at Sunningdale'.[11] Instead Sunningdale turned sour with the collapse of the power-sharing executive, and Cosgrave turned his back on the North, leaving the SDLP high and dry. Initially the Taoiseach was inclined to blame the British, but then he turned his ire on the IRA. His ministers 'made matters worse for themselves by adopting attitudes towards the SDLP which betrayed a curious ignorance of elementary psychology ... the SDLP leaders who had been received with great warmth and hospitality in Dublin while the executive lasted now found their welcome very much cooler'.[12]

In any case a 'greener' Fianna Fáil policy had emerged in October 1975 when the party called on the British government 'to declare Britain's commitment to implement an orderly withdrawal from her involvement in the Six Counties of Northern Ireland'. The declaration was meant, its advocates claimed, to 'concentrate the minds' of unionists. The fact that it occurred in the middle of a vital by-election in a traditionally 'republican' west of Ireland constituency suggested a certain degree of opportunism. In the event Fianna Fáil lost to a government party 'grappling with huge economic difficulties and imposing severe law-and-order measures'.[13] It was indicative of a slow-burning crisis inside Fianna Fáil on policy towards Northern Ireland. The Northern issue dogged Lynch when he was returned as Taoiseach following the 1977 general election, which Fianna Fáil won with the biggest majority ever recorded in the history of the state. Lynch correctly predicted that such a majority would cause problems for his party. When Fianna Fáil performed badly in the first direct elections to the European Parliament in June 1979 – it won only 35 per cent of the vote compared to 50 per cent in 1977 – the die was cast. The election of the former Fianna Fáil minister Neil Blaney in Connacht–Ulster was interpreted by the hawkish faction within the party as 'a verdict on Lynch's Northern policy rather than as a thank you vote from sheep breeders'.[14] After Fianna Fáil lost two by-elections in Cork, one in the Taoiseach's own constituency, Lynch resigned on 5 December 1979.

He was succeeded by Charles Haughey who 'defeated George Colley by forty-four votes to thirty-eight in an election conducted in a 'sulphurous' atmosphere. Colley's immediate response, 'acknowledging loyalty to Haughey as Taoiseach, but not as leader of the party, on the grounds that Haughey had intrigued against Lynch, reflected more credit on his human than on his political instincts'.[15] So the stage was set for perpetual, bitter infighting inside Fianna Fáil that lasted beyond Haughey's demise as leader. It was an atmosphere that was not conducive to dealing with the Northern conflict in a rational and non-confrontational manner. The fact of the matter was that Haughey's politics and lifestyle provoked strong reactions. Conor Cruise O'Brien believed that 'if conditions ever became rife for a characteristically Irish Catholic form of dictatorship, Charles J. Haughey would make a

plausible enough Taoiseach/Duce'.[16] In a Dáil debate on the day
that Haughey was elected Taoiseach, the Fine Gael leader, Garret
FitzGerald, attacked his 'flawed pedigree' because, as FitzGerald explained later, 'he differed from all his predecessors in that his motives
had been and were widely impugned, most notably, although not exclusively, by people close to him within his own party ... and they
attributed to him an overwhelming ambition not simply to serve the
state but to dominate it and even to own it'.[17]

Haughey attempted to redefine Fianna Fáil's policy. By December
of 1980 he attempted to exploit the Northern question at a time when
the economy was dominating the domestic agenda, a reflection of the
fact that the governments 'of the 1970s mortgaged the future of the
country at first for narrowly partisan reasons, but ultimately in order to
avoid national bankruptcy ... It was their successors in the 1980s, and
indeed after, who ultimately paid the price.'[18] Public opinion polls at
the time indicated that the electorate believed that unemployment and
inflation should be the politicians' top priorities, with no more than 5
per cent putting Northern Ireland in that category.

Following the second Anglo-Irish summit in Dublin on 8 December
1980, a fateful phrase – the totality of relationships within these islands
– entered the lexicon.[19] In a Dáil debate three days later Charles
Haughey interpreted these words as meaning 'that the special consideration to which our next meeting will be devoted does not exclude
anything that can contribute to achieving peace, reconciliation and stability and to the improvement of relationships within these islands'.[20]
The rhetoric of a Taoiseach besieged by a faltering economy inevitably
raised the temperature in Northern Ireland, which was already at fever
pitch on account of the hunger-strike campaign. The hunger strike was
to dominate events during 1981 and do untold damage to the political
process. Despite the fact that his interpretation of the December summit had been rebuffed by Thatcher and that Anglo-Irish relations had
been damaged in consequence, Haughey used Northern Ireland again
when, on 21 May 1981, he called a general election 'because of the
grave and tragic situation in Northern Ireland'. He was seeking a clear
and definite mandate based on his policy. But it was the economy that
dominated the electorate's mind, and Haughey and Fianna Fáil went
out of power.[21]

The strains on bipartisanship meant that the SDLP had to move with
some stealth in the Republic. They had been working on the fiction
that they were neutral between the Republic's parties, a position that
was difficult to maintain given the close identification of the SDLP's
deputy leader, Seamus Mallon, with Charles Haughey. Fianna Fáil was

divided. Cosgrave's successor as leader of Fine Gael, Garret FitzGerald, was more sympathetic to the Northern party's plight. The defeat of Conor Cruise O'Brien in the 1977 election eased tensions between the SDLP and the Irish Labour Party. But the mood of the general public was not one of re-engaging with the North.

The position in London was not dissimilar. In the previous chapter we noted Labour's growing antipathy to Irish nationalism and its dependence on Ulster unionism at Westminster. But it may have been deeper than that. There was, as was also seen in the previous chapter, a tremendous amount of misperception between Dublin and London. Yet at the highest institutional levels Dublin and London may have shared the view that Northern Ireland belonged to the 'too difficult' category. That was a position suggested by a former Permanent Secretary in the Northern Ireland Office, Sir Frank Cooper, when it was put to him that his problem would have been getting the British cabinet to give Northern Ireland a high enough priority. He responded that that was not the case in the early part of the Troubles: 'What happens in the British Cabinet system of government is that people will try over a period of time to deal with a particular issue. Then it gets too difficult. You're not going to have a solution. So they put it, to use an old Irish phrase, "on the long finger" – and they don't think it's going to be soluble. They don't think it's going to be popular in terms of votes, that it's going to cause nothing but trouble.'[22] The 'nothing but trouble' school enjoyed some support from influential commentators. From 1976 onwards the *Daily Mirror* argued that Britain could not solve the 'problem of Ireland' and saw an 'independent Ulster' as the answer; by 1978 it was suggesting that the troops needed to be brought home, and by 1981 it was spelling out the logic of Irish reunification.[23] Others expressed their exasperation with Northern Ireland. Ferdinand Mount, for example, described Ian Paisley as 'probably the most widely disliked man in Great Britain', and summed up one parliamentary performance thus: 'The religious tone, the menacing prophecy, the homely detail, the promise of a huge turnout – P.T. Barnum and Elmer Gantry live on.'[24]

THE NEW IRELAND FORUM

Political opportunism was not the way to deal with the Northern conflict. Both governments realised as much when they set out on the Anglo-Irish route from 1980 onwards. But both were aware, too, of the huge depth of emotions attached to the conflict and, equally, of their own superficial grasp of the detail of history and of policy. As early as 1973 Fine Gael's John Kelly had warned the Dáil that the early 1960s 'were years in which it is possible to comb the Dáil Reports without finding so much as a single reference to the disabilities of the Northern minority'; anyone undertaking such a search 'will find it very hard to assemble half a dozen instances when the House concerned itself in the 1960s until the situation in the North exploded'.[25] Indeed it was not until 1990 that the Dáil debated Articles 2 and 3 of the constitution.[26] Less than a decade earlier, on 27 September 1981, the Taoiseach, Garret FitzGerald, launched a 'constitutional crusade' because he believed that 'this part of the country has slipped into a partitionist attitude with institutions which are acceptable to people living down here but could never be the basis to enter discussions with Unionists in Northern Ireland'. He placed his remarks in a republican context: 'What I want to do is to lead a crusade – a Republican crusade – to make this a genuine Republic on the principles of Tone and Davis.'[27]

The magnitude of the undertaking soon manifested itself. The Fianna Fáil leader, Charles Haughey, stated that the Taoiseach was guilty of self-abasement and attempting to placate unionists, who would merely use his 'reckless' statements as a propaganda weapon to oppose unity: 'I regard it as a serious undermining of our national position – the equivalent of sabotage of our national policy of unity – to attack the Constitution in the way that Dr FitzGerald has done, to attack the bona fides of politicians of all parties in the South and to attempt to suggest that our State has a sectarian basis.'[28] Here a clear line was drawn between the two leading parties in the Republic in their attitude towards Irish unity, a fissure which was to dominate the New Ireland Forum a few years later. An opinion poll in the *Sunday Tribune* in October 1981 suggested that a majority of people in the Republic disapproved of constitutional change ahead of Irish unity (52 per cent) and were against allowing divorce (53 per cent); and by a plurality of 46 per cent to 35 per cent they disapproved of dropping the constitutional claim to Northern Ireland.[29] Attitudes among the Protestant minority in the Republic were mixed. The Archbishop of Dublin, Henry McAdoo, welcomed FitzGerald's remarks, whereas another Church of Ireland bishop placed them in the context of alleged discrimination against Protestant schools in the Republic.[30] The response in Northern Ireland was equally mixed – the most strident being that of the deputy leader of the DUP, Peter Robinson MP: 'There's nothing he can do, even if he turns it upside down, which could make Protestants want to join an all-Ireland Republic. That doesn't mean that the Republic shouldn't clean out its own house.'[31] In his autobiography

FitzGerald accepted that his 'constitutional initiative was stillborn', a victim to some extent of 'the sharp swing to the right in religious as well as political affairs that had marked the first half of the 1980s'. Nevertheless he was convinced that the 'battle lines were drawn on 27 September 1981' and that his vision was 'not dead but sleeping'.[32] Many of the issues in that vision were to be revisited over the next sixteen years.

Another vision was floundering about the same time. As we saw in the previous chapter, James Prior's attempt at rolling devolution met with stout resistance from Irish nationalists. The initial response had been favourable,[33] but the Prior plan got enmeshed in Tory Party in-fighting, the Falklands campaign and ensuing worsening Anglo–Irish relations. Following four lengthy meetings with Prior the SDLP dismissed his initiative on 26 April 1982; and in a lengthy press interview John Hume made no attempt to hide his exasperation. He thought that 'Britain's problem would appear to be their psychological incapability of accepting Ireland as an independent sovereign State' and said that '"irresponsible" is not too severe to describe the British Government's failure to consult the Irish Government in the preparation of its proposals. Because, after all, the Irish Government and the people in the Republic are paying substantially in both finance and manpower because of the failure of the British Government to provide stability on a part of this island over which the people of the South have no jurisdiction.'[34] Both the SDLP and Sinn Féin contested the Assembly elections on 20 October 1982, when Sinn Féin bit into SDLP support, but neither took up its seats in the Assembly.

The process

The SDLP was now without a role, although it had built the potential for one into its manifesto for the Assembly elections. It argued that a solution could be found in the Anglo–Irish framework, and that British governments had allowed their policies 'to be dictated by the intransigence of Unionism'. Hence it was up to constitutional nationalists to spell out their proposals:

> Towards that end it is the intention of the SDLP following the election to propose to the Irish Government the setting up of a Council for a New Ireland made up of members of the Dáil and those mandated in this election. The Council should have a limited life and have the specific task of examining the obstacles to the creation of a New Ireland and producing for the first time on behalf of all the elected democratic parties in this country who believe in a New Ireland, an

agreed blue-print so that a debate on real alternatives can begin within the Anglo-Irish framework.[35]

The 'Council for a New Ireland' metamorphosed into the 'New Ireland Forum' following a meeting between Garret FitzGerald (Taoiseach and leader of Fine Gael), Dick Spring (Tánaiste and leader of the Labour Party), Charles Haughey (leader of Fianna Fáil) and John Hume (leader of the SDLP) on 21 April 1983. The metamorphosis reflected FitzGerald's concern that a 'council' might recall the ill-fated Council of Ireland of Sunningdale fame. He also wanted to ensure that participation would be 'open to all democratic parties which reject violence, and which have members elected or appointed to the Oireachtas or the Northern Ireland Assembly'.[36] Hume readily agreed to this and sold the idea to Haughey. But FitzGerald wanted to extend the consultations beyond an Irish nationalist constituency. In this he failed. The biconfessional Alliance Party refused 'to participate in its deliberations because the stated views of some of its leading participants indicated that its objective was to provide a forum for Nationalists to draw up a blueprint for a United Ireland'.[37] There were to be individual (and unofficial) submissions from two members of the Ulster Unionist Party and there were others who represented the Northern Protestant case. There was even a suggestion that the UDA planned to make a written submission (on Ulster independence) but, following the murder of three Pentecostalists by the Irish National Liberation Army at a Gospel hall on 21 November 1983, the offer was withdrawn.[38]

In essence the New Ireland Forum was to be an Irish nationalist exercise. That is not to say that each of the participating parties shared the same outlook. We have noted already profound disagreements between Fine Gael and Fianna Fáil over FitzGerald's 'constitutional crusade' and over what role unionists might play in Anglo-Irish negotiations. But there were also tensions within the different nationalist parties. FitzGerald had been taken aback when he initially took the proposal to establish the forum to his government on 22 February and had it rejected by twelve votes to two: 'they feared that if my proposal went ahead my deep concern about Northern Ireland could distract me from what they saw – with some reason – as exceptionally pressing domestic problems'.[39] It took some persuasion – and an 'incorporeal' meeting of the government – to bring them round. The Labour Party, too, had its difficulties. It was led by Dick Spring, a thirty-two-year-old barrister who had entered the Dáil in 1981 and who had to negotiate his first government in December 1982, only a few months after becoming party leader: 'The party he led into the [24 November] 1982 election was demoralised, terribly split, and above all, a virtual stranger to its leader.'[40] While the SDLP appeared to have a united front, two of its delegation were close to the Fianna Fáil leader. As the forum exercise progressed, it became obvious that only Fianna Fáil presented a united front.

These differences manifested themselves in the opening statements by the party leaders at the first public session on 30 May 1983. The Taoiseach set a deadline of the end of the year for the forum's work, declaring: 'if we are not seen to tackle it with this kind of deadline for the completion of our work, we should have no credibility with those who, in Northern Ireland, are suffering from [the conflict's] corrosive effects'.[41] He placed it, too, in the context of Anglo-Irish relations, 'given that there will be a newly-elected Government in Britain' (the UK general election was just ten days away). FitzGerald's conciliatory tone contrasted sharply with Charles Haughey's combative contribution. In his opening paragraph he announced that their purpose 'was to construct a basic position, which can then be put to an all-round constitutional conference, convened by the Irish and British Governments *as a prelude to British withdrawal*' [emphasis added]. He allowed that the discussions 'must be founded on respect for the unionist tradition, but also and equally on respect for our own'. He challenged the belief 'that we would have to jettison almost the entire ethos on which the independence movement was built and that the Irish identity has to be sacrificed to facilitate the achievement of Irish unity'. In respect of political and religious minorities in the Republic he claimed that if 'there have been blemishes, they are small ones and not necessarily all on the one side'. The Labour leader, Dick Spring, was more self-questioning. He recognised the magnitude of the challenge that faced them by quoting from the legendary socialist James Connolly and said: 'They [these words] can make us recall the historical deficiencies of political evolution in Ireland, encourage us to examine whatever social and constitutional progress we have made, and stimulate us to identify the relationship, if any, between various formal political attitudes and the daily lives and aspirations of ordinary people.' He highlighted the need to discuss and analyse church–state relations, and asserted that the forum represented 'an alternative approach, which hopefully will recognise the fundamental differences but must strive to ensure that these differences do not act as obstacles either to reconciliation or political development'. The theme of John Hume's remarks could be summed up in his phrase 'flag-waving will no longer do' and his promise that the SDLP 'shall not place either the short-term or the long-term political interest of our party above the common goal … There is no room, there is no time for opportunism or righeousness or, indeed, for what is normally understood as "politics". Only thus will those who doubt our good intentions (the unionists and British) take us seriously and start to take their own responsibilities seriously.' He displayed a similar attitude when he entered into prolonged dialogue with Gerry Adams a few years later: reconciliation was to be the way forward.

These opening statements identified the centrifugal pull at the heart of the exercise and they have to be examined in the context of the prevailing political climate. Seldom has such a radical concept been born with such scepticism. The *Irish Times* (31 May 1983) caught the mood of despondency when it set the process in the context of a very divisive campaign to introduce a constitutional amendment to prohibit abortion and reminded its readers that 'the Forum takes place in the shadow of the abandoning by Fianna Fáil and Fine Gael of a serious concern for minority views on delicate matters of religion and conscience'. A few weeks earlier the paper had suggested that the proposed amendment be referred to the forum – an early indication of how unpredictable the process could become.[42] With the exception of the *Irish News* and, to a lesser extent, the *Guardian* and the *Financial Times* it is difficult to find any medium which greeted the forum with enthusiasm and optimism. The Northern Ireland Assembly had rejected it roundly as early as 15 March. It received some neutral reportage in the United States.[43]

Since all parties were moving into uncharted territory and since they were moving implicitly from the aspirational to the operational the exercise held out great risks for leadership. Perhaps Haughey had given most by agreeing to participate – the Fianna Fáil position on Northern Ireland had been that everything should be on a negotiating table at an all-party conference, and that nationalist Ireland should not weaken its hand before then. Moreover, once Fianna Fáil were sucked into the process they might lose their independence lest they desert the SDLP in the battle against Sinn Féin. They shared with the remaining parties in the Republic the temptation to do nothing about the North in case they risked all – precisely that which they were to accuse Britain of in the forum's final report. There was the further danger that the forum would have a destabilising effect on a fragile polity because it presupposed a critical examination of society in the Republic. Had the leaders been aware initially that they were expected to put a phenomenal amount of time into the forum it is conceivable that they would have turned their backs on it.

The SDLP had much to gain but everything to lose if the forum went wrong. It feared a republican resurgence – Sinn Féin took 10.1 per cent of the vote in the 1982 Assembly elections (from an electoral base of zero) and 13.4 per cent at the 1983 general election, when Gerry Adams won West Belfast for the first time. The SDLP had abandoned the Assembly; it had grave doubts about the commitment beyond rhetoric of the Southern parties to a new Ireland; and it had to ensure that it maintained its delicate, even-handed approach to its forum partners. Yet it also needed to establish its presence among the newer generation of Dáil politicians. In that last respect it succeeded. Seán Farren, a member of the SDLP delegation, noted that the 'Labour Party in the South distrusted us. They saw the SDLP as a sectarian party . . . Our relations with Southern parties apart from leadership level were not cemented until the New Ireland Forum.' His colleague Paddy O'Hanlon concurred. Critical of the lack of Southern involvement in the Northern Ireland question since partition, he saw the forum as 'the first sign of genuine coherent interest in the problem. The fact that they [Southern parties] had come in from the cold was enough for me. I just wanted them to address this problem regarding the conflict. Symbolically [the forum's report] was a very important document, and really committed them to what has become a much more urgent process where they feel there is something in it for them too.'[44]

Discussion of the final report is to get ahead of the narrative; it did not appear until 2 May 1984. In all there were twenty-eight private sessions, thirteen public sessions, fifty-six meetings of a steering group, and numerous meetings of subgroups which examined economic issues and alternative constitutional structures in detail. It was obvious from the outset that this was a hazardous undertaking. Following the opening session one commentator suggested that if the four leaders held rigidly to their opening public positions 'then this latest political initiative is set to fail'.[45] There were even problems about choosing a chairman. The Fianna Fáil leader vetoed two of the names put forward: Declan Costello, a High Court judge and former Fine Gael politician, and T.K. Whitaker, former Secretary of the Department of Finance. There was agreement on a third: Colm Ó hEocha, president of University College Galway and a distinguished marine scientist with no known political affiliation. He had his work cut out: 'As chairman he had the wisdom to employ a very loose rein in handling his four headstrong steeds.'[46] In trying to set the tone at the opening session he quoted some Scots Gaelic words, 'Mo shúile togam súas' ('I raise my eyes') – the inscription on the crest of the University of Calgary, Alberta – in an effort to show some empathy with Northern Protestants as well as to exhort the Forum participants to get 'away from the immediate problem, lift up our eyes and seek to become innovative and imaginative'.[47] Ó hEocha avoided the temptation of becoming the 'fifth voice' in the forum. His was a self-effacing, even-tempered and patient role which made a positive contribution to the demeanour of the public and private proceedings.

A second operational consideration was the composition of the secretariat. An eight-man team emerged, led by Jack Tobin, who was appointed secretary. Tobin, formerly Clerk to the Senate, was at the head of a young and dynamic team. In the beginning his fastidious approach irritated some of his younger colleagues but, on reflection, they acknowledged that his painstaking manner and old-fashioned courtly approach served as a useful restraint on their enthusiasm. The coordinator of the secretariat was Wally Kirwan from the Taoiseach's department, who was recognised by all as one of the key players. Kirwan had been at Sunningdale in 1973 and was married to a Northern Catholic. He had a keen interest in the issue and played an important role in drafting various documents and the final report.[48] Among others who were influential were Colm Larkin, considered to be close to the SDLP and a Eurocrat who had worked in the *cabinets* of two Irish European Commissioners, Dick Burke and Michael O'Kennedy; Ted Smyth, who was seconded from the Department of Foreign Affairs; Richard O'Toole, seconded from the Organisation for Economic Cooperation and Development; and Ciaran Murphy from University College Galway, the choice of Colm Ó hEocha. The remaining two members, Hugh Finlay and Frank Sheridan, were drawn from the Irish civil service. The secretariat were considered to reflect the diverse political views of the delegates themselves, and all had to be agreed by the party leaders. One view of their role was that in times of crisis some of them – particularly Kirwan, Smyth and O'Toole – were proactive: 'There was one occasion about four months ago, when members were wondering whether they should just go ahead and take the Fianna Fáil option of a unitary state and not bother with anything else. Immediately the secretariat started drawing up documentation on *all* the other options, joint authority, federal state etc. Ó hEocha took their lead.'[49]

A third consideration was the size of each party delegation. John Hume was anxious to secure as many positions for his Assembly members as possible since they had forfeited their Assembly salaries. After two meetings of the party leaders on 14 and 21 April 1983 it was agreed that each party would send delegates and alternates in proportion to their parliamentary representation. Hence Fianna Fáil secured nine delegates and four alternates, Fine Gael eight and three, and Labour and the SDLP five delegates, although the SDLP had five alternates to Labour's two. Each party also appointed a secretary to its delegation, and as a result eleven of the SDLP's fourteen Assembly members found themselves in gainful employment for the lifetime of the forum.

Fianna Fáil's was the most disciplined delegation. They all followed the party line throughout, and three of their alternates uttered not a word during the entire proceedings of the forum's plenary sessions. In addition some of their more senior members played a low-key role. With the exception of David Andrews the Fianna Fáil team was in the Haughey mould. The delegation was dominated by Haughey and Ray MacSharry, a former Tánaiste and Minister for Finance, with support from Brian Lenihan.[50] One Fianna Fáil member who impressed as being independent-minded was Jimmy Leonard, who represented the border constituency of Cavan–Monaghan and hence was much closer to the Northern conflict.

The Fine Gael team did not always speak with one voice. Peter Barry's position as Minister for Foreign Affairs ensured that he could not always be present. Jim Dooge, who had been Minister for Foreign Affairs in 1981–2 and was a close ally of the Taoiseach, was relatively muted, and Myra Barry, the young TD for Cork East – physically as far removed from Northern Ireland as was possible – played no visible role. It was two of the newer generation of Fine Gael politicians, Maurice Manning and Enda Kenny, along with the three alternates (Nora Owen, David Molony and Ivan Yates) who made a big impression. Two members of the Fine Fael delegation who would have been expected to figure prominently – Paddy Harte and John Kelly – were surprisingly quiet. Harte had been in the Dáil since 1961 representing Donegal North-East, the constituency that shared the border with Derry. He had single-handedly made contact with many unionists of all tendencies, from paramilitaries to Ian Paisley. He had co-authored with FitzGerald a seminal Fine Gael document on the conflict.[51] Yet he appeared to be unhappy with the process. FitzGerald considered that he might have been losing some perspective 'and I had subsequently found it wise to distance him to some degree from the Northern Ireland issue. He never quite came to terms with the Forum project.'[52] Kelly, an academic lawyer, was a cerebral individualist. We have noted already how critical he had been of the lack of attention to the North on the part of successive Irish governments. His demeanour irritated the Taoiseach: 'At times I felt it difficult to keep patience with this persistent attempt to question the whole rationale of the Forum.'[53] Like Harte, Kelly failed to play a prominent role in the forum, and even those sympathetic to his liberal credentials bemoaned the fact that he absented himself for a crucial period of the deliberations when chapters 4 and 5 of the final report were being negotiated.

None of this would have been visible to the naked eye. Initially the Irish public generally showed little interest in the proceedings of the forum. Indeed it is not certain that all of the participants went into it believing that it would be anything more than a talking shop.[54] There were particular concerns about the attitude of Charles Haughey. One commentator quoted 'some people who have attended the private sessions' who feared 'that he sees it less as an instrument for promoting Irish unity, than for spreading egg all over the face of Garret Fitz-Gerald. Position papers prepared by the Forum's fulltime secretariat have been dismissed by the Fianna Fáil leader as irrelevant. Meanwhile, members of his party have taken up a considerable amount of time at the Forum's private meetings raising questions about the Irish language and the position of the GAA in a United Ireland.'[55] Yet Fianna Fáil participation was soon to be challenged. On 18 August 1983 the *Irish Press* carried in full a leaked document, 'Framework for Discussion of Fundamental Problems', which had been tabled at the forum on 10 August.[56] The document stated bluntly that the 'work of the Forum is neither academic nor abstract. It takes place against a background of deep division and threatening violence. The crisis which the Forum attempts to address involves intolerable human misery. It follows that the *Forum must be prepared to consider all options, including those which have hitherto not been examined*, once they meet the criteria of pragmatism, durability and justice' (emphasis added). It asked pointedly: 'how could we demonstate with the maximum credibility that we are, with the support of our people, ready to face some of the more expensive or otherwise uncongenial adjustments that this would involve for the Irish Constitution and the Irish State as at present structured and administered? For example, in the difficult area of Church–State relations as they affect family law, education and the administration of the health services?'

Three points can be made about the leaked document. The first, which relates to the particular significance of the church–state comment, is that this issue was being raised in the middle of a divisive referendum campaign on abortion – a point that was raised by political commentators at the time.[57] The second is that the document was an early indication of how serious and far-reaching was this exercise; it suggested that the forum could go beyond a stale reiteration of the case for a united Ireland and look at several options.[58] The third is that the leak led to much closer control of the process by the party leaders. That may have damaged a growing collegial spirit: certainly when the forum resumed after the summer break some delegates felt that too much power had been retained by the leaders.[59]

Even before the forum resumed after the summer recess another important decision had been taken. On 15 September the economic consultants Davy Kelleher McCarthy were commissioned to prepare a study that 'should examine by comparison with the existing situation the possibilities, costs, and benefits to each of the parties involved in integrated economic planning and coordination in Ireland' for each of the following scenarios: (a) a unitary Irish state; (b) a federal/confederal state in Ireland; (c) joint Irish/British authority in Northern Ireland.[60] From the outset then it was evident that this was going to be a thorough investigation that would spread well beyond a traditional exposition of the Irish nationalist case.

Another dose of realism was imposed at the first public session of the forum on 21 September when two economists, Sir Charles Carter and Professor Louden Ryan, presented their pessimistic analysis of a unitary Ireland's economic prospects. In place of the formal vote of thanks moved by the other three leaders the Fianna Fáil leader offered his own prognosis of the economists' analyses: 'These two eminent economists have painted in varying degrees a bleak and depressing picture. We must take this into account in our thinking. I would like to suggest to the Forum that we look on that more as a challenge or difficulty to be overcome rather than as a dismal fate to be accepted passively. In that connection this Forum must reject positively certain concepts that were put before us this morning.' Haughey's philippic was not well received by the other leaders and it was noticeable that he made no such attempt at any of the remaining public sessions. He lost support, too, with elements of Northern nationalism. An erstwhile supporter, the *Irish News*, in a strong leader agreed heartily with Haughey's rebuke, adding 'we would question his timing'.[61]

One other aspect of the proceedings of that day deserves comment in the light of reaction to the Anglo-Irish Agreement of November 1985. Towards the end of his submission Sir Charles Carter commented that economic considerations point the same way as the judgement of political realities:

> this is a problem which has always had a British dimension as well as an Irish dimension and there is no solution which sacrifices one to the other. That may mean that your search for constitutional innovation has to be along novel paths, paths it would be impertinent for me to speculate about, but I would suggest that you must search for a solution within the constraint that you must leave good ground for a continuing British economic responsibility for the welfare of those who are and wish to remain British subjects.[62]

It might be suggested that that was precisely what the architects of the Anglo-Irish Agreement put in place two years later, and yet by then Carter was in the forefront of a new 'clerisy' denouncing the agreement and all its works.[63] It is a point to which we shall return.

The debate about economic prospects has to be set alongside another contentious political reality – a conservative reaction to a 'liberal agenda' that played out in the Republic through much of the 1980s and 1990s. The

> high points of this particular struggle were the 'moral' referenda on the constitution – abortion in 1983, divorce in 1986, abortion again in 1992 and divorce again in 1995. More generally, party political differences over these and related issues – usually between what is portrayed as the social conservatism of Fianna Fáil on the one side, and the liberalism of Labour, sometimes of Fine Gael and more latterly of the Progressive Democrats on the other – served as important axes of differentiation in Irish electoral politics for much of the last three decades.[64]

The forum session on the economy occurred just two weeks after 67 per cent (in a 54 per cent turnout) voted in favour of a constitutional prohibition on the legislation of abortion. This statistic can be read in the wider context of decline in religious practice: 'Certain indicators of Catholic affiliation have shown substantial decline in recent years (weekly church attendance, for example, which in the early 1970s had been practised by more than 90 per cent of Catholics in Ireland had fallen to almost 80 per cent by the late 1980s and to below 65 per cent by 1995 ...). The Catholic Church had also been badly hit by sexual scandals in the 1990s, especially regarding child sexual abuse by clergy.' Another indicator was the growth in non-marital births. They accounted for less than 3 per cent of all births in the early 1960s: 'By 1996, one in four births (24.7 per cent) took place outside of marriage. In 1992 (the most recent year for which relevant data are available), 34.6 per cent of *first* births (that is, of new family formations) took place outside of marriage.'[65]

The 1983 abortion referendum was one of the battles in this conflict between liberal and conservative visions of Ireland's future – and it was being fought at an embarrassing time for those who wanted the forum to succeed. The *Sunday Times* was not slow to make connections: 'The Irish referendum decision, making abortion unconstitutional in the Republic as well as illegal, is one more sign that the idea of Irish unity is dead ... The SDLP, as the constitutionally-minded Catholic party, should stop hankering after unattainable change and start work in his [James Prior's] frozen assembly.'[66] The *Financial Times* was much more upbeat. It detected new thinking coming out of the forum which 'has begun to turn away from visionary ideas of a unitary state and to become more practical'. It raised, possibly for the first time, the concept of joint sovereignty and commented that it would be 'a recognition that merely to stick with the *status quo* is unsatisfactory'.[67]

The new thinking illustrated the distance between Fianna Fáil and the other forum teams. With the introduction of options other than Irish unity, the traditional Fianna Fáil position had to be protected. The party's head of research, Dr Martin Mansergh, who played a key role throughout the forum exercise, was called in to bat against the 'revisionists'. One of the high priests of this black art was Dr John Bowman, whose *De Valera and the Ulster Question 1917–1973* was published in 1982. It was a book of some influence and was awarded the Christopher Ewart-Biggs Memorial Literary Prize for the contribution it made towards improving Anglo-Irish relations and fostering peace and reconciliation in Ireland. But it was revisionist. According to Mansergh it did not recognise 'the Fianna Fáil position [as] enunciated by Eamon de Valera which sought a united Ireland in the form of a unitary state'. Bowman's crime was that he had 'been propagating the notion that de Valera was a federalist'. Mansergh was concerned: 'Indeed, Bowman contrives to present de Valera half seriously as the founding father of revisionism, while simultaneously censuring him as a blinkered irredentist. It would be about as sensible for party followers to take de Valera's Northern policy from Bowman, as it would be for Christians to take their religion from Voltaire.'[68]

This was not simply a matter of two distinguished historians disagreeing on interpretation. It really had become an article of faith inside Fianna Fáil that there could be no movement beyond the unitary state model. An alternative model – joint sovereignty – was being discussed seriously as early as November 1983. On the eve of a meeting between Garret FitzGerald and Margaret Thatcher London Weekend Television devoted an hour to Northern Ireland.[69] The programme's presenter, Brian Walden, interviewed three prominent Conservative MPs, Sir Humphrey Atkins (a former Secretary of State for Northern Ireland), Brian Mawhinney and Peter Bottomley (both of whom were to become ministers in Northern Ireland), on the topic of joint sovereignty. The fact that there was no unanimity was less important than that it was on the agenda and that London was beginning to take seriously the forum exercise. Joint sovereignty also made an appearance at the forum early in December when it was raised by two academics and (very impressively) by the Irish Information Partnership, a London-based research group. In its turn that led to some media speculation.[70]

By February 1984 the Fianna Fáil leader was raising questions about whether an agreed conclusion on the major constitutional issues could be reached.[71] Later that month there was acrimony at a private session of the forum, with Fianna Fáil 'insisting that the Forum's report should be a clear call for a unitary State', whereas the other parties 'are in favour of a report which would set out a range of alternative structures and relationships, including various forms of joint sovereignty for the North'.[72] There was also speculation of a split in the SDLP along the same lines.[73]

We have spent some little time sketching in the prevailing conditions for two reasons. One is to highlight the tensions existing within the forum, tensions that were to be reflected in the final report in May 1984 and the subsequent selling of it. An internal draft document from as early as 8 November 1983 gives some indication of the manner in which the forum sought to handle these tensions. A 'Digest of Discussions by Forum' was broken down into four sections.[74] Section (1) dealt with 'The need for a major reassessment by Britain of its policy in Northern Ireland with an emphasis on the growth in alienation among Northern nationalists in the previous three years', and the 'factor of inertia whereby, it is always easier to do nothing than to do something'. Section (2), 'The Unionist Tradition and the Loyalist Ethos', admitted that it 'is not enough to say that nationalists do not discriminate against religious minorities in the Republic' and acknowledged 'that it will take a very long time for this feeling of being under threat to wane'. Section (3), 'The Nationalist Aspiration', was further subdivided into 'Southern Nationalism', 'Northern Nationalism', and 'Nationalist Aspirations, North and South'; section 3 discarded the notion of discussing only power-sharing for the North since 'this would be opposed by the unionists because they would regard it as a back door to Irish unity'. Section (3) also recognised that it was the security forces who took the brunt of the violence, but added that 'violence can also be an expression of the way people feel about a situation and an expression of hopelessness' – here was the opening gambit in the talks which were to begin with Sinn Féin some years later. The fourth section recognised that unionists might feel that if the political situation was reversed nationalists would treat them in a similar fashion to their own treatment over the previous sixty years: 'This is not an insoluble problem but the Forum will have to take adequate cognisance of it.' Given the welter of evidence and historical prejudice with which they were confronted it is not entirely surprising that unanimity did not prevail in the end.

That brings us to the second reason, and it is a question of time

– why did the exercise take so long? The simple, and obvious, reason lay in the complexity of the issues and the process. A senior Fianna Fáil source maintained that it was impossible 'to reach a solution to the problem of centuries within a schedule of weeks'; it was quite unrealistic, he argued, 'to expect politicians in what amounted to a spare time Assembly to reach agreement on fundamentals in so short a period'.[75] Nevertheless two important deadlines were missed. The Taoiseach had hoped to be in a position to present the forum's final report during his annual St Patrick's Day visit to Washington. Secondly, and more importantly, many in the forum wanted the publication of their report to coincide with that of a report on Northern Ireland commissioned by the European Parliament – the Haagerup Report.[76] What both the United States visit and Haagerup had in common was the international dimension to the forum exercise.

Haagerup's initial report was first debated at the Political Affairs Committee in Brussels in January, where it was warmly welcomed by all parties including, surprisingly, the British Conservatives.[77] It stressed the need for increased economic aid and Anglo-Irish co-operation to bring about 'a political system with an equitable sharing of Government responsibilities'. It was adopted by the committee on 29 February, although the two Northern Ireland unionist MEPs, Ian Paisley and John Taylor, voted against it. In the meantime the work of the forum was praised by New Zealand's Prime Minister, Robert Muldoon, on a visit to Dublin.[78] In March the forum was endorsed by 100 members of Congress, and most emphatically by President Reagan two days later.[79] Finally at the end of March the Haagerup Report was adopted by the European Parliament by 124 votes to 3, with 63 abstentions. The three who voted against were the two unionist MEPs and the Independent Fianna Fáil MEP, Neil Blaney. The abstention bloc was that of the British Conservatives in deference to Margaret Thatcher's belief that the European Parliament should have no say in Northern Ireland's future. Nevertheless the report was historic in that it was 'the first official policy declaration on Northern Ireland by an EEC institution'.[80]

Before we consider the forum report we need to refer to one other study commissioned by the forum and to one other public session. The study, *The Cost of Violence Arising from the Northern Ireland Crisis Since 1969*, appeared four days before a London summit between FitzGerald and Thatcher in November 1983. In that respect it fitted into the Anglo-Irish context, which some read in a cynical fashion.[81] Others showed little sympathy. The DUP's Chief Whip, Jim Allister, said: 'Considering that the authorities in the Republic spawned the terrorism which they now find rather costly to contain, one finds it difficult to excite any sympathy for them.' His Alliance Party counterpart, John Cushnahan, said: 'While it may be useful to know the exact cost of terrorist violence, the more important question that the report fails to answer is how to create a set of political circumstances in which the effects of terrorism can be minimised.' His answer was that 'a solution can only be based on a power-sharing settlement in Northern Ireland'.[82] The study calculated that the total costs of the violence were £11 billion sterling – £9 billion for the British exchequer and £2 billion for the Irish.[83] Beyond these bald statistics the real message of the study was in the human and social costs: more than 2,300 people had died as a result of the violence since 1969; more than 24,000 had been injured or maimed in 43,000 incidents of terrorism. Those killed included 722 members of the security forces (including prison officers), 278 paramilitaries and 1,297 civilians. Republicans were responsible for 1,264 deaths, loyalists for 613 and the security forces for 264 (the discrepancy in the figures comes about because of a 'non-classified' heading). The analysis highlights the extent to which Catholics were the victims of their *soi-disant* republican protectors. No less than 703 of the civilian fatalities were Catholics; and if we examine the major centres of violence and its economic consequences a similar picture emerges – the Catholic working class has suffered the most.

The public session that requires some attention was the presentation by the Irish Episcopal Conference delegation on 9 February 1984, the very last such event before the presentation of the report itself on 2 May. One of the features of the public sessions was the attempt to engage unionist and Protestant opinion. Hence the forum heard from a high-powered Church of Ireland group representing both sides of the border; a prominent Methodist minister, Rev. Sydney Callaghan; a former Moderator of the Presbyterian Church, Dr S.J. Park; Rev. William T. McDowell representing the Presbyterian Synod of Dublin; and Dr George Gordon Dallas on behalf of an interdenominational Bible study group based at Clonard Monastery in Belfast whose simple message was the need for spiritual preparation in readiness for a unitary state. The unionist case was put by, among others, Christopher and Michael McGimpsey and Sir John Biggs-Davison, a Conservative back-bencher.[84] But despite these voices the forum's deliberations lacked a significant unionist input and its report suffered accordingly.

That the Catholic bishops came in at the very end was an interesting fact in its own right. They came in very reluctantly and very hurriedly – their submission came in five parts, each typed on a different typewriter and believed to be the work of a separate group of bishops. The forum had approached the Catholic bishops in October 1983. They eventually produced their hurried written submission in January 1984, – citing communication problems, the bureaucratic structure of the hierarchy and the fact that Christmas was 'one of the busiest times in the Church's calendar' as reasons for the delay. They also explained that they could not make an oral submission in the near future 'because the panel members have now made other commitments'.[85] Not surprisingly, their submission, particularly in its opposition to divorce law in a united Ireland, drew criticism from the unionist parties as well as the SDLP and Sinn Féin.[86] To compound matters, in a radio interview on 15 January the Archbishop of Armagh, Cardinal Tomás Ó Fiaich, said that people might be morally justified in joining or supporting Sinn Féin if they did it for 'local community activities'.[87] Hence there was huge interest when they did make an appearance in February. The very contentious 1983 referendum on abortion was still in people's minds. The moral climate was changing,[88] and it would be interesting to gauge how the hierarchy was responding. But more profoundly the encounter would be historic because the 'Republic of Ireland is one of the few remaining nations of Christendom where the overlapping presence of Church and state are almost equally visible ... and where the contrast between the new pluralism on the surface of Irish political society and the confessionalism still underlying it' needed to be probed.[89]

The bishops' submission dealt with five issues: ecumenism; the family; pluralism; Alienation of Catholics in Northern Ireland; and the Catholic school system in Northern Ireland. In essence their views were based on an assessment of how the 'common good' is defined and how that affected majority–minority relationships:

> To require in the name of pluralism that public policy tolerate or even facilitate forms of public morality of which the majority of the citizens could not approve may sometimes be reasonable in the interests of the common good of harmony between all the citizens; but where the offence to the moral principles of the majority of the citizens would be disproportionately serious it is not unreasonable to require sacrifice of minorities in the interests of the common good.[90]

To reinforce the point, the submission cites a judgement given by Mr Justice Frankfurter of the US Supreme Court in 1943 in which he stated that 'to deny the political power of the majority to erect laws concerned with civil matters simply because they may offend the conscience of a minority really means that the consciences of a minority are more sacred and more enshrined in the Constitution than the consciences of a majority'. What the submission failed to point out was that this was a minority judgement and was repudiated by the judgements of a majority of the court. In fact the Supreme Court decision 'completely refutes the Hierarchy's argument for majority rule in matters affecting conscience'.[91] In some senses that set the tone for the oral submission.

The bishops' performance was described as 'politically brilliant, occasionally spectacular. At the end of the day, they left it up to the politicians to make up their minds about the shape of a New Ireland. But if they don't like it they'd probably be just as happy to live within the old partitionist mould, and speak out against whatever they objected to.'[92] That was a fair assessment of the political schizophrenia on display – such as divorce rights for Northern Protestants but not for their Southern counterparts. And when the Bishop of Down and Connor, Dr Cahal Daly, diverted a question from Fine Gael's John Kelly on the grounds that it was a 'political question' he received the reply: 'It is not a political question, but I do agree that it is probably the first time since St Patrick arrived in Ireland that the representatives of the Hierarchy were asked to think on their feet.'[93] That retort symbolised the collapse of deference in church–state relations in Ireland. But the session was important for more reasons than that. Firstly, it was important that it happened at all. Even sceptical commentators accepted that 'it shows how valuable the Forum can be in opening up a dialogue on Church-State relations, particularly in the South'.[94] Secondly, it dealt unequivocally with the question of the 'armed struggle' when Cahal Daly stated: 'I declare in the name of the whole Episcopal Conference that it is totally unjustified, immoral.'[95] Finally, it dealt with the Irish constitution when Cahal Daly accepted that there 'is no way that the Constitution we now have could be imposed on Northern Ireland Unionists'.[96] The *Economist* described that remark as 'pregnant with significance within Ireland' because 'the elected and spiritual leaders had publicly and formally cast doubt on the Irish republic's constitution'. In other words, the forum 'had done what its inventors hoped. It had addressed a sign of friendship and co-operation not only to Ulster Unionists – nobody expected them to be much impressed by the hierarchy's views – but to the government and people of the United Kingdom within which the Unionists insist on remaining.'[97]

The report

After the meeting with the Irish Episcopal Conference speculation grew that the forum process was nearing completion. The fact that it was to take nearly another three months was indicative of the intensity of the debate. In early April there were indications that 12 April had been tentatively decided as a date by which the final recommendations should be published.[98] But by mid-April there were indications that the Minister for Foreign Affairs, Peter Barry, was contemplating that they might not reach full agreement on all aspects of the report and that, whereas the Fianna Fáil leader would prefer an agreed report, Charles Haughey's room for manoeuvre was limited by those in his party who insisted on a unitary state and a rejection of all other 'models'.[99] By this stage it was clear that there was a stand-off between Haughey and the other three party leaders – as well as some consternation inside Fianna Fáil itself among a faction concerned that a hard-line approach could be damaging to the process.[100] An optimistic construction could be placed on this divergence of opinion: 'it could mean that the members were using their grey matter on the North as they had not done for sixty years ... They had to leave aside much of the rhetoric of the decades and address themselves to practical considerations. They had much to unlearn.'[101] Despite the varying quality of its final report, the New Ireland Forum was a serious exercise in 'unlearning' and in catharsis.

Eventually agreement was reached that the report would be published on 2 May. Given the number of leaks there was little in the report that had not been predicted. Indeed from the outset opponents of the process such as Robert McCartney argued that it would not be a catalyst for change, that there was little likelihood of it 'being able to produce a blueprint for pluralism in the teeth of opposition from the Church and partitionist republicanism'.[102] McCartney was but one of a long line of critics who insisted on viewing the forum as a giant public relations exercise in starry-eyed nationalism. There was some truth in this but it presupposed a uniformity in approach by the party leaders which, as we have seen, was lacking from the outset. Friend and foe agreed that the report was a *nationalist* report, replete with a nationalist interpretation of Irish history. There is in the report, however, a general acceptance that partition can be overcome only through consent and that the unionist sense of British identity must be preserved and protected.[103] Once the latter point was accepted 'a new objective was then set out: to broaden the definition of Irish identity so as to include the hitherto denied or execrated identity of the Ulster Unionist'.[104] This 'very acknowledgement of Ulster Unionist parity represented a striking change in several senses' ... 'First, it accepted a subjective basis for self-identification ... Secondly, to face the fact that northern Unionists defined themselves as British, Protestant and intermeshed socially and economically with the motherland may have been merely to face the obvious. It was none the less a radical departure, a recognition of how things actually were, and therefore a mental admission of the true proportions of the problem. Last but far from least, the volte face constituted an *implicit* confession of past error and arrogance.'[105]

We need to pause at this point to consider the import of these remarks by reference to critical appraisals of the New Ireland Forum. Paul Bew and Henry Patterson dismiss the report as 'singularly banal and traditional on the central question of Ulster Unionism'.[106] Clare O'Halloran placed the forum in the context of previous full-scale propaganda initiatives, the North-Eastern Boundary Bureau in the 1920s and the All-Party Anti-Partition Conference thirty years later: 'it merely clothed traditional values and aspirations in a new language of pluralism and deferred the question of fundamental change. Its attraction lies in its ambiguities and the fact that it is open to diverse interpretation'; and it succeeded in 'bringing anti-partition rhetoric to a new level of sophistication'.[107] On the other hand, Arthur Aughey took a slightly broader approach when he argued that while 'there was little that was new in the Forum Report ... it helped to put the Irish dimension back into focus'.[108] That last remark at least had the merit of paying some obeisance to the wider picture and of showing some understanding of political process. Of course there were ambiguities, and of course final status issues were deferred. It is true, for example, that the forum did not spell out what it meant by 'consent', but the concept was now open for discussion, and its relevance increased with the signing of the Anglo-Irish Agreement eighteen months later.[109] Politicians are no different from the rest of us in avoiding the harshness of unpalatable realities. But this much can be said: the considerable amount of work undertaken by the forum to flesh out the bones of a hitherto very basic demand for Irish unity was to feed into the political debate over the following fifteen years.

It is indisputable that a constitutional nationalist perspective pervades the report, particularly since the unitary state model took pole position: 'The particular structure of political unity which the Forum *would* wish to see established is a unitary state, achieved by agreement and consent, embracing the whole island of Ireland and providing irrevocable guarantees for the protection and preservation of both the unionist and nationalist identities.'[110] We are entering the realm of textual exegesis here. It is interesting to compare a draft of the report dated 27 April and the final report five days later. The changes made during these few days are indicative of the stand-off between Fianna Fáil and the rest. The use of the conditional in relation to the unitary state model in paragraph 5.7

(quoted above) is a case in point.[111] Other last-minute changes can be found in paragraphs 5.1(3), 5.2(3), 5.10, 6.1, 6.4 and 6.7. Space does not permit us to examine these in detail but a few points can be made. Besides constitutional issues the changes are concerned with church–state, language and cultural matters. They go back to the original centrifugal pull in the leaders' opening addresses and the extent to which there were 'blemishes' (to quote Charles Haughey) in the Republic in respect of political and religious minorities. The Fianna Fáil position was uncomplicated: put the strongest case for the ideal of the unitary state and waste no time on other considerations.

In many respects – in terms of an ongoing process – the key paragraph became 5.10: 'The Parties in the Forum also remain open to discuss other views which may contribute to political development.' The insertion of the word 'also' created major problems for Fianna Fáil. In interview one of the party's senior delegates told me that the whole paragraph was 'superfluous'. Others held the view that constitutional nationalists could not engage the British government if the forum emphasis remained on the unitary state and the removal of the British guarantee. The word was contested right to the very end: 'It became the real crunch in terms of "also" being there . . . It's the fourth open-ended option.'[112] It was an option which reappeared when the House of Commons debated the forum's report two months later and the SDLP leader challenged the Northern Secretary on the government's views of the three options: 'Let us hear what they think of those proposals. Let us not hide behind the Unionists.' Hume went on to say that 'only within a British–Irish framework can the solution be found'; and, significantly: 'The most important aspect of the report is not the three options, but the views of Irish Nationalists about the ways in which realities must be faced if there is to be a solution.'[113]

Before we move on to consider how the report was received let us make a few positive points about the process. Echoing Hume's parliamentary remarks above, Oliver MacDonagh wrote that it is 'of some interest that for the first time – at any rate since de Valera's abortive Document No. 2 – Irish nationalists have produced a specific constitutional scheme or agenda for negotiation with Great Britain'. Concentrating on the broader picture and bringing to bear 'a distant historical perspective', MacDonagh detected the 'beginnings of a profound change of mind and attitude on the part at least of one of the key parties to the imbroglio. The Irish constitutional nationalists had shifted their hereditary ground, had thrown over received assumptions.' He saw three alterations as being particularly significant:

First, not only was violence repudiated conjointly with unprecedented solemnity and finality but so also – and much more significantly – was even psychological coercion of the Ulster Unionists.

Secondly, the case for the basic common interests of North and
South was both elaborated and placed in the foreground. This was
new. In place of vague, bloated assertion, a specific argument of advantage was moderately pressed in terms of needless duplication . . .
All this emblemized an earnestness in the attempted reconciliation,
and a turning away from the horrid rhetoric of rights and right-
eousness. The third changed state of mind, the crucial one, was the
directly political . . . Even Proposal 1 (the unitary state) had no real
precedent in modern Irish history. The revolutionary change was the
open gratuitous acknowledgement by the Forum that the Ulster
Unionist identity was both fundamentally different and a permanent
condition. This represents surely the first breaking of the ideological
ice jam.[114]

In light of the burgeoning Anglo-Irish relationship and particularly the
historic compromise (between unionism and nationalism/republican-
ism) of the 1998 agreement, this analysis is pertinent.

THE AFTERMATH

Any possibility of a cool and reasoned debate on the report itself was
shattered when Charles Haughey distanced himself from the other
party leaders on the day of publication by arguing that a unitary state
was the only solution to the island's problems and that nobody was
entitled to deny the national unity of the country. Neither of the other
two suggested arrangements – joint authority and a federal arrangement – would bring peace and stability, which were the forum's ob-
jectives: 'In my view the right answer to the problem is the
establishment of a unitary state, the constitution for which would be
written by an all-round conference called by the British and Irish governments, as set out in the report.'[115] Within a day he was appealing to
politicians and commentators to concentrate on the broad areas of
agreement achieved by the forum.[116] Two days later the influential
Fianna Fáil TD (and forum delegate) Ray MacSharry was restating
Fianna Fáil orthodoxy; and later that week Fianna Fáil were accusing
the Irish government of 'walking away from the Forum Report'.[117]
This view was clearly out of kilter with the opinions of the other party
leaders and indeed most of Irish nationalist opinion (including some
within Fianna Fáil).[118] Unionist opinion formers made much of the
division.[119] Generally, however, British editorial opinion was favourable, as a perusal of the *Daily Express, Daily Mirror, Guardian, Observer,*

Financial Times, New Statesman and *Economist* demonstrates. A common theme was that the British government had to give the Irish issue a high priority.[120] Generally the report received a fair wind in the British political establishment, which an *Irish Times* editorial perceived as 'evidence of British willingness to learn, to think afresh, to admit past mistakes'.[121]

More importantly, the report received widespread and positive international coverage in all the EEC countries, Japan, Canada and the US. The *Washington Post* (7 May) described it as 'an opening statement in what its writers hope will be a continuing debate'; the Baltimore *Sun* (7 May) called it 'a remarkable political gesture and a positive development'; and the *Philadelphia Inquirer* (6 May) said that it constituted 'an act of courageous realism, an extraordinary accomplishment in the context of Ireland's mortal passions'. It was welcomed, too, by leading Irish-American politicians and by the US State Department.[122] All of that would have been to the satisfaction of the forum architects who had planned a diplomatic offensive. The Minister for Foreign Affairs, Peter Barry, who had flown to Washington to brief US politicians, said that he was 'very pleased that men of Senator Kennedy's and President Reagan's stature in world politics show an interest in Ireland's progress', and that he was 'not in any sense trying to line up the US administration against the UK Government'.[123] In light of Fianna Fáil's more aggressive stance that latter statement from Peter Barry was especially significant because the New Ireland Forum process was both endogenous and exogenous – endogenous in that it was drawing to a close civil war politics in the Republic and was beginning to address the Northern Ireland conflict in a rational and calculated manner for the first time; exogenous in that it was maintaining that the Northern Ireland conflict was in reality an Anglo-Irish conflict writ small. Before we turn to the exogenous we need to make a final comment on the forum's impact.

One of the strange ironies of the process was that it spawned a cottage industry of constitutional speculation. The UUP and DUP reacted with pre-emptive responses: *Devolution and the Northern Ireland Assembly: The Way Forward* and *Ulster: The Future Assured* respectively. In addition there was an academic critique by Kevin Boyle and Tom Hadden, *How to Read the New Ireland Forum Report: Searching Between the Lines for a Realistic Framework for Action* (June 1984); a report from a joint Liberal/Social Democratic Party commission chaired by Lord Donaldson (who had been a junior Northern Ireland Office minister in 1974–6), *What Future for Northern Ireland?* (July 1985); a Conservative Party Research Department document, *Politics Today* (August 1984); a report from what was described as 'an independent study group' headed by Sir Patrick Macrory, *Britain's Undefended Frontier: A Policy for Ulster* (1984); Sir John Biggs-Davison's Conservative *and* Unionist strategy, *United Ireland: United Islands?*; *Northern Ireland: Report of an Independent Inquiry* chaired by Lord Kilbrandon (the terms of reference of which were 'to consider the Report of the New Ireland Forum, examine the practicality of any proposals made in the Report or by other sources, and make recommendations') (November 1984); and the travel writer Dervla Murphy's *Changing the Problem: Post-Forum Reflections* (1984). This list is by no means exhaustive

We cannot do justice to all of these in the context of this chapter. Instead we will concentrate on Kilbrandon, which was particularly important for a number of reasons. Firstly, its remit refers specifically to the Report of the New Ireland Forum. Secondly, while it 'had no official status, nor did it have the political weight of the Forum', its significance, according to Aughey, 'lies in its intellectual tone and the indication of a style of thinking in the British establishment sympathetic to those ideas which were to find expression in the [Anglo-Irish] Agreement'.[124] That might suggest some kind of conspiracy. In an Assembly debate the deputy leader of the DUP, Peter Robinson, referred to 'the so-called independent inquiry'. He went on to say that he did 'not believe that this document is accidental or merely promoted by the well-meaning academics that the list on the front page would suggest. It is being deliberately promoted as part of an overall campaign to force Northern Ireland towards a particular political goal: joint sovereignty and joint authority.'[125] Some weight might be given to the conspiracy theory in that a majority of the Kilbrandon Committee opted for a form of joint authority – 'co-operative devolution' – made up of a five-person devolved executive 'consisting of the Secretary of State for Northern Ireland or his deputy, the Minister for Foreign Affairs of the Republic of Ireland or his deputy, and three members elected by the voters of Northern Ireland (which would reflect the majority/minority division – possibly Northern Ireland's three MEPs)'.[126] And, as we have seen earlier, joint authority was a concept that was getting an airing. On the other hand some observers felt that the Kilbrandon Committee 'really is an independent body, even though some ill-informed people think it's a dark British Government plot to float ideas in a covert way'.[127]

Thirdly, the Kilbrandon Report made an impact in at least two respects. Aughey has alluded above to the first; to that we could add the fact that the Donaldson Commission digested its contents before producing their own report – what both had in common was a sense of urgency and a strong belief that there needed to be joint action by both governments. Kilbrandon was not unanimous in it recommendations. There was agreement on the analysis of the situation but a difference on the 'appropriate degree of the association of the Republic with the administration of the province'.[128] Secondly, the Kilbrandon Report made an immediate impact, as coverage in the three major Dublin newspapers – all devoted editorials and many column inches to it – as well as the *Irish News, News Letter, Guardian, Daily Telegraph, Financial Times* and *Times* confirm. An *Irish Independent* leader considered that 'its considerable value lies in the fact that it originates in Britain and is the result of intensive study by British citizens. Because of this and of the high standards of its findings the Inquiry's work ought to be taken into consideration by the British Government when it presents its first considered reaction to our own Forum Report.'[129] In addition it was given some degree of official sanction when it was debated in the Lords and the government welcomed its contribution to the process.[130] In sum, Aughey is correct to see it as part of a 'persuasive intellectual consensus . . . in favour of joint action by both governments as a *first step* towards the resolution of the Ulster crisis'.[131]

THE ANGLO-IRISH AGREEMENT

Before we move to an examination of the Anglo-Irish Agreement we need to be aware of the endogenous and exogenous factors at play between 1984 and 1985. These include the attempts by the SDLP to mobilise enough support for its position in order to persuade the British government that negotiation would be a prudent course of action. SDLP mobilisation has to be set against unionist *reaction* including the divisions between the UUP and DUP as to the utility of the Northern Ireland Assembly. And the exogenous factor – the Falklands/Malvinas conflict – resulted in strained Anglo-Irish relations and a consequent unionist confidence that the Thatcher government would face down constitutional nationalism's mobilisation efforts. These attempts at mobilisation took three forms: John Hume's efforts in the US and the EEC to stimulate debate, interest and support for the position of Irish *constitutional* nationalism; intergovernmental cooperation through the Anglo-Irish process begun in May 1980; and the New Ireland Forum process. The last mentioned has to be seen as an agenda rather than a blueprint; as a challenge to British policy-makers; and as a process that ran in parallel with the Northern Ireland Assembly.

Unionists believed that issues such as Haagerup, Kilbrandon, Anglo-Irish dialogue and American 'interference' were designed to undermine the Union. The DUP, in particular, placed its faith in the Assembly which the Reverend Ian Paisley described as 'a bulwark for the union'; he pleaded with all unionists 'to regard this assembly as a real opportunity for devolution and to make sure that they do not embark upon any course which is going to assist the SDLP, the IRA, Dr FitzGerald and all the rest in attaining their goal'.[132] Despite this plea the Northern Ireland Assembly never succeeded in moving on to the second stage in rolling devolution – progress towards legislative and executive devolution. Their concern with the 'gradualist scenario' of Anglo-Irish relations was best expressed in the Assembly by the DUP Chief Whip, Jim Allister:

> the exercise of shared and joint authority will evolve by degree, rather than decree. The key is to be found in the infamous Anglo-Irish process whereby all-Ireland harmonisation is to be perfected, not instantly, but over a period of time. What started in the Dublin summit declaration of December 1980 with the examination of the totality of relationships within these islands has moved through joint talks to joint studies to joint action and will assuredly move to joint sovereignty and joint institutions ... Already, on the security front, the secretary of state has declared his support for an Anglo-Irish security commission. That indeed would be a definite and sinister step ... Once the joint studies and joint institutions steps have been taken it is, indeed, only a short step to joint sovereignty.[133]

They watched the burgeoning Anglo-Irish relationship with some dismay. We have seen that the process began in May 1980 when Thatcher and Haughey reached agreement on 'new and close political cooperation'. A few days later the Chief Constable of the RUC and the Garda Commissioner met for the first time to discuss improved cross-border security arrangements. In December Haughey and Thatcher met again in Dublin, where they contemplated an examination of 'the totality of relationships within these islands' and agreed to establish Anglo-Irish studies on matters of common concern. The joint studies reported in November 1981 and recommended, *inter alia*, the establishment of an 'Intergovernmental Council' which was to give institutional expression to the 'unique character of the relationship between the two countries'. It was duly established, but met on only seven occasions during 1982.

Unionists took some initial comfort from a breakdown in Anglo-Irish relations as a result of the Falklands issue. At the 1980 session of the UN General Assembly Ireland had been elected to serve a two-year term as a representative of the West European Grouping on the UN Security Council. Following the Argentinian invasion of the

Falklands/Malvinas on 2 April 1982, the Irish Permanent Representative at the UN, Noel Dorr, was required to respond. Traditionally
Ireland's position on the Falklands had been implicitly anti-British, in
keeping with its anti-colonial record at the UN. There was a substantial
Irish diaspora in Argentina, and for eighteen years after 1947 Buenos
Aires was the only Latin American capital in which Ireland maintained
a full diplomatic presence. The anti-British line had softened by the
time the Falklands issue was discussed at the UN in 1976. On the in-
structions of the Fine Gael-led coalition the Irish delegation abstained,
perhaps in deference to its EEC partnership with the UK and in protest
against allegations of human rights abuses emanating from Argentina
at the time. When Argentina invaded the Falklands in early April 1982,
a Fianna Fáil government led by Charles Haughey had been in office
for less than a month. This was its first major challenge in the foreign
policy domain and one which would receive global attention.

Dorr told the Security Council Ireland reserved its position on 'the
merits of the basic dispute about the island' but condemned the
Argentinian invasion. It supported the adoption of the British-inspired
Resolution 502 (which called for the implementation of sanctions)
based on a 'commitment to the authority of the Security Council rather than support for the British case as such'.[134] But there were those
who were concerned about Ireland's traditional position on neutrality
and on the efficacy of sanctions. It became obvious that Haughey was
far from enthusiastic about their initial imposition: 'In the week following the adoption of resolution 502 the *Taoiseach* caused some bewilderment by appearing to suggest that the delegation had acted in the
matter without having fully consulted with Dublin and that the terms
of Ireland's condemnation of Argentina and the support for the resolution were not entirely accurate expressions of the government's
position.'[135] Nevertheless, the Irish announced on 10 April that they
would support sanctions 'in the interests of EEC solidarity'. Yet by
2 May – and hours *before* news reached Europe about the sinking of the
Belgrano – an Irish cabinet statement 'indicated a move towards an even
greater emphasis on the importance of the United Nations in the search
for a diplomatic solution. And, significantly, it ended with "the Government (wishing) to reaffirm Ireland's traditional role of neutrality in
relation to armed conflicts".'[136] The sinking of the *Belgrano* allowed
Ireland to break free from its original stance: 'The Irish Government
chose to criticize Britain for its action and take a call for an immediate
cease-fire to the UN Security Council ... Within the EEC Ireland also
argued that the sanctions against Argentina should be discontinued
forthwith. There were clear expressions of concern from Germany and

Denmark. Italy which has close connections with Argentina was particularly unhappy.'[137] In other words, Britain's international support
was in danger of crumbling. It didn't, but it certainly eroded. The
Security Council did not follow up on Ireland's call for an immediate
ceasefire; and the best that the EEC's meeting of foreign ministers could
agree on was that sanctions would be renewed weekly on a voluntary
basis. Ireland and Italy opted out.

The Falklands campaign complemented complications over the
hunger strikes, the Prior initiative and a British attempt to block EEC
farm-price rises – the latter a further example of Margaret Thatcher
finding herself in a minority of one. But, at a more fundamental level,
the Anglo-Irish differences reflected a clash of nationalisms personified
in two conviction politicians: the 'born-again' nationalism of Margaret
Thatcher and the more familiar, weary dirge of Irish victimhood rehearsed by Charles Haughey. The former was captured in an over-
blown *Times* editorial on 5 April 1982, that is two days after the historic
(Saturday) Commons debate on the Falklands. The *Times* drew comparisons with another crisis: 'As in 1939, so today ... The Falkland
Islands are British territory. When British territory is invaded, it is not
just an invasion of our land, but of our whole spirit. We are all Falk-
landers now.'[138] Anglo-Irish relations got back onto a relatively even
keel with the defeat of the Haughey government in November 1982:
'Not only was Haughey replaced but he was replaced by the most
persistent and articulate public critic of his approach to the Falklands
crisis. At the European summit in Stuttgart in June 1983, Mrs Thatcher
and Dr FitzGerald concluded the necessary Anglo-Irish "peace" and a
formal and evidently cordial summit subsequently took place.'[139]

Unionists may have misread the situation. The Prime Minister had
been rebuked in that famous Commons showcase debate for allowing
the debacle to have occurred in the first place:

> She was shamed, yet she was also dared, even taunted into action, in
> particular by Enoch Powell:
>
>> The Prime Minister, shortly after she came into office, re-
>> ceived the soubriquet as the 'Iron Lady'. It arose in the context
>> of remarks which she made about defence against the Soviet
>> Union and its allies. But there was no reason to suppose that
>> the Right Honourable Lady did not welcome and, indeed,
>> take great pride in that description. In the next week or two
>> this House, the nation and the Right Honourable Lady herself
>> will learn of what metal she is made.
>
> Apparently Thatcher nodded her head in agreement.[140]

The 'Iron Lady' proved her metal in the Falklands. The assumption was that she would do the same in the North. She had told parliament that 'Northern Ireland is part of the United Kingdom – as much as my constituency is'. Unionism's unpreparedness for the Anglo-Irish Agreement has been attributed to Powell's influence on the UUP leader, James Molyneaux; and it is conceivable that Powell overestimated his influence on the Prime Minister. That was the view of a well-informed journalist who believed that Powell's remarks 'were pretentious and she realised that'. Moreover he 'has clearly lost his spell: not just on this subject [the Northern Ireland conflict] but on many subjects he has become meandering over the past few years'.[141] It was the view, too, of Richard Needham, the longest-serving minister in Northern Ireland, who described the Prime Minister's approach to Northern Ireland as 'one of exasperated despair. She would have liked somehow to get rid of the problem. She did not like or trust the unionists and never forgave Enoch Powell, rightly in my view, for his highly personal, exaggerated attacks on her.'[142] Needham also recorded that 'Jim Molyneaux still believed that he had a route to the PM that could derail the [Anglo-Irish] process. Both he and Enoch Powell misjudged the influence of Ian Gow and his friends.'[143] Gow had served as Thatcher's parliamentary private secretary from May 1979 until November 1985, when he resigned in protest over the Anglo-Irish Agreement. His friend Alan Clark recorded in his diary in 1983 that Gow must have seen more of Margaret Thatcher over the previous four years than anybody else except her husband, Denis: 'He was enormously influential, too.' By late 1985 Alan Clark is quoting 'a cruel piece by Peter Riddell in the *Financial Times* . . . "[Gow's] career is already in decline", etc., etc., and other unwelcome truths'.[144] The rot began with the Falklands campaign.

The Falklands campaign ensured that Margaret Thatcher was to dominate the country for the next decade. Charles Haughey was not so fortunate. Fianna Fáil was defeated in a general election in November 1982 and a new Fine Gael–Labour coalition was appointed on 14 December. This change of government was a boost for Anglo-Irish relations. After three general elections in only eighteen months, Irish politics entered a period of stability and continuity. The new government was to remain in office for over four years, until February 1987. It was led by the more sympathetic Dr Garret FitzGerald and had key personnel in place who were committed to the Anglo-Irish process: besides the Taoiseach, these included the Tánaiste (Dick Spring), the Minister for Foreign Affairs (Peter Barry) and the Minister for Justice (Michael Noonan), all of whom were to have key roles in the upcoming negotiations. Equally the Conservatives' resounding victory in the

June 1983 general election – they won 397 seats and had a majority of 144 over all other parties combined – placed Thatcher in a position to do something about Ireland.[145] The process began after June 1983 when Thatcher and FitzGerald had a meeting at the European Council at Stuttgart. She agreed to exploratory talks between Sir Robert Armstrong and Dermot Nally, talks that led to eighteen months of intense negotiations from the release of the New Ireland Forum Report in May 1984 to the signing of the Anglo-Irish Agreement in November 1985.

One of the strangest aspects of the whole process was the degree of secrecy that surrounded it. The negotiations were the property of a tiny group of people – besides the two prime ministers, two foreign ministers and the Northern Ireland Secretary the remainder were officials: the British side was represented by Sir Robert Armstrong, David Goodall (seconded from the Foreign Office to the Cabinet Office), Sir Robert Andrew of the Northern Ireland Office, Christopher Mallaby (seconded from the Foreign Office to the Cabinet Office) and Sir Alan Goodison (British Ambassador in Dublin); the Irish team was led by Dermot Nally and included Seán Donlon (Secretary of the Department of Foreign Affairs), Michael Lillis (head of the Anglo-Irish section at the Department of Foreign Affairs) and Noel Dorr (Irish Ambassador in London). Strong personal ties were formed, in particular between Armstrong and Nally, and Goodall and Lillis. The British were lavish in their praise of the Irish negotiating team; and on the day that the agreement was signed one of them ventured the opinion about his own (British) side: 'I don't think that we could have produced man for man a more powerful team.'[146] There was also the unusual circumstance that three of those involved in the negotiations – FitzGerald, Goodall and Goodison – were amateur theologians. These personal contacts should not be underestimated, as Nally confirms:

> The negotiation of the Agreement was, in my experience, unique in the way in which, over time, understandings developed between officials on both sides: one side would argue for the other's case so that the entire effort became concentrated on making the Agreement not simply a record of hard won compromises between two opposing sides but a composite accord aimed at achieving an end to which both sides could fundamentally subscribe.[147]

The same could be said at the political level, especially in the post-agreement days: after Margaret Thatcher became less than enamoured by the agreement much depended on the personal chemistry between the two foreign ministers, Sir Geoffrey Howe and Peter Barry. Indeed it has been suggested to me in private interview that Howe played a 'steadying role' throughout the negotiations.

Two things are interesting about the above list: the numbers involved and the absence of a Northern Ireland voice. An agreement as comprehensive as that signed in 1985 called for the expertise of more than those named above. Many officials were consulted but very, very few were able to grasp the bigger picture. It was noteworthy that this operation had been taken away from the 'dead hand' of the Northern Ireland Office and placed in the hands of the Cabinet Office and Foreign Office, although the circle was widened in the autumn of 1984 to include senior officials from the Northern Ireland Office. In effect the Cabinet Office was given a role it had not enjoyed before, and the Secretary to the Cabinet became almost an emissary of the Prime Minister. The absence of Northern Ireland voices was deliberate too. The architects realised that the final outcome would be controversial and they were conscious that there had been allegations of leaks during the Ulster Workers' Council strike.[148] Even the head of the Northern Ireland civil service, Kenneth Bloomfield, was kept in the dark until near the very end. The same applied to John Houston, Geoffrey Howe's private secretary and a native of Northern Ireland.[149] Until virtually the very last minute opinion-formers and the media were kept in the dark as well.[150] BBC and UTV were made aware during the week the agreement was signed that there might be a 'happening' and were asked, 'just supposing' there was, would they be in a position to cover it. At that stage the venue was being kept a secret: Dublin and Shannon airport were mentioned. Hillsborough was confirmed only twenty-fours hours before the ceremony and the BBC's outside broadcast unit was housed overnight in the Maze Prison.[151] In the circumstances there may have been advantages in ignorance. This was very much a London–Dublin show, a cabinet-to-cabinet operation, an attempt by two of the 'solitudes' to corral the third. The lessons of Sunningdale had been learnt – any new institutions arising out of the negotiations would have to be resistant to boycotts.

Serious negotiations got under way in the period after the publication of the New Ireland Forum Report.[152] There had been a stocktaking Anglo-Irish summit between Thatcher and FitzGerald in November 1983 but that had simply repaired relations. It led, however, to a period of intense negotiation. William Shannon calculated that by the time the agreement was signed there had been 'two summit meetings of the prime ministers, their four informal meetings on the margins of European common market conferences, six meetings of cabinet ministers, and 35 among officials at lower levels'.[153] There had also been a parliamentary response to the forum at Westminster when on 2 July 1984 the Commons debated its report 'and several other documents' in the first major debate on Northern Ireland in prime time since 1974. In fact virtually all the debate concentrated on the forum's report, with some obeisance paid to the UUP's document *The Way Forward*. Thatcher recognised the significance of the occasion by sitting in on the speech by her Northern Secretary, James Prior, but the debate attracted less than eighty members, most of whom disappeared after Prior's statement, leaving a hard core of those who interested themselves in Northern Ireland. Prior did not close any doors irrevocably and the most positive spin that could be put on his remarks was that he recognised (implicitly) the validity of paragraph 5.10 of the report, in which, as we have seen, the parties to the forum stated that they remained open to discussing other views that may contribute to political development. There were predictable outbursts from hard-liners like the Tory back-bench MP Ivor Stanbrook – 'I believe that the report is a humbug, a deceit, a snare and a delusion.'[154] There were also more thoughtful interventions; the Tory back-bencher Fred Silvester called for joint activity with the Republic and cautioned about how 'we talk about sovereignty',[155] while the junior Northern Ireland Office minister Nicholas Scott spoke of recognising nationalist 'alienation' and the need for 'dialogue'.[156] Prior considered that his own statement 're-presented a considerable step forward in the Government's approach. It was accepted by the House of Commons, and gave some pleasure in Dublin, without at the same time causing any major problems in the Unionist camp.'[157]

Dublin's pleasure did not last too long, and Prior was out of office in little over two months. He resigned from government in September. Since he was not to be offered one of the major departments of state he decided to move on. His departure brought much pleasure to his enemies in Conservative *and* unionist circles. Earlier in 1984 T.E. Utley had analysed the Thatcher–Prior relationship and concluded that it survived on 'mutual terror': 'Mrs Thatcher, in her own expression, is "frit" to let him go, in case he should organise an effective back-bench rebellion.' So she kept him in the 'Irish bog' where, according to Utley and his ilk, 'he has contributed precisely nothing'. Utley described the Thatcher–Prior relationship as 'this perpetually renewed shotgun marriage' in which 'Mrs Thatcher bears the mark of one who has been willing to sacrifice the interests of the one part of the Kingdom which is attacked by terrorism for the sake of low considerations of political expediency'.[158] By the autumn of 1984 Prior lacked the inclination to lead a back-bench revolt, effective or not. Integrationists, and their high-priest Enoch Powell, must have relished the moment. Their joy was compounded following a further Anglo-Irish summit at Chequers on 18–19 November when it seemed that Thatcher had rejected the New Ireland Forum and all its works.

Initially the November summit was notable for the Irish reaction to Thatcher's press conference following the summit. There she seemed to reject the three forum options with such vehemence that the *Irish Press* commented that she made 'out' sound like a four-letter word.[159] Headlines in the *Irish Times* over the following days captured the Irish sense of bewilderment: 'British offensive, Taoiseach tells FG party meeting' (22 November); 'Dublin pessimistic of any progress with Thatcher' (23rd); 'SDLP may decide that it cannot "do business" with Thatcher' (26th). In stark contrast unionists were ecstatic. At an emergency meeting of the Northern Ireland Assembly the DUP leader, Ian Paisley, called on the SDLP to accept that the forum was now 'dead and buried'; and his deputy, Peter Robinson, asserted that the forum proposals 'are now in the burial plot somewhere in Chequers'.[160] And on the eve of the UUP annual conference the following weekend Enoch Powell said that Margaret Thatcher had broken out of a 'vicious spiral' constructed by civil servants in the Foreign Office and Northern Ireland Office: 'We are entitled once again to assume that, as in days long ago, the Conservative Party, when it declares itself to be Unionist, is sincere and determined. We may, therefore, with good heart and conscience say to one another – rejoice, rejoice; there is work to do.'[161]

There were others who read the summit in a more positive light by concentrating on the communiqué itself although the SDLP deputy leader, Seamus Mallon, noted that the two prime ministers had met for nine hours and he assumed that much more was discussed than appeared in the communiqué. He derived three very important points from the communiqué: '[Firstly,] that the minority identity of the nationalist community must have its identity recognised within political structures. Secondly, it does recognise that the same applies to the court and judicial system ... an implicit recognition of the degree of alienation which exists among the nationalist community. And thirdly, the confidence that each section of the community must have that its rights are being protected ... I look forward to seeing the ways in which that can be done and how that will be promoted by the two sovereign governments.'[162] Mallon's third point was particularly tantalising because it alluded to a form of joint authority. In turn the Irish government noted that at her press conference Thatcher had rejected joint authority because it 'is a derogation from sovereignty'. But there could be some scope for negotiation if joint authority could be developed in a way that did not affect British sovereignty.[163] Finally, there was the influence of the exogenous factor. In two strong editorials the *New York Times* and the *Washington Post* were especially critical of Thatcher.[164] And, intriguingly, some seven months after the forum had reported, President Reagan issued a statement to 'commend the Irish statesmen for their courageous and forthright efforts recently embodied in the report of the New Ireland Forum'. He went on to encourage 'the people of Ireland, north and south, and the Governments of Ireland and Great Britain to pursue a constitutional and peaceful solution to the terrible problems that have so long plagued the Emerald Isle'.[165] The statement fits in with the information supplied to the Policy Coordinating Committee at Stormont before the Anglo-Irish Agreement was signed (that the government was concerned with its international standing). Its timing was significant in another sense: 'After the Chequers summit, Mrs Thatcher visited the United States and was told by Ronald Reagan of his interest in the New Ireland Forum initiative and of his support for a concerted attack on terorrism.'[166]

Those zealots who assumed that Thatcher's press conference was the end of the Anglo-Irish affair had missed two vital points – the influence of the exogenous and the significance of process. There is evidence that as early as September 1984 a conflict existed within the Northern Ireland Office between officials – 'If you are standing blindfolded on a cliff-top it is not a good idea to take a step in *any* direction' – and ministers: 'We take a risk ... instead of Dublin urging us to "do something", we say to Dublin "This is what we intend to do, now will you make the gesture that renders it possible." '[167] We can trace the beginning of the latter policy in the fallout from Chequers. As early as 23 November the Minister for Foreign Affairs, Peter Barry, was declaring that the government was pressing ahead with its efforts to win British agreement for a viable political initiative.[168] And the message coming out of 'reliable Conservative sources' in London was that the current rift in Anglo-Irish relations was regrettable but probably ultimately beneficial in what was seen as 'a necessary process of bringing the Irish nationalist parties to significantly lower expectations'.[169] What mattered was that the process was back on track, and when Thatcher met FitzGerald at a European Community summit in Dublin early in December the Armstrong–Nally line was reopened.[170]

We have dwelt on the November breakdown because it was a defining *public* rift that obscured the significance of the process. It is not our purpose to follow the tortuous path of the process during 1985 but simply to highlight a few landmarks along the way.[171] One was the

annual trek to Washington to celebrate St Patrick's Day when Speaker
Tip O'Neill assured FitzGerald and Hume of Reagan's financial support 'once the ink is dry'; a second was the appointment of a British
cabinet committee which included William Whitelaw, Geoffrey
Howe and Douglas Hurd to supervise the negotiations; and a third was
the EC summit meeting in Milan in June where 'Mrs Thatcher dropped
her skeptical and detached approach to the negotiations and appeared
for the first time to appreciate FitzGerald's sense of urgency and importance of doing something constructive about the north before Sinn
Féin made irreversible gains and displaced the SDLP as the political
spokesman for a majority of northern Catholics'.[172] Before the summer recess the British cabinet discussed the upcoming agreement and
one commentator noted the diverse opinions. Whitelaw remained
sceptical, John Biffen was nervous. The Lord Chancellor, Lord Hailsham, poured cold water on proposals for mixed North–South courts.
'The Prime Minister herself, while sharing the scepticism, agreed that it
was better to go ahead than to abandon the talks. She wanted to be able
to indicate to a sceptical President Reagan that Britain was trying to co-
operate with Dublin.'[173] Alan Clark recorded a conversation with Ian
Gow around the same time: 'He is peevish and fussed about Ireland . . .
Ian said the pressure to concede everything to Dublin (and thus expose
the decent Loyalists in Ulster to the full force of IRA terrorism) is
coming from the Foreign Office, who are themselves reacting to pressure from Washington.'[174]

Eventually the Anglo-Irish Agreement was signed at Hillsborough
Castle, the seat of British power in Northern Ireland, on 15 November
under a huge security presence. The communiqué that followed recognised the historic significance of the occasion with its reference to 'a
formal and binding Agreement between their two Governments,
which will enter into force as soon as each Government has notified the
other of acceptance'. The Dáil ratified it on 21 November by eighty-
eight votes to seventy-five, with Fianna Fáil voting against. Charles
Haughey stated his opposition: 'We are deeply concerned that by
signing this Agreement the Irish Government are acting in a manner
contrary to the Constitution of Ireland by fully accepting British sovereignty over a part of the national territory and by purporting to
give legitimacy to a British administration in Ireland.'[175] Interestingly
this approach harmed Fianna Fáil's electoral strength. An *Irish Times*/
MRBI poll (23 November) revealed that only 52 per cent of Fianna Fáil
supporters approved of Haughey's stance, whereas 59 per cent of the
electorate supported the signing of the agreement, with a disapproval
rate of only 29 per cent. A second poll ten weeks later (12 February

1986) showed an increase of 10 per cent in support. The Commons approved the agreement on 27 November by 473 to 47, the biggest majority in the Thatcher era. It came into effect on 29 November and was registered under Article 102 of the Charter of the UN on 20 December 1985.

It was short document of only thirteen articles. It was boosted by a strong institutional framework. Article 2 (a) established an 'Intergovernmental Conference' which would be 'concerned with Northern Ireland and with relations between the two parts of the island of Ireland' and would deal, 'on a regular basis, with: (i) political matters; (ii) security and related matters; (iii) legal matters, including the administration of justice; (iv) the promotion of cross border cooperation'. The structures of the agreement were built to withstand boycotts, physical threats, general strikes, or whatever. The permanent Anglo-Irish secretariat (staffed by six senior personnel from Dublin and London and housed, symbolically, on Northern Ireland soil) was a manifestation of its rigour. There was also a degree of flexibility – or ambiguity – built into it. Article 1, for example, attempted to reassure unionists that the existing constitutional status of Northern Ireland was assured unless a majority of the people there wished otherwise. (Nonetheless, unionists interpreted that article, and the agreement *in toto*, differently.[176]) In Article 2 (b) the 'United Kingdom Government accept that the Irish Government will put forward views and proposals relating to Northern Ireland within the field of activity of the [Intergovernmental] Conference in so far as those matters are not the responsibility of a devolved administration in Northern Ireland'. Articles 4 (b), 5 (c) and 10 (b) were to act as catalysts towards achieving devolution in place of an enhanced role for the Intergovernmental Conference. Article 11 arranged for a review of the working of the Intergovernmental Conference 'to see whether any changes in the scope and nature of its activities are desirable' at the end of three years, or earlier, if requested by either government. Finally, Article 10 (a) saw the potential of promoting economic and social development to regenerate a belaboured Irish economy by considering 'the possibility of securing international support for this work'. The US, Canada and New Zealand contributed to an International Fund for Ireland (IFI). The sums were relatively small but the fund's symbolic importance, as an earnest of international goodwill, was significant. Further, a board of the IFI was appointed from both parts of the island and with one observer each from the United States and Canada to administer the fund's resources. The special problems of Northern Ireland were recognised in the decision to spend approximately three-quarters of the resources there, with the remainder going to the six border counties in the Republic. In the fourteen years following its foundation the IFI was associated with investing £1.1 billion.

But it was about more than structure: process was equally important. One commentator noted that

> never before has Britain formally acknowledged that Ireland has a legal role to play in governing the north. Although it is far short of an acceptance of the principle of a united Ireland, the agreement contradicts cherished beliefs of the unionist majority in Northern Ireland: the belief that the north is exclusively British territory, that its affairs are purely an internal British concern, and that the Republic of Ireland, although a neighbor, is to be regarded as in all respects a foreign country.[177]

The Intergovernmental Conference, chaired by the Northern Ireland Secretary and the Minister for Foreign Affairs, represented both structure and process. Its dual purpose was alluded to a few years later by the British Ambassador to Ireland, Sir Nicholas Fenn, when he stated that there could be 'no return to the dictatorship of the majority'.[178] Fenn recognised that the agreement remained controversial and had profoundly alienated the unionist majority. Then he made a telling point: 'But it reflected a fundamental change in the politics of the North. I have no hesitation in saying that it was one of those rare diplomatic instruments which changes the game thereafter.'

CONCLUSION

At the beginning of this chapter we mentioned four personalities – FitzGerald, Hume, Haughey and Thatcher. The missing element was Gerry Adams, who personified the physical force movement. In a 1985 Christmas message to its supporters the IRA described the Anglo-Irish Agreement as 'a highly sophisticated counter-revolutionary plan' designed to isolate republicans and as the 'most elaborate and determined of schemes yet contrived by Britain in the past 16 years'.[179] Gerry Adams initially described the agreement as a disaster that would copperfasten partition; later he felt it necessary to admonish unionists for playing into the hands of Dublin and the SDLP by overreacting to the agreement.[180] We must never underestimate how much the agreement was about security,[181] but we need to enter two caveats. The first is that the Irish resented very strongly the suggestion that they were not pulling their weight on the security front.[182] And the second is that early in 1984 the Armstrong–Nally conduit agreed that besides security, constitutional change and governmental institutions would equally be on the agenda.

In all the welter of Anglo-Irish detail and political violence we need to remember, too, that there was fundamental change going on through political initiatives whose 'intellectual origins were deeply rooted within the processes of modernization in the Irish state'.[183] This was recognised by Desmond O'Malley, who had been expelled from Fianna Fáil when he refused to tow the Haughey line, when he challenged the Fianna Fáil perspective on republicanism:

> I am certain of one thing in relation to partition – we will never see a Thirty-Two County Republic on this island until, first of all, we have here a Twenty-Six County Republic in this part we have jurisdiction over today, which is really a Republic practising real Republican traditions. Otherwise, we can forget about persuading our fellow Irishmen in the North to join us. 'Republican' is perhaps the most abused word in Ireland today ... There is an immediate preconceived notion of what it is. It consists principally of Anglophobia. Mentally, at least, it is an aggressive attitude towards those who do not agree with our views on what the future of this island should be. It consists of turning a blind eye to violence, seeing no immorality, often, in the most awful violence, seeing immorality only in one area, the area with which this Bill deals.[184]

Charles Haughey did not have the vision to recognise this change.

Finally we need to acknowledge that the Anglo-Irish Agreement was about fundamental and attitudinal change – hence the epigraph to this chapter from a former American Ambassador to Ireland, William Shannon. But it was also about transcendence, about a tiny step in making the break with violence. In the final chapter we shall see how far it has succeeded.

10

CONFLICT TRANSFORMATION

These are the martyrs
Who die for a future buried in the past.

RICHARD MURPHY[1]

The past invades the present,
The present lives in the past,
The future will never come.

ROBERT GREACEN[2]

History is never more valuable than when it enables us, standing as on
a height, to look beyond the smoke and turmoil of our petty quarrels,
and to detect in the slow developments of the past the great
permanent forces that are steadily bearing nations onwards to
improvement or decay.

W.E.H. LECKY[3]

In this final chapter we revisit many of the themes which have informed this book: the 'solitudes'; political paranoia; political violence;
inclusion and exclusion; geopolitical influences; the endogenous and
the exogenous; time and space; and, finally, transcendence. Our starting-point will be the 1985 Anglo-Irish Agreement, and closure will be
the 1998 Belfast Agreement and its fallout. The chapter will be more
chronological than most: resistance to (and problems with) the 1985
agreement; tentative movement towards dialogue through 'the talks
about talks' process initiated by the Secretary of State for Northern
Ireland, Tom King, in 1987 to re-engage the unionist parties; the SDLP–
Sinn Féin dialogue of 1988 leading (eventually) to the Hume–Adams
declaration of 1993; the Downing Street Declaration of December
1993; the republican and loyalist ceasefires of 1994; the Framework

Document of February 1995; and finally the 1998 agreement. We need to consider whether the 1985 agreement delivered 'peace, reconciliation and stability'; the political environment that enabled politicians to take risks for peace; and the role of prestigious third parties and of unofficial diplomacy.

A common thread wending its way through the previous chapter and this one is the capacity to turn the conflict around – that is, to move towards conflict transformation in the journey to conflict resolution. In other words we recognise that the absence of violence does not in itself create the conditions for a permanent peace, merely the space to create such conditions. Conflict transformation calls to mind yet again the issue of time-scales and the significance of process. It accepts that a 'peace agreement is merely one element of a larger peace process, an element that may create some new opportunities but hardly alters all aspects of the conflict'.[4] We are not suggesting that the Hillsborough Agreement represented a peace agreement – overwhelming opposition to it suggests otherwise. But we do well to consider William Shannon's prescient comments (quoted as an epigraph at the opening of the last chapter) that the agreement represented a type of intergovernmental cooperation that was unique in international relations, and that it might take until the end of the (twentieth) century to judge whether it had succeeded or not. We need to keep in mind, too, the remarks (quoted at the end of the last chapter) made by Sir Nicholas Fenn, the British Ambassador to Ireland, in June 1988, that the agreement was 'one of those rare diplomatic instruments which changes the game thereafter'. Formally, 1985 placed the conflict in a wider setting. It moved it beyond the 'narrow ground' and placed it in an international context; informally, through the International Fund for Ireland's economic programme for Northern Ireland and the six northern counties of the Republic, it gave some respectability to the concept of the 'North of Ireland' and to the blurring of boundaries.

The 1985 agreement raised the question of when is the optimum moment to engage conflicting parties in mediation and negotiation. Obviously government has no choice but to be engaged at all times if only to regulate the conflict. More important is when a government judges that it has a proactive role to play and that the time is ripe for prestigious third-party intervention. There is a school of thought which asserts that there may be a 'ripe moment' for intervention in conflicts 'composed of a structural element, a party element, and a potential alternative outcome – that is, a mutually hurting stalemate, the presence of valid spokespersons and a formula for a way out'. But it may be more prudent to view the 'ripe moment' as a process rather than a specific point in time: 'While the "ripe moment" deals with the shift, theories on possible settlement are dealing with the end product. This leaves the highly important interim period inadequately studied'.[5] In the Northern Ireland conflict that interim period began some time late in 1985. At the turn of the century it is still too early to say whether it has come to an end.

REACTION AND RECESSION

Belfast

Perhaps the most poignant expression of unionist bewilderment at the Hillsborough Agreement was a speech from the UUP MP Harold McCusker during a two-day Commons debate on the issue in late November 1985. He described how, on the day the agreement was signed, he stood outside Hillsborough Castle in the rain 'like a dog and asked the Government to put in my hand the document that sold my birthright'. His anger was compounded by the fact that the Irish Labour Party had already produced its official response to the agreement with a covering letter from its leader, Dick Spring, dated 15 November. And he wondered whether all his time as an MP had been wasted years: 'Why did not successive Governments tell me that I would never be treated with equality? If I had been told, my attitude over the past 12 years would have been different.' He regretted that he had brought up his children to believe in British traditions: 'It would have been better if they had never looked at the Union flag or thought that they were British or put their trust in the House of Commons than spending the rest of their lives knowing that they are now some sort of semi-British citizens.' He called for a UK-wide referendum, adding that if 'the people of the United Kingdom say to me that they no longer want me, it will simply be echoing what the Government are saying anyway'. As for sovereignty, it 'is what the Government decides it is'.[6] This was a powerful and dignified speech that deserves analysis at two levels.

The first concerns the speaker himself. McCusker was one of the more independent-minded unionists. He had, for example, voted with the Labour government in the confidence vote that led to the collapse of the Callaghan government in 1979. A year after the 1985 agreement he had distanced himself to some extent from his own party. He told the Belfast *News Letter*: 'I make my judgements. I have reservations at times about the commitment of my party to oppose the agreement. That is why right from day one I said I would make my own protest, because I did not want to risk being tied to people who, when the crunch came, would maybe come to terms with the agreement.'[7] In the same interview he argued that British governments 'have never been honourable. The only thing that motivates an Englishman is his self-interest and comforts. The double standards which exist at Whitehall and Westminster are incredible.' These two statements encapsulate the confusion and isolation prevalent within the unionist community in the aftermath of November 1985.

This leads to the second consideration: why were unionists so surprised by the turn of events? Ian Paisley and James Molyneaux began their campaign against this phase of Anglo-Irish cooperation only in August 1985. One Whitehall insider expressed the view that unionists exaggerated 'the degree of their own ignorance. They were certainly given enough nods and winks and nudges to know that something big was up; but what were we to do? We couldn't tell them.'[8] The simplest explanation is post-Falklands hubris. Even Molyneaux's (very sympathetic) biographer had little to add: 'His peculiar characteristic of being able to have a "long view" and of recognising the eventual outcome of a policy even before it has left the drawing board failed on this occasion.'[9] They underestimated Margaret Thatcher's determination.[10] The *Listener* (26 September 1985) was suggesting that 'suffice to say that she seems unlikely to shrink from adding Dr Paisley's scalp to those of Arthur Scargill and General Galtieri'.[11] The unionists' pre-emptive strike had been a report written by Sir Fredrick Catherwood, the Ulster-born Conservative MEP and a future president of the Evangelical Alliance. In the opinion of Arwel Ellis Owen, the report's proposals 'were contained in less than three pages and reflected the paucity of ideas and the despondent mood of the Unionists at this critical time in their history'.[12]

That failure led to an enormous loss of confidence within the unionist community and a curious cross-class alliance. For example, reflecting in the late 1980s on his professional career, the historian A.T.Q. Stewart believed that his preoccupation with his chosen period – the late eighteenth century – had the advantage of keeping him out of trouble: 'Like Carlyle, I believed that the beauty of the past was precisely that it had none of the problems of the present in it.' But the changing circumstances, in particular the outbreak of violence, meant 'an instant realignment of familiar assumptions about order in society. I felt as a French historian might have felt in the Paris of 1789, distracted by noises in the street as he toiled over a history of the monarchy.'[13] Like many in the unionist professional class he, too, was to be distracted by noises in the street. In an article anticipating the first anniversary of the agreement he wrote: 'The road to reform, and indeed even to the recovery of basic democratic freedom, has been firmly closed. The hour for determined resistance is past, yet an implacable British Government is driving [unionists] towards violence as inexorably as a sheepdog driving a flock of sheep.'[14] That last phrase encapsulated unionism's sense of fatalism and its return to a particular form of mobilisation – extra-parliamentary protest. It had worked after 1912 and again in 1974. Admittedly it had failed in 1977, but unionism was not united then. There was no reason, unionists believed, that it could not succeed after 1985: 'What we have we hold.'

There was every reason why it might fail. Their 'success' in 1974 had made successive British governments more wary; international opinion had been garnered in favour of the agreement; and Paisley's comparing the Prime Minister to 'Jezebel who sought to destroy Israel in a day' was not the way to win friends and influence people.[15] More importantly unionists did not have the Westminster support they had held during the Third Home Rule Bill crisis. The forty-seven MPs who voted against the agreement were a *mélange* of Ulster unionists, the Labour Left and dissident Conservatives. From the unionist perspective the dissident Tories were the key group. They have been described as 'generally to be found to the right of the party and within that section of the right whose principal concerns are, or have been, non–economic; imperial, moral, religious and national concerns being prevalent.'[16] Yet they numbered only twenty-one, and only one minister – Ian Gow – was sufficiently opposed to the agreement as to resign from government, whereas three MPs resigned from government in protest against Prior's proposed legislation on a Northern Ireland Assembly. With the passing of time their influence became even more marginal. By the early 1990s five of this small group's articulate and consistent dissidents were no longer on the scene: John Biggs–Davison died in 1988; Gow was assassinated in 1990; Julian Amery, Michael McNair-Wilson and Ivor Stanbrook did not contest the 1992 election. In the wider community in Britain support for unionism was on the wane. A *Guardian/*ICM poll of November 1993 was summarised thus: 'traditional support for unionism among supporters of what was once (sic) the Conservative and Unionist Party seems to be almost dead. Only 23 per cent believe Northern Ireland should remain part of the UK and 52 per cent prefer solutions that loosen the link with Britain.'[17]

Formal connections between the Conservatives and the UUP were severed after the 1985 agreement: 'By 1986 the last organizational linkage between the two parties, joint youth membership, was broken after the Anglo-Irish Agreement.'[18] Admittedly unionists continued to enjoy some support in the right-wing press. In an amazing piece of hyperbole Andrew Alexander warned in the *Spectator*: 'if Mrs Thatcher does not want her legacy to be the destruction of the United Kingdom, then she needs to end the Hillsborough Agreement . . . Hillsborough is as pregnant with danger for Britain as Munich once was.'[19] Alexander represented a strain of media opinion that was to act as an irritant at critical moments in Anglo-Irish relations over the next fifteen years. These sceptics were to be found in the *Daily Telegraph*, the *Sunday Telegraph*, the *Times* and the *Spectator* and included Matthew d'Ancona, Charles Moore and Noel Malcolm but crucially they did not carry enough weight to swing the argument against the rationale underlying the 1985 agreement. Some of them were to be found, too, among the 'Friends of the Union' established in June 1986 to 'increase knowledge and understanding of the need to maintain the union of Great Britain and Northern Ireland'. Sixteen Conservative MPs and eight peers were listed as trustees or patrons of the body. That was part of its problem. Some unionists were suspicious of any organisation emanating from the Palace of Westminster, and the group was never to have the impact its founders had desired.[20]

In a wistful phrase Aughey contends that during the Home Rule crisis, 'the fate of Ulster concentrated the mind of a whole political generation in Britain and confronted it with a challenge of political principle which was taken to be profoundly significant'. He adds that 'the principle is the same today, but the cause of Ulster is an esoteric one'.[21] There can be little doubt that a significant segment of the political establishment sided with the unionist cause during that period. What had been absent in the meantime was a lack of self-reflection, an inability to engage in dialogue. According to Norman Porter:

> It is ideally via dialogue that we become clearer about who we are, that we express what is important to us, that we check out the intelligibility and the appropriateness of our goals and purposes, and so forth. Dialogue is the vehicle *par excellence* of the search for authentic self-interpretations, not least because it is constituted by relations of reciprocity and recognition. Such relations are so important because their absence goes a long way towards explaining why individually or collectively we often find ourselves struggling with frustrating self-interpretations, perhaps ones that demean us.[22]

Porter's remarks are pertinent in two respects: they serve as an antidote to Aughey's myopia; and they serve as a reminder of why unionism got it so wrong in 1985. Unionists ignored the bigger picture and fell back on their own solitude. Porter was attempting to divert them from that narrowness. In the meantime they had indulged in a form of mobilisation that eschewed self-reflection. It was only after mobilisation had patently failed that unionism began to consider dialogue seriously.

It was a painful journey of self-discovery. The campaign against the Anglo-Irish Agreement is too well known to need repetition.[23] Mass demonstrations produced a sense of solidarity (and continuity with 1974 and 1912), but they were unpredictable and often degenerated into mindless delinquency. The decision of the Northern Ireland Assembly in December 1985 to suspend normal sittings and to set up a committee to examine the implications of the agreement 'for the government and future of Northern Ireland' led to the withdrawal of the Alliance Party and was counterproductive. A decision by the cabinet's Overseas and Defence Committee, with the Prime Minister in the chair, to suspend the Assembly received the royal assent on 25 June 1986. The decision by all unionist MPs to resign their Westminster seats and force a series of by-elections scheduled for 23 January 1986 was bizarre – moving the writ for the fifteen by-elections at Westminster Sir Peter Emery claimed that the occasion qualified for the *Guinness Book of Records*, and the unionist parties had to create four bogus candidates called 'Peter Barry' to ensure that there were fifteen contests. In any case it backfired in that the UUP's Jim Nicholson lost the Newry–Armagh seat to the SDLP's Seamus Mallon, and (with a drop in the Sinn Féin vote of 5.4 per cent) his colleague Eddie McGrady received the boost he needed to go on and defeat Enoch Powell in the 1987 general election. The unionists' policy of abstention from Westminster had collapsed by March 1987 and had antagonised potential allies in the Commons. Even when the close result of the 1992 general election, 'coupled with the fractiousness of the Conservative Party (over Europe in particular), once again gave the Unionists a pivotal position in British politics', there were limits on their influence. A senior Conservative remarked in July 1993: 'They can have anything they want short of the Anglo-Irish Agreement which they know we cannot abandon.'[24]

Unionists who had begun a policy of adjourning local council meetings – to thwart Sinn Féin after it won fifty-nine seats at the May 1985 local government elections – intensified their policy after the agreement was signed: for example, when the fourth Intergovernmental Conference met on 11 March 1986 the mayoral chains of thirteen unionist councils were hung on the barbed wire at Stormont. It became part of a wider anti-agreement campaign of civil disobedience launched in May 1986, which included a rent and rates strike, economic sanctions against the Republic of Ireland and the resignation of unionists from area boards. By September 1986 the campaign was under pressure, and by mid–February 1987 it was effectively at an end.[25] The adjournment campaign highlighted yet again the potency of localism in Northern Ireland politics, and, in its turn, localism underlined the constraints on political leadership in a demotic culture.

One of the strands running through the campaign was a growing unease in UUP circles with more militant actions. One of the most celebrated occasions was the invasion of the border village of Clontibret in County Monaghan in August 1986 by Peter Robinson and two hundred supporters in protest at lax security on the Republic's side of the border. Two gardaí were injured, and Robinson was fined IR£15,000. The *Irish Times* (8 August 1986) commented: 'Peter Robinson wanted to find out what security was like on this side of the border. Now he knows.' It was in line with earlier actions. When the Northern Secretary banned an Apprentice Boys' parade on Easter Monday 1986 – a parade normally held in Bangor but switched to Portadown, the scene of the biggest riot in the 1985 marching season – Paisley and Robinson assembled three thousand marchers and marched the route in the early hours of the morning. But more ominous than the militant fringe activities (such as the damage to 149 shops and the looting of 14 of them during the first anniversary anti-agreement rally at Belfast City Hall) was the formation of groups such as the Ulster Clubs and Ulster Resistance. The former predated the agreement but supplied a cutting edge to the protests after November 1985. By January 1986 it claimed to have eight thousand members in forty-eight branches. The picketing of the homes of alleged 'collaborators' was one of its activities. Ulster Resistance was launched at an invitation-only rally at the Ulster Hall on 10 November 1986 which was attended by Paisley, Robinson, Belfast Lord Mayor Sammy Wilson and Rev. Ivan Foster, all prominent DUP members. The standards of nine Ulster divisions were dedicated, and, in language redolent of earlier crises, the audience 'resolved to band together to take whatever steps are necessary . . . [and to] embark on a province-wide recruitment of men willing and prepared to take direct action as and when required'. A few days later Paisley was introduced at a rally in Kilkeel, County Down, as 'the head of Ulster's newest army'.[26] The DUP began to distance itself from Ulster Resistance shortly afterwards and when a major arms find was discovered in November 1988 the party issued a statement saying that all formal contacts with the group had ceased after the summer of 1987. It was the formation of such 'citizens' armies' which brought the campaign into disrepute. The unionist slogan 'Ulster Says No' encapsulated stagnation on the political landscape. Extra-parliamentary protest was a poor substitute for political discourse. With the emergence of the new groups loyalist paramilitary killings increased. In 1984 fewer than ten deaths were ascribed to loyalist groups. In 1988–90 they claimed an annual average of twenty victims, and in both 1991 and 1992 double that number were killed by loyalists. Other means had to be found.

Two deserve some attention. In January 1987 the UDA's think-tank, the New Ulster Political Research Group, produced a remark-able document, *Common Sense*. The title was borrowed from Thomas Paine, the late-eighteenth-century English republican, and an unlikely source for Ulster loyalism. It explored questions of identity and displayed sensitivity towards minorities. It argued for an agreed process of government for Northern Ireland based on co-determination, power-sharing, a bill of rights and a mutually agreed system for the administration of justice. It accepted the reality that the whole com-munity was part of the process, that an exclusivist mentality was counterproductive and that the Anglo-Irish Agreement could act as a catalyst.[27] *Common Sense* may have had its own catalytic effect in goading the mainstream unionist parties into seeking positive alter-natives to Hillsborough. The first fruit of this process was the publica-tion in July 1987 of *An End To Drift*, the report of a unionist task force made up of Frank Millar and Harold McCusker MP (UUP) and Peter Robinson MP (DUP). The report recognised the 'inadequacies of the existing protest campaign' and the 'limits of Unionism's negotiation strength'; it rejected integration – 'we cannot believe that constitutional security is to be found in a campaign to persuade mainland political parties to extend their organisation to Northern Ireland' – and acknowledged that 'membership of the United Kingdom or mem-bership of an Irish Republic are *not* the only options available to the people of Northern Ireland'.[28] Only the first part of the report was published; the second was reported to be highly critical of the leadership – who proceeded to sit on its recommendations.

Frank Millar and Peter Robinson resigned their positions as UUP general secretary and DUP deputy leader respectively as a consequence. Robinson's resignation on 7 October 1987 was a severe blow to the DUP. He was central to the DUP apparatus. After Ian Paisley he was the DUP's most successful politician, with a career built on 'efficiency, articulate and unrelenting extremism, and frequently declared loyalty to his party boss'.[29] He was re-elected by the DUP executive on 8 January 1988, a meeting which he did not attend. His return was an acknowledgement that the anti-agreement campaign had run into the sands and that a new strategy was needed.[30] By April he was revisiting the task force report and asserting that the union he supported 'is a union that protects Unionist interests'; unionists, he said, would never acquiesce in the Anglo-Irish Agreement – 'acquiescence is the brother of surrender'.[31]

The need for a change in direction had been clear since mid-1987. At the British general election on 11 June the Conservatives were returned with a majority of 101, Enoch Powell was defeated in South Down, and the unionist vote was down by 2 per cent. Unionists had campaigned in the expectation of a minority administration after the election, and themselves in the role of power brokers. In Northern Ireland the election had been conducted on issues arising out of the Anglo-Irish Agreement, but that was not how the electorate saw it – 71 per cent said that the state of the economy was of greater importance than the agreement.[32] All of these constraints on the unionists' room for manoeuvre created the conditions for a new dialogue with the British government.

DUBLIN AND LONDON

If unionists had had the benefit of foresight they might have reconsidered their strategy. Firstly, one of the features of Anglo-Irish co-operation in the first three years after Hillsborough was the degree of bickering between the two governments, especially on security and the administration of justice. We will pursue that in greater detail later. Secondly, cooler heads may have persuaded them that Hillsborough was not a sell-out. One analyst asserted that 'the Anglo-Irish Agreement is not formal joint authority, neither a formal notice to Unionists of eventual reunification, nor the formal abandonment of territorial irredentism by the Irish Republic'. He moved from the negative to the positive by considering what its constitutional significance was: 'First, it is the formalisation of inter-state co-operation; second, a formal notice that while the Unionist guarantee remains Unionists have no veto on policy formulation within Northern Ireland; and, third, the formalisation of a strategy which binds the Irish Republic to a constitutional mode of reunification which is known to be practically infeasible, and therefore facilitates the end of the Nationalist monolith in the Republic's politics.'[33] Thirdly, had they considered that the nationalist monolith was being undermined in the Republic they might have paid closer attention to the political stance on the agreement adopted by the Fianna Fáil leader, Charles Haughey. There they would have found an unlikely ally.

In an epilogue to his *Irish Journey* written in 1967, thirteen years after his first visit to the country, Heinrich Böll commented on the vast changes that had occurred in the meantime 'in an Ireland that has caught up with two centuries and leaped over another five'. He regretted that 'a certain something has now made its way to Ireland, that ominous something known as The Pill ... and to know that His Majesty The Pill will succeed where all the Majesties of Great Britain have failed – in reducing the number of Irish children – seems to me to be no cause for rejoicing'.[34] Böll was a whimsical and compelling social commentator who was reading the runes well before many Irish politicians. We do not know whether Charles Haughey had read him, but Haughey gave the impression that he was committed to a form of whimsy – Fianna Fáil's traditional (and conservative) social values that echoed the *mores* of traditional Ireland. As early as June 1980, speaking about the prospects for the North within a united Ireland, he declared: 'It's quite possible to have completely different sets of social legislative provisions in one area from the other.'[35] Four years later he was still procrastinating on the issue of marital breakdown in the Republic.[36] He demonstrated insensitivity, too, towards Northern Ireland when an invitation to the Alliance Party leader, John Cushnahan, to speak at a Young Fianna Fáil meeting was withdrawn.[37] It was as if he was going to great lengths to distance himself from his immediate Fianna Fáil predecessors – Seán Lemass and Jack Lynch – and identify himself with the world of Eamon de Valera of the 1930s and 1940s.

We noted in the previous chapter his heterodox position on the New Ireland Forum and the Hillsborough Agreement. It led to some problems with the SDLP, problems that began to be addressed properly only a year later.[38] It led famously to the expulsion of Des O'Malley from Fianna Fáil on 26 February 1985, with O'Malley speculating that he might have to set up a new party. While the vote to expel O'Malley was carried comfortably (73–9), Haughey was not short of critics, including the former Taoiseach Jack Lynch and various leader writers.[39] And that was storing up trouble for Fianna Fáil.[40] It may have persuaded some unionists that they could do business with Haughey: 'A Haughey election victory within a year or a year and a half of the signing of the Agreement might be the required shock to Anglo-Irish relations that would save the day for the unionists.' But there was a problem with this wishful thinking because 'as opinion polls in the Republic showed, the Agreement was popular, and it was unlikely that such a consummate populist as Haughey would hasten to incur the displeasure of his electorate by undermining it'.[41] The test came when Fianna Fáil won the Irish general election on 14 February 1987 and Haughey became Taoiseach for the third time. It took him three weeks to put together a minority administration. When Garret FitzGerald pledged Fine Gael's full support if the agreement was allowed to continue untouched Haughey replied by 'accepting that the Anglo-Irish Agreement was an accord . . . accepted as binding . . . Ireland and Britain are so much involved with each other . . . governments must strive to have the best possible relationships'.[42] One of his first tasks was to make the annual St Patrick's Day pilgrimage to Washington. Eighteen months earlier he had tried to persuade the US administration to withhold its support for the pending Hillsborough Agreement: 'There was no doubt that the St Patrick's Day meeting with President Reagan was a difficult one for Haughey. FitzGerald and John Hume were present to witness and help the taoiseach through this difficult manoeuvre.'[43]

Unionists might also have paid closer attention to Irish public opinion if they were seeking reasurances. One survey by Bernadette Hayes and Ian McAllister indicates that by the 1990s Irish opinion had changed, 'this time in favour of a much-reduced preference for unity, and a renewed interest in maintaining the union between the province and Britain. Indeed, in 1991, Irish unity was only 18 percentage points ahead of the union as the preferred option.'[44] One outcome of all this was a dramatic decline in support for retaining Articles 2 and 3 of the Irish constitution. The same survey found considerable disinterest among the British public as a result of bipartisanship, which had had the effect of removing the Northern Ireland problem from informed political debate. Hayes and McAllister conclude that at 'the end of the day, continued disinterest by British public opinion, coupled with a new flexibility in Irish public opinion, may well create the best preconditions for the resolution to the problem in a quarter of a century'.[45] This flexibility was to be found in the creation of the 1998 agreement but its antecedents go back to the 1985 agreement.

That is not to say that the operation of the Hillsborough Agreement was not without its problems. There is an asymmetry in Margaret Thatcher's description of how the agreement operated in practice; she was obsessed with the security issue and paid much less attention to justice matters: 'we hoped for a more co-operative attitude from the Irish Government, security forces and courts. If we got this the agreement would be successful.' Alas, it was not to be: 'Our concessions alienated the Unionists without gaining the level of security co-operation we had a right to expect.'[46] In some respects the position was reversed with the Irish: 'The Republic of Ireland had signed the Anglo-Irish Agreement in the belief that it would lead to changes in the administration of justice.' There were changes, but there was also much disagreement on issues such as extradition, 'mixed' courts, the role of the Ulster Defence Regiment, the rejection of the 'Birmingham Six' appeal, concerns about the perversion of the course of justice in what became known as the Stalker–Sampson affair, the killing of three IRA members by the SAS at Gibraltar and other incidents. The degree of Irish dissatisfaction in these matters was best summed up in a comment by Mary Holland in the *Irish Times* (21 October 1986): 'one year after Hillsborough the British have virtually reneged on Article 8'.[47] After the failure to reform the court system it seemed as if 'Ireland had all the burdens of co-reponsibility for what was happening north of the border, but no authority to change things.'[48]

Yet, despite dissatisfaction by both the British and Irish, the agreement remained in place. The statistics on violence suggest that it failed to deliver 'peace, reconciliation and stability'. During 1988 there were ninety-four conflict-related deaths, precisely the same number as 1987, and thirty more than 1986; with fifty-three deaths in 1985, the trend was upward. Other factors have to be borne in mind as well. The first is the rise in sectarian civilian killings by loyalist paramilitaries (two in 1985, sixteen in 1986, fourteen in 1987 and eighteen in 1988), bringing them back to their 1977 level of nineteen but well below their 1976 peak of 110 civilians killed. A second is the nature of republican violence. It changed in two respects: during 1988 the army replaced the police as the main republican target; and of fourteen civilians killed by the IRA eleven were acknowledged as 'mistakes' – an unacceptably high level for an organisation that relied on tacit public support.[49] The governments might have insisted that this rise was to be expected in the land of the self-fulfilling prophecy and that many organisations had an interest in undermining the agreement. On the other hand some would insist that 'ultimately, the Agreement led republicans to reconsider their strategy and goals. They ceased to believe that they, or the IRA, could win a united Ireland through war, or indeed through war and electoral competition ... Not the least of the achievements of the Agreement was that Sinn Féin's activists sought to internationalize their struggle, in America and Europe, through appeals to the discourses of international law, self-determination and democracy.'[50] It might also be said that the regular meeting of the Anglo-Irish Intergovernmental Conference demonstrated a capacity for conflict management during a period when Dublin–London relations encountered major problems, including, as we have seen, perceived miscarriages of justice, differences on extradition and concerns about improving the quality of life in Northern Ireland.

The British and Irish governments' official verdict on the viability of the Anglo-Irish Agreement came on 24 May 1989 when they published the *Review of the Working of the Conference* in line with Article 11 of the agreement. The publication illustrated the extent to which Charles Haughey had come on board. In January 1987, with a general election looming, Haughey outlined his party's position on the Anglo-Irish Agreement: 'We do not accept the constitutional implications of Article 1. What we do about it is something we will have to consider.'[51] Yet two years later he had no problem signing up to the following: 'the two governments reaffirm their firm commitment to all of the provisions of the agreement and to the shared understandings and purposes set out both in the preamble and in the agreement itself as well as in the Hillsborough communiqué of November 15th, 1985'. In short, the agreement was on full throttle. The review moved the process up a notch with its concentration on functional cooperation.[52] The penultimate paragraph (29) displayed a healthy measure of flexibility: 'If in future it were to appear that the objectives of the Agreement could be more effectively served by changes in the scope and nature of the working of the Conference, consistent with the basic provision and spirit of the Agreement, the two governments would be ready in principle to consider such changes.' In other words, only an arrangement which would meet with the approval of both governments and transcended the agreement in importance would be considered. Finally, and fundamentally, it returned to first principles in the second sentence of the second paragraph: 'They reaffirm their belief in the need for political dialogue at all levels in achieving progress and an end to violence.' That last sentence should be read in conjunction with Porter's comment about dialogue being constituted by relations of reciprocity and recognition;[53] it also points to the necessity to move beyond the exclusivism of the 'solitude' and to embrace inclusion.

COMMUNICATION

Communication entails recognition of the other, and 'the awareness of being separate and different from and strange to one another' opens up potentials of creative search for dialogue and for understanding each other. This is also the essence of negotiations. Reaching common ground is not necessarily a product of similar opinions.

SASSON SOFER[54]

If the first phase of the Anglo-Irish Agreement was about dialogue between governments then the second was an attempt to widen the communicative dimension. Success for the latter has been attributed to

Peter Brooke who became Secretary of State for Northern Ireland in July 1989, although the groundwork had been done by his predecessor, Tom King, in what became known as the 'talks about talks' process. Initially it ran from 7 July 1987 until 26 January 1988. Evidence of unionist procrastination surfaced at a meeting between Tom King and the two unionist leaders at the beginning of 1988 when according to unionist sources 'Mr King told Mr Paisley and Mr Molyneaux that the British cabinet did not consider it worthwhile continuing talks about suspending the Anglo-Irish Agreement unless the unionist parties were ready to come forward with more realistic proposals about the future government of Northern Ireland'.[55] The next formal meeting between the three of them did not occur until 11 May 1988; by then relations had improved considerably, and Molyneaux took the initiative in seeking preliminary contact with the Taoiseach, Charles Haughey, to consider developing North–South contacts. When King, Molyneaux and Paisley met again in London on 26 May it was clear that the UUP leader had been freelancing and was not speaking on behalf of the joint unionist policy committee (a ten-man think-tank established by the two leaders in January). It was Paisley who reiterated the traditional stance when he stated that a devolved government must be set up in Belfast *before* talks could be held with the Republic about relationships between the two parts of Ireland. In any case the SDLP was engaged in dialogue with Sinn Féin at this time, and that was anathema to the unionist parties (and many more besides). All of this uncoordinated activity illustrated that, at the very least, the parties were removing themselves from the boxes they had withdrawn into in November 1985.[56]

To make some sense of this subterranean movement we can move ahead to what became known as the Brooke initiative. He was not considered one of the big hitters of the Conservative front bench. He was party chairman between 1987 and 1989 and came from Anglo-Irish stock, but he did not bring with him a reputation like that of Whitelaw or Prior. An early indication of his political intent surfaced after 100 days in office when he stated that an abandonment of violence by the IRA could lead to 'imaginative steps' by the government; in turn Sinn Féin's Martin McGuinness described him as the first Northern Secretary 'with some understanding of Irish history'. These were the first steps in a minuet that culminated in an IRA cessation of violence on 31 August 1994. In a speech in his Westminster constituency on 9 November 1989 Brooke claimed that Britain had no economic or strategic interest in the union with Northern Ireland; that it would accept Irish unification by consent; and that there would be a place in any Northern Ireland settlement for non-violent republicanism. These were not the sentiments of a man who had come to Northern Ireland for a quiet life. His message was not picked up immediately because commentators concentrated on style rather than substance, on a carefully cultivated sense of bewilderment and a delivery based on understatement. Hence at Methodist College Belfast on 6 December he declared that he had 'no secret plan, no hidden agenda'; and he advised Bangor Chamber of Commerce on 9 January 1990: 'I would not wish to raise hopes unduly.'[57]

While none of these amounted to a modern version of the Gettysburg Address, raise hopes was precisely what he had done. The Bangor speech was the beginning of his initiative. In retrospect we can see that it was based on learning from the mistakes of previous constitutional initiatives, and on seduction – he was careful to find something positive to say about the four major constitutional parties. Perhaps the key phrase referred to rescuing unionism from its 'internal exile'. The Brooke initiative was to be about creating the conditions whereby the Anglo-Irish Agreement could be transcended by a new agreement engaging *all* of the parties to the problem by taking seriously paragraph 29 of the 1989 review. He was assisted in this by John Hume, who, in a series of speeches and interviews (most notably with the *Irish Times* on 13 January 1989), asserted that the agreement was not written on tablets of stone and that it could be replaced by something which transcended it in importance.

Brooke's first success was ending unionism's 'internal exile' by making three concessions. He was prepared to consider an alternative to the agreement; he agreed to a predetermined gap between meetings of the Intergovernmental Conference to allow negotiations to get under way; and he suggested that during those negotiations officials of the Anglo-Irish secretariat would be gainfully employed. These concessions were made with the acquiescence of the Irish government and the SDLP. They recognised the significance of the initiative in that it had changed the political vocabulary. In his Bangor speech Brooke had referred to the three relationships – the North–South dimension as well as the intercommunity and intergovernmental dimensions.

By July 1990 Brooke thought that he had reached some understanding with all of the parties and was ready to make a statement announcing the start of talks to the Commons before the summer recess. But he was blocked by the SDLP and Dublin, who were unhappy with two substantive points. Firstly, they needed some clarification on when the talks would move on to the North–South dimension (i.e. Strand 2). They suspected that unionist insistence on 'substantial progress' being made on talks internal to Northern Ireland (i.e. Strand 1) would encourage procrastination and enable the unionists to avoid direct talks with Dublin. Secondly, since they believed that unionism's relationship with the rest of the island went to the heart of the matter, they were unhappy with the idea of unionists attending Strand 2 under the umbrella of a UK delegation. They believed, too, that Brooke had gone back on a commitment between the two governments, made on 19 April, that the talks should proceed 'in unison'.

It was not until 26 March 1991 that the Northern Secretary was able to announce that Intergovernmental Conference meetings would be suspended for a period of about ten weeks from mid-April to allow bilateral talks to take place and set an agenda for the talks proper. Everyone recognised the historic import of the talks – the *Irish Times* (27 July 1990) described them as 'potentially the most significant political discussions in all of Ireland since the treaty of 1921' – as well as the considerable role played by Peter Brooke in getting them to that point. It was agreed that the talks would begin on 30 April with a series of bilaterals to finalise housekeeping arrangements; these were expected to be fairly brisk. That did not prove to be the case, and the first plenary session did not commence until 17 June. The talks whimpered to a collapse on the evening of 2 July, when Peter Brooke brought them to a close in order to avoid further recrimination. Essentially the talks had not moved beyond the procedural level. They foundered on essentially technical matters such as the location of the meetings and the issue of chairmanship. Brooke refused to be downcast. He told the Commons on 3 July that 'foundations have been laid for progress in the future which neither cynics nor men of violence will be able to undermine'. He said that he would be listening 'for rustling in the undergrowth' and that he hoped to pick up the process in the autumn.[58] In fact the talks did not begin until 29 April 1992, that is after the British general election and under the chairmanship of a new Secretary of State for Northern Ireland, Sir Patrick Mayhew.

The bizarre events and posturings that scuttled Brooke's initiative might seem like the equivalent of two bald men fighting over a comb. But that does an injustice to the deep-seated animosities that paralysed the protagonists. All had made concessions to get to the negotiating table. All were aware of the paranoia in their respective communities, and of belonging to a culture which had eschewed the art of political negotiation in the past. When the talks were brought to a close the *Irish Times* (4 July 1991) suggested that the 'Brooke talks have reached a hiatus, not a conclusion'. This optimism was supported by the results of an opinion poll in Britain, Ireland and Northern Ireland which was commissioned by the Rowntree Reform Trust and published on 12 July. It demonstrated that 80 per cent of the electorate wanted the talks to continue 'as soon as possible' because they 'were potentially vital to the future of Northern Ireland'.[59] The Brooke round of talks was a painful and necessary exercise in catharsis involving retreats from previously stated positions to less 'extreme' positions, as perceived by the adversaries. It has been argued that the 'end result of the [Anglo-Irish] Agreement was to create the context for a real attempt at dialogue', and that the motivation of the Brooke talks was a desire to bring the unionist parties and Sinn Féin out of their respective cul-de-sacs.[60]

We have lingered over the Brooke initiative at some length because this chapter is concerned with conflict transformation. If we assume that this entails three elements – analysis, negotiation and implementation – we can say confidently that we are only on the nursery slopes of implementation. Elements of all three were to be found in the crash course set by both governments after 1985. We have to acknowledge, too, that diplomacy is not a precise science, so we have to allow for the role of unpredictability, of serendipity, of randomness and, above all, of *confusion*. Having no cognitive framework about a conflict is perhaps better than having a wrong cognitive framework, 'which is what happens when you prematurely close in on an understanding. There are no correct understandings but there are very bad ones.'[61] Much of Anglo-Irish diplomacy since the 1970s falls into this category of confusion, and a great deal of time was spent on trying to make sense of what was going on. There was a specific role for analysis and it was to be found in several exercises in 'Track Two' (or unofficial) diplomacy. This is not a substitute for government-to-government or leader-to-leader contact, but can assist in complementing such contact. At a more general level 'it seeks to promote an environment in a political community, through the education of public opinion, that would make it safer for public opinion to take risks for peace'.[62] But it was difficult for public opinion to take risks in the midst of a campaign of violence.

That called for political leadership. There were some signs that this might be forthcoming. Sinn Féin produced a policy statement in February 1992, *Towards a Lasting Peace In Ireland*, which gave some indication that it was beginning to appreciate the complexity of politics. The Northern Secretary, Sir Patrick Mayhew, in a major speech at the University of Ulster at Coleraine on 16 December 1992, sent a coded message to the wider nationalist community when he acknowledged past British wrongs. He paid obeisance to the historic figures of constitutional nationalism and commented that Sinn Féin had excluded itself from the talks: 'if its cause does have a serious political purpose, then let it renounce unequivocally the use and threat of violence, and demonstrate over a sufficient period that its renunciation is for real'. He described the British government's role as that of a 'facilitator' with no separate political agenda of its own: 'the Government is just as plainly the facilitator of the will of the people in Northern Ireland democratically expressed, as terrorism is its enemy'.[63]

The origins of all this movement can be traced to two separate sets of talks: the SDLP–Sinn Féin dialogue that began in 1988 and the secret meetings between Sinn Féin and the British government that began in 1990. The timing of the 1988 development was significant because it came on the back of a huge public relations disaster for the IRA (and implicitly Sinn Féin) following the massacre of eleven innocent civilians at a Remembrance Day ceremony in Enniskillen in November 1987.[64] The SDLP leader, John Hume, decided that this was a good psychological moment to challenge the armed struggle. In a letter to Sinn Féin's president Gerry Adams, dated 17 March 1988, he pointed out that the IRA campaign was doing more damage to the people whom they claimed to be protecting; that it was too simplistic to state that the 'cause of all the violence is the British presence in Ireland'; that it was the people, rather than the territory, of Ireland that had to be united; and that the IRA 'methods and their strategy have actually become more sacred than their cause'.[65] There followed a series of meetings between the two parties which ended in September when it became clear that the gap between them could not be bridged.

The process was interesting for several reasons. Firstly, it was the first time that Sinn Féin policies had been scrutinised so closely by a party which sought the same end of Irish unity. A curious juxtaposition arose during the dialogue. It was the SDLP that emerged as the *republican* party as it sketched out the implications of postnationalism.[66] It was the SDLP that invoked the ghosts of the republican past to challenge Sinn Féin's claim to be the heirs of non-sectarianism. The SDLP reminded Sinn Féin that Wolfe Tone and Patrick Pearse had called off the armed struggle rather than commit their people to further bloodshed. Secondly, the dialogue had an educative effect and shifted the debate away from moral certitude. Over the next few years Sinn Féin had much more contact with those who did not support the armed struggle. Thirdly, the dialogue rehearsed many of the issues which were to appear in the Downing Street Declaration of the two prime ministers (John Major and Albert Reynolds) of December 1993 by removing the debate about self-determination from its theological plinth and placing it in the harsh political world of the late twentieth century. Some of these realities were faced in Sinn Féin's 1992 discussion paper, *Towards a*

Lasting Peace in Ireland. It recognised that unionist fears would have to be addressed, and it accepted that British withdrawal would only be brought about by a process of cooperation between both governments in consultation with all parties in Northern Ireland. This represented movement on Sinn Féin's part because now it recognised the legitimacy and role of the Irish government as well as the rights of Northern Protestants. Finally, the document raised its eyes above the parapet by taking account of the international dimension and the political implications of the process of European integration.

The secret meetings between Sinn Féin's Martin McGuinness and an emissary of the British government need not detain us because, essentially, they were about building up trust. We can assume that enough was established; otherwise republicans would not have bought into the process that led to their ceasefire announcement of 31 August 1994. In any case the details of these contacts were put on the public record when Sinn Féin published a forty-seven-page pamphlet, *Setting the Record Straight*, in January 1994. Its subtitle accurately portrays its contents: 'A record of communication between Sinn Féin and the British government October 1990–November 1993'. What mattered was that communication had been established. Contact between Sinn Féin and the SDLP was not renewed until April 1993, when the Hume–Adams talks began.[67] Following a few meetings a joint statement was issued in late April which read, initially, like a stale reiteration of Irish nationalism. But it was couched in the language of accommodation and recognised that any 'new agreement is only achievable and viable if it can earn and enjoy the allegiance of the different traditions of this island by accommodating diversity and providing for national reconciliation'.[68] The Hume–Adams contacts continued through the summer and culminated in a joint statement – the broad principle of which would be 'for consideration between the two governments' – being forward to Dublin on 25 September.[69]

TOWARDS INCLUSION

At this stage the peace process was broadened onto an intergovernmental level if only because of Dublin and London's insistence on distancing themselves from proximity to Sinn Féin in order to assuage unionist fears.[70] It was an appropriate moment because two of the leading players had departed the scene: Margaret Thatcher in November 1990 and Charle Haughey in February 1992. In keeping with their styles of politics both of their resignations were dramatic and controversial. Both individuals had dominated their respective parties, but the manner of their departures illustrated the deep damage they had done to their parties as well. The Northern Ireland conflict had played a central role during their years in office. Ironically it was one of Margaret Thatcher's greatest triumphs. The signing of the Anglo-Irish Agreement in 1985 was one of the defining moments in the long and bitter relationship between the two islands. But as her memoirs (and hindsight) revealed, it was a reluctant triumph. Haughey could claim no such triumph. Again it is an irony that for someone who had devoted so much commitment to the problem he got poor returns. History will not be kind on his stewardship. He misread the North as early as the gun-running episode. His republicanism owed more to Eamon de Valera than to the more fluid positions of Seán Lemass and Jack Lynch. Too much of his time had been devoted to looking over his shoulder at a putative Sinn Féin electoral threat. He was too dismissive of the liberal agenda in Southern politics and did not appreciate how it could impact on the Northern question. Finally, he had little feel for developments in Irish-American politics and failed to influence the US administration. For the most part his Northern policy was that which was imposed on him. It was his personal tragedy that he was forced out of office just when he had begun to take extensive soundings within the republican movement; this initiative might be seen as the first tentative steps in the peace process, but it was Haughey's successor, Albert Reynolds, that was able to claim the benefits of this policy.[71]

Discussions between British and Irish officials gathered pace in late 1993, and there were three separate Anglo-Irish meetings in December before a joint declaration was launched by Prime Minister John Major and Taoiseach Albert Reynolds in London on 15 December. The Downing Street Declaration was a very personal affair – there were more references in it to the two prime ministers than to their respective governments. Major and Reynolds represented the new guard. Both had taken leadership of their parties and governments when their more charismatic predecessors were forced to resign in controversial circumstances. When Reynolds called an election in November 1992 Fianna Fáil dropped nine seats and 5 percentage points. He was forced into coalition with Dick Spring's Labour Party, who took six of the fifteen cabinet posts. When Spring became Tánaiste and Minister for Foreign affairs he re-established a line of continuity in Anglo-Irish affairs because, it will be remembered, he had been a central player in the process that led to the signing of the Anglo-Irish Agreement in 1985. His was the most experienced voice in the new coalition.[72] It was clear from the outset that the new government was giving Northern Ireland a very high priority. In their *Programme for Partnership Government*

Fianna Fáil and Labour said they would mobilise 'all the resources of the Government which can contribute to this process [and was working towards] an accommodation of the two traditions in Ireland, based on the principle that both must have equally satisfactory, secure and durable, political, administrative and symbolic expression and protection as set out in the Forum Report'[73] – an embryonic outline of what was to appear in the Belfast Agreement.

Reynolds's standing with elements of his own party was suspect. The same could be said about John Major. After the 1992 election the Conservatives held a majority of twenty-one seats over all other parties, and with by-election slippages inevitable in the course of any parliament the thirteen unionists were in a position of some influence. Moreover, as time went on Major found himself to be a figure of contempt among traditional Thatcherites. Reynolds and Major were deal-makers who liked, and needed, each other. Hence the Prime Minister's tone when he told the Commons on 15 December 1993 that when he met the Taoiseach at Downing Street 'two years ago, we both agreed on the need to work together to try to bring about peace in Northern Ireland and in the Republic . . . we both knew that, after 25 years of killing, we had to make it a personal priority both to seek a permanent end to violence and to establish the basis for a comprehensive and lasting political settlement'.[74]

The Downing Street Declaration did establish the basis for a comprehensive and lasting peace. That may not have been obvious at the outset because the declaration was a (deliberate) piece of tortuous syntax that defies textual exegesis. One of the more astute commentaries on the declaration comes, as we have seen, from Sir David Goodall, a former High Commissioner to India, but more importantly one of the chief architects of the 1985 agreement. Goodall understands the nuances, the actors and the dynamics of the Northern Ireland conflict. He notes the declaration's skilful drafting and abundant use of coded language allowed for constructive ambiguity. Hence it is 'a minor diplomatic masterpiece . . . [which] is not a formal agreement or treaty setting the framework for a comprehensive constitutional settlement: it is a political statement of attitude and intent directed primarily at the IRA. The two heads of government have carefully shelved all the difficult longer term issues . . . in order to make a bid for an IRA ceasefire.'[75]

Three distinct aspects of the declaration deserve comment. The first concerned Europe: there are two references to developments within Europe in the declaration. The first is in paragraph 3, which acknowledges that 'the development of Europe will, of itself, require new approaches to serve interests common to both parts of the island of

Ireland, and to Ireland and the United Kingdom as partners in the European Union'. The second is in paragraph 9, which states that any new structures or institutions that may be set up in Northern Ireland would take account 'of newly forged links with the rest of Europe'.[76] Placing it in this wider context allowed for the blurring of boundaries and distancing from the three solitudes. The second aspect concerns dialogue and inclusion. As a result of the declaration a Forum for Peace and Reconciliation was established in Dublin with the task of making 'recommendations on ways in which agreement and trust between both traditions in Ireland can be promoted and established'.[77] Ten parties and a number of independent senators participated when the first session met in Dublin Castle on 28 October 1994, following the republican and loyalist ceasefires. Its role was unlike the New Ireland Forum of the previous decade in that its primary purpose was to bring Sinn Féin into the democratic process. That was a significant development. The forum was to be a victim of the breakdown in the IRA ceasefire but it did valuable work in the interim.

The third aspect concerned the attitudes of the paramilitaries. The loyalist ceasefire was conditional on the IRA maintaining its ceasefire. That ceasefire did not come without its problems.[78] When the IRA announced its cessation of violence it refused to use the word 'permanent' nor did it accept the Joint Declaration. It was not prepared to countenance decommissioning of weapons prior to being involved in meaningful all-party talks. Nevertheless Major accepted as a 'working assumption' that the IRA had renounced violence for a good three months after the cessation and his officials began a series of bilateral talks with Sinn Féin to be followed later by meetings with ministers. Matters did not rest there. Republicans sought clarification of certain aspects of the declaration. The government view was that it was a free-standing document which needed no further comment. Sinn Féin demurred. Eventually the government responded in May 1994 to twenty questions from Sinn Féin. Question 18 (a) asked specifically: 'The British Government has called upon Sinn Féin to renounce violence. What does this mean?' The response was a fudged reiteration of paragraph 10 of the declaration, itself a fudge that makes no mention of decommissioning. Republicans asserted that the absence of violence and their democratic mandate were all that were needed to ensure all-party talks. In the meantime Sir Patrick Mayhew provided a further clarification of what was meant by the renunciation of violence in the United States in March 1995. It was dubbed the 'Washington 3' speech because it contained three elements on decommissioning: the acceptance of the principle of disarmament; the modalities by which it could be achieved; and the necessity to make some gesture of decommissioning as an act of good faith prior to all-party talks. Both sets of paramilitaries baulked at this last point. They read it as a new precondition and believed that to accept it would be construed as surrender. This was to be the major hurdle blocking the peace process. The IRA ceasefire broke down in February 1996 with the bombing of Canary Wharf in London.

Before that happened both governments published on 22 February 1995 *Frameworks for the Future*, better known as the 'Joint Framework Document', which was in fact two separate documents. The first, *A Framework for Accountable Government in Northern Ireland*, was concerned with matters internal to Northern Ireland. The second, *A New Framework for Agreement*, had a significant subtitle: 'A shared understanding between the British and Irish Governments to assist discussion and negotiation involving the Northern Ireland parties'. Here was a further recognition that agreement entailed the support of the two governments as well as the two communities in Northern Ireland. As with paragraph 9 of the Joint Declaration, the new document recognised the need to cooperate with the EU. To give substance to this interest the EU Commission had created a special task force in the autumn of 1994 to look further into ways in which it could give practical assistance to Northern Ireland and the border counties in the peace process. Arising from the work of the task force, the commission announced a proposal for a special support programme (the 'Delors package'). The EU Special Support Programme for Northern Ireland and the Border Counties (referred to as the Peace and Reconciliation Programme) would run for five years with a budget of 300 million ECUs for the first three years and with finance for the final two years subject to a review based on a commission report to the Council. 80 per cent of the funds would be spent in the North and 20 per cent in the South but with a minimum of 15 per cent allocated to cross-border projects. The respective Departments of Finance in Dublin and Belfast were given responsibility for drafting and negotiating a detailed programme. These were announced on 28 June 1995. Here was one small example of how managing change in the international system had moved on from old-fashioned notions about the role of the nation-state and power politics and from spheres of responsibility and spheres of abstention to that of 'functional regimes'.

The two governments attempted to break the decommissioning impasse when they launched a 'twin track' process on 28 November 1995 to make progress in parallel on the decommissioning issue and all-party negotiations. An international decommissioning panel, chaired by former US Senator George Mitchell who was joined by Canadian General John de Chastelain and a former Finnish Prime Minister Harri Holkeri, was created. It produced an impressive report on 22 January 1996 that made the stark point that 'success in the peace process cannot be achieved solely by reference to the decommissioning of arms' (paragraph 51). Instead it decoupled the issue of decommissioning through the enunciation of six principles with the need for confidence-building measures during all-party negotiations.[79] To attain the latter the government called elections for 30 May 1996 to create a forum that would be 'a deliberate body [whose] purpose will be the discussion of issues relevant to promoting dialogue and understanding within Northern Ireland'. 110 members were to be elected on the basis of all eighteen Northern Ireland constituencies electing five members each under the D'Hondt formula, with the top ten parties selecting a further two from a regional list. The only advantage in this exercise was that it enabled fringe parties such as the Progressive Unionist Party, the Ulster Democratic Party and the Women's Coalition to participate in the process. Only Sinn Féin emerged with an enhanced mandate. With 15.5 per cent of the vote it achieved its highest poll ever in Northern Ireland but since the IRA had not reinstated its ceasefire Sinn Féin was denied entry into negotiations.[80]

Suffice it to say that mistrust, a precarious Conservative majority in the Commons and a fundamental disagreement on the nature of de-commissioning all combined to undermine the process. One ex-amination of the Major government's strategy depicts a contradictory picture of important confidence-building measures combined with the erection of 'an ever-changing obstacle course to inclusive multi-party negotiations'; a picture of a Prime Minister in thrall to his Europhobic and ultra-unionist right wing and to David Trimble's (UUP leader from September 1995) forays in procrastination.[81] The IRA did not an-nounce 'a complete cessation of military operations' until 19 July 1997, that is only after Labour won the May 1997 general election with a majority of 179. No sooner had Tony Blair become Prime Minister than he received a call from President Clinton at 4 a.m. on 2 May with a request for fresh negotiations on Ireland. This has been placed in the context of the creation of a new 'special relationship': 'With the demise of John Major, the last remnant of the "special relationship" of old is gone. With Blair and Clinton on the world stage, will there be a vital international Centre?'[82] The new government set the multi-party talks deadline for one year later. The process had been assisted, too, by the appointment of George Mitchell as chair of the multi-party talks on 11 June 1996. He displayed tremendous patience and diplomacy throughout the talks. With Sinn Féin's entry into the talks in September 1997 the process had become more inclusive. On 25 March 1998 Mitchell set 9 April as the date for agreement between the parties; and on 7 April he published his own draft paper. The talks failed to meet the deadline but agreement was reached early on the morning of 10 April – hence the Good Friday Agreement – an agreement that was endorsed by 71.1 per cent of Northern Ireland's voters and 94.39 per cent of the Republic's voters on 22 May 1998.

What is of interest to students of conflict transformation has been the role played by prestigious third parties.[83] It is impossible to imagine a 1998 agreement without the full-hearted support of the Clinton administration and the international commissioners, Senator George Mitchell, General John de Chastelain and Harri Holkeri.[84] Equally, it is inconceivable that such an explosive issue as a new policing service for Northern Ireland could have been tackled if left solely in the hands of Northern Ireland's politicians. Instead 'An Independent Commission on Policing for Northern Ireland' was established under the terms of the 1998 Agreement which had sought 'a new beginning to policing in Northern Ireland with a police service capable of attracting and sustaining support from the community as a whole'. The commission had been chaired by Christopher Patten, former Governor of Hong Kong and (Conservative) Cabinet Minister and drew its membership from civic society in Northern Ireland, a former Deputy Commissioner of the Metropolitan Police, and international experts from the United States and South Africa. The commission was established in June 1999 and reported in Sepember 1999. The Police (Northern Ireland) Bill, based on most of the 175 Commission recommendations, trundled through parliament and became law in November 2000.

CONCLUSION

The profound significance of the 1998 agreement has been noted by Joseph Ruane and Jennifer Todd by comparing it with the 1973 Sunningdale Agreement: 'The Belfast Agreement offers a fuller recognition of the right of the people of Northern Ireland to determine their constitutional future. It is much more inclusive of the range of political opinion and more supportive of equality and human rights. Crucially, it offers something which Sunningdale could not: a complete end to political violence. These differences reflect profound differences in the contexts of the two agreements.[85] The genius of the 1998 agreement can be traced to a few innocuous words. The question of identity is dealt with in subsection (vi) of the opening paragraph which recognises 'the birthright of all the people of Northern Ireland to identify themselves and be accepted as Irish or British *or both*' (emphasis added); and in paragraph 6 of the section dealing with the Northern Ireland Assembly which states that at their first meeting 'members of the Assembly will register a designation of identity – nationalist, unionist *or other*' [emphasis added]. Here was the culmination of a movement away from exclusion and towards polycentric identities and a blurring of boundaries. In that respect the 1998 agreement drew on the experience of the previous quarter-century of conflict management exercises.

But we need to be conscious of the very provisional nature of the Good Friday Agreement. Drawing on a comparative study of peace agreements Robert Rothstein states:

> One thing that is imperative is to establish realistic expectations about how much and how quickly a weak and tentative peace agreement can alter the basic nature of a long and profoundly bitter conflict. It is also important for the leaders on both sides to recognise that the game has changed, that the behaviour necessary to get to a provisional agreement is not always the behaviour appropriate for the post-agreement period: needs and priorities change, interests must be redefined or revisioned, and a joint learning process must be institutionalised and accelerated.[86]

We may need to revise William Shannon's timetable when he allowed fifteen years to gauge whether the Anglo-Irish Agreement would succeed. As Ruane and Todd illustrated above, it is the complete end to political violence that is the new factor. But we need to enter two caveats: violence is not at a complete end, as low-level punishment beatings and a loyalist paramilitary feud on the Shankill Road in Belfast in the late summer of 2000 illustrates;[87] and we must never underestimate what Byron Bland has called 'the ritual of small differences' – the annual marching season guarantees that that is never far from our minds. The distance between the end of violence and a proper 'peace' manifested itself, too, in the whole morass of symbolism as evidenced by the controversy over the Patten Report on policing.[88] Those opposed to the agreement have eaten into David Trimble's majority. In May 2000 Trimble, with only 53 per cent of the vote, narrowly carried a motion at the Ulster Unionist Council to go back into government with Sinn Féin; and on 21 September 2000 his party lost the Westminster seat of South Antrim to a DUP candidate on a 43 per cent turnout.

On the positive side we can allow for a less fatalistic general public, a more tolerant civic society, burgeoning economic opportunities, and a sense of shame at our past. Politics is now more concerned with equity issues. A sense of civic consciousness is being developed aided by a Civic Forum created by the government under the terms of the Agreement. North–South cooperation has been improved immensely.[89] And the agreement has been heralded as a model for other societies coming out of conflict.[90] Finally we should bear in mind that the agreement should be read alongside the constitutional innovation inherent in the devolution debate in the rest of the United Kingdom. Vernon Bogdanor has highlighted the historic irony of the Agreement which

> offers, in essence, a return to the past, a return to Gladstone's original conception of Home Rule in a form suited to modern conditions . . . the proposals for devolution, together with the North–South Council, giving institutional form to the Irish dimension, and the British–Irish Council offers a chance of realizing the underlying theme of Gladstonian thinking, i.e. recognition both of the various and distinctive national identities within these islands, and also of the close and complex links between them . . . The British–Irish Council is an expression of the belief that the manifold links which exist between Britain and the Irish Republic can no longer be contained within a formal framework which, in theory at least, makes the two countries as foreign to each other as Russia and Brazil.[91]

NOTES

CHAPTER 1

1 A.J.P. Taylor, *English History 1914–1945* (Oxford: Oxford University Press, 1965), p. 161.
2 John Whyte, *Interpreting Northern Ireland* (Oxford: Clarendon Press, 1990), p. 246.
3 Eddie McAteer, leader of the Nationalist Party, quoted in W.H. Van Voris, *Violence in Ulster: An Oral Documentary* (Amherst: Massachusetts University Press, 1975), p. 14.
4 J.G.A. Pocock, 'The Limits and Divisions of British History: In Search of the Unknown Subject', *American History Review*, 87, 2 (1982), p. 318.
5 Con Cremin, 'Northern Ireland at the United Nations August/September 1969', *Irish Studies in International Affairs*, 1, 2 (1980), p. 69. A similar opinion was expressed more diplomatically in the Downing Street Declaration of August 1969 (agreed by the Prime Ministers of the United Kingdom and of Northern Ireland). The second paragraph read that the 'United Kingdom Government again affirms that responsibility for affairs in Northern Ireland is entirely a matter of domestic jurisdiction. The United Kingdom Government will take full responsibility for asserting this principle in all international relations.' Quoted in Appendix 6, Richard Deutsch and Vivien Magowan, *Northern Ireland 1968–72:*

A Chronology of Events, vol. 1, 1968–71 (Belfast, Blackstaff Press, 1973), p. 152.
6 Quoted in K. Boyle, T. Hadden and P. Hillyard, *Law and State: The Case of Northern Ireland* (London: Martin Robertson, 1975), p. 171.
7 Nicholas Mansergh, *The Prelude to Partition: Concepts and Aims in Ireland and India,* The 1976 Commonwealth Lecture (Cambridge: Cambridge University Press, 1978), p. 45.
8 *HC Deb.*, 127, cols. 928–30 (29 March 1920).
9 Nicholas Mansergh, *The Government of Northern Ireland: A Study in Devolution* (London: Allen and Unwin, 1936), p. 314.
10 D.S. Johnson, 'The Northern Ireland Economy 1914–39', in L. Kennedy and P. Ollernshaw (eds.), *An Economic History of Ulster, 1820–1940*, (Manchester: Manchester University Press, 1985), p. 191.
11 J.J. Lee, *Ireland 1912–1985: Politics and Society* (Cambridge: Cambridge University Press, 1989), p. 45. Lee is scathing in his criticism of unionist acquiescence in this arrangement, suggesting that it dented the unionists' cherished 'self-image of men whose word was their bond' and that it 'counts as the basest of all "betrayals" of the period' (p. 44–5). For a candid explanation of why unionists accepted six rather than nine counties see the statement by their Westminster spokesman, Sir James

Craig, in *HC Deb.*, 127, cols. 990–1 (29 March 1920). In his dispassionate account Whyte (*Interpreting Northern Ireland*, pp. 163–4) describes their acceptance as 'a clear example of unionist reluctance to deal fairly'.

12   R.F. Foster, *Modern Ireland 1600–1972* (London: Allen Lane, 1988), p. 53.

13   A good account of the expectations and outcome of the Boundary Commission can be found in Lee, *Ireland*, pp. 140–50.

14   Clare O'Halloran, *Partition and the Limits of Irish Nationalism* (Dublin: Gill and Macmillan, 1987), p. xiii.

15   See Richard Rose, *Governing Without Consensus: An Irish Perspective* (London: Faber and Faber, 1971), pp. 449–52.

16   Frank Wright, *Northern Ireland: A Comparative Analysis* (Dublin: Gill and Macmillan, 1987), p. 53.

17   *ibid.*, pp. 28 and 48.

18   Whyte, *Interpreting Northern Ireland*, pp. 124–5.

19   Patrick Keatinge, 'Unequal Sovereigns: The Diplomatic Dimension of Anglo-Irish Relations', in P.J. Drudy (ed.), *Ireland and Britain Since 1922* (Cambridge: Cambridge University Press, 1986), p. 139.

20   Quoted in H.E. Chehabi, 'Self-Determination, Territorial Integrity, and the Falkland Islands', *Political Science Quarterly*, 100, 2 (1985), p. 219.

21   Lee, *Ireland*, p. 77.

22   Denis Ireland, *From the Jungle of Belfast* (Belfast: Blackstaff Press, 1973), p. 18.

23   See, for example, *The Situation in the SIX COUNTIES of North-East Ireland by the Taoiseach, Jack Lynch, Tralee, 20 September 1969* (Dublin: Government Publication, 1969). By 1973, admittedly, Irish government documents referred to 'Northern Ireland': see the agreed communiqué following the Sunningdale Conference on 6–9 December 1973. Quoted in Deutsch and Magowan, *Northern Ireland 1968–72*, vol 2, pp. 376–8.

24   Dennis Kennedy, *The Widening Gulf: Northern Attitudes to the Independent Irish State 1919–49* (Belfast: Blackstaff Press, 1988), p. 231.

25   All material is extracted from *Irish Times*, 3 January 1978, 2 January 1980, 5 January 1983 and 3 January 1984. As an extreme example see a football report of Northern Ireland's 3–1 victory over Austria in September 1983 by Sam Duddy in *Ulster: Voice of the Ulster Defence Association*, October 1983. The tone of the report is epitomised in the penultimate sentence: 'It would not be too much to ask of the players, irrespective of their religious persuasion, to wear a combination of red-white-and-blue, and play in the ULSTER International Soccer team.'

26   Patrick Buckland, *The Factory of Grievances: Devolved Government in Northern Ireland 1921–39* (Dublin: Gill and Macmillan, 1979), p. 180.

27   Kennedy, *Widening Gulf*, p. 69.

28   Ronan Fanning, *Independent Ireland* (Dublin: Helicon, 1983), pp. 25–6.

29   See *Irish Times*, 4 January 1980, and *Irish News*, 1 January 1991. On the Chequers conference see Fanning, *Independent Ireland*, pp. 87–92.

30   Kennedy, *Widening Gulf*, p. 97. The earlier quotations are taken from pp. 17 and 19. A similar picture emerges from the BBC in Northern Ireland: see Rex Cathcart, *The Most Contrary Region: The BBC in Northern Ireland 1924–1984* (Belfast: Blackstaff Press, 1984), *passim*.

31   Lee, *Ireland*, pp. 266 and 218.

32   See O'Halloran, *Partition*, pp. 57–92.

33   John Whyte, 'The Permeability of the United Kingdom–Irish Border: A Preliminary Reconnaisance' (unpublished paper, 1983), pp. 3 and 14.

34   'Ireland is an island behind an island'; Jean Blanchard, French political commentator on Irish affairs, quoted in Basil Chubb, *The Government and Politics of Ireland*, 2nd edn, (London: Longman, 1982), p. 8.

35   Johnson, 'Northern Ireland Economy', pp. 216-17.

36   *ibid.*, p. 204. But see A.H. Birch, 'A Note on Devolution', *Political Studies*, 4, 2 (1956), p. 311, who argues that that is precisely what it did not do.

37   Tom Wilson, *Ulster: Conflict and Consent* (Oxford: Oxford University Press, 1989), p. 77. See his table 9.1 on p. 84 for the comparison of identifiable public expenditure per head.

38   Whyte, *Interpreting Northern Ireland*, p. 161.

39   Lee, *Ireland*, pp. 77 and 536.

40   David Fitzpatrick, *The Two Irelands 1912–1939* (Oxford: Oxford

University Press, 1998), pp. 205–42.

41   See, for example, Denis Ireland, *From the Jungle of Belfast*, for a comfortable Northern bourgeois view of the South: and a richly splenetic exposition of the 'myth' of Northern propserity in the Sinn Féin weekly, *Young Ireland*, August 1921, quoted in O'Halloran, *Partition*, p. 17.

42   I am aware that it may not be possible to speak of a single political culture in Northern Ireland. See Arend Lijphart, 'The Northern Ireland Problem: Cases, Theories and Solutions', *British Journal of Political Science*, 5, 1 (1975), pp. 83–106.

43   Kennedy, *Widening Gulf*, pp. 5 and 9.

44   Quoted in Lee, *Ireland*, p. 105. Brian Farrell qualifies the remark in his *The Irish Parliamentary Tradition* (Dublin: Gill and Macmillan, 1973), p. 23, by saying that the Irish leaders were no revolutionaries in the political sense but may have been in the cultural sense.

45   See, for example, T.K. Daniel, 'Griffith on his Noble Head: The Determinants of Cumann na nGaedheal Economic Policy, 1922–32', *Irish Economic and Social History*, 3 (1976), pp. 55–65.

46   Fitzpatrick, *Two Irelands*, p. 214.

47   Lee, *Ireland,* p. 375.

48   Wright, *Northern Ireland*, p. 145.

49   Fitzpatrick, *Two Irelands*, p. 216.

50   Kerby A. Miller, 'Emigration, Capitalism and Ideology in Post-Famine Ireland', in Richard Kearney (ed.), *Migrations: The Irish at Home and Abroad* (Dublin: Wolfhound Press, 1990), p. 92.

51   Whyte, *Interpreting Northern Ireland*, p. 153. The figures for Northern Ireland are extracted from Whyte, p. 65.

52   Lee, *Ireland*, p. 379.

53   *ibid.*, p. 187.

54   Much of what follows is based on Paul Arthur, 'Policing and Crisis Politics: Northern Ireland as a Case Study', *Parliamentary Affairs*, 39, 3, (July 1986), pp. 341–53.

55   Charles Townshend, *Political Violence in Ireland: Government and Resistance Since 1848* (Oxford: Oxford University Press, 1983), p. 102.

56   *ibid.*, p. 96.

57   Eanna Mulloy, *Emergency Legislation: Dynasties of Coercion,* Field Day Pamphlet No. 10 (Derry, 1986). The emphasis of his remarks is contained in his subtitle.

58   Michael Farrell, *Emergency Legislation,* Field Day Pamphlet No. 11 (Derry, 1986) p. 6.

59   *ibid.,* p. 25. See, too, Liam de Paor, 'Partition and ambiguity', *Irish Times*, 25 October 1984.

60   Fitzpatrick, *Two Irelands*, p. 237.

61   Pocock, 'Limits and Divisions of British History', p. 317.

62   *ibid.*, p. 334.

63   J.G. Bulpitt, *Territory and Power in the United Kingdom: An Interpretation* (Manchester: Manchester University Press, 1983), pp. 160, 238, 237 and 59.

64   *ibid.*, pp. 81–2, 96–7, (157).

65   *ibid.*, p. 98.

66   David W. Miller, *Queen's Rebels: Ulster Loyalism in Historical Perspective* (Dublin: Gill and Macmillan, 1978), p. 5. Miller writes that this formulation reduces political obligation to a simple matter of private ethics: one ought to be loyal to the king for the same reason that one should keep ordinary bargains. If the ruler defaults on his side of the bargain the subjects are absolved of their duty to obey his laws. It resembles even more closely the peculiarly Scottish variant of contractarian thought and practice, covenanting, in which the proper course for subjects whose king violates his bargain (or refuses to undertake it in the first place) is not to repudiate his regime, but to refuse compliance with his laws or try to coerce him into keeping (or making) the bargain. Such contractarian theory was used to rationalise the Glorious Revolution of 1688 by a resolution of the Commons of the English Convention in 1689. See pp. 5 and 27.

67   Quoted in Eric A. Nordlinger, *Conflict Regulation in Divided Societies* (Cambridge, Mass: Center for International Affairs, Harvard University, 1972), p. 3. See, too, Miller, *Queen's Rebels*, p. 66 on definitions of the 'nation' supplied by Karl Deutsch and Rupert Emerson. These definitions lead Miller to query whether 'Ulster Protestants [had] come to trust the whole people of the United Kingdom, as represented in its democratic regime, as a satisfactory guarantor of their civil rights?'

68   Pocock, 'Limits and Divisions of British History', p. 322.
69   Miller, *Queen's Rebels*, pp. 12 and 25.
70   *ibid.*, p. 132.
71   Wright, *Northern Ireland*, p. 48, and Bulpitt, *Territory and Power*, p. 146.
72   Pocock, p. 320.
73   Peter Gibbon, *The Origins of Ulster Unionism* (Manchester: Manchester University Press, 1975); J.C. Beckett, 'Northern Ireland', in B. Crozier and R. Moss (eds.), *The Ulster Debate: Report of a Study Group* (London: Bodley Head, 1972), pp. 11–26.
74   Rose, *Governing Without Consensus*, p. 215.
75   Tom Nairn, *The Breakup of Britain: Crisis and Neo-nationalism* (London: New Left Books, 1977), pp. 240–1.
76   Walker Connor, 'A nation is a nation, is an ethnic group, is a . . .', *Ethnic and Racial Studies*, 1, 4 (1978), pp. 377–400.
77   Quoted in R. Wallis, S. Bruce and D. Taylor, *No Surrender! Paisleyism and the Politics of Ethnic Identity in Northern Ireland* (Belfast: Department of Social Studies, Queen's University Belfast, 1986), p. 3.
78   Miller, *Queen's Rebels*, pp. 130 and 103. Others have commented on a loyalist sense of anti-Englishness. See Patrick Buckland, 'The Unity of Ulster Unionism 1886–1939', *History*, 60 (June 1975), pp. 219–22; and Rosemary Harris, *Prejudice and Tolerance in Ulster: A Study of Neighbours and 'Strangers' in a Border Community* (Manchester: Manchester University Press, 1972), p. 188.
79   Ian Budge and Cornelius O'Leary, *Belfast: Approach to Crisis – A Study of Belfast Politics, 1613–1970* (London: Macmillan, 1975), p. 143. See, too, A.G. Donaldson, 'The Constitution of Northern Ireland: Its Origins and Development', *University of Toronto Law Journal*, 11, 1 (1955), p. 42, where he discusses whether the United Kingdom parliament had partially abdicated its sovereignty.
80   See Patricia Jalland, 'United Kingdom Devolution 1910–14: Political Panacea or Tactical Diversion?', *English Historical Review*, (October 1979) pp. 757–85. See, too, Vernon Bogdanor, *Devolution* (Oxford: Oxford University Press, 1979), p. 46: 'In June 1914 Lord Crewe, the Lord Privy Seal, introduced on behalf of the government a proposal that the nine counties of Ulster could, on the basis of co-option, vote themselves out of a Dublin parliament for a period of six years after the Act came into force . . . the Lords transformed the temporary exclusion of Ulster into permanent exclusion.'
81   Mansergh, *Prelude to Partition*, pp. 29–30.
82   John McColgan, *British Policy and the Irish Administration 1920–22* (London: Allen and Unwin, 1983), p. 132. Sir Ernest Clark (1864–1951) was described by a future Prime Minister of Northern Ireland, Lord Brookeborough, as the 'midwife to the new province of Ulster'. He had had previous experience as Assistant Under-Secretary in the Inland Revenue and in South Africa, both of which were regarded as good qualifications for the practical working of Home Rule institutions: 'As a person the Ulster Unionists found fit to organise the Ulster Special Constabulary and perform the spadework for a future government of Northern Ireland, he was the administrative expression of the Ulster dimension of Britain's Irish policy' (pp. 32–3).
83   Miller, *Queen's Rebels*, p. 128.
84   *HC Deb.*, 127, col. 1333 (31 March 1920).
85   Miller, *Queen's Rebels*, p. 103.
86   Kenneth Pyper, the central character in Frank McGuinness's play *Observe the Sons of Ulster Marching Towards the Somme* (London: Faber, 1986).
87   Lord Brookeborough quoted in Van Voris, *Violence in Ulster*, p. 4.
88   Rose, *Governing Without Consensus*, p. 214.
89   Arthur Aughey, *Under Siege: Ulster Unionism and the Anglo-Irish Agreement* (Belfast: Blackstaff Press, 1989), p. 10.
90   McColgan, *British Policy*, p. 137.
91   *HC Deb. (NI)*, 1, 174.
92   Lord Killanin and Michael V. Duignan, *The Shell Guide to Ireland*, 2nd edn (London: Ebury Press, 1967), p. 115.
93   C.E.B. Brett, *Buildings of Belfast 1700–1914*, 2nd edn (Belfast: Friars Bush Press, 1985), p. 65. The other 'architectural monument of consequence' named by Brett is the Royal Courts of Justice.

94 Anthony Cronin, *Irish Times*, 10 September 1976. Note his use of the term 'Six County State'. Cronin did not pretend to be a disinterested party. As well as being a poet, novelist and literary critic, he also acted as cultural adviser to Taoiseach Charles Haughey during the 1980s.

95 Brian Faulkner, *Memoirs of a Statesman* (London: Weidenfeld and Nicolson, 1978), p. 26.

96 Claire Palley, *The Evolution, Disintegration and Possible Reconstruction of the Northern Ireland Constitution* (Belfast: Barry Rose Publishers in conjunction with the Institute of Irish Studies, 1973), p. 389.

97 Kenneth Bloomfield, 'Constitution-Making in Northern Ireland: A Look Around the Monuments', (Bass Ireland Lecture, University of Ulster, Jordanstown, 28 February 1991).

98 Frank Newsam, *The Home Office* (London: Allen and Unwin, 1955), p. 172.

99 *Belfast Telegraph*, 29 April 1965.

100 C.E.B. Brett, *Long Shadows Cast Before: Nine Lives in Ulster 1625–1977* (Edinburgh: John Bartholomew, 1978), p. 135. Later (p. 139) he writes with some restraint: 'A dozen times since then I have been reproached by friends in the British Labour Party, one at least today a cabinet minister, with the words: "Why ever did you not warn us of what was coming?" I have never yet succeeded in finding words adequate to reply to that question.' Earlier evidence suggests continuing Home Office bias. Buckland, *Factory of Grievances*, p. 266, quotes a letter from the Home Secretary, William Joynson-Hicks, to Craig in December 1928 after he had received a deputation from the NILP complaining about the decision of the Belfast government to abolish proportional representation in parliamentary elections: 'I don't know whether you would care at any time to discuss the matter with me; of course I am always at your disposal. But beyond that "I know my place", and don't propose to interfere.' Patrick Keatinge, *A Place Among the Nations: Issues of Irish Foreign Policy* (Dublin: Institute of Public Administration, 1978), pp. 106–8, cites instances of hostile Home Office reaction in the 1930s; and Ronan

Fanning, 'The Response of the London and Belfast Governments to the Declaration of the Republic of Ireland, 1948–49', *International Affairs*, 58, 1 (1981–2), pp. 94–114, produces similar evidence for the 1940s.

101 John A. Oliver, *Working at Stormont: Memoirs* (Dublin: Institute of Public Administration, 1978), pp. 47 and 20. Admittedly he was writing of his experiences when he entered the service in 1937.

102 Derek Birrell and Alan Murie, *Policy and Government in Northern Ireland: Lessons of Devolution* (Dublin: Gill and Macmillan, 1980), p. 266.

103 Bloomfield, 'Constitution-Making', p. 14.

104 Oliver, *Working at Stormont*, p. 39.

105 Paul Bew, Peter Gibbon and Henry Patterson, *The State in Northern Ireland, 1921–72: Political Forces and Social Classes* (Manchester: Manchester University Press, 1979), p. 78. See, too, Birrell and Murie, *Policy and Government*, p. 266: 'Even between the wars, when the financial environment was most restrictive, the Northern Ireland government often rejected the cautious and compliant advice of the Ministry of Finance and pursued policies which that ministry felt went beyond what was possible.'

106 Martin Wallace, *Northern Ireland: 50 Years of Self-Government* (Newton Abbott: David and Charles, 1971), p. 157.

107 *Royal Commission on the Constitution 1969–1973 [Kilbrandon Commission]*, Cmnd 5460 (London: HMSO, 1973), paras. 1272–1314.

108 Buckland *Factory of Grievances*, p. 45.

109 Bew, Gibbon and Patterson, *State in Northern Ireland*, pp. 81 and 106.

110 Birrell and Murie, *Policy and Government*, p. 287. Admittedly they are writing of more recent years but their next sentence is crucial for an understanding of the period before direct rule: 'The Home Office had no officials specialising in Northern Ireland affairs.'

111 Deirdre McMahon, *Republicans and Imperialists: Anglo-Irish Relations in the 1930s* (New Haven: Yale University Press, 1984), pp. 240–1. See, too, Buckland, *Factory of Grievances*, pp. 45, 73–7.

112 Buckland, *Factory of Grievances*, p. 92. The 'minus contribution' referred to

the imperial contribution. The idea that not only would Northern Ireland not contribute to the imperial exchequer but it would be reimbursed by it had until then been dismissed as unthinkable because it would require legislation and have implications for relations with the Irish Free State.

113 *ibid.*, p. 113.

114 McMahon, *Republicans and Imperialists*, pp. 278–9.

115 Birrell and Murie, *Policy and Government*, pp. 28–9.

116 *HC Deb.*, 488, col. 631 (1 June 1950). The Home Secretary continued: 'but I hope – and I repeat this – that Northern Ireland will listen to this debate rather more, perhaps, to the spirit that has animated us than sometimes to the exact words which have been uttered, so that we may get nearer to the time when the full co-operation of every citizen in Northern Ireland in the government of that province may be assumed'. More than two decades later a Conservative government found it necessary to adopt a more robust approach in an effort to get full cooperation. The full debate can be found between at cols. 557–647.

117 R.H.S. Crossman, *The Diaries of a Cabinet Minister*, vol. III, (London: Hamilton and Cape, 1977), p. 187.

118 This paragraph relies on David Harkness, *Northern Ireland Since 1920* (Dublin: Helicon, 1983), pp. 106–8.

119 A.F. Madden, ' "Not For Export": The Westminster Model of Government and British Colonial Practice', *Journal of Imperial and Commonwealth History* 8 (Oct. 1979), p. 22. See, too, Bloomfield, 'Constitution-Making', p. 17.

120 Janet Morgan (ed.), *The Backbench Diaries of Richard Crossman* (London: Hamilton and Cape, 1981), pp. 439–40 and 499–500.

CHAPTER 2

1 Albert Camus was writing about the final stages of the civil war in Algeria. The quotation is taken from Hermann Giliomee and Jannie Gagiano (eds.), *The Elusive Search for Peace: South Africa, Israel and Northern Ireland* (Cape Town: Oxford University Press, 1990), p. 1.

2 Edmund Burke, *A Letter to the Sheriffs of Bristol on the Affairs of America* (1777), in B.W. Hill (ed.) *Edmund Burke on Government Politics and Society* (London: Fontana, 1975), p. 189

3 Paul Theroux, referring to Northern Ireland in *The Kingdom by the Sea* (Harmondsworth, Penguin Books, 1984), p. 255.

4 Belinda Loftus, *Mirrors: William III and Mother Ireland* (Dundrum: Picture Press, 1990).

5 Louis MacNeice, 'Carrickfergus' (1936), *The Collected Poems of Louise MacNeice*, ed. E.R. Dodds (London: Faber and Faber, 1979), p. 89–90.

6 Seamus Heaney, 'An Ulster Twilight', *Station Island* (London: Faber and Faber, 1984), p. 39.

7 Conor Cruise O'Brien, 'Imagination and Politics', in Conor Cruise O'Brien and William Dean Vanech, *Power and Consciousness* (London: London University Press, 1969), p. 211.

8 Lionel Trilling, quoted in O'Brien, 'Imagination and Politics', p. 211.

9 John Whyte, *Interpreting Northern Ireland* (Oxford: Clarendon Press, 1990), pp. 258–9.

10 Oliver MacDonagh, *States of Mind: A Study of Anglo-Irish Conflict 1780–1980* (London: Allen and Unwin, 1983), pp. 22 and 26.

11 D.S. Johnson, 'The Northern Ireland Economy 1914–39', in L. Kennedy and P. Ollernshaw (eds.) *An Economic History of Ulster, 1820–1940*, (Manchester: Manchester University Press, 1985) p. 215.

12 Frank Wright, *Northern Ireland: A Comparative Analysis* (Dublin: Gill and Macmillan, 1987), p. xiii.

13 John Darby, *Intimidation and the Control of Conflict in Northern Ireland* (Dublin: Gill and Macmillan, 1986), pp. viii–ix, 10 and 30.

14 See Arend Lijphart, *Democracy in Plural Societies: A Comparative Exploration* (New Haven: Yale University Press, 1977), pp. 147–50. See, too, R.H. Dekmejian, 'Consociational Democracy in Crisis: The Case of Lebanon', *Comparative Politics*, 10, 2, (1978), pp. 251–65; and Donald Horowitz, 'Dual Authority Politics', *Comparative Politics*, 14, 3, (1982), pp. 329–49.

15 David W. Miller, *Queen's Rebels.*

Ulster Loyalism in Historical Perspective (Dublin: Gill and Macmillan, 1978), pp. 68–9.

16 Wright, *Northern Ireland*, pp. 153–4.

17 Geraint Parry, 'Tradition, Community and Self-Determination', *British Journal of Political Science*, 12, 4 (October 1982), pp. 401–2.

18 Rosemary Harris, *Prejudice and Tolerance in Ulster: A Study of Neighbours and 'Strangers' in a Border Community* (Manchester: Manchester University Press, 1972), p. 168. The expression 'exclusive dealing' is borrowed from Wright, *Northern Ireland*, p. 29.

19 Wright, *Northern Ireland*, p. 155. The Cameron Report was concerned with the reasons for the outbreak of civil disturbances late in 1968. See, too, Harris, *Prejudice and Tolerance*, pp. 146–7, on the need to stick to neutral topics in conversation.

20 Seamus Heaney, 'Among Schoolchildren', (John Malone Memorial Lecture, Queen's University Belfast, 9 June 1983), p. 8.

21 Theroux, *Kingdom by the Sea*, p. 233.

22 Parry, 'Tradition', pp. 413–14.

23 See, for example, Richard Jenkins, Hastings Donnan, Graham McFarlane, *The Sectarian Divide in Northern Ireland Today* (London: Royal Anthropological Society of Great Britain and Ireland, Occasional Paper No. 41, 1986.)

24 Frank Burton, *The Politics of Legitimacy: Struggles in a Belfast Community* (London: Routledge and Kegan Paul, 1978), pp. 10 and 125.

25 *ibid.*, p. 37. He credits the civil rights movement (p. 121) with having 'exposed the social practices behind telling by making explicit discriminatory practices'. For an account of telling in another context see David Beresford's report on South African apartheid in *Guardian*, 13 June 1991.

26 Heaney, 'Among Schoolchildren', p. 9.

27 Burton, *Politics of Legitimacy*, p. 69. For another study of generational conflict in Northern Ireland see Paul Arthur, *The People's Democracy 1968–1972* (Belfast: Blackstaff Press, 1974).

28 Colm Keena, *Gerry Adams: A Biography* (Cork: Mercier Press, 1990), pp. 16 and 23. See, too, Harris,

Prejudice and Tolerance, p. 199: 'It seemed that even the adults' attitudes to children and adolescents were made more friendly by the strength of the recognition that it was on them that adults had to count for the fulfilment of their political hopes, and for this if for no other reason everyone was anxious to involve the young in community life.'

29 Simon Winchester, *In Holy Terror* (London: Faber, 1974), p. 35.

30 Eamonn McCann, *War and an Irish Town* (Harmondsorth: Penguin Books, 1974), pp. 18–19.

31 Rex Cathcart, *The Most Contrary Region: The BBC in Northern Ireland 1924–1984* (Belfast: Blackstaff Press, 1984), pp. 262, 36 and 263. I have looked at this issue in greater detail in 'The Media and Politics in Northern Ireland', in Jean Seaton and Ben Pimlott (eds.), *The Media in British Politics* (Aldershot: Gower, 1987), pp. 201–14.

32 V.S. Pritchett, *Midnight Oil* (Harmondsworth: Penguin Books, 1974), p. 115.

33 Sean O'Faolain and Paul Henry, *An Irish Journey* (London: Readers' Union, 1941), p. 246.

34 *Irish Times*, 7 October 1976.

35 In J. Ronsley (ed.), *Myth and Reality in Irish Literature* (Waterloo, Ontario: Wilfrid Laurier University Press, 1977), p. 327. J.J. Lee, *Ireland 1912–1985: Politics and Society* (Cambridge: Cambridge University Press, 1989), p. 320 and *passim,* pursues the idea of a culturally moribund Ireland (especially in the 1950s).

36 John Hewitt, *Art in Ulster: 1* (Belfast: Blackstaff Press, 1977), pp. 3, 78–9 and 131. See, too, Mike Catto, *Art in Ulster: 2* (Belfast: Blackstaff Press, 1977).

37 Sam Hanna Bell, *The Theatre in Ulster* (Dublin: Gill and Macmillan, 1972), p. 92.

38 Tom Nairn, *The Breakup of Britain: Crisis and Neo-nationalism* (London: New Left Books, 1977), p. 233. See, too, John Hewitt's 1945 article 'The Bitter Gourd' in Tom Clyde (ed.), *Ancestral Voices: The Selected Prose of John Hewitt* (Belfast: Blackstaff Press, 1987), p. 113–14, where he writes about 'an extroverted, stubborn, inarticulate society with well-defined material values and, for the most part,

a rigid creed', and of 'that very inarticulateness of the Protestant block' which 'had this strange consequence that the best articulators of the general passion that Ulster was and should persist as a separate entity were not themselves Ulstermen'; or Tom Paulin who finds 'very little in the way of an indigenous cultural tradition of its own in Ulster Protestantism', and writes of 'the contradictory, self-pitying, childish and festering sense of grievance which is at the centre of the Loyalist mentality' in *Ireland and the English Crisis* (Newcastle upon Tyne: Bloodaxe Books, 1985), pp. 17 and 119. We are not suggesting that the picture was totally bleak for Protestant Ulster. Perhaps the most optimistic and realistic account can be read in Sam Hanna Bell (ed.), *The Arts in Ulster: A Symposium* (London: Harrap, 1951), especially his introductory essay, 'A Banderol', pp. 13–21.

39   Patrick Kavanagh, 'In Memory of Brother Michael', from Paul Muldoon (ed.), *The Faber Book of Contemporary Irish Poetry* (London: Faber and Faber, 1986), p. 70.

40   Seamus Heaney, 'The Ministry of Fear', from *North* (London: Faber, 1974), p. 64 and 65.

41   Heaney, 'Among Schoolchildren', p. 7.

42   John Hewitt, 'Alec of the Chimney Corner', in Clyde, *Ancestral Voices*, p. 42. See, too, Dennis Kennedy, *The Widening Gulf: Northern Attitudes to the Independent Irish State 1919–49* (Belfast: Blackstaff Press, 1988), p. 24, on those few dissenting magazines within the 'broadly Unionist Protestant community'. Besides Hewitt we should acknowledge, too, the 'subversive' activities of other literary figures such as John Boyd, Bertie Rodgers and Sam Hanna Bell. See Sean McMahon, *Sam Hanna Bell: A Biography* (Belfast: Blackstaff Press, 1999).

43   Public Record Office of Northern Ireland (PRONI) D1327/7/16.

44   John Dunlop, 'The Self-Understanding of Protestants in Northern Ireland', in Enda McDonagh (ed.), *Irish Challenges to Theology* (Dublin: Dominican Publications, 1986), pp. 6–9.

45   Steve Bruce, *God Save Ulster: The Religion and Politics of Paisleyism* (Oxford: Clarendon Press, 1986), pp. 8 and 12. For an account of the *lack* of democracy in Free Presbyterianism see Ed Moloney and Andy Pollak, *Paisley* (Dublin: Poolbeg Press, 1986), pp. 231–8.

46   Bruce, *God Save Ulster*, pp. 192–3. Armstrong's story is told in David Armstrong and Hilary Saunders, *A Road Too Wide: The Price of Reconciliation in Northern Ireland* (Basingstoke: Marshall, Morgan and Scott, 1985).

47   Dunlop, 'Self-Understanding of Protestants', pp. 18–20.

48   Eric Gallagher and Stanley Worrall, *Christians in Ulster 1968–1980* (Oxford: Oxford University Press, 1982), p. 93.

49   Quoted in Moloney and Pollak, *Paisley*, p. 282.

50   Barry White, *John Hume: Statesman of the Troubles* (Belfast: Blackstaff Press, 1984), p. 54. See, too, Bob Purdie, *Politics in the Streets: The Origins of the Civil Rights Movement in Northern Ireland* (Belfast: Blackstaff Press, 1990), p. 52, for a description of a similar organisation in County Tyrone.

51   Ian Budge and Cornelius O'Leary, *Belfast: Approach to Crisis – A Study of Belfast Politics, 1613–1970* (London: Macmillan, 1973) p. 355; see, too, pp. 249–63 and 284–318.

52   Patrick Buckland, *The Factory of Grievances: Devolved Government in Northern Ireland 1921–39* (Dublin: Gill and Macmillan, 1979), p. 6.

53   On patronage in the Republic see Paul Sacks, *The Donegal Mafia: An Irish Political Machine* (New Haven: Yale University Press, 1976); Mart Bax, *Harpstrings and Confessions: Machine-Style Politics in the Irish Republic* (Assen: Van Gorcum, 1976); R.K. Carty, *Electoral Politics in Ireland: Party and Parish Pump* (Dingle, Co. Kerry: Brandon Books, 1983); Richard Roche, 'The High Cost of Complaining Irish Style', *Irish Business and Administrative Research* 12 (October 1982), pp. 98–108.

54   Nicholas Mansergh, *The Government of Northern Ireland: A Study in Devolution* (London: Allen and Unwin, 1936), pp. 179 and 176. The comparable figures for the Dáil and

Westminster were just over 10 per cent and about 8 per cent respectively. As late as 1971, when there were only eighteen cabinet ministers in the United Kingdom; Northern Ireland had fifteen; see Derek Birrell and Alan Murie, *Policy and Government in Northern Ireland: Lessons of Devolution* (Dublin: Gill and Macmillan, 1980), p. 31.

55   Whyte, *Interpreting Northern Ireland*, p. 169. For a rich account of life in the Northern Ireland civil service see the memoirs of one of the 'collaborators' – Patrick Shea, *Voices and the Sound of Drums: An Irish Autobiography* (Belfast: Blackstaff Press, 1981).

56   T.E. Utley, *Lessons of Ulster* (London: Dent, 1975), p. 7. On the party system see Paul Arthur, 'The Party System in Northern Ireland Since 1945', in A. Seldon (ed.), *UK Political Parties Since 1945* (London: Philip Allen, 1990), pp. 110–22.

57   Mansergh, *Government of Northern Ireland*, p. 253.

58   Purdie, *Politics in the Streets*, pp. 93–4. For a critical account of nationalist party politics in Northern Ireland see Michael McKeown, *The Greening of a Nationalist* (Dublin: Murlough Press, 1986).

59   Wright, *Northern Ireland*, p. 301, fn 78.

60   Cynthia Enloe, *Ethnic Conflict and Political Development* (Boston: Little, Brown and Co., 1973), pp. 169–71.

61   J.L.P. Thompson, 'Ethnicity, Class and Incorporation: Political Mobilisation and Social Structures in Northern Ireland,' (unpublished manuscript), p. 122.

CHAPTER 3

1   Anthony Cronin, 'Belfast Notebook – 1', *Irish Times*, 9 September 1976.

2   John Hewitt, 'Planter's Gothic', in Tom Clyde (ed.), *Ancestral Voices: Selected Prose of John Hewitt* (Belfast: Blackstaff Press, 1987), p. 10.

3   Louis MacNeice, 'Ode' (1934), from *Collected Poems* (London; Faber and Faber, 1989), p. 56.

4   Eamonn McCann, *War and an Irish Town*, (Harmondsworth: Penguin Books, 1974), p. 87.

5   William Whitelaw quoted in Cecil King, *The Cecil King Diary 1970–1974* (London: Jonathan Cape, 1975), p. 194.

6   R.H.S. Crossman, *The Diaries of a Cabinet Minister*, vol. III (London: Hamilton and Cape, 1977), p. 80.

7   Tony Benn, *Office Without Power: Diaries 1968–72* (London: Hutchinson, 1988), p. 197.

8   *Royal Commission on the Constitution 1969–1973* [Kilbrandon Commission], Cmnd. 5460 (London: HMSO, 1973), paragraph 1287.

9   *ibid.*, paragraph 1261.

10   *Report of the Committee on Representational Services Overseas* [Plowden Report], Cmnd 2276 (London: HMSO, 1964).

11   *Report of the Committee on Overseas Representation* [Duncan Report], Cmnd 4107 (London: HMSO, 1969).

12   Crossman, *Diaries*, vol. III, p. 620.

13   Cardinal Richelieu, *Testament Politique* (Paris: Laffonte, 1947), p. 104.

14   Ken Heskin, *Northern Ireland: A Psychological Analysis* (Dublin: Gill and Macmillan, 1980), p. 100.

15   *ibid.*, p. 101.

16   James Callaghan, *A House Divided: Dilemma of Northern Ireland* (London: Collins, 1973), p. 2.

17   *ibid.*, pp. 62–3.

18   Michael J. Cunningham, *British Government Policy in Northern Ireland: Its Nature and Execution* (Manchester: Manchester University Press, 1991), p. 23, quoting from the Downing Street Declaration.

19   K. Boyle, T. Hadden and P. Hillyard, *Law and State: The Case of Northern Ireland* (London: Martin Robertson, 1975), p. 132, my italics.

20   R.J. Lawrence, S. Elliott and M.J. Laver, *The Northern Ireland General Elections of 1973*, Cmnd 5851 (London: HMSO, 1975), p. 48.

21   *Report of the Advisory Committee on Police in Northern Ireland* [Hunt Report], Cmd 535 (Belfast: HMSO, 1969).

22   *Violence and Civil Disturbances in Northern Ireland: Report of Tribunal of Inquiry* [Scarman Report], Cmd 566 (Belfast: HMSO, 1972), paras 3.1, 3.2 and 3.7.

23   Eric Gallagher and Stanley Worrall, *Christians in Ulster 1968–1980* (Oxford: Oxford University Press, 1982), p. 68.

24   David Watt, *Financial Times*, 19 May 1972.

25   Patrick Shea, *Voices and the Sound of*

Drums: An Irish Autobiography
(Belfast: Blackstaff Press, 1981); John
A. Oliver, *Working at Stormont:*
Memoirs (Dublin: Institute of Public
Administration, 1978).

26   Lord Windlesham, 'Ministers in
Ulster: The Machinery of Direct
Rule', *Public Administration*, 51
(Autumn 1973), p. 270.

27   Steve Bruce, *The Red Hand: Protestant*
Paramilitarism in Northern Ireland
(Oxford: Oxford University Press,
1992), p. 59.

28   Brendan O'Leary and John McGarry,
The politics of Antagonism:
Understanding Northern Ireland
(London: Athlone Press, 1993), p. 16.

29   *ibid.*, p. 20.

30   *ibid.*

31   David Apter, 'A View from the
Bogside', in Hermann Gilomee and
Jannie Ganiano (eds.), *The Elusive*
Search for Peace: South Africa, Israel and
Northern Ireland (Capetown: Oxford
University Press, 1990), p. 164.

32   Frank Burton, *The Politics of*
Legitimacy: Struggles in a Belfast
Community (London: Routledge and
Kegan Paul, 1978), p. 10.

33   Richard Rose, *Governing Without*
Consensus: An Irish Perspective
(London: Faber and Faber, 1971),
p. 306.

34   J. Bowyer Bell, 'Aspects of the
Dragonworld: Covert
Communication and the Rebel
Ecosystem', *Intelligence and*
Counterintelligence, 3, 1 (1990),
pp. 15–43.

35   Quoted in Henry Patterson, *The*
Politics of Illusion: Republicanism and
Socialism in Modern Ireland (London:
Hutchinson Radius, 1989), p. 12.

36   J.J. Lee, *Ireland 1912–1985: Politics and*
Society (Cambridge: Cambridge
University Press, 1989), p. 375.

37   *ibid.*, p. 406.

38   A.S. Cohan, *The Irish Political Elite*
(Dublin: Gill and Macmillan, 1972),
pp. 37–8.

39   See, for example, Seán Ó Tuama and
Thomas Kinsella (eds.), *An Duanaire:*
Poems of the Dispossessed 1600–1900
(Portlaoise: Dolmen, 1981).

40   Denis Donoghue, *Warrenpoint*
(London: Jonathan Cape, 1991),
p. 124.

41   This comment was an epigraph to
Frank McGuinness's play, *Baglady*.
Czeslaw Milosz, *Nobel Lecture,*

8 Dec. 1980.

42   Frank Wright, *Northern Ireland: A*
Comparative Analysis (Dublin: Gill and
Macmillan,1987), pp. 130 and 124.

43   David W. Miller, *Queen's Rebels:*
Ulster Loyalism in Historical Perspective
(Dublin: Gill and Macmillan, 1978).
See chapter 1 above for treatment of
this issue.

44   John Darby, *Intimidation and the*
Control of Conflict in Northern Ireland
(Dublin: Gill and Macmillan, 1986).
See chapter 2 above for treatment of
this issue.

45   Wright, *Northern Ireland*, p. 122.

46   Eileen Fairweather et al., *Only the*
Rivers Run Free: Northern Ireland – The
Women's War (London: Pluto, 1984)
p. 49.

47   Maurice Hayes, *Minority Verdict:*
Experiences of a Catholic Public Servant
(Belfast: Blackstaff Press, 1995).

48   These remarks are no substitute for a
detailed discussion of the campaigns
of violence. There is no shortage of
such narratives. For an overview see
my '"Reading" Violence: Ireland', in
David Apter (ed.), *The Legitimization*
of Violence (London: Macmillan in
association with the United Nations
Research Institute for Social
Development, 1997), pp. 234–91.

49   The definition is that of Byron Bland,
Marching and Rising: The Rituals of
Small Differences and Great Violence in
Northern Ireland (Stanford, Calif.:
Center for International Security and
Arms Control, Stanford University,
1996).

50   The quotations in both the Parker
and Wilson cases come from David
McKittrick, Seamus Kelters, Brian
Feeney and Chris Thornton, *Lost*
Lives: The Stories of the Men, Women
and Children who Died as a Result of the
Northern Ireland Troubles (Edinburgh:
Mainstream Publishing, 1999),
pp. 1098 and 232–3. This book is a
fitting and poignant memorial to the
dead.

51   David Moss, 'Analysing Italian
Political Violence as a Sequence of
Communicative Acts: The Red
Brgades, 1970–1982', *Social Analysis*,
13 (May 1983), p. 85.

52   Gerry Adams, *The Politics of Irish*
Freedom (Dingle, Co. Kerry: Brandon
Books, 1986), pp. 64–5.

53   Burton, *Politics of Legitimacy*, pp. 9 and
19.

54   Quoted in Desmond Hamill, *Pig in the Middle: The Army in Northern Ireland 1969–1984* (London: Methuen, 1985), pp. 233–41.

55   Quoted in McKittrick et al., *Lost Lives*, p. 996.

56   Quoted in Richard Kearney, *Transitions: Narratives in Modern Irish Culture* (Manchester: Manchester UP, 1988), p. 313.

57   Moss, 'Analysing Italian Political Violence', p. 86.

58   Donoghue, *Warrenpoint*, p. 227.

59   T.M. O'Keeffe, 'Suicide and Self-starvation', *Philosophy*, 59, 229 (1984), p. 355.

60   Padraig O'Malley, *Biting at the Grave: The Irish Hunger Strikes and the Politics of Despair* (Belfast: Blackstaff Press, 1990), p. 182.

61   *Irish News*, 20 October 1992.

CHAPTER 4

1   Quoted in Ronan Fanning, 'The Anglo-American Alliance and the Irish Application for Membership of the United Nations', *Irish Studies in International Affairs*, 2, 2 (1986), p. 46.

2   See, for example, Leo Rosten, *The Joys of Yiddish* (Harmondsworth: Penguin Books, 1971), in which Yiddish is celebrated because it 'favours paradox, because it knows that only paradox could do justice to the injustice of life; adores irony, because the only way the Jews could retain their sanity was to view a dreadful world with sardonic, astringent eyes' (p. xvii).

3   Fanning, 'Anglo-American Alliance', p. 46.

4   Tom Garvin, *The Evolution of Irish Nationalist Politics* (Dublin: Gill and Macmillan, 1981), p. xi.

5   Quoted in Gary Wills, 'Goodbye Columbus', *New York Review of Books*, 37, 18 (22 November 1990), p. 6.

6   Ronan Fanning, 'Anglo-Irish Relations: Partition and the British Dimension in Historical Perspective', *Irish Studies in International Affairs*, 2, 1 (1985), p. 3.

7   Keith Middlemas, *Politics in Industrial Society: The Experience of the British System Since 1911* (London: André Deutsch, 1979), p. 45. Later (p. 51) he writes: 'The intractable position taken up by each side in Britain over the question of Irish Home Rule seemed to prove beyond question the failure of the classical two-party political system.'

8   John Gallagher, *The Decline, Revival and Fall of the British Empire* (Cambridge: Cambridge University Press, 1982), p. 98.

9   *ibid.*, pp. 96–7 and 86–7.

10   A.F. Madden, 'Constitution-Making and Nationhood: The British Experience – An Overview', *Journal of Commonwealth and Comparative Politics*, 36, 2 (July 1988), p. 127.

11   Ronan Fanning, *Independent Ireland* (Dublin: Helicon, 1983), p. 39. J.J. Lee, *Ireland 1912–1985: Politics and Society* (Cambridge: Cambridge University Press, 1989), cautions (pp. 68–9) that we should keep the scale of conflict in perspective. He compares it with the much more bloody Finnish Civil War in 1918.

12   Lee, *Ireland*, pp. 390–1.

13   *ibid.*, p. 627.

14   *ibid.*, p. 629.

15   Oliver MacDonagh, *Ireland: The Union and its Aftermath* (London: Allen and Unwin, 1977), pp. 125 and 137.

16   Quoted in T.C. Salmon, *Unneutral Ireland: An Ambivalent and Unique Security Policy* (Oxford: Clarendon Press, 1989), p. 85.

17   Fanning, *Independent Ireland*, pp. 82–3.

18   Some of de Valera's predecessors – Daniel O'Connell, Isaac Butt and John Redmond – were 'imperially-minded'. See Patrick Keatinge, *A Place Among Nations: Issues of Irish Foreign Policy* (Dublin: Institute of Public Administration, 1978), pp. 32–3.

19   *ibid.*, p. 72.

20   Eamon de Valera in May 1921, quoted in John Bowman, *De Valera and the Ulster Question 1917–1973* (Oxford: Oxford University Press, 1982), p. 48.

21   Keatinge, *A Place Among the Nations* p. 2. We shall see that this issue was a little more complicated than Aiken's statement suggests.

22   Salmon, *Unneutral Ireland*, p. 164.

23   See Stephen Barcroft, 'Irish Foreign Policy at the League of Nations 1929–1936', *Irish Studies in International Affairs*, 1, 1 (1979), pp. 19–37. Note that Barcroft states that 'Contemporary Ireland was not often preoccupied with international

affairs, and that, when it was, the frontier of interest was usually London rather than Geneva' (p. 19). See, too, Keatinge, *A Place Among the Nations*, pp. 172–3: 'The League itself was viewed with varying degrees of suspicion as an instrument of its imperialist "leaders", Britain and France, particularly while Fianna Fáil was in opposition from 1927 to 1932.'

24   Again Frank Aiken can be taken as an exponent of this position. See a speech he made to the UN General Assembly on 6 October 1960 when he quoted Parnell proclaiming the principle that 'the cause of nationality is sacred, in Asia and Africa as in Ireland'. Keatinge, *A Place Among the Nations*, pp. 173–4.

25   Evgeny M. Chossudovsky, 'The Origins of the Treaty on the Non-proliferation of Nuclear Weapons: Ireland's Initiative in the United Nations (1958–61)', *Irish Studies in International Affairs*, 3, 2 (1990), pp. 111–35.

26   Fanning, 'Anglo-American Alliance', p. 37. See, too, Norman MacQueen, 'Ireland's Entry to the United Nations 1946–56', in Tom Gallagher and James O'Connell (eds.), *Contemporary Irish Political Studies* (Manchester: Manchester University Press, 1983), pp. 65–79. We shall see that 'national security' and 'sovereignty' are recurring themes.

27   *Seanad Éireann Deb.*, 44, 4, cols. 373–4 (25 November 1954).

28   William Wallace, *The Foreign Policy Process in Britain* (London: Royal Institute of International Affairs, 1975), pp. 31 and 215.

29   Keatinge, *A Place Among the Nations*, pp. 211 and 270.

30   Quoted in Lee, *Ireland*, p. 30.

31   *ibid.*, pp. 87, 105, 106 and 198.

32   David Harkness, 'The Constitutions of Ireland and the Development of National Identity', *Journal of Commonwealth and Comparative Politics*, 36, 2 (July 1988), p. 143.

33   The Donoughmore Commission (1928) raised doubts about the Westminster model in Westminster itself. See A.F. Madden, ' "Not For Export": The Westminster Model of Government and British Colonial Practice', *Journal of Imperial and Commonwealth Politics*, 8, 1 (October

1979), pp. 20–1. Richard Rose has noted that British democracy has deviated from the Westminster model and asserts that New Zealand is now 'the only example of the true British system left'. Rose is quoted in Arend Lijphart, 'The Demise of the Last Westminster System? Comments on the Report of New Zealand's Royal Commission on the Electoral System', *Electoral Studies*, 6 (1987), pp. 97–103.

34   See Brian Farrell (ed.), *The Irish Parliamentary Tradition* (Dublin: Gill and Macmillan, 1973), p. 214; and Brian Farrell, *The Founding of Dáil Éireann: Parliament and Nation-Building* (Dublin: Gill and Macmillan, 1971), *passim*.

35   Garvin, *Evolution of Irish Nationalist Politics*, p. 12.

36   Eric Gallagher and Stanley Worrall, *Christians in Ulster 1968–1980* (Oxford: Oxford University Press, 1982), p. 5.

37   '[A]s the Irish language was increasingly abandoned in favour of English by the mass of the population, religion was left as the only significant cultural marker for the majority of Irish Catholics, whether at home or in exile'. M.A.G. Ó Tuathaigh, 'Religion, Nationality and a Sense of Community in Modern Ireland', in M.A.G. Ó Tuathaigh (ed.), *Community, Culture and Conflict: Aspects of the Irish Experience* (Galway: Galway University Press, 1986), p. 68.

38   Oliver MacDonagh, *States of Mind: A Study of Anglo-Irish Conflict 1780–1980* (London: Allen and Unwin, 1983), pp. 97–101.

39   Ó Tuathaigh, 'Religion, Nationality and a Sense of Community', p. 68.

40   See John Whyte, *Catholics in Western Democracies: A Study in Political Behaviour* (Dublin: Gill and Macmillan, 1981), p. 64; and also p. 15 where he draws our attention to the fact that such activity was unusual in the Anglo-American world: 'On the whole, however, the clergy have been more circumspect about engaging in politics in the Anglo-American world than they have been in continental Europe.' See also MacDonagh, *States of Mind*, *passim*, who illustrates the cautious nature of the clergy's extensive power.

41   See John Whyte, *Church and State in Modern Ireland 1923–1979*, 2nd edn. (Dublin: Gill and Macmillan, 1980), pp. 1–23. See, too, Ó Tuathaigh, 'Religion, Nationality and a Sense of Community', p. 72: 'The prominence of Protestants among the theorists of Irish nationalism, and the tinge of anti-clericalism which has long marked Irish republicanism as a result of the Catholic Church's consistent condemnation of secret oath-bound societies (like the Fenians) alert us to the error of assuming that the terms Catholic and Nationalist are in any simple way synonymous from the nineteenth century forward.'

42   Ó Tuathaigh, 'Religion, Nationality and a Sense of Community', p. 73.

43   Quoted in Pro Mundi Vita, 'The Irish Conflict and the Christian Conscience', *The Furrow*, 24, 9 (September 1973), p. 24.

44   Barbara Wootton, *Contemporary Britain* (London: Allen and Unwin, 1971), p. 67.

45   Quoted in Salmon, *Unneutral Ireland*, p. 230. For further thoughts on the 'spiritual dominion' see pp. 167–8 and 189–90.

46   Seamus Heaney, 'Among Schoolchildren' (John Malone Memorial Lecture, Queen's University Belfast, 9 June 1983), p. 12.

47   James Hogan, *Elections and Representation*, (Cork: Cork University Press/Oxford: B.H. Blackwell, 1945), p. vi.

48   David Harkness, *The Restless Dominion: The Irish Free State and the British Commonwealth of Nations 1921–31* (London: Macmillan, 1969), p. 21.

49   *ibid.*, p. 21. Harkness is quoting from *Encyclopaedia Britannica* (1963 ed.) VI, p. 172.

50   Harkness, *Restless Dominion*, pp. 21–2.

51   *ibid.*, p. 19.

52   *ibid.*, pp. 23–5.

53   Tom Nairn, *The Enchanted Glass: Britain and its Monarchy* (London: Radius Books, 1988), p. 10. The Nairn thesis is concerned with the 'awesomeness' and 'near-hypnotic impact' of the Crown on the state: 'the Crown is a crucial element in Constitution, Law and Government' (pp. 89–90).

54   Tom Nairn, *The Break up of Britain: Crisis and Neo-nationalism* (London: New Left Books, 1977), p. 42 and p. 40, fn 27. McKenzie and Silver were discussing the 'deference' ideology of lower-class Conservation in their book *Angels in Marble: Working-Class Conservatives in Urban England* (1968). Further, in relation to Irish policy, the 'people' can be a nuisance: 'A part of the blame for what Dicey saw as the folly of Liberal policy towards Ireland lay, he believed, in the combination of an ignorant electorate with the operation of party machines to produce an influence on political life that was fickle, venal and tyrannical' – quoted in Rodney Barker, *Political Ideas in Modern Britain* (London: Methuen, 1978), p. 109.

55   Nairn, *Enchanted Glass*, p. 366.

56   Nairn, *Breakup of Britain*, p. 36.

57   On Scotland, see Keith Webb, *The Growth of Nationalism in Scotland* (Harmondsworth: Pelican, 1978), pp. 51, 55–6 and 59ff. On Wales, see David Williams, *A History of Modern Wales* (London: John Murray, 1977), especially pp. 246–85. Both studies emphasise that their politics were less turbulent than the Irish, and that there were often sharp religious differences. On the persisting significance of religion in the structure of modern party politics, see Nairn, *Breakup of Britain*, pp. 66–7, fn 43.

58   Philip Dodd, 'Englishness and the National Culture', in Robert Colls and Philip Dodd (eds.), *Englishness: Politics and Culture, 1880–1920* (London: Croom Helm, 1986), p. 3. Nairn (*Enchanted Glass*, pp. 68–9) concurs when he writes that 'what the contemporary Anglo-British idiom really does is to fuse literacy with aristocracy: a democratic need is at once fulfilled and nullified by the generalization of a form of class speech . . . it is more accurately described as the slurred, allusive, nasal cawing of the English gentry. Great Britain's accepted tongue is the ultra-distilled by-product of drawing-room, shoot and London club, a faded aristocratic *patois* remarkable for its anorexic vowels and vaporized consonants. It is social geography that links this vernacular to the London–Oxford–Cambridge triangle; while the social power of the same locality

has turned it into the inevitable emblem of authority, acceptance, literacy and nationality.'

59   Nairn, *Enchanted Glass*, p. 183.

60   Referring to Britain's recent entry into the EEC Nairn (*Breakup of Britain*, p. 78) states that the 'debate surrounding the event demonstrated that "nationalism" in the familiar disparaging sense is by no means confined to the smaller nations. "Narrowness" has nothing whatever to do with size . . . greater nations remain grandly unaware of their narrowness, because their size, their culture, or their imagined centrality makes them identify with Humanity or Progress *tout court*.'

61   Harkness, 'Constitutions of Ireland', p. 138. He acknowledges that in due course 'the Irish Free State did give expression to Ireland's special genius'.

62   Harkness, *Restless Dominion*, pp. 249–50. McGilligan's speech is quoted on pp. 247–8. Fanning (*Independent Ireland*, p. 85) summarises the Statute of Westminster as having laid down 'that no law made by the United Kingdom Parliament should extend to any of the dominions other than at their request and with their consent. Its effect, claimed the then minister for external affairs, Patrick McGilligan, would be "to destroy as a matter of law what had already been destroyed as a matter of practice, the legal sovereignty of the British parliament in the commonwealth".'

63   Farrell, *Founding of Dáil Éireann*, p. 83.

64   Garvin, *Evolution of Irish Nationalist Politics*, p. 193. They were to be matched by politicians who 'were puritanical, idealistic and austere and were adherents of the politics of national redemption rather than the politics of compromise, bargaining and pay-offs' (p. 199).

65   Frank Munger, *The Legitimacy of Opposition: The Change of Government in Ireland in 1932*, Contemporary Political Sociology Series, vol. 1, (London: Sage Professional Papers, 1975), p. 27. Of the forty-eight highest ranking officials in 1914 thirty-eight 'were Irish in origin. These were divided equally between Catholic and Protestant. The proportions of native Irish and of Catholics undoubtedly were higher in the lower ranks' (p. 26).

66   Lee, *Ireland*, p. 107.

67   *ibid.*, p. 109.

68   Munger, *Legitimacy of Opposition*, p. 11.

69   Lee, *Ireland*, p. 336.

70   Fanning, *Independent Ireland*, p. 117. The doctrine of 'external asociation' had been enunciated first by de Valera during the Treaty debates (1921–2) in which he argued that the source of all authority in an Irish constitution would be the *Irish people*; that external association inside the Commonwealth would be established on the basis of equality of rights; and that the British monarch would be recognised as head or president, so to speak, of the association. See, too, Lee, *Ireland*, pp. 48 and 51.

71   Quoted in Basil Chubb, *The Government and Politics of Ireland*, 2nd edn (London: Longman, 1982), p. 46.

72   John Kelly, the pre-eminent legal authority on the constitution, in Harkness, 'Constitutions of Ireland', p. 144.

73   Michael McInerney, *Irish Times*, 30 December 1977.

74   Lee, *Ireland*, has commented on the contradictions of a constitution which claimed jurisdiction over the whole of Ireland but was not submitted to the whole people of Ireland (p. 206), although he allows that Article 15 – which permitted the 'creation or recognition of subordinate legislatures' – made provision for the possible 'recognition' of Stormont in the event of unification (p. 204).

75   Fanning, *Independent Ireland*, p. 89.

76   Bowman, *De Valera*, p. 284. Indeed when two Northeners – Austin Currie (SDLP) and John Cushnahan (Alliance) – transferred to Fine Gael in the late 1980s their Northern background was initially a drawback. Currie, for instance, who was elected as a Fine Gael TD, was once advised in the Dáil by a Fianna Fáil backbencher to 'go back' to the North; and when he stood as the Fine Gael candidate for the Irish presidency in 1990 private polls suggested that his Northern background was a serious deficiency even among Fine Gael voters.

77   *ibid.*, p. 108. Bowman is quoting from Joseph Frankel, *National Interest* (London: 1970), pp. 32–3.

78   John A. Murphy, *Ireland in the Twentieth Century* (Dublin: Gill and Macmillan, 1975), p. 90.

79   Dennis Kennedy, *The Widening Gulf: Northern Attitudes to the Independent Irish State 1919–49* (Belfast: Blackstaff Press, 1988), p. 173, although the *Church of Ireland Gazette* (7 May 1937) adopted a less sanguine view.

80   Whyte, *Church and State*, p. 51.

81   Quote in Bowman, *De Valera*, p. 155.

82   Whyte, *Church and State*, p. 58: 'The imposition of compulsory Irish in the schools aroused much Protestant resentment'; Kennedy, *Widening Gulf*, pp. 178 and 182–4, shows that the Irish language policy was 'a real bonus' to the unionists.

83   Deirdre McMahon, *Republicans and Imperialists: Anglo-Irish Relations in the 1930s* (New Haven: Yale University Press, 1984), p. 289.

84   Garvin, *Evolution of Irish Nationalist Politics*, p. 189. Garvin uncovers a political culture when he quotes a veteran Fianna Fáil TD (and former IRA leader from the 1919–21 period): 'At times I hate politicians. Part of me had a strong dislike of politicians. I was a soldier basically and the whole business of politics was too slow ... The funny thing is I always believed the old boy [de Valera] would re-unite Ireland ... I was always convinced he had a plan.'

85   Bowman, *De Valera*, p. 138.

86   McMahon, *Republicans and Imperialists*, p. 83. This is the best source for Anglo-Irish relations for the period. It is particularly good on tensions within the Irish Situation Committee and between the Dominions Office and the Home Office.

87   I borrow that term from Robert Fisk, *Ireland, Ulster and the Price of Neutrality 1939–1945* (London: André Deutsch, 1983), p. 34. (Emphasis is Fisk's.)

88   Interestingly the negotiations highlighted tensions between the British and Northern Ireland governments: see Keatinge, *A Place Among the Nations*, pp. 107–8.

89   Patrick Keatinge, *A Singular Stance: Irish Neutrality in the 1980s* (Dublin: Institute of Public Administration, 1984), p. 16.

90   Salmon, *Unneutral Ireland*, pp. 97 and 98.

91   Introduction to William A. Carson, *Ulster and the Irish Republic* (Belfast: Cleland, 1957), p. ii. The introduction is a masterpiece of invective which repays rereading since it raises some of the major myths in the triangular relationship.

92   See Eunan O'Halpin, 'Intelligence and Security in Ireland, 1922–45', *Intelligence and National Security*, 5, 1 (1990), pp. 50–83. Continuing security cooperation after the war is mentioned in Salmon, *Unneutral Ireland*, p. 170.

93   Salmon, *Unneutral Ireland*, p. 126.

94   Fanning, 'Anglo-American Alliance', p. 36. On Ireland's ideological commitment to the NATO ideal see an Irish military intelligence report (1952) quoted in Ian McCabe, 'New light shed on army stance towards NATO', *Irish Times*, 29 January 1991.

95   Bowman, *De Valera*, p. 268. CAB 128/13 176, 15 December 1948.

96   Ronan Fanning, 'London and Belfast's Response to the Declaration of the Republic of Ireland, 1948–49', *International Affairs*, 58, 1 (1981–2), p. 113.

97   Quoted in Ronan Fanning, 'The Response of the London and Belfast Governments to the Declaration of the Republic of Ireland, 1948–49', *International Affairs*, 58, 1 (1981–2), p. 99. See, too, Ian McCabe, 'Not British ... but not foreign either', *Irish Times*, 17 October 1988.

98   David Vital, *The Making of British Foreign Policy* (London: Allen and Unwin, 1968), p. 99.

99   'The Catholic Church, apart from the British Commonwealth, was the one international institution which had a liberal sprinkling of Irishmen throughout the world. The Irish were strongly represented in the international hierarchies of America, Australia, New Zealand and Canada.' Dermot Keogh, *The Vatican, the Bishops and Irish Politics 1919–1939* (Cambridge: Cambridge University Press, 1986), pp. 18–19.

100   Quoted in Barker, *Political Ideas*, p. 172.

101   Roy Jenkins, *British Foreign Policy Since 1945, Proceedings of the British Academy* (Oxford: Oxford University Press, 1972), p. 6.

102   Gallagher, *Decline, Revival and Fall of the British Empire*, p. 128.

103   *ibid.*

104   *ibid.*, p. 149.

CHAPTER 5

1   *Report of the International Body on Arms Decommissioning* [Mitchell Report] (Belfast: Northern Ireland Office, 24 January 1996), para. 16.
2   Oliver MacDonagh, 'Time's Revenges and Revenge's Time: A Review of Anglo-Irish Relations', *Anglo-Irish Studies*, 4 (1979), p. 15.
3   Norman Porter, *Rethinking Unionism: An Alternative Vision for Northern Ireland* (Belfast: Blackstaff Press, 1996), p. 8.
4   Quoted in David W. Miller, *Queen's Rebels: Ulster Loyalism in Historical Perspective* (Dublin: Gill and Macmillan, 1978), p. 123.
5   The Taoiseach, Jack Lynch TD, *Speeches and Statements on Irish Unity, Northern Ireland, Anglo-Irish Relations: August 1969–October 1971* (Dublin: Government Information Bureau, 1971), p. 35.
6   Quoted in Susan Baker, 'Nationalist Ideology and the Industrial Policy of Fianna Fáil (1955–72): The Evidence of the *Irish Press*', *Irish Political Studies*, 1 (1986), p. 65.
7   See Patrick Keatinge, 'Unequal Sovereigns: The Diplomatic Dimension of Anglo-Irish Relations', in P.J. Drudy (ed.), *Ireland and Britain Since 1922* (Cambridge: Cambridge University Press, 1986), pp. 139–60.
8   IBEC Technical Services Corporation, *Industrial Potentials of Ireland: An Appraisal* (New York, 1952), p. 27. See, too, T.C. Salmon, *Unneutral Ireland: An Ambivalent and Unique Security Policy* (Oxford: Clarendon Press, 1989), table 6.2 and pp. 171–2 for a discussion of Ireland as an 'economic satellite' of Britain. A whimsical account of Ireland in the mid-1950s can be found in Heinrich Böll, *Irish Journal: A Traveller's Portrait of Ireland* (London: Abacus, 1983).
9   John Horgan, *Seán Lemass: The Enigmatic Patriot* (Dublin: Gill and Macmillan, 1997), p. 252. The simplicity lay in the belief that a solution lay solely in British hands. The failure lay in the inability to recognise 'that the fissile combination of Northern unionism and Southern irridentism could not be defused only by actions taken by another government in another country'.
10   *ibid.*, p. 350.
11   Quoted in John Bowman, *De Valera and the Ulster Question 1917–1973* (Oxford: Oxford University Press, 1982), p. 325. A discussion of the report can be found at pp. 323–6. This committee was the first of many attempts to examine the validity of Articles 2 and 3 in the changing dispensation. The revised article had been written by John Kelly, a professor of law and a member of Fine Gael who would be elected to the Dáil in 1973. He was not on the committee but passed it on to one of its members.
12   Jack Lynch, 'My Life and Times', *Magill*, November 1979, p. 43.
13   I say the 1940s because, as Bob Purdie points out, the popular perception is that it began in 1948, was essentially an affair of Southern politics and was an outcome of the jostling between Fianna Fáil and the interparty government following de Valera's defeat in the general election of 1948. In fact, according to Purdie (p. 67), 'it began in 1945, not 1948, and was not confined to the political establishment in the South but emerged in the North, with the establishment of the Irish Anti-Partition League'. See Bob Purdie, 'The Irish Anti-Partition League, South Armagh and the Abstentionist Tactic 1945–58', *Irish Political Studies*, 1 (1986), pp. 67–77.
14   See Donal Barrington, 'Uniting Ireland', *Tuairim* (Dublin, n.d.), *passim*.
15   Michael Gallagher, *The Irish Labour Party in Transition 1957–82* (Manchester: Manchester University Press, 1982), p. 126. See, too, Horgan, *Lemass*, pp. 281–3, 288 and 342 for evidence of animosity between Eddie McAteer, leader of the Nationalist Party 1964–9, and Seán Lemass in the aftermath of the visit to O'Neill and comments made in Belfast in 1969. In that respect Lemass was following the lead of his predecessor, Eamon de Valera: 'most of the evidence, public and private, suggests great inhibition on de Valera's part in his relations with northern nationalists'. See Bowman, *De Valera*, p. 132.
16   In the context of the Republic's political culture Kelly's views were

idiosyncratic and ahead of their time. His position was that Ireland had not used its independence dynamically; and as a result it had 'a society left over from the Britain of fifty years ago and frozen in the conventional wisdoms of Asquith and Lloyd George'. If, on the other hand, it reoriented its young people 'towards an understanding of, and familiarity with, the civilisation and the standards of the larger Europe, not just the UK [it would] achieve Irish unity as a by-product, as the rise of this republic to something that the rest of the world can envy [would destroy] the deepest psychological barrier which repels the unionist from us.' See John Fanagan (ed.), *Belling the Cats: Selected Speeches and Articles of John Kelly* (Dublin: Moytura Press, 1992), pp. 4 and 35.

17   See Senator Mary Robinson (another academic lawyer and a future President of Ireland), 8 July 1970; R.C. Geary, 20 July 1970; Michael Sweetman, 24 July 1970; and Hugh Munro, 31 August 1970 (all *Irish Times*). Only Geary adopted an anti-national position when he described Articles 2 and 3 as 'a national menace'; and all of them sought a solution within the island's boundaries.

18   Dick Walsh, *The Party: Inside Fianna Fáil* (Dublin: Gill and Macmillan, 1986), p. 4.

19   *ibid.*, p. 6.

20   A.S. Cohan, *The Irish Political Elite* (Dublin: Gill and Macmillan, 1972), p. 72.

21   Tom Garvin, 'The Growth of Faction in the Fianna Fáil Party, 1966–1980', *Parliamentary Affairs*, 34, 1 (1981), p. 121.

22   *ibid.*, pp. 110–11.

23   Walsh, *The Party*, p. 101. As if to challenge this *canard* a very fat publication (pp. xlii + 1216) appeared in 1986: Martin Mansergh (ed.), *The Spirit of the Nation: The Speeches and Statements of Charles J. Haughey* (Cork: Mercier Press, 1986). It traces Haughey's musings on partition back to 1962. In the 1840s the Young Irelanders, in honour of the memory of Theobald Wolfe Tone, produced a book with the same title. If nothing else Haughey was finding his place in the pantheon.

24   Kevin Boland quoted in Walsh, *The Party*, p. 101.

25   Aontacht Éireann attracted only one Fianna Fáil TD, Seán Sherwin. Its thirteen candidates took less than 1 per cent of the vote at the 1973 general election and it had disappeared by 1976. Essentially Blaney's party served as his regional base in Connacht–Ulster to ensure his return to the Dáil and (after 1979) to the European Parliament.

26   Small libraries have been produced on the Haughey legacy. Two of the best books are Joe Joyce and Peter Murtagh, *The Boss: Charles J. Haughey in Government* (Dublin: Poolbeg Press, 1983) and Shane Kenny, *Go Dance on Somebody Else's Grave* (Dublin: Kildanore Press, 1990).

27   Richard Sinnott, *Irish Voters Decide: Voting Behaviour in Elections and Referendums Since 1918* (Manchester: Manchester University Press, 1993), p. 37. The crisis serves as metaphor for the total disarray within the Southern political elite. Potentially it was the greatest threat to the legitimacy of the state since the period 1922–32. As an analogue see Frank Munger, *The Legitimacy of Opposition: The Change of Government in Ireland in 1932*, Contemporary Political Sociology Series, vol. 1, (London: Sage Professional Papers, 1975).

28   *Irish Times*, 11 November 1982.

29   See Sinnott, *Irish Voters*, p. 177 and p. 178, table 7.4.

30   A.S. Cohan, 'The Question of a United Ireland: Perspectives of the Irish Political Elite', *International Affairs*, 53, 2 (1977), p. 248 and *passim*. The article was based on a series of interviews carried out in 1968–9 and followed up in March and December 1975.

31   Its share of the vote increased from 15.4 per cent in 1965 to 17 per cent in 1969 but it actually lost four seats, down from twenty-two to eighteen. Its vote rose considerably in Dublin but that did not compensate for the loss of seats in rural areas, and that was to be a bone of contention. Besides Dr Conor Cruise O'Brien, its successful intellectuals included David Thornley and Justin Keating (two television personalities), Dr Noël Browne and Dr John O'Donovan. See Cornelius O'Leary, *Irish Elections 1918–1977: Parties, Voters and Proportional Representation* (Dublin:

Gill and Macmillan, 1979), pp. 72–4.

32   Indeed O'Brien must be one of the earliest of that rare breed, 'the traveller'. I say 'rare' but from the 1970s onwards they spawned and spread their wings throughout the North. Essentially, the traveller was an official from the Department of Foreign Affairs whose role was to gather information and intelligence on conditions on the ground in Northern Ireland. In the early days of the conflict this was vital because the department was groping around for a sense of what was happening. Some of the most impressive Foreign Affairs officials began their apprenticeships as travellers. For O'Brien's role see Conor Cruise O'Brien, *States of Ireland* (London: Hutchinson, 1972), pp. 142–5.

33   *ibid.*, p. 145. That would suggest a certain degree of institutional, if not intellectual, schizophrenia on O'Brien's part if others' long memories are to be believed: 'a quarter of a century earlier, as an official of the Department of Foreign Affairs, he had been an exponent of the sterile anti-partition propaganda line that I had rejected all my life'. Garret FitzGerald, *All in a Life: An Autobiography* (London: Macmillan, 1991), p. 197, recalling a meal he had with O'Brien and Norman St John Stevas MP in a Dublin restaurant in the 1950s.

34   See Conor Cruise O'Brien, *Memoir: My Life and Themes* (London: Profile Books, 1998), p. 243.

35   Gallagher, *Irish Labour Party*, p. 152, and pp. 135–53 for a 'colour' of the whole debate.

36   *ibid.*, pp. 210–11.

37   O'Brien, *Memoir*, pp. 350 and 349. His reference to not being a practising Catholic occurred at a cabinet meeting when the Irish government considered whether to support a Council of Ireland as well as a power-sharing government in Northern Ireland. O'Brien – and O'Brien alone – opposed the idea of a Council of Ireland.

38   Sinnott, *Irish Voters*, p. 56.

39   Salmon, *Unneutral Ireland*, p. 201. The figures and other quotations in this paragraph are taken from the same source pp. 193–201.

40   Two months earlier, the *Daily Telegraph* (31 August) warned that an Anglo-Irish war was 'an ultimate possibility which cannot be logically excluded'.

41   *ibid.*, pp. 241–5.

42   Eoin Neeson, 'The overnight information drive – how the world was won over', *Irish Times*, 12 August 1994.

43   Dublin had been uncertain who to turn to for advice in Northern Ireland. Nationalist politics was going through a trauma as a new leadership emerged from the civil rights campaign. Some – notably the Belfast socialists Gerry Fitt and Paddy Devlin – distrusted Fianna Fáil, and others were engaged in more nefarious activities with the re-emergence of the IRA. The contact with Hume was crucial.

44   Keatinge, 'Unequal Sovereigns', p. 150.

45   For Cosgrave quotation see Paul Arthur, 'Anglo-Irish Relations Since 1968: A "Fever Chart" Interpretation', *Government and Opposition* 18, 2 (1983), p. 162. The name of Dublin's Department of External Affairs was changed to the Department of Foreign Affairs in August 1971. One commentator notes that after October 1968 Dublin tried 'to persuade the British to carry out jurisdictional acts *within* Ireland, to bring about reforms or changes in Northern Ireland'. This placed the Irish government in a contradiction. On the one hand the 1937 constitution accepts some obligation to speak on behalf of the people of Northern Ireland; on the other Dublin 'has in effect also recognised British rights in Ireland, and this entangles them in the implications of the constitutional claim'. See Liam de Paor, 'The case of the retention of Articles 2 and 3', *Irish Times*, 4 September 1981.

46   Denis Healey, *The Time of My Life* (Harmondsworth: Penguin Books, 1990), p. 343.

47   Cecil King, *The Cecil King Diary 1970–1974* (London: Jonathan Cape, 1975), p. 23.

48   See chapter 3 above and James Callaghan, *A House Divided: Dilemma of Northern Ireland* (London: Collins, 1973), p.2.

49   See chapter 3 above.

50 John Peck, *Dublin from Downing Street* (Dublin: Gill and Macmillan, 1978), pp. 16–17 and 116. This section draws on my 'Anglo-Irish Relations Since 1968: A "Fever Chart" Interpretation', pp. 157–74, to explain the anomalous relationship.

51 Hugh Shearman, *How Northern Ireland is Governed* (Belfast: HMSO, 1963), p. 31.

52 For a concise and lucid account of this phenomenon see R. Wallis, S. Bruce and D. Taylor, *No Surrender!: Paisleyism and the Politics of Ethnic Identity in Northern Ireland* (Belfast: Department of Social Studies, Queen's University Belfast, 1986).

53 Richard Rose, *Governing Without Consensus: An Irish Perspective* (London: Faber and Faber, 1971), p. 193. Interestingly only 13 per cent of Catholics approved of 'any measures' to end partition.

54 See Richard Deutsch and Vivien Magowan, *Northern Ireland 1968–73: A Chronology of Events. Vol. 1, 1968–71* (Belfast: Blackstaff Press, 1973), p. 13.

55 In 1938 a Progressive Unionist Party contested twelve Stormont seats on a non-sectarian and radical economic programme but it failed to unseat any of the official candidates. Some working-class constituencies elected maverick candidates but virtually all of them were contained within the party straitjacket.

56 He has been described as a 'man of considerable integrity who would accept a straight answer when the facts were put to him'. A senior public servant offered the following political obituary: 'It is a pity too that Faulkner, whose life had been a preparation for the highest office, should have enjoyed it so briefly and in such difficult times. He was unquestionably the most effective minister in Northern Ireland, he had filled post after post with ability and distinction, he had adapted to changing times, he had built strong personal relationships, and he was not given time to build the stable and fair society to which he was finally committed.' See Maurice Hayes, *Minority Verdict: Experiences of a Catholic Public Servant* (Belfast: Blackstaff Press, 1995), pp. 58 and 204.

57 See Brian Barton, 'Relations Between Westminser and Stormont during the Attlee Premiership', *Irish Political Studies*, 7 (1992), pp. 1–2.

58 *ibid.*, pp. 18, 13 and 3.

59 Quoted in Miller, *Queen's Rebels*, pp. 153–4, my emphasis.

60 Trevor Smith and Alison Young, *The Fixers: Crisis Management in British Politics* (Aldershot: Dartmouth, 1996), p. 68. Arnold Goodman had acted as an intermediary in the Rhodesia crisis for both Harold Wilson and Edward Heath.

61 Hayes, *Minority Verdict*, pp. 222–3.

62 Molyneaux had succeeded Harry West as leader of the Ulster Unionists after the latter's dismal showing in the first direct elections to the European Parliament in 1979. West had been an undistinguished leader between 1974 and 1979, being overshadowed by Ian Paisley, Enoch Powell and William Craig. In any case Molyneaux had been leader of the UUP MPs at Westminster since 1974 following West's defeat in the October general election. Molyneaux had nearly thirty years' attendance at Westminster as an MP between 1970 and 1997 before his elevation to the Lords. In fact, he had acted as Sir Knox Cunningham's (MP for South Antrim 1955–70) agent before 1970.
    During the lifetime of the 1974–9 Labour government Molyneaux had two big opportunities to display his parliamentary skills. One occurred in 1977 when the Labour minority government needed, at the very least, the acquiescence of the eight Ulster Unionists. Following a series of meetings between Molyneaux, Enoch Powell and Harry McCusker on one side and Roy Mason, Michael Foot and the Prime Minister on the other, the Unionists won a major concession when the government agreed that there would be an increase in Northern Ireland representation at Westminster; this marked a complete U-turn in the government's attitude from the year before. The second was on the vote of confidence which brought the Labour government down in 1979; on this occasion two Ulster Unionists voted with Labour but they still lost by one vote. Both of these incidents, by demonstrating that such a small parliamentary

grouping could have extraordinary influence, reinforced in Molyneaux a belief in the importance of the Westminster scene. Yet we shall see that he misread the situation in the mid-1980s. On increased representation see Alistair Michie and Simon Hoggart, *The Pact: The Inside Story of the Lib-Lab Government, 1977–8* (London: Quartet Books, 1978), pp. 30–4, 42–4, 53, 58–9; and Mary Holland, 'Ulster learns the score', *New Statesman*, 25 March 1977, p. 390. On the fall of the government see Roy Hattersley, *Who Goes Home? Scenes from a Political Life* (London: Little, Brown and Company, 1995), pp. 208–10.

63   Unionist Task Force, *An End to Drift: The Task Force Report* (Belfast: Task Force Report, 1987).

64   See *Irish Times*, 30 May 1991. One can have some sympathy with the latter point. He is described as being 'appalled by the bigotry, drunkenness and stupidity of the Unionist Party in Ulster' after returning from the North in April 1971. See King, *Diary*, p. 99.

65   About the only other example of an 'external' intervention was that of Sir Fred Catherwood, former Conservative MEP but more importantly an Ulsterman who was president of the Evangelical Alliance. Trusted by Paisley, he had advised the unionist-dominated Northern Ireland Assembly in 1985 and 1986.

66   Alvin Jackson, *Ireland 1798–1998* (Oxford: Blakwell, 1999), pp. 411–21.

67   John Campbell, *Edward Heath: A Biography* (London: Jonathan Cape, 1993), pp. 426–7.

68   Miller, *Queen's Rebels*, pp. 148–9.

69   Campbell, *Heath*, p. 428.

CHAPTER 6

1   Tom Nairn, *The Breakup of Britain: Crisis and Neo-nationalism* (London: New Left Books, 1977), p. 93.

2   Frank Wright, *Northern Ireland: A Comparative Analysis* (Dublin: Gill and Macmillan, 1987), p. 218.

3   Clive R. Symmons, 'The Anglo-Irish Agreement and International Precedents: A Unique Experiment in Inter-State Co-operation on Minority Rights', in J. Hayes and P.

O'Higgins (eds.), *Lessons from Northern Ireland* (Belfast: Servicing the Legal System Publishers, 1990), pp. 221–2. The lawyer he quotes is John O'Conner (in *Irish Times*, 21 November 1985).

4   A.H. Birch, 'Minority Nationalist Movements and Theories of Political Integration', *World Politics*, 303 (1978), p. 341.

5   Quoted in George Quigley, 'Of Three Minds', in Richard Kearney (ed.), *Migrations: The Irish at Home and Abroad* (Dublin, Wolfhound Press, 1990), p. 75.

6   Daniel Moynihan, 'The Irish Among Us', *Reader's Digest*, January 1985, pp. 63 and 62. This theme of the Catholic–Protestant division (and myths about the Irish diaspora) is explored by Donald Harman Akenson. See his 'Data: What is Known about the Irish in North America?', in Oliver MacDonagh and W.F. Mandle (eds.), *Ireland and Irish-Australia: Studies in Cultural and Political History* (London: Croom Helm, 1986), pp. 1–17; and his *Half the World from Home: Perspectives on the Irish in New Zealand 1860–1950* (Ontario: Langdale Press, 1990).

7   Quigley, 'Of Three Minds', p. 74.

8   Quoted in Charles McC Mathias Jr, 'Ethnic Groups and Foreign Policy', *Foreign Affairs*, 5 (Summer 1981), p. 977.

9   Stephen Hartley, *The Irish Question as a Problem in British Foreign Policy 1914–18* (Basingstoke: Macmillan, 1987), p. 193.

10   Quoted in *ibid.*, p. 19.

11   Quoted in Mathias, 'Ethnic Groups', p. 982.

12   Owen Dudley Edwards, *Eamon de Valera* (Cardiff, GPC Books, 1987), p. 86.

13   Despite its flaws the best source on American foreign policy towards Ireland is Seán Cronin, *Washington's Irish Policy 1916–1986* (Dublin: Anvil Books, 1987).

14   On the evolution of the relationship see David Vital, *The Making of British Foreign Policy* (London: Allen and Unwin, 1968); for a sceptical appraisal see Ferdinand Mount (ed.), *The Inquiring Eye: A Selection of the Writings of David Watt* (Harmondsworth: Penguin Books 1988); on recent academic surveys see

David D. Newsom, 'US–British Consultation: An Impossible Dream?', *International Affairs*, 63, 2 (1987), pp. 225–38, and David Reynolds, 'A "Special Relationship"?: America, Britain and the International Order Since the Second World War', *International Affairs*, 62, 1 (1985–6), pp. 1–20.

15 Quoted in Mount, *Inquiring Eye*, p. 118.

16 David Reynolds, 'Rethinking Anglo-American Relations', *International Affairs*, 65, 1 (1988–9), pp. 89 and 110.

17 This checklist is borrowed from Mount, 'Inquiring Eye', Reynolds, 'Rethinking', and D.A. Low, *Eclipse of Empire* (Cambridge: Cambridge University Press, 1991), p. 328.

18 Low, *Eclipse of Empire*, pp. 6–7. The figures are borrowed from Low. He cites the demographic explanation in contrast to the 'treacherous loss of national nerve' thesis.

19 *ibid.*, p. 333.

20 *ibid.*, p. 19.

21 *ibid.*, pp. 329–31.

22 T.C. Salmon, *Unneutral Ireland: An Ambivalent and Unique Security Policy* (Oxford: Clarendon Press, 1989), p. 287.

23 Quoted in *ibid.*, p. 240.

24 Christopher Tugendhat, *Making Sense of Europe* (Harmondsworth: Viking, 1986), p. 118. As a former Vice-President of the European Commission Tugendhat is obviously an 'enthusiast'. Nonetheless his book is a model of clarity and brevity.

25 Quoted in *ibid.*, p. 33.

26 Robert S. Jordan and Werner J. Feld, *Europe in the Balance: The Changing Context of European International Politics* (London: Faber and Faber, 1986), p. 113.

27 *ibid.*, p. 114.

28 Tugendhat, *Making Sense of Europe*, p. 117.

29 *ibid.*, p. 116.

30 *ibid.*, p. 119.

31 See William Wallace, 'Foreign Policy and National Identity in the United Kingdom', *International Affairs*, 67, 1 (1991), pp. 67–80.

32 Chris Cook and Mary Francis, *The First European Elections* (London: Macmillan,1979), p. 23.

33 Some 67.2 per cent of the turnout voted 'Yes' with 32.8 per cent voting 'No'. Only Shetland and the Western Isles voted 'No' in the United Kingdom, although Northern Ireland with a 'Yes' vote of 52.1 per cent had the smallest pro-European vote among the 'national segments' in the United Kingdom. One reason for the lukewarm reception in Northern Ireland was that 'Europe' posed a general threat to British sovereignty, and it was seen as a largely Roman Catholic organisation. See Steve Bruce, *God Save Ulster: The Religion and Politics of Paisleyism* (Oxford: Clarendon Press, 1986), pp. 226–7, 229; and Paul Hainsworth, 'Political Parties and the European Community', in A. Aughey, P. Hainsworth and M.J. Trimble, *Northern Ireland in the European Community: An Economic and Political Analysis* (Belfast: Policy Research Institute, 1989), pp. 51–72.

34 Tugendhat, *Making Sense of Europe*, p. 120. He takes a critical look at the UK's performance at pp. 116–27.

35 This line of argument is pursued by Lord Cockfield, 'The Constitution in Transition: Brussels and Westminster', in Norman Lewis (ed.), *Happy and Glorious: The Constitution in Transition* (Milton Keynes: Open University Press, 1990), pp. 6–17.

36 Joseph H.H. Weiler, 'The European Community in Change: Exit, Voice and Loyalty', *Irish Studies in International Affairs*, 3, 2 (1990), pp. 18–19.

37 *ibid.*, p. 22.

38 F.H. Hinsley, *Sovereignty*, 2nd edn (Cambridge: Cambridge University Press, 1986), p. 234.

39 William Wallace, 'What Price Independence? Sovereignty and Interdependence in British politics', *International Affairs*, 62, 3 (1986), p. 14.

40 Quoted in J.J. Lee, *Ireland 1912–1985: Politics and Society* (Cambridge: Cambridge University Press, 1989), p. 463

41 *ibid.*

42 Quoted in *ibid.*, pp. 463–4.

43 Wallace, 'What Price Independence?', p. 19.

44 Wallace, 'Foreign policy', pp. 70 and 67.

45 *ibid.*, p. 76.

46 Bernard Crick, 'The Sovereignty of Parliament and the Irish Question', in

D. Rea (ed.), *Models of Political Co-operation in Divided Societies* (Dublin: Gill and Macmillan, 1982), pp. 239 and 232. Elsewhere he describes the 'myth of parliamentary sovereignty' as being essentially Hobbesian: 'if you do not surrender all power to Parliament we cannot stop you getting your throats cut by Catholic Highlanders or bog-dwelling Irish peasants'. See his 'The Concept of Consent and the Agreement', in Charles Townshend (ed.), *Consensus in Ireland: Approaches and Recessions* (Oxford: Clarendon Press, 1988), p. 119.

47   Quoted in Wallace, 'What Price Independence?', p. 1.

48   Friedrich Kratochwil, 'Of Systems, Boundaries, and Territoriality: An Inquiry into the Formation of the State System', *World Politics*, 39, 1 (October 1986), p. 27.

49   *ibid.*, pp. 42–3.

50   Michael Ó Corcara and Ronald J. Hill, 'The Soviet Union in Irish Foreign Policy', *International Affairs*, 58, 2 (1982), p. 260. See, too, Marcus Wheeler, 'The Dublin–Moscow Accord', *The World Today*, 29, 11 (November 1973), pp. 458–60; and Marcus Wheeler, 'Soviet Interest in Ireland', *Survey: A Journal of East and West Studies*, 21, 3 (1975), pp. 81–93.

51   Eamon Gallagher, 'Anglo-Irish Relations in the European Community', *Irish Studies in International Affairs*, 2, 1 (1985), p. 35.

52   Wright, *Northern Ireland*, p. 222.

53   Kratochwil, 'Of Systems, Boundaries and Territoriality, pp. 47, 47–8, 48–9.

54   *HC Deb.*, vol. 998, col. 557 (9 July 1980).

CHAPTER 7

*   The phrase comes from James Joyce, *Ulysses* (New York: Random House, 1961), p. 329.

1   Stanley B. Greenberg,'Social Differentiation and Political Violence', *Journal of Conflict Resolution*, 19, 1 (1975), p. 178. He maintains that political activity among Catholic groups in Northern Ireland is influenced by developments in Boston as well as in Ireland, and that the 'conflict within Northern Ireland cannot be understood without an appreciation for the English Reformation and the Glorious Revolution' (p. 183).

2   Former Speaker Tip O'Neill describing his childhood in a largely working-class neighborhood in North Cambridge, Massachusetts. Quoted in Andrew J. Wilson, *Irish America and the Ulster Conflict 1968–1995* (Belfast: Blackstaff Press, 1995), p. 131.

3   The *Times*' opinion of Anglo-American diplomacy when the Clinton administration granted a visa to Gerry Adams for the first time. Quoted on the back cover of Conor O'Clery, *The Greening of the White House: The Inside Story of How America Tried to Bring Peace to Ireland* (Dublin: Gill and Macmillan, 1996).

4   Donald T. Regan, *For the Record: From Wall Street to Washington* (London: Hutchinson, 1988).

5   See O'Clery, *Greening*; Eamon Mallie and David McKittrick, *The Fight for Peace: The Secret Story Behind the Irish Peace Process* (London: Heinemann, 1996) pp. 276–94; Tim Pat Coogan, *The Troubles: Ireland's Ordeal 1966–1995 and the Search for Peace* (London: Hutchinson, 1995), pp. 325–405; Wilson, *Irish America*.

6   Martin Fletcher, Philip Webster and Nicholas Watt, 'US links with Britain "worst since 1973" ', *Times*, 16 August 1996. The same article carried a comment from David Wilshire MP, vice-chairman of the Conservative Party back-bench Northern Ireland committee: 'Hallelujah! At long last a note of realism in America. At last someone is putting people's lives above grubbing for votes. I applaud him for it. He is absolutely right.' It is doubtful whether Wilshire's applause even extended beyond his constituency.

7   This close relationship was demonstrated when the Conservatives intervened in the 1992 presidential election campaign to assist George Bush's bid for re-election. A good luck message on the eve of the poll from the Foreign Secretary, Douglas Hurd, to Baker, who was in charge of the President's re-election effort, was leaked to the media. In it Hurd referred to a hunting expedition they had shared when he expressed the hope that Baker might 'shoot down all his

ducks' on election day. See O'Clery, *Greening*, pp. 24–5. One commentator has suggested that as a result of such interference 'Bill Clinton could rightly say to himself that whatever fealty he owed the special alliance with Britain, his obligation to the then sitting British government was a big fat zero'. See Ray O'Hanlon, *The New Irish Americans* (Boulder, Colo.: Roberts Rinehart, 1998), p. 200.

8   Henry Kissinger, *The White House Years* (London: Weidenfeld and Nicolson, 1979), p. 90.

9   All quotations in this paragraph come from Carl M. Cannon, 'When Clinton *Wasn't* Boastful', *National Journal*, 23 May 1998, pp. 1184–5.

10   Wilson, *Irish America*, p. 129.

11   Editor's Foreword, 'Northern Ireland: The International Dimension', *Cambridge Review of International Affairs*, 1997, p. 5

12   R. Maidment and A. McGrew, *The American Political Process* (London: Longman, 1986), p. 135.

13   Nathan Glazer and Daniel Patrick Moynihan, *Beyond the Melting Pot: The Negroes, Puerto Ricans, Jews, Italians and Irish of New York City* (Cambridge: MIT Press, 1963), p. v.

14   Quoted in Charles McC Mathias Jr., 'Ethnic Groups and Foreign Policy', *Foreign Affairs* 59 (1981), p. 979.

15   Glazer and Moynihan, *Beyond the Melting Pot*, 1970 edn, p. 310.

16   Quoted in D.S. Broder, *Changing of the Guard: Power and Leadership in America* (Harmondsworth: Penguin Books, 1984), p. 74.

17   John Hume, 'The Irish Question: A British Problem', *Foreign Affairs*, 58, 2 (1979), p. 312.

18   That figure would have shocked most commentators. In February 1980 a distinguished correspondent, knowledgeable about the conflict and about the state of Irish-America, had calculated that there were about 20 million US citizens who defined themselves as Irish-Americans, and that 'most estimates put the number of politically conscious Irish-Americans at about 100,000 at best – scattered through a nation of 220 million'. See Harold Jackson, 'The strengths and weaknesses of Irish America', *Guardian*, 22 February 1980.

19   This is reflected in the final editorial of the *Boston Irish News* (June 1990) where the editor and publisher Don Mooney commented that the more he 'became involved with Irish affairs in America, the less I liked what I saw. Too many political assumptions were taken for granted and there was a dearth of self-criticism. Nobody defied the conventional view or questioned the self-appointed spokespersons. The consensus was overbearing.'

20   *Boston Irish News*, December 1989.

21   See Jeffrey Donaldson, 'The U.S.A. Effect', in Ulster Young Unionist Council, *Selling Unionism: Home and Away* (Belfast, 1995), pp. 19–25. Donaldson was then one of the (four) honorary secretaries of the Ulster Unionist Council; since 1997 he has been MP for Lagan Valley. His article was a belated plea for proper UUP representation in North America and served as a backhanded compliment to Irish diplomacy and his political rival John Hume.

22   *New York Times*, 26 May 1978. Quoted in Wilson, *Irish America*, p. 146.

23   Maidment and McGrew, *American Political Process*, pp. 147 and 151.

24   It is a constant theme which runs through his *Personal Views: Politics, Peace and Reconciliation in Ireland* (Dublin: Town House, 1996). See, too, Barry White, *John Hume: Statesman of the Troubles* (Belfast: Blackstaff Press, 1984), *passim*.

25   *New York Times*, 17 March 1977.

26   See Jack Holland, *The American Connection* (New York: Viking Press, 1987), p. 129: the 'Irish diplomatic mission is second only to that of the Israelis'. US *News and World Report* (17 June 1984) listed the Irish Republic as the fifth largest group lobbying the United States government, based on its reputed $5.5 million expenditure in 1984.

27   Edward Kennedy, 'The Protestant Irish Heritage in America', *Congressional Record – Senate*, S13235 – S13237.

28   Wilson, *Irish America*, p. 139, my emphasis.

29   Quoted in *ibid.*, p. 140.

30   Eugene McEldowney, 'O'Dwyer: obvious parallels between Ireland and Vietnam', *Irish Times*, 21 June 1978.

31 Conor O'Clery, 'Tremendous turnaround in attitudes to NI – Jay', *Irish Times*, 20 January 1978. The date of the interview is significant for two reasons. Firstly, it followed the 1977 St Patrick's Day statement but was conducted *before* the more critical 1978 statement. Hence British diplomacy was taking a more benign view of Irish-America. Secondly, the interview stressed Dublin-London relations a full two years before that relationship was formalised.

32 David McKittrick, 'Horsemen of the Irish apocalypse', *Irish Times*, 6 September 1979. McKittrick described O'Neill's relationship with the White House as follows: 'He treats the President's men – up to and including the Chief of the White House staff, Hamilton Jordan, just like little boys, and he doesn't care who knows it.'

33 See Gary Wills, *The Kennedy Imprisonment: A Meditation on Power* (Boston: Little, Brown and Company, 1981), pp. 194–6 and 292–4.

34 Quoted in McKittrick, 'Horsemen'.

35 David McKittrick, 'Biaggi thought the British army was in the Republic', *Irish Times*, 5 September 1979. The peace forum which is mentioned was an attempt by Biaggi to bring loyalist and republican paramilitaries to Washington; it is discussed below.

36 See Jimmy Carter, *Talking Peace: A Vision for the Next Generation* (New York: Puffin Books, 1995), pp. 21–8.

37 David McKittrick, 'Stopping the gunrunning no simple task', *Irish Times*, 26 March 1977.

38 Amnesty International, Report of an Amnesty International Mission to Northern Ireland (28 November 1977).

39 Tip O'Neill *et al.*, Mimeograph, (17 March – 6 December 1977) Amnesty International 1978: both quotes from p. 70.

40 Quoted in Wilson, *Irish America*, p. 156.

41 For the O'Neill visit to London and the RUC licence issue, see *ibid.*, pp. 154–62.

42 McKittrick, 'Horsemen'.

43 McKittrick, 'Biaggi'. McKittrick is quoting a republican supporter in the United States.

44 Wilson, *Irish America*, pp. 147–9.

45 Ian Paisley, 'If you had given me a visa . . .', *Washington Post*, 1 August 1982, p. A23.

46 Ken Heskin, *Northern Ireland: A Psychological Analysis* (Dublin: Gill and Macmillan, 1980), p. 100.

47 J. Enoch Powell, 'Dev and devolution', *Spectator*, 8 January 1983, pp. 19–20. See, too, David McKittrick, *Despatches from Belfast* (Belfast: Blackstaff Press, 1989). McKittrick describes Powell's analysis as a 'conspiracy theory more grandiose, more fantastic, more breathtaking than anything ever propagated by Ian Paisley' (p. 62).

48 Of course, this is not to be taken too literally. Shakespeare's play was entitled *The Tragedy of Antony and Cleopatra*. Neither the President nor the Prime Minister dispayed a similar public ardour. Nor could one say of President Reagan as Philo says of Antony in the opening scene:

> His captain's heart,
> Which in the scuffles of great
>   fights hath burst
> The buckles on his breast, reneges
>   all temper,
> And is become the bellows and the
>   fan
> To cool a gipsy's lust.

All the same Ronald Reagan's official biographer implies that their relationship was platonic. See Edmund Morris, *Dutch: A Memoir of Ronald Reagan* (New York: Random House, 1999), p. 392 (and 777).

49 Margaret Thatcher, *The Downing Street Years* (London: HarperCollins, 1993), pp. 157, 68–9, 324–5, 158.

50 *ibid.*, pp. 435 and 770–1. One White House insider drew comparisons between the two: 'both conservatives and both political dark horses who have won office and the grudging respect of their enemies against the odds, [they] truly like and admire each other'. Regan, *For the Record*, p. 16.

51 Regan, *For the Record*, p. 259. He may have exaggerated the closeness of their relationship. He recalls (p. 34) a meeting at Camp David: 'As usual, they met alone, without aides for several hours of intensive conversation.' Yet in her memoirs Thatcher makes a telling point about

an early meeting with President Bush: 'For all the friendship and co-operation I had had with President Reagan, I was never taken into the Americans' confidence more than I was during the two hours or so I spent that afternoon at the White House' (*Downing Street Years*, p. 820). Nevertheless Reagan's Secretary of State, George Shultz, described the Anglo-American relationship as 'now closer than at any time since World War II'; this closeness was manifested on a personal level – 'The president had immense confidence in her, and her views carried great weight' – and on an ideological level – 'Freedom in political and economic life was her trademark. In that regard she and Ronald Reagan were soul mates.' George P. Shultz, *Turmoil and Triumph: My Years as Secretary of State* (New York: Scribners, 1993), pp. 152, 509 and 153.

52   Thatcher, *Downing Street Years*, pp. 156–7.

53   Quoted in Dilys M. Hill and Phil Williams, 'The Reagan Presidency: Style and Substance', in Dilys M. Hill, Raymond Moore and Phil Williams (eds.), *The Reagan Presidency: An Incomplete Revolution?* (Basingstoke: Macmillan in association with the Centre for International Policy Studies, University of Southampton, 1990), pp. 3 and 10.

54   Thatcher, *Downing Street Years*, pp. 330–3. In a revealing vignette she recalls a telephone call from the President when 'he began by saying, in that disarming way of his, that if he was in London and dropped in to see me he would be careful to throw his hat through the door first' (p. 332).

55   *ibid.*, p. 447.

56   *ibid.*, p. 158.

57   Joe Carroll, 'Reagan biographer plays down "apparent airhead" remark', *Irish Times*, 2 October 1999.

58   Garret FitzGerald, *All in a Life: An Autobiography* (London: Macmillan, 1991), p. 577. George Shultz (Turmoil and Triumph, p. 353) recalls 'putting on a little show' to get Reagan's attention and involvement: 'With Mike Deaver as the impresario, we selected people to play the parts of Mitterrand, Thatcher, Trudeau, Kohl, Nakasone, Fanfani, and Thorn

... and let the president interact with them. We would have a little drama and fun ... By the time we got to Williamsburg, he was in top form, limber and well prepared in his mind for the interplay of issues and personalities.'

59   Hedrick Smith, *The Power Game: How Washington Works* (New York: Ballentine Books, 1996), p. 618.

60   Morris, *Dutch*, p. xi. His biographer recalls the malign influence of his drunken Irish Catholic father and the fact that he was reared as a Protestant. Morris records an interview he had with former Governor Edmund T. Brown when both he and Reagan were campaigning for Harry Truman in 1948: 'I said to him, "Good to meet another Irish Catholic." He said pleasantly, yet very deliberately, "Mr Brown, I'm of Irish descent, but my mother raised me as a Protestant" ' (p. 337).

61   Chester A. Crocker, *High Noon in Southern Africa: Making Peace in a Rough Neighborhood* (New York: Norton, 1992), pp. 96–9.

62   Smith, *Power Game*, p. 590. The troika consisted of James Baker, Chief of Staff; Mike Deaver, Deputy Chief of Staff; and Edwin Meere, Attorney-General. Their formidable powers are described by Smith on p. 412.

63   *ibid.*, p. 593. Smith notes that Clark 'projected the boyish modesty of a tall, lanky rancher who gave up a sunny life on the Californian Supreme Court to help his old friend, Ron Reagan [but] he was not shy about exercising power'. Morris, *Dutch*, pp. 455–8, paints a fascinating picture of the Reagan–Clark relationship.

64   Quoted in Seán Cronin, 'Paisley visa galvanises Irish issue', *Irish Times*, 12 December 1981.

65   Regan, *For the Record*, p. 277.

66   Morris, *Dutch*, p. 466.

67   Quoted in Wilson, *Irish America*, p. 180.

68   Thatcher, *Downing Street Years*, pp. 165–6.

69   Shultz, *Turmoil and Triumph*, p. 646.

70   'Britain is trampling precious rights to fight IRA', *Newsday*, 26 October 1988.

71   See Paul Arthur, 'The Media and Politics in Northern Ireland', in Jean Seaton and Ben Pimlott (eds.), *The*

Media in British Politics (Aldershot: Gower, 1987), pp. 208–11.

72   Joseph Ruane and Jennifer Todd, *The Dynamics of Conflict in Northern Ireland: Power, Conflict and Emancipation* (Cambridge: Cambridge University Press, 1996), pp. 278–9.

73   The first public announcement appeared in the *Irish Echo*, 10 November 1984: 'Caucus proposes new initiative to stop discrimination in NI'.

74   See, for example, Steve Lohr, 'Push on hiring bias in Ulster', *New York Times*, 4 September 1986, pp. D7–8; Elliott D. Lee, 'Activist holders target Northern Ireland: campaign against US firms stirs concern', *Wall Street Journal*, 20 January 1987; Robert England, 'Antidiscrimination campaign takes aim at the least biased', *Insight*, 4 May 1987, pp. 26–8; Pamela Sherrid, 'Why Irish eyes frown at US help', *US News and World Report*, 24 August 1987, p. 32.

75   'Sean MacBride – International Statesman', interview by Michael Farrrell, *Irish America*, April 1986, p. 35.

76   See his testimony before the Joint Committee of the Finance and State Government of the Pennsylvanian House of Representatives on 15 September 1987 (mimeograph).

77   See two contrasting views: Harrison J. Goldin, 'Stopping discrimination by US companies', *Irish America*, April 1987, pp. 14–15; and John P. McCarthy, 'The MacBride Principles are not helpful', *Irish America*, May 1987, pp. 14–15. Goldin was comptroller for the city of New York and McCarthy a professor of history at Fordham University in New York.

78   For his pains he received the epithet of 'England's main propaganda expert in the United States of America', in a letter from Fr Seán McManus to the *Derry Journal*, 17 March, 1987. See, too, Brian Donaghy, 'MacBride Principles could cause splits between unions', *Irish Times*, 29 May 1987.

79   Fr Seán McManus interview with the author, 13 May 1986.

80   Steven Erlanger, *Boston Globe*, 2 May 1986. Her speech to Congress can be found in *British Information Service News Release*, 20 February 1985.

81   Morris, *Dutch*, pp. 535–6.

82   Fr Seán McManus interview with the author, 13 May 1986.

83   An insightful article on Irish-American resistance to the treaty is Christopher Hitchens, 'Attacking an IRA refuge', *Spectator*, 5 October 1985. Hitchens describes McManus as 'a burly, plausible charmer [who] hadn't been raised as a clerical apologist for nothing'. Hitchens admitted to spending 'a long and, to be perfectly frank, rather enjoyable afternoon with Father McManus in his Capitol Hill office'. Hitchens makes the critical point that if the supplementary treaty became law it 'would consummate the special relationship in a most memorable and decisive way. It would make the United Kingdom, of Great Britain and particularly of Northern Ireland, the only country in the world which could reclaim its refugee opponents from the United States. Reclaim them, moreover, not as opponents but as criminal fugitives.' Given the trauma of the hunger strikes, those last remarks should have sent a warning to the British authorities. Certainly Hitchens was aware of the significance of the extradition issue. He closed his article thus: 'And it should surprise nobody that the Irish who came to this country to escape British rule will bust every sinew and call in every debt before they let anyone be returned to it.' Prophetic words!

84   Joe Biden, Press release, 1 August 1985.

85   Thomas O. Melia, 'Killing confusion', *New Republic*, 2 June 1986, pp. 12–14. The subtitle is 'The Senate waffles on the IRA'.

86   See Paul D. Colford, 'An Irish symbol in an NY prison', *Newsday*, 27 April 1987, pp. 4–5 and 12.

87   Brian O'Dwyer interview with the author, 11 March 1998. O'Dwyer was an attorney and the son of the veteran civil rights activist, Paul. He had been heavily involved in a campaign for immigration reform to protect young illegal immigrants and was co-chair of the Emerald Isle Immigration Center in New York.

88   *ibid.*

89   This section borrows from O'Hanlon, *New Irish Americans*, pp. 27–9.

90   See *ibid.*, pp. 96–110.

91 Quoted in *ibid.*, p. 99.
92 Tim Hames, 'Impotence of being Tony', *Times*, 24 February 2000.
93 Arwel Ellis Owen, *The Anglo-Irish Agreement: The First Three Years* (Cardiff: University of Wales Press, 1994), p. 16.
94 Mallie and McKittrick, *Fight for Peace*, p. 278.
95 John Major, *The Autobiography* (London: HarperCollins, 1999), p. 499. Indeed one of the President's closest aides described Major as 'a delightful and very decent person'. Private information.
96 Private information.
97 David Goodall, 'Terrorists on the spot', *The Tablet*, 25 December 1993/ 1 January 1994, p. 1676.
98 Interview with Tom Moran and Bill Flynn, 11 March 1998. Moran and Flynn were respectively chief executive officer and former chief executive officer of Mutual of America.
99 *Irish America* was first published in 1985 by a young Irish emigrant, Niall O'Dowd. It was a glossy magazine designed to convey the message that Irish-Americans had come of age. In its premier issue it compiled a list of 'The Top 100 Irish-Americans'. It focussed on two prerequisites: 'first on those who have taken an interest in the condition of their fellow religionists in Northern Ireland, and have sought to find a peaceful solution for all sides there, and secondly on the tremendous role the Irish have historically and presently played in education in the US'. Religion was a major headache since 'over 35 per cent of the bishops and major ecclesiastical figures in the US are of Irish extraction'. This listing became an annual feature of the magazine.
100 Patricia Harty, 'Business 100', *Irish America*, (1996), p. 32.
101 Charles McC Mathias Jr, 'Ethnic Groups and Foreign Policy', *Foreign Affairs*, 59 (Summer 1981), p. 984.
102 Interview with Brian O'Dwyer, 11 March 1998.
103 Much of the following information on the NSC and the State Department is drawn from Smith, *Power Game*.
104 Morris, *Dutch*, p. 786.
105 Morris (*ibid.*, p. 437) refers to the State Department as 'the striped pants set'.
106 Interview with Nancy Soderberg, 5 November 1997.
107 Niall O'Dowd, 'Clinton's foreign policy credentials will rest on his role in Irish peace process', *Irish Times*, 10 November 2000.
108 *ibid.*
109 On the role of Jean Kennedy Smith see O'Clery, *Greening*, pp. 74–90, and Coogan, *Troubles*, pp. 352–3 and 371–2.

CHAPTER 8

1 Tom Paulin 'An Ulster Unionist Walks the Streets of London', *Fivemiletown* (London: Faber, 1987), p. 42.
2 *Northern Ireland: Statement by the National Executive Committee to the 1981 Conference* (London: Labour Party, 1981), p. 5.
3 Bernard Donoghue, *Prime Minister: The Conduct of Policy under Harold Wilson and James Callaghan* (London: Jonathan Cape, 1987), p. 159.
4 See Billy McCarrick, 'The British Labour Party, British Politics and Ireland' (D. Phil thesis, University of Ulster, 1992); *passim.*
5 Donoghue, *Prime Minister*, p. 132.
6 Brendan O'Duffy and Brendan O'Leary, 'Violence in Northern Ireland, 1969–June 1989', in John McGarry and Brendan O'Leary (eds.), *The Future of Northern Ireland* (Oxford: Oxford University Press, 1990), p. 331.
7 Northern Ireland Act 1974, ch. 28, s. 2.
8 *The Government of Northern Ireland: A Working Paper for a Conference*, Cmnd 7763 (London, HMSO, 1979).
9 *Northern Ireland: A Framework for Devolution*, Cmnd 8541 (London, HMSO, 1982).
10 McCarrick, 'British Labour Party', pp. i and 329. McCarrick was writing about the crucial period in the Labour Party's evolution between 1918 and 1924.
11 Austen Morgan, *Harold Wilson* (London: Pluto Press, 1992), p. 365.
12 See Tam Dalyell, *Devolution: The End of Britain?* (London: Jonathan Cape, 1977), where he draws on the Irish analogy at pp. 285–94.
13 See Bob Purdie, 'The Friends of Ireland: British Labour and Irish Nationalism, 1945–49', in Tom

Gallagher and James O'Connell (eds. *Contemporary Irish Studies* (Manchester University Press, 1983, pp. 81–94.

14 That can be found even among those who were sympathetic to the party. See, for example, an editorial, 'End-Game in Ulster', *New Statesman*, 28 May 1976, where there was an assumption that Labour was preparing for withdrawal.

15 Donoghue, *Prime Minister*, felt that Rees's problem was that 'he could not always see the wood for the trees' (p. 131); and Maurice Hayes, *Minority Verdict: Experiences of a Catholic Public Servant* (Belfast: Blackstaff Press, 1995), found him to be 'a haverer who found it hard to make up his mind on anything' (p. 176). There is an apocryphal story about one of his senior advisers who didn't mind Rees wrestling with his conscience but did object that it always ended up in a draw. There was a feeling, too, that he was unduly influenced by his Permanent Under-Secretary, Frank Cooper, with whom he had served in the RAF during World War II. One Irish politician described Cooper as 'a combination of Cardinal Richelieu and Machiavelli' (private information). Everyone who came into contact with Rees was agreed on one point – he was impossible to dislike.

16 Merlyn Rees, *Northern Ireland: A Personal Perspective* (London: Methuen, 1985), p. 31. Yet on p. 43 he writes, 'On my first day in the province I met the leaders of the Executive and emphasised that our aim was to implement Sunningdale.'

17 *ibid.*, p. 90. Interestingly the leader of the Alliance Party, Oliver Napier, concurs with this view: 'The two people I blame – and both were superb at Sunningdale – are Garret FitzGerald and John Hume. They were going out to negotiate the best possible deal they could get from Faulkner for the nationalist tradition and to hell with everything else, and they did it very well.' See Joe Carroll, 'Hume and Garret crucified Faulkner at Sunningdale', *Sunday Tribune*, 7 October 1984. Garret FitzGerald, *All in a Life: An Autobiography* (London: Macmillan, 1991), pp. 209–24, gives a detailed account of the Sunningdale negotiations.

18 Rees, *Northern Ireland*, p 39. The fact that Orme described the same people as 'bigots' and 'fascists' seems to have escaped Rees's attention. His remarks were made in relation to the UWC strike. See Robert Fisk, *The Point of No Return: The Strike Which Broke the British in Ulster* (London: André Deutsch, 1975), pp. 63–4 and 81.

19 'Unusually', Bernard Donoghue informs us, 'Joe Haines and I were not involved in the speech-writing; it was drafted by the Northern Ireland Office and Mr Wilson himself inserted the reference to scroungers' (*Prime Minister*, p. 130). That seems to be confirmed by Harold Wilson in his memoirs, *Final Term: The Labour Government 1974–1976* (London: Weidenfeld and Nicolson and Michael Joseph, 1979), p. 76, where he explains why he came to use these words which he accepts might be seen as 'provocative and bitter'.

20 Rees, *Northern Ireland*, pp. 73 and 89–90.

21 *ibid.*, p. 90. The Prime Minister suffered from no such delusions. It was 'an undeniably political strike, arguably the first in the history of the United Kingdom'. See Wilson, *Final Term*, p. 74.

22 Rees, *Northern Ireland*, p. 107. He describes the convention period at pp. 183–210 and 251–82.

23 Hayes, *Minority Verdict*, p. 211. Hayes acted as adviser to the chairman of the Constitutional Convention, where he found that there was 'very little real communication ... and very little real contact between the groups' (p. 224).

24 Rees, *Northern Ireland*, p. 280.

25 See *ibid.*, pp. 149–81, 217–19. See Garret FitzGerald, 'Preconditions for an Irish peace', *London Review of Books*, 8 November 1979, pp. 1–4, for an account of Dublin's displeasure: 'The damage done by these repeated contacts with terrorist leaders or representatives can scarcely be overestimated. The boost to the morale of the IRA, with whom no government of the Republic has had truck, was inestimable.'

26 Donoghue, *Prime Minister*, pp. 130–1. A similar theme can be found in Robert Fisk, *Point of No Return, passim*; see, too, Desmond Hamill, *Pig in the Middle: The Army in Northern Ireland 1969–1984* (London: Methuen, 1985),

pp. 145–54 for the army version of
the UWC strike. Hamill is particularly
interesting because he is sympathetic
to the army viewpoint: 'However a
question mark was to remain over the
Army's decision [that dealing with a
civil strike was the responsibility of
the police] which was never removed'
(p. 145). He illustrates a certain
amount of condescension visited on
the Northern Secretary: ' "Merlyn
was a nice chap to work with", said
one staff officer, "but he didn't really
terrify the chief constable" ' (p. 149).

27 John Hume, 'A case of exploding
myths once again in Ulster', *Irish
Times*, 15 November 1975. This was a
review of Fisk's book *The Point of No
Return*. Stan Orme was the only
member of the direct rule team to
escape Hume's wrath. See, too, Sir
Oliver Napier, 'Where Merlyn Rees
got it wrong', *Belfast Telegraph*, 24
October 1985. Napier, the leader of
the Alliance Party and a member of
the power-sharing executive, was
reviewing Rees's memoirs.

28 See Gerard Murray, *John Hume and the
SDLP: Impact and Survival in Northern
Ireland* (Dublin: Irish Academic Press,
1998), pp. 60–8.

29 See, for example, Robert Fisk,
'Ulster fears the economic screw',
New Statesman, 6 February 1976,
p. 151.

30 Rees, *Northern Ireland*, pp. 60–1; Roy
Mason, *Paying the Price* (London:
Robert Hale, 1999), p. 125. Barbara
Castle, who was Social Services
Secretary in the Labour government,
describes the 'strained inquest' in
cabinet on 25 April 1974: 'But that
india–rubber little man hardly seemed
perturbed. It would take more than
that major gaffe to shake his
complacency,' *The Castle Diaries
1974–76* (London: Weidenfeld and
Nicolson, 1980), p. 89. Others have
commented on Mason's size. One
Northern Ireland politician described
him as 'the 5 foot three John Wayne'.
Hayes describes him as 'a small man in
every respect' (*Minority Verdict*,
p. 235).

31 Fisk, *Point of No Return*, p. 191.

32 Mason, *Paying the Price*, p. 161.

33 *ibid.*, p. 162. Interestingly, the two
senior Northern Ireland civil servants
who have produced their memoirs of
that period – Hayes (*Majority Verdict*,

pp. 236–40) and Sir Kenneth
Bloomfield (*Stormont in Crisis: A
Memoir* [Belfast: Blackstaff Press,
1994], p. 265) – give Melchett ringing
endorsements.

34 Donoghue, *Prime Minister*, p. 131.

35 Mason, *Paying the Price*, pp. 190–1. He
puts it down, not to frivolity, but 'to
the tension we were under'. Andrew
Lloyd Webber's *Evita* was a hugely
successful musical at the time and
'Don't cry for me, Argentina' was its
most popular song.

36 That was in sharp contrast to Merlyn
Rees's earlier statement that he did
not see 'any circumstances in which
extra representation for Northern
Ireland with its history would be a
means of bringing the peace that we
all want'. Quoted by Patrick
Wintour, 'Britain's Ulster Gamble?',
New Statesman, 9 March 1979.

37 *HC Deb.*, 5, cmlxi, vol. 961, col. 1834
(12 January 1978).

38 David McKittrick, 'Mason whips up
SDLP anger', *Irish Times*, 10 February
1979.

39 Fitt's no vote 'was probably the price
we paid for our reactionary Irish
policy'. Donoghue, *Prime Minister*,
p. 185. Interestingly, Roy Hattersley,
*Who Goes Home? Scenes from a Political
Life* (London: Little, Brown and
Company, 1995), pp. 208–11, argues
that the government could have
secured all the UUP votes for the price
of a gas pipeline from Scotland to
Northern Ireland.

40 An interesting literary exercise would
be a comparison between Mason's
memoirs, *Paying the Price*, and those of
the former head of the Northern
Ireland civil service, Sir Kenneth
Bloomfield, *Stormont in Crisis*. Both
open with violence – or the threat of
violence. In Bloomfield's case it was
palpable in an IRA bomb that
destroyed his home and very nearly
killed all of his family. He tells the
story quietly and with feeling. But
that is it. He moves on to discuss his
professional life. Mason's preface is
entitled 'Targeted for Assassination'
and ends: 'In the words of one Provo
godfather, I was the minister who
"kicked the shit" out of the terrorists.
Their desire for vengeance is
implacable. My family have been
living with the consequences for
more than twenty years.' The closing

two sentences of the book read: 'And I've managed to survive being thrust into the maelstrom of politics, religion and terrorism. I can't complain.'

41   Mark Urban, *Big Boys' Rules: The Secret Struggle against the IRA* (London: Faber, 1992), pp. 12, 81.

42   *Report of the Committee of Inquiry into Police Interrogation Procedures in Northern Ireland* [Bennett Report], Cmnd 7497 (London: HMSO, 1979).

43   Peter Taylor in *New Statesman*, 9 March 1979.

44   Mason, *Paying the Price*, pp. 170–1.

45   David McKittrick, 'The man who thought he had done it', *Irish Times*, 16 May 1979.

46   Bloomfield, *Stormont in Crisis*, p. 243, 'felt acutely that Northern Ireland had been taken for a ride'. Mason (*Paying the Price*, pp. 218–22) puts up a spirited defence in which most of the blame is shifted to his Conservative successors for their lack of detailed, hands-on supervision and their lethargy.

47   Hayes (*Minority Verdict*, p. 235) describes Atkins as 'totally invisible and lazy'. One journalist found him to be a 'cultivated and courteous man who seems to think that Northern Ireland demands the same levels of political skills as a Young Conservatives' garden fete'. See Mary Holland, 'South of the border', *New Statesman*, 7 September 1979, p. 330.

48   Urban, *Big Boys' Rules*, p. 85.

49   *The Government of Northern Ireland: A Working Paper for a Conference*, Cmnd 7763 (London: HMSO, 1979), p. 2.

50   SDLP Mimeograph (Belfast, 16 December 1977), p. 2.

51   *The Government of Northern Ireland: Proposals for Further Discussion*, Cmnd 7950 (London: HMSO, 1980).

52   *HC Deb.*, vol. 988, col. 557 (9 July 1980).

53   See Chapter 3 above and Dick Walsh, 'Secret report casts doubt on new British initiative on North', *Irish Times*, 14 May 1979.

54   Gerry Adams, *The Politics of Irish Freedom* (Dingle, Co. Kerry: Brandon Books, 1986), pp. 67–8, 71.

55   See the 1987 survey quoted in Padraig O'Malley, *Biting at the Grave: The Irish Hunger Strikes and the Politics of Despair* (Belfast: Blackstaff Press, 1990), p. 131.

56   Adams, *Politics of Irish Freedom*, p. 87.

57   *Republican News*, 16 September 1982.

58   Adams, *Politics of Irish Freedom*, p. 151. We should not underestimate the huge significance for the republican movement of electoral politics: 'In the case of the IRA and Sinn Féin, internal debates regarding the role of electoral politics resulted in disastrous splits in 1928, 1933, 1945 and 1969 ... So damaging was the 1969–70 split within the IRA and Sinn Féin that, following the regrouping in the Provisional IRA and Sinn Féin of those who rejected participation in parliamentary politics, the question of participating in elections was not raised again until 1983 when delegates to the annual Sinn Féin *ard fheis* (party conference) passed a motion proposing that "no aspect of the constitution and rules be closed to discussion".' Cynthia L. Irvin, 'Parties against the State: Militant Nationalism in Ireland and Spain' (D. Phil. thesis, Duke University, 1993), p. 10. Sinn Féin's constitution was duly amended in 1986.

59   Margaret Thatcher, *Downing Street Years* (London: HarperCollins, 1993), p. 384.

60   Dick Spring, 'Everything was black or white, never grey', *Irish Times*, 24 November 1990, my emphasis. In the same issue his predecessor, Michael O'Leary, stated: 'I was never persuaded that she had any real interest in the Northern Ireland question ... She found, I believe, the politics and problems of Northern Ireland alien and un-English, however loudly she might protest her loyalty to the union.' The Irish may have been too sensitive about her disparaging opinions. She expressed her prejudices freely. For her opinion on Scotland, for example, see her *Downing Street Years*, pp. 618–24.

61   See David McKittrick, 'It's make or break time for Jim Prior', *Irish Times*, 29 September 1981. McKittrick recounts the public humiliation of Prior in February 1980 when Thatcher explained in a television interview that he had made a mistake: 'I think it was a mistake and Jim Prior was very, very sorry indeed. He was very apologetic. But we don't just sack a person for one mistake.'

62   *Northern Ireland: A Framework for*

Devolution, Cmnd 8541 (London: HMSO, 1982).

63 For a description of 'rolling devolution' see Sydney Elliott and W.D. Flackes, *Northern Ireland: A Political Directory 1968–1999*, 5th edn (Belfast: Blackstaff Press, 1999), pp. 610–13. For an account of the work of the Northern Ireland Assembly see Cornelius O'Leary, Sydney Elliott and R.A. Wilford, *The Northern Ireland Assembly 1982–1986: A Constitutional Experiment* (London: Hurst, 1988).

64 See David McKittrick, 'Tory filibuster on Prior bill showed gulf in party', *Irish Times*, 26 June 1982.

65 Maev-Ann Wren, 'Prior's thinking is on well-worn tracks', *Irish Times*, 23 January 1982.

66 Margaret van Hattem, *Financial Times*, 6 April 1982.

67 Alvin Jackson, *Ireland 1798–1998* (Oxford: Blackwell, 1999), p. 380.

68 Michael Gallagher, *The Irish Labour Party in Transition 1957–82* (Manchester: Manchester University Press, 1982), p. 197. 'In the event, prices rose by about 90 per cent during the first four years of the Coalition's term.'

69 Gemma Hussey (Fine Gael politician and Minister for Education in the 1980s) quoted in Jackson, *Ireland*, p. 379. Jackson writes that it 'is scarcely an exaggeration to suggest that the economic crisis of the 1970s helped to shape some of the fundamental features of Irish politics not just at the time but for much of the next 20 years'. See, too, J.J. Lee, *Ireland 1912–1985: Politics and Society* (Cambridge: Cambridge University Press, 1989), pp. 465–7.

70 A flavour of his philosophy can be found in a speech he made during the 1973 election campaign: 'We must resolutely defend and protect our great Christian heritage, and this can only be done if we improve, rather than alter, the present system.' Quoted in Brian Harvey, *Cosgrave's Coalition: Irish Politics in the 1970s* (London: Selecteditions, 1980), p. 23.

71 Mary Holland, 'Ulster – the drift to disaster', *New Statesman*, 5 December 1975.

72 See FitzGerald, *All in a Life*, pp. 196–7.

73 *ibid.*, pp. 197–8. In a famous put-down O'Brien describes FitzGerald's 'darker side' and says that 'it was one of Garret's strengths that he himself was unaware of any darker side. He lived in the sunny confidence that he was invariably acting for the common good which, by a happy coincidence, often coincided with his own good.' Conor Cruise O'Brien, *Memoir: My Life and Themes* (London: Profile Books, 1998), pp. 347–8.

74 'Among the smaller European Union members with a broadly comparable range of international interests and obligations – such as Belgium, Denmark, Finland, Greece, Portugal, Sweden – all have more than twice as many mssions and twice as many diplomatic staff as Ireland.' Department of Foreign Affairs, *Challenges and Opportunities Abroad: White Paper on Foreign Policy* (Dublin: Stationery Office, 1996), pp. 320–1. See, too, pp. 52–3 for a discussion on relations with Britain.

75 FitzGerald, *All in a Life*, p. 196.

76 *ibid.*, pp. 252–3, 273–4.

77 Rees, *Northern Ireland*, p. 320. This seemed a rather odd position to be adopted by a public representative of a liberal democratic government. After all the European Court of Human rights did find against Britain for degrading and inhuman treatment. John Whale in the *Sunday Times* (5 September 1976) argued that interrogation techniques used by the army when internment was introduced 'were designed, in plain terms, to send men out of their minds'. The charges had been first raised in 1971 but were not finally settled until January 1978. There is no doubt that the charges poisoned Anglo-Irish relations during these years.

78 'When British territory is invaded it is not just an invasion of our land, but of our whole spirit'. Editorial in *Times*, 5 April 1982. By a strange coincidence I happened to be reading Nicholas Mansergh's *Britain and Ireland* (London: Longman, 1942) when writing this section and came across the following (p. 95): 'By temperament and by religion, the Southern Irish are peculiarly fitted to constitute a bridge-head between the English-speaking and the Latin world.' By an even stranger

coincidence the Taoiseach was being advised by Professor Mansergh's son, Martin, then and since. There is no evidence that the Irish were able to apprise Margaret Thatcher of the Latin temperament.

CHAPTER 9

1   James Prior, *A Balance of Power* (London: Hamish Hamilton, 1986), p. 52.
2   Byron Bland, *Marching and Rising: The Rituals of Small Differences and Great Violence in Northern Ireland* (Stanford, Calif.: Center for International Security and Arms Control, Stanford University, 1996), pp. 10–11.
3   William Shannon, 'The Anglo-Irish Agreement', *Foreign Affairs*, 64, 4 (1986), p. 870. Shannon, a former American Ambassador to Ireland, was commenting on the Anglo-Irish Agreement signed the previous November.
4   Leo Tolstoy, *War and Peace* (Harmondsworth: Penguin Books, 1971), p. 1342.
5   Arend Lijphart, *Democracy in Plural Societies: A Comparative Exploration* (New Haven: Yale University Press, 1977), pp. 1 and 66.
6   Brian Barry, 'Political Accommodation and Consociational Democracy', *British Journal of Political Science*, 5, 4 (1975), p. 494.
7   Karl Popper, *The Open Society and its Enemies* (London: Routledge, 1960), vol. 1, p. 117.
8   Peter Hennessy, *Cabinet* (Oxford: Basil Blackwell, 1986), p. 22. One Whitehall insider argued that under Margaret Thatcher they had, temporarily at least, 'a form of presidential government in which she operates like a sovereign in her court' (*ibid.*, p. 99). In those circumstances Armstrong's role became more vital. See, too, Garret FitzGerald, *All in a Life: An Autobiography* (London: Macmillan, 1991). He describes Armstrong as 'a man with a sense of history and a deep commitment to Anglo–Irish relations' (p. 469).
9   See Geraldine Kennedy, 'The perfect civil servant', *Irish Times*, 19 December, 1992; and Joe Carroll, 'A civil service mandarin with a mastery of cabinet secrets', *Irish*

Times, 23 June 1990.
10   In a review of the South's economic fortunes in 1982, T.K. Whitaker, the key figure in Irish economic thinking during the period, pointed out that by 1981 the UK 'was the destination of 43 per cent of our exports as against 55 per cent in 1973, whereas the Continental EEC takes 32 per cent as against 21 per cent . . . On a general review of EEC membership one must conclude that the overall benefits to the Irish economy, and particularly to agriculture, have been substantial.' While poverty still persisted and social inequality had not been removed, 'the typical Irish family now enjoys a real income about three times that of its forerunner in the early 1920s. The gross national product per head has more than doubled in the last twenty years, and the Republic now ranks among the twenty-five richest countries in the world. By all indices of material progress . . . we are consistently moving up the scale.' Whitaker, in his Louvain Lecture to the Irish Club in Belgium, reported in *Irish Times*, 25 March 1982. By the end of the century only 25 per cent of Irish exports were going to the UK. See Stephen Collins, 'Harney is wrong. We owe the EU a huge debt', *Sunday Tribune*, 30 July 2000.
11   James Downey, *Them and Us: Britain, Ireland and the Northern Ireland Question 1969–1982* (Dublin: Ward River Press, 1983), pp. 180 and 163. Downey is aware that this is very much a minority view. But it does have validity. A senior official in Dublin told me in an interview in the summer of 1985 that, whereas Lynch had kept Liam Cosgrove fully briefed on Northern Ireland when the latter was leader of the opposition, this was not reciprocated when Cosgrave became Taoiseach in 1973.
12   *ibid.*, p. 140. Cosgrave's handling of the North does not receive a warm press. One of the themes in FitzGerald's memoir, *All in a Life*, is clashes between Cosgrave and himself on Northern Ireland, especially in the earlier days. Arnold, *What Kind of Country*, p. 107, maintains that for 'Cosgrave, Northern Ireland had not been, nor was, a central political issue. His belief in unity as an attainable

ideal was perfunctory, and his thoughts, either on how it might be attained, or on what might be done in preparation within the Republic, were severely limited by the prior claims of preserving the institutions of the State. This not only meant the institutions of law and order, and security, but also the Catholic Church, to which his devotion acted as a barometer in respect of what was acceptable legislative, constitutional, social or ideological change. The prospect of a form of government being restored to Northern Ireland which appeared to offer the stability and fairness of Unionists working with the Alliance Party and the SDLP was enormously attractive. It gave him bi-partisanship without the bother of negotiating with Jack Lynch. It satisfied the minority within his own administration who believed in action on Northern Ireland, and it reflected primarily upon him as the leader responsible for achieving the breakthrough.' Lee's summary (*Ireland*, p. 486) is equally devastating: 'His courage under fire stood the country in good stead. When he was not under fire, there was nothing in particular he wanted to do. He dreamed no dreams. The game was about possession, not performance. He was essentially a local politician operating at national level .'

13   Arnold, *What Kind of Country*, p. 120. See, too, Downey, *Them and Us*: pp. 165–6.

14   Lee, *Ireland*, p. 495. He continues: 'this restiveness was exploited when Síle de Valera, a young Fianna Fáil TD, grand-daughter of Eamon de Valera, chose the Liam Lynch [chief of staff of the anti-Treaty IRA in the Irish Civil War] annual commemoration ceremony in September to portray Lynch's increasing cooperation with the British government on cross-border surveillance . . . as collaboration, thus revealing the depths of the smouldering resentments in the party'.

15   *ibid.*, p. 498.

16   Conor Cruise O'Brien, *States of Ireland* (London: Hutchinson, 1972), p. 189. O'Brien's pen portrait of Haughey is coruscating, and prescient

more than a quarter of a century before Haughey's private affairs became a matter for public scrutiny.

17   FitzGerald, *All in a Life*, pp. 340–1.

18   Alvin Jackson, *Ireland 1798–1998* (Oxford: Basil Blackwell, 1999), p. 380.

19   See Margaret Thatcher, *The Downing Street Years* (London: HarperCollins, 1993), p. 390: 'This meeting did more harm than good because, unusually, I did not involve myself closely enough in the drafting of the communiqué and, as a result, allowed through the statement that Mr Haughey and I would devote our next meeting in London "to special consideration of the totality of relationships within these islands" . . . it was a red rag to the Unionist bull.'

20   Martin Mansergh (ed.), *The Spirit of the Nation: The Speeches and Statements of Charles J. Haughey* (Cork: Mercier Press, 1986) p. 411.

21   See Bruce Arnold, *What Kind of Country: Modern Irish Politics 1968–1983* (London: Jonathan Cape, 1984), pp. 158–61 for an account of the election. He writes: 'It was an implausible basis for an election strategy, since no one knew what Northern Ireland policy was, and since there were few if any signs that it was going to bring the hunger strike to an end, an obvious prerequisite for more fundamental change (p. 158).

22   Hennessey, *Cabinet*, p. 168.

23   See, for example, 'Mirror comment: Ulster: Bring home the troops', *Daily Mirror*, 14 August 1978, and an interview with Joe Haines, *Mirror* leader-writer and Harold Wilson's press secretary for seven years, with Martin Collins, *New Labour and Ireland*, 2, 5 (1981).

24   Ferdinand Mount, 'Dr Paisley's laughter', *Spectator*, 21 November 1981; see, too, Peter Kellner, 'The most subsidised people on earth', *New Statesman*, 22 May 1981.

25   *DE Deb.*, vol. 265, cols. 623 and 625 (8 May 1973).

26   *ibid.*, 403, cols. 994–1032 (4 December 1990). Opening the debate the leader of the Workers' Party, Proinsias De Rossa, described it as 'without doubt, an historic occasion. First, it is the first time for more than 50 years that the question of Articles 2 and 3 of the Constitution has been

debated in the Dáil, and, second, because potentially there are sufficient Deputies in this House convinced that they should be revised and amended' (col. 997).

27 'FitzGerald wants crusade against "sectarian Republic" ', *Irish Times*, 28 September 1981. One commentator pointed out the significance of such a crusade: 'It is, indeed, a singular paradox of history that, as things stand, it is the South at least as much as the North, which has to make up its mind how much it will do towards unity.' Claud Cockburn, 'Bookies take bets on "crusade" ', *Irish Times*, 21 October 1981. It may be more accurate to say that the crusade was launched when the Taoiseach gave an interview to the *Cork Examiner*, 22 September 1981.

28 Dick Walsh, 'Haughey accuses FitzGerald of national sabotage', *Irish Times*, 29 September 1981.

29 See Geraldine Kennedy, 'As good as the Taoiseach could reasonably have expected . . .', *Sunday Tribune*, 18 October 1981.

30 See 'FitzGerald's view welcomed by Dr McAdoo', *Irish Times*, 29 September 1981; and 'Bishop tells Taoiseach "fine words" not enough', *Irish Times*, 5 November 1981.

31 See Ed Moloney, 'Taoiseach's crusade welcomed in North', *Irish Times*, 29 September 1981; and 'FitzGerald's move unlikely to bring unity, say Unionists', *Belfast Telegraph*, 28 September 1981.

32 FitzGerald, *All in a Life*, p. 380. His account of the crusade can be found at pp. 376–80. See, too, R.F. Foster, 'Garret's crusade', *London Review of Books*, 21 January–3 February 1982, pp. 6–7. Foster delineates changing attitudes in Irish society: 'It remains nonetheless true that, despite decades of institutionalised Anglophobia and chauvinism under the de Valera dispensation, the Republic has emerged as a comfortable, *petit-bourgeois*, culturally mongrel, English-speaking, European-inclined, inflation-ridden EEC state, closely linked to Britain by economic ties and citizenship laws.'

33 See 'Prior may head new NI Executive, says Hume', *Irish Times*, 18 January 1982. See, too, Prior, *Balance of Power*, p. 196.

34 Ed Moloney, 'NI devolution plans "doomed to fail" ', *Irish Times*, 14 July 1982. This was a clear indication of the emphasis that the SDLP put on the need for a firmer Anglo-Irish framework. Prior's account can be found in *Balance of Power*, pp. 177–201.

35 'SDLP election manifesto', quoted in Gerard Murray, *John Hume and the SDLP: Impact and Survival in Northern Ireland* (Dublin: Irish Academic Press, 1998), p. 124.

36 FitzGerald, *All in a Life*, pp. 164–6.

37 *Alliance Party News*, June 1984. See, too, a paper delivered by its Chief Whip, John Cushnahan, at the University of the Sorbonne, n.d., in which he argued that 'the narrow stated objective of its leading participants strangled it at birth'. FitzGerald (*All in a Life*, pp. 466–7) suggests that it was statements by Haughey and Seamus Mallon of the SDLP that upset Alliance, although he concedes that he may have displayed some insensitivity at a meeting with the Alliance Party.

38 See Ed Moloney, 'Killings halt planned UDA submission to Forum', *Irish Times*, 24 March 1984.

39 FitzGerald, *All in a Life*, pp. 464–5. The two Fine Gael members who supported him were Peter Barry and Michael Noonan.

40 Fergus Finlay, *Snakes and Ladders* (Dublin: New Island Books, 1998), p. 1. Finlay describes Spring as 'a taciturn, reserved Kerryman' whom the party turned to 'more in hope than in confidence. He was young, inexperienced and largely unknown.' The party had been riven with ideological battles for many years. An apocryphal story has it that when Frank Cluskey was leader (1977–81) he inquired about the absence of a senior member from a crucial meeting. When informed that he was in Central America on a human rights mission Cluskey allegedly commented: 'Typical, when it's a question of saving the world or saving the Labour Party he takes the easy option.'

41 All quotations in this paragraph are from *New Ireland Forum*, Public Session, Monday 30 May 1983.

42 'Last chance', *Irish Times*, 10 May 1983.

43 See Jon Nordheimer, 'Irish leaders seek blueprint for reunion', *New York Times*, 31 May 1983; and 'In search of a blueprint: Amid bombs and boycotts, a unity forum is born', *Time*, 13 June 1983. A more upbeat piece came from the distinguished American broadcaster Dan Rather, who said that the forum had two essential tasks: 'For one, it means to take a stand at acknowledging the problems which lie at the heart of the fears and mistrust of the Protestants of the North . . . Second, the Forum means to force the politicians of the Republic to define just what a unified Ireland could consist of . . . Clearly they have their work cut out for them, but the fact that they are working at all seems inherently hopeful. It's a thing to be watched.' 'Commentary', Station WCBS, New York, 28 July 1983.

44 Murray, *John Hume and the SDLP*, pp. 56 and 141. In a series of interviews I conducted with members of all parties participating in the exercise there was a general consensus that relations with the SDLP improved immensely during the course of the forum.

45 Joseph O'Malley, 'Forum doomed unless leaders do a U-turn', *Sunday Independent*, 5 June 1983.

46 FitzGerald, *All in a Life*, p. 467.

47 Michael Finlan, 'Raising our eyes to an ideal', *Irish Times*, 3 June 1983. As the exercise dragged on the chairman may often have reflected that one raises one's eyes in exasperation as well.

48 FitzGerald, *All in a Life*, p. 489, gives a practical example of Kirwan at work on a particularly sensitive issue. See, too, Emily O'Reilly and Vincent Browne, 'Inside the Forum: Haughey's Provos and Paisley's Posters', *Sunday Tribune*, 6 May 1984.

49 Anonymous source quoted in Emily O'Reilly, 'The professional chairman', *Sunday Tribune*, 22 April 1984. A senior forum official told me in an interview that a Fianna Fáil aide had claimed that there was a feeling that the secretariat was proselytising for 'joint authority'. He said that was 'a fair comment'.

50 MacSharry impressed political opponents. In interview one described him to me as 'a textual man'

with an enormous grasp of his brief. The same source was amazed at the ignorance of senior Fianna Fáil members such as John Wilson and Gerry Collins when it came to consideration of federal/confederal models. That opinion was confirmed by two representatives of another political party.

51 Garret FitzGerald and Paddy Harte, *Ireland – Our Future Together* (Dublin: Fine Gael, 1979).

52 FitzGerald, *All in a Life*, p. 482. See, too, 'Majority against unity, says Harte', *Irish Times*, 1 October 1983. He is quoted as having said that he would resign from the forum if it failed to work towards a peaceful and prosperous society.

53 FitzGerald, *All in a Life*, p. 482. In the end Kelly refused to sign the forum's report. See Dick Walsh, 'Kelly declines to sign Forum report', *Irish Times*, 5 May 1984.

54 This became clear to me after I interviewed several of the participants from across the party spectrum.

55 Mary Holland, 'Haughey's strategy', *Magill*, August 1983, p. 12. Conor Cruise O'Brien had already dismissed it as 'The let's pretend forum', *Irish Times*, 21 June 1983. He was writing his column from south Wexford, where he had visited a place called 'Place Forlorn': 'It would have been an appropriate venue for that forum.'

56 John Wallace, 'Forum sets out price of unity', *Irish Press*, 18 August 1983.

57 See, for example, an interview with Paddy Harte TD on *News at 1.30*, RTÉ Radio 1, 18 August 1983, and *Saturday View*, RTÉ Radio 1, 20 August 1983.

58 Mary Holland ('Haughey's strategy', p. 13), concluded her article thus: 'It is now fairly generally accepted that the Forum is unlikely to come up with any single united strategy as to the political route that should be pursued to reach the New Ireland. What its supporters are still optimistic about is that an agreed report will at least lay out the obstacles to Irish unity and suggest a number of possible political options ranging from a unitary state, as advocated by Fianna Fáil, to joint sovereignty over Northern Ireland.'

59 I base this remark on a number of interviews I had with representatives from all the parties. See Fergus Pyle,

'Fears voiced over Forum confidentiality', *Irish Times*, 21 September 1983.

60 New Ireland Forum, *The Macroeconomic Consequences of Integrated Economic Policy, Planning and Co-ordination in Ireland* (Dublin: Stationery Office, 2 May 1984), p. 15.

61 'A better day', *Irish News*, 22 September 1983. It continued: 'It smacked of the opportunism the Forum can do well without. It would be far better if all the Forum leaders waited until they drew up their final report before passing judgement on the respective submissions.' In any case, no one should have been too surprised at the economists' pessimism. The Department of Finance in Dublin had been monitoring the two economies for some time and knew how bleak the actual picture was (private (information).

The quotation from Charles Haughey is taken from *Spirit of the Nation*, p. 772.

62 New Ireland Forum, *Report of Proceedings*, Public Session No. 2, 21 September 1983, p. 7.

63 See Sir Charles Carter, *Two Years of Peace, Stability and Reconciliation?: A Commentary on the First Two Years of the Anglo-Irish Agreement* (London: Policy Search and Friends of the Union, 1987). Indeed, as early as 1972 he had advocated a condominium proposal. See Charles Carter, 'Permutations of Government', *Administration*, 20, 4 (Winter 1972), pp. 50–7.

64 Tony Fahey, 'Progress or Decline?: Demographic Change in Political Context', in William Crotty and David E. Schmitt (eds.), *Ireland and the Politics of Change* (London: Longman, 1998), pp. 51–2.

65 *ibid.*, pp. 64 and 59.

66 'Different again in Ireland', *Sunday Times*, 11 September 1983.

67 'New wind from Ireland', *Financial Times*, 20 September 1983.

68 Martin Mansergh, 'What Dev really stood for', *Sunday Press*, 27 May 1984.

69 'Northern Ireland: A new way forward?', *Weekend World*, 6 November 1983. In an interview some weeks earlier the Northern Secretary, James Prior, dismissed the unitary state option but said that what 'we have to do is find a situation or find a position which enables unionists to go on upholding their unity with the United Kingdom and yet at the same time allows nationalists to seek their aspirations for a united Ireland'. He also acknowledged that it would be impossible to engage nationalists 'in the general affairs of the province' until the forum had ended its deliberations. Interview with Brian Redhead, *Today*, BBC Radio 4, 14 October 1983.

70 See, for example, Fergus Pyle, 'Joint sovereignty in clearcut perspective', *Irish Times*, 10 December 1983. Pyle quotes one forum supporter thus: 'It is important to get away from the traditional legal idea of nationality and find a new way to accommodate two different ideas of community.' See New Ireland Forum, *Report of Proceedings*, Public Session No. 10, 8 December 1983, for a report of the presentations given by Dr Bernard Cullen and Dr Richard Kearney (pp. 20–39), and of the Irish Information Partnership (pp. 47–65).

71 *Irish Times*, 6 February 1984.

72 'FF provokes angry Forum exchanges', *Irish Times*, 18 February 1984.

73 Ed Moloney, 'Hume–Mallon split emerges at SDLP talks', *Irish Times*, 20 February 1984. See, too, Olivia O'Leary, 'The John Hume show', *Magill*, March 1984, pp. 16–23, where she writes that the forum process 'risked splitting the SDLP along the lines which have for 60 years divided Fianna Fáil and Fine Gael. [Hume] has stretched the SDLP across the San Andreas fault of the South's differences in Northern Ireland and already the cracks are beginning to show.' O'Leary reveals that Seamus Mallon threatened to resign on 16 February when the SDLP decided to back an 'all-options' forum report rather than the Fianna Fáil unitary state model.

74 'A Digest of Discussions', New Ireland Forum, internal document, 8 November 1983.

75 Dick Walsh, 'Forum leaders seek to avert split', *Irish Times*, 20 February 1984.

76 Niels J. Haagerup, *A Report on Northern Ireland* (Strasbourg: European Parliament, 1984).

Haagerup was a Danish Liberal MEP.

77 Rebecca Franceskides, 'Blanket welcome for report', *Irish Times*, 27 January 1984.

78 'Muldoon praises Forum', *Irish Times*, 17 February 1984.

79 Dick Walsh, 'Forum's work endorsed by 100 members of Congress', *Irish Times*, 15 March 1984; and Dick Walsh, 'Reagan endorses Forum, praises Anglo-Irish links', *Irish Times*, 17 March 1984.

80 John Cooney, 'Haagerup urges respect for both Northern traditions', *Irish Times*, 30 March 1984. The Irish Minister for Foreign Affairs, Peter Barry, described the report as 'sensitive, fair and generous' and said that it was a 'valuable contribution to heightening European awareness of the Northern Ireland conflict'.

81 See a *Belfast Telegraph* leader, 'Counting the cost' (4 November 1983), which mused: 'The intention must be to alert British taxpayers to the sums they have paid out – and will continue to pay – to keep the lid on the Irish problem. If the reaction is one of horror, perhaps Mrs Thatcher would commit herself to a radical reappraisal of present policy?' The editorial claimed that the report 'errs always on the side of exaggeration'.

82 'Reaction to "terror cost" study muted', *Belfast Telegraph*, 4 November 1983. Cushnahan was being premature because (as the final report stated) this study and two others – *The Economic Consequences of the Division of Ireland since 1920* and *A Comparative Description of the Economic Structure, North and South* – contribute to an understanding of the problems involved and provide an important point of reference'. New Ireland Forum, *Report* (Dublin: Stationery Office, 2 May 1984), p. 3.

83 See Richard Ford, 'Ulster violence "has cost UK £9 bn"', *Times*, 4 November 1983; and Tom Rowley and Chris Glennon, 'Violence in North costs us £2¼ b.', *Irish Independent*, 4 November 1983.

84 The McGimpsey brothers were acting in a personal capacity, a fact that was brought home to me when I attended the 1984 UUP conference: the McGimpseys received a very hostile reception from most of the delegates.

85 'Dr Daly says criticism is not justified', *Irish Times*, 14 January 1984.

86 Ed Moloney, 'Church stand on divorce meets hostile NI response', *Irish Times*, 14 January 1984.

87 See John Whale, 'Bishops confirm Protestant fears', *Sunday Times*, 22 January 1984.

88 See Damian Hannan, 'Ireland's new social and moral dilemmas', *New Society*, 18 November 1982, pp. 291–3.

89 'Where church meets state', a *Times* leader, 13 February 1984. One of the more interesting submissions that was *not* scrutinised in a public session was that from the Irish Theological Association – 'a professional body whose ordinary members are engaged in theological teaching and research in Ireland, North and South. These ordinary members are both Catholic and Protestant. Associate membership includes a wide range of interested lay people of the different Churches.' – who had produced a prescient report and series of recommendations way back in 1972. It anticipated many of the church–state problems that were to arise in the Republic in the following decades. Their forum submission can be read as the antithesis to the Irish Episcopal Conference's thesis.

90 Irish Episcopal Conference, *Submission to the New Ireland Forum* (Dublin: Veritas Publications, January 1984), p. 18.

91 See a letter from R.L. McCartney QC in *Irish Times*, 3 February 1984. McCartney, who is the leader of the United Kingdom Unionist Party and MP for North Down, closes his letter with a further quotation from Mr Justice Frankfurter in the same case: 'The validity of secular laws cannot be measured by their conformity to religious doctrines. It is only in a theocratic State that ecclesiastical doctrines measure legal right or wrong.'

92 Dick Walsh, 'What the bishops left unsaid', *Irish Times*, 14 February 1984. Alf McCreary, 'A very Catholic gathering', *Belfast Telegraph*, 10 February 1984, said their performance was 'like trying to pin jelly to a wall'.

93 New Ireland Forum, *Report of*

Proceedings, Public Session No. 12, 9 February 1984, p. 46.

94   'Viewpoint', *Belfast Telegraph*, 10 February 1984.

95   New Ireland Forum, *Report of Proceedings*, Public Session No. 12, 9 February 1984, p. 7. He made his views abundantly clear one week earlier when he delivered the Monsignor Arthur H. Ryan Memorial Lecture at Queen's University Belfast on the subject of 'War: The Morality, the Reality, the Myths', where he argued that the IRA campaign failed the tests of 'competent authority' and 'just means' (pp. 20–3).

96   New Ireland Forum, *Report of Proceedings*, Public Session No. 12, 9 Febuary 1984, p. 39.

97   *Economist*, 18 February 1984.

98   *Irish Times*, 4 April 1984.

99   John Cooney, 'Forum leaders face crucial meeting today', *Irish Times*, 16 April 1984.

100 Dick Walsh, 'Party wants to be consulted', *Irish Times*, 17 April 1984. This was an issue that arose first when the 'extensive and uncongenial' changes document had been leaked in August 1983: see Denis Coghlan, 'Forum document "for discussion", says Tunney', *Irish Times*, 19 August 1983. At one meeting between the leaders 'Mr Haughey is said to have muttered: "I have to go back now and sell this to the Provos" – meaning the hardliners in his ranks'. Emily O'Reilly and Vincent Browne, 'Inside the Forum: Haughey's Provos and Paisley's Posters', *Sunday Tribune*, 6 May 1984.

101 'One Voice', *Irish Times*, 17 April 1984.

102 Robert McCartney QC, in *Unionist Review*, 1 (Autumn 1983).

103 See Oliver MacDonagh, 'What was new in the New Ireland Forum?', *Crane Bag*, 9, 2 (1985), pp. 166–70. MacDonagh is particularly critical of the historical framework of the report: 'For the most part [it] is a simplistic repetition of the received popular orthodoxy of the 1930s or at best 1950s.' He was critical, too, of *all* the blame being laid on the British but allowed that 'beneath all this lay a tacit admission that one essential pre-supposition of traditional Irish nationalism was erroneous' – the identification of Irish national identity with the values of 'what we might loosely term the Catholic–Gaelic culture '. In addition, 'the report recognized a distinct Ulster Unionist identity with at least three alien elements of first importance – its Britishness, its Protestantism and its presumption of economic dependence on the link with Britain'.

104 *ibid.*, p. 167. There was a significant practical outcome in all of this: 'Formally at least the Forum reconstituted after sixty or some might even say, ninety years, the Popular Front which has been the norm of nineteenth-century constitutional nationalism ... This was a significant development ... To measure its significance it is enough to recall that the major constituents of the Forum, Fianna Fáil and Fine Gael, were descendants of factions which had fought a civil war in 1922–3 upon the very question of the fundamental nature of the Irish state' (p. 166).

105 *ibid.*, pp. 167–8. His remarks were addressed particularly at Fianna Fáil.

106 Paul Bew and Henry Patterson, 'The New Stalemate: Unionism and the Anglo-Irish Agreement', in Paul Teague (ed.), *Beyond the Rhetoric: Politics, the Economy and Social Policy in Northern Ireland* (London: Lawrence and Wishart, 1987), p. 44. They refer to their earlier, more detailed, critique – *The British State and the Ulster Crisis: From Wilson to Thatcher* (London: Verso, 1985), pp. 127–35. In fact the earlier critique is not as swingeing and simplistic: it does allow that 'the Forum represents only the most hesitant beginning' in deepening a self-critical politics of conciliation that would act to reduce 'British and Ulster – based opposition to re-unification'. (p. 134) The more strident tone of their article in the Teague volume may be explained by the different dates of the two publications: *The British State and the Ulster Crisis* was published in 1985 and was a serious misreading of the state of Anglo-Irish relations: 'The Thatcher–FitzGerald summit of November 1984 appeared to mark the end of an era: an era when discussion had been dominated by highly speculative proposals of the joint authority type' (p. 135). Their

1987 piece was part of their sustained attack on the Anglo-Irish Agreement. It seemed to affect the manner in which they wrote about Northern Ireland. The easiest example is to compare and contrast their (with Peter Gibbon) *The State in Northern Ireland, 1921–72: Political Forces and Social Classes* (Manchester: Manchester University Press, 1979) with *Northern Ireland 1921–1996: Political Forces and Social Classes* (London: Serif, 1996) by the same three authors. The 1996 edition is an updated version of a book from the same publisher in 1995 that brought the narrative up to 1994. The significant break with their path-breaking 1979 book is their dereliction of their Marxist gurus, Althusser and Poulantzas, and the interminable, internal debates attached to that approach. They became more accessible, but also more engaged – as was demonstrated by their contribution to the Teague volume in 1987.

107 Clare O'Halloran, *Partition and the Limits of Irish Nationalism* (Dublin: Gill and Macmillan, 1987), pp. 194 and 195. This view is challenged in John Whyte's magesterial *Interpreting Northern Ireland* (Oxford: Clarendon Press, 1990), p. 140. He accepts that, given the divergence of opinion among the party leaders and the fudging on critical points, 'the report can be interpreted in this way. But in my view, the innovations in its approach decisively outweigh the continuities with old-style nationalist views. Despite what Mr Haughey said in his opening statement, the report does not see the British presence as being at the heart of the Northern Ireland problem. The core is seen as lying in the clash of the two identities.'

108 Arthur Aughey, *Under Siege: Ulster Unionism and the Anglo-Irish Agreement* (Belfast: Blackstaff Press, 1989), p. 50. Aughey makes no claim to be impartial (p. vii). And he takes no prisoners in his onward journey towards an integrationist thesis. He rails against the 'crypto-racism of Sinn Féin and the ethno-geographical determinism of modern constitutional nationalism' (p. vii); against 'the British intelligentsia – 'if

there is such a thing . . . it suffers from the same disease as the political establishment; an imperviousness to novel ideas and a conceited complacency which passes for wisdom' (p. 157); against the SDLP, which, 'apart from the reworked clichés of the defunct Nationalist Party, it is a party without ideas' (p. 196); and against John Hume, 'a persistent and tireless hawker of platitudes' whose role in Anglo-Irish cooperation 'is ultimately . . . peripheral and expendable' (p. 115). On the other hand he devotes almost twenty pages to a peripheral pressure group, the Campaign for Equal Citizenship, 'formed in 1985 to promote and mobilise support for the rights of citizens in Northern Ireland to join and vote for the major United Kingdom political parties' (p. xiii) and its erstwhile intellectual mentor, Robert McCartney QC, 'one of the most intelligent and articulate of the unionist politicians to emerge in the 1980s . . . a man able to "speak out" and put into words the inarticulate feelings of the honest Ulster Unionist' (p. 160). There is no record of how the 'honest Ulster Unionist' felt about being patronised in these tones. A devastating critique of the integrationist case can be found in Whyte, *Interpreting Northern Ireland*, pp. 218–21, where he dismisses the 'threadbare nature of their case '.

109 'Consent' is a contested concept well beyond the Anglo-Irish imbroglio. See P.H. Partridge, *Consent and Consensus* (London: Macmillan, 1971). He identifies seven forms of consent (pp. 32–6), and presents a more modern overview: 'consent has come to be viewed, not as an original act or a series of discrete and repeated acts, but as a continuous process of interaction between the governed and the government by means of which governments become relatively more responsive to the interests, demands and initiatives of their subjects . . . in short, the processes of consent tend to coincide in the end with almost the whole of the mechanism of liberal parliamentary democracy' (pp. 44–5). In the Nothern Ireland context unionists may have rued the fact that they never attempted to win post-facto consent. See, too, Bernard

Crick, 'The Concept of Consent and the Agreement', in Charles Townshend (ed.), *Consensus in Ireland: Approaches and Recessions* (Oxford: Clarendon Press, 1988), pp. 110–27, where he argues that 'we need both Hobbes and Locke. Hobbes is the precondition for any kind of political order, Locke for a just and consenting political order (when happily possible)' (p. 127).

110   New Ireland Forum, *Report*, paragraph 5.7, emphasis added. Interviewed on LWT's *Weekend World* on 6 May, the Taoiseach, Garret FitzGerald, spoke about the *aspiration* to a unitary state: 'It is what any Irish nationalist would wish to see; and "would" is an important condition in addition to the word "wish" . . . It would be foolish of us not to state that, dishonest of us not to state that.' Dick Walsh, 'Cost of fourth green field', *Irish Times*, 10 May 1984, comments that in place of the Taoiseach's 'aspiration' Charles Haughey 'sees "unitary state model" as a formula embracing a singular, incontrovertible ambition: a right that is not to be denied'. Walsh also comments on the economic report that accompanied the report, which estimated that Britain's subvention amounts to 8 per cent of the GNP of the whole of Ireland per annum. The price to be paid for recovering Northern Ireland would be dauntingly high: 'And it will put a stop to all but the most raucous singer in the most crowded pub.' Incidentally, none of the academic critics – Bew and Patterson, Aughey, O'Halloran – refer to this economic report, nor indeed to any of the reports emanating from the forum process.

111   When I pointed this out to a senior Fianna Fáil delegate he referred me to paragraph 5.9, where the other two models are diminished to the status of 'structural arrangements'. A Labour Party delegate agreed by saying that '5.9 was hard fought but we lost'. The one concession the other parties secured in this paragraph was that options other than the unitary state model were treated as 'proposals' rather than mere 'suggestions' – as Fianna Fáil would have had it.

112   Interview with senior Labour

Party delegate.

113   *HC Deb.*, vol. 63, col. 57 (2 July 1984). The debate can be found in cols. 23–106. The Northern Ireland Assembly had had a 150-minute debate on the forum on 8 May 1984. It can be found in *Official Report*, 10, 3, pp. 91–122. A theme in both debates was the meaning of 'consent'. See, too, the reaction of the two main Protestant churches in Ireland. Appendix II of the 1985 annual report of the Presbyterian Church in Ireland is an analysis presented by its Government Committee (pp. 16–20). The General Assembly expressed 'deep disappointment at the general contents of the Report'. The Role of the Church Committee of the Church of Ireland published its thoughts in the 1985 report (pp. 146–52) where specific reference is made to paragraph 5.10 (p. 151).

114   MacDonagh, 'What was new in the New Ireland Forum?', pp. 168–70.

115   Renagh Holohan, 'Haughey calls on Britain to back all-Ireland talks', *Irish Times*, 3 May 1984. See, too, Charles Haughey, 'Onus is now on British', *Irish Independent*, 3 May 1984.

116   Dick Walsh, 'Haughey plays down divergence on unitary state', *Irish Times*, 4 May 1984.

117   Ray MacSharry, 'Why F.F. is satisfied with the Forum', *Sunday Press*, 6 May 1984; and Denis Coghlan, 'FF claims Government abandoning Forum plan', *Irish Times*, 11 May 1984.

118   A leader in Ireland's largest-selling newspaper called Haughey's opinion 'nothing less than an act of national sabotage [which put Fianna Fáil] on a par with the Provisional Sinn Féin': 'A trust forfeited', *Sunday Independent*, 6 May 1984; and a senior Fianna Fáil senator expressed concern over the manner in which the forum was being interpreted – see Denis Coghlan, 'Ryan criticises interpretations of report', *Irish Times*, 7 May 1984; and Willy Clingan, 'FF chief whip discounts split over Forum report', *Irish Times*, 14 May 1984.

119   See Mervyn Pauley, 'Haughey sinks the Forum', *News Letter*, 3 May 1984, and 'Dublin pie in the sky', *News Letter* leader of the same day; and *Belfast Telegraph* leader, 'Forum failure', 3 May 1984. Others who

expressed the same negativism included a *Daily Telegraph* leader, 'An Irish mouse', 3 May 1984; and Sinn Féin, which described it as 'toothless and wishy-washy' – 'A "toothless" report, says Sinn Féin', *Irish Times*, 3 May 1984.

120 See, for example, 'The way from the Forum', *Financial Times* leader, 3 May 1984: 'No British policy will get anywhere if it is half-hearted and low on the political agenda. Mrs Thatcher has an opportunity denied to almost all her predecessors. She should make an Irish settlement a priority'; and George Gale, 'Now I beg Mrs Thatcher to concentrate her mind and energies upon the Irish problem', *Daily Express*, 3 May 1984: 'The Forum constitutes an offer to compromise. It is an offer which the British Government must not spurn.'

121 'Learning', *Irish Times*, 7 May 1984; and David McKittrick, 'Thatcher gives mixed verdict on Forum report', *Irish Times*, 7 May 1984.

122 See Niall O'Dowd, 'US welcome for study's finding', *Irish Press*, 3 May 1984; Seán Cronin, 'Report will strengthen Anglo-Irish ties, says US', *Irish Times*, 5 May 1984; Nicholas Ashford, 'Reagan will urge Britain to examine unity proposal of Irish Forum', *Times*, 5 May 1984, where he concludes: '[Tip] O'Neill was undoubtedly speaking for more than his fellow Irish-Americans when he said: "now it is up to the British Government and the Unionists to consider this report with open hearts and open minds. Permitting the status quo in Northern Ireland to continue is simply intolerable" '; and 'Jay says Forum a rare window of opportunity', *Irish Times*, 5 May 1984, which cites an article in the *Times* by the British Ambassador in Washington where he refers to that newspaper's 'disdainful leader' on the report and declares that history would judge harshly those who 'fluff this rare window of opportunity' in Irish affairs.

123 Denis Coghlan, 'Barry briefs US politicians on report', *Irish Times*, 4 May 1984. See, too, John Cooney, 'Forum diplomatic offensive planned', *Irish Times*, 26 April 1984, and John Cooney, 'Pressure for new British initiative to follow Forum',

Irish Times, 28 April 1984.

124 Aughey, *Under Seige*, p. 50. See, too, Brigid Hadfield, 'More reports on Northern Ireland: Panaceas or Pandora's Box?', *Public Law* (Summer 1985), pp. 240–50, for a discussion on the New Ireland Forum Report, Kilbrandon, *Britain's Undefended Frontier*, and reports from the UUP, DUP and Alliance Party to the Northern Ireland Assembly's non-statutory Devolution Report Committee in the summer of 1984.

125 *Official Report*, 12, 3, col. 137 (14 November 1984). The debate can be found at cols. 112-39. His colleague, Jim Allister, considered that it 'would be easy to dismiss it as the rantings of lofty academics, but perhaps in reality it is more the poison of malevolent academics' (col. 116). In fact only four of the twelve-person team were academics – the deputy chairman, Anthony Kenny (Master of Balliol College, Oxford), myself, Gillian Peele (Lady Margaret Hall, Oxford) and A.T.Q. Stewart (Queen's University Belfast). Besides the chairman, Lord Kilbrandon (who had chaired the Royal Commission on the Constitution which reported in 1973), there were two MPs – Alf Dubs (Labour) and David Howell (Conservative, formerly Secretary of State for Energy and for Transport, and a junior minister at the Northern Ireland Office 1972–3); two (Labour) peers – Lady Ewart-Biggs and Lord Underhill; John Roberts (a former chairman of the Welsh Liberal Party); Sara Morrison (director of GEC); and Simon Jenkins (political editor of the *Economist* and former editor of the *Times*). It had been appointed in April 1984 at the invitation of the British–Irish Association.

126 *Northern Ireland: Report of an Independent Inquiry* [Kilbrandon Report] (London, 1984), ch. 12, pp. 46–53.

127 David McKittrick, 'Committee mirroring Northern Ireland divide', *Irish Times*, 3 November 1984. He goes on to say: 'This independence was reflected in a willingness to take a long and hard look at the fundamentals of the problem. Unfortunately, it was also reflected in a final report, much of which has absolutely no chance of acceptance in

the grim Northern Ireland political world.'

128 Kilbrandon Report, p. 5. The majority view (eight members) is set out in ch. 12 – 'Co-operative Devolution' – and the minority view (four members) is set out in ch. 13 – 'Functional Co-operation'.

129 'Facing facts', *Irish Independent*, 2 November 1984. The leader concluded: 'This kind of Report would have been inconceivable even five years ago. The fact that some British politicians and scholars have come so far is an encouraging sign for those watching Downing St. for reaction.'

130 See *HL Deb.*, 457, 13 cols. 1178–1202.

131 Aughey, *Under Seige*, p. 52, emphasis added. We need not concern ourselves with the detailed recommendations in Kilbrandon embracing such issues as security and political symbolism. We are concerned here with the wider picture.

132 *Official Report*, 5, 24, p. 901 (15 March 1983).

133 *Official Report*, 9, 16, p. 762 (4 April 1984).

134 Norman MacQueen, 'The Expedience of Tradition: Ireland, International Organization and the Falklands Crisis', *Political Studies*, 33, 1 (1985), p. 42.

135 *ibid.*, pp. 42–3. MacQueen dismisses as 'groundless' the imputation of lack of consultation, and suggests that 'the episode carried a clear message: Haughey now regarded the Falklands crisis as a policy area within which he wished to retain a wide freedom of initiative'.

136 *ibid.*, p. 46. This position was reiterated at a press conference on 6 May when the Taoiseach said 'sanctions complementing military action are not acceptable to us as a neutral country' (p. 47).

137 Lawrence Freedman, *Britain and the Falklands War* (Oxford: Basil Blackwell and the Institute of Contemporary History, 1988), p. 55.

138 Quoted in Anthony Barnett, *Iron Britannia: Why Parliament Waged its Falklands War* (London: Allison and Busby, 1982), p. 97. Barnett asserts (correctly) that it was this debate that transformed Thatcher from being a 'misfit' and 'elevated her into the war leader of a bi-partisan consensus. Or rather a multiparty unanimity' (pp. 18–19). It was from that date that she took on her Churchillian mode. Barnett captures the vainglorious nature of it all by opening his book with a quote from the Prime Minister in the *Daily Express* (26 July 1982): 'I had the winter at the back of my mind. *The winter.* What will the winter do? The wind, the cold. Down in South Georgia the ice, what will it do? It beat Napoleon at Moscow'; and he closes with her speech at a Conservative rally at Cheltenham race course on 3 July, where the Churchillian spirit was reinvoked. Her closing words were: 'Britain found herself again in the South Atlantic and will not look back from the victory she has won' (p. 153).

139 MacQueen, 'Expedience of Tradition', p. 53. MacQueen comments that 'whatever its intrinsic flaws, the [Irish] government's position remained close to the mood of the country' (p. 50); and he could not guage what damage, if any, Ireland's performance had done to its position in the UN and EEC: 'Ireland's position was certainly warmly regarded by the Latin Americans and elements in the non-aligned group' (p. 54).

140 Barnett, *Iron Britannia*, p. 19.

141 Interview with Malcolm Rutherford, *Financial Times*, 23 June 1986. See, too, Feargal Cochrane, *Unionist Politics and the Politics of Unionism Since the Anglo-Irish Agreement* (Cork: Cork University Press, 1997), pp. 124–5.

142 Richard Needham, *Battling For Peace* (Belfast: Blackstaff Press, 1998), p. 217. Needham served in Northern Ireland from 1985–92.

143 *ibid*, p. 80.

144 Alan Clark, *Diaries* (London: Weidenfeld and Nicolson, 1993), pp. 35 and 121. Clark agreed with Riddell's prognosis: 'I think it is probably true that she was getting irritated with him in his closing months as her Secretary. Like many men who find their love unrequited, he was becoming more and more subservient and attentive. The stooping, obsequious family retainer, speaking very often in a special high-pitched tone that was almost tearful

... ' (p. 122).

145 As early as December 1982 she intimated that if she was returned to office she would 'like to do something about Ireland'. Quoted in Bew, Gibbon and Patterson, *Northern Ireland*, p. 210.

146 *Irish Times*, 16 November 1985.

147 Dermot Nally, quoted in Gareth E. Ivory, 'The Political Parties of the Republic of Ireland and the Nothern Ireland Question, 1980–1995' (Ph.D. thesis, University of Wolverhampton, 1999), p. 265.

148 See Robert Fisk, *The Point of No Return: The Strike which Broke the British in Ulster* (London: André Deutsch, 1975), p. 212.

149 In an interview with me Houston expressed his exasperation at the implied lack of trust in him. For Bloomfield see a remark made by Tom King (who was Northern Secretary at the time of the signing of the Anglo-Irish Agreement) when he announced in April 2000 that he would be retiring from Parliament at the next election: he told BBC Northern Ireland's *Good Morning Ulster* on 4 April 2000 that he regretted that there had not been enough consultation during Anglo-Irish negotiations and he mentioned specifically that Kenneth Bloomfield had been brought in late. See, too, Kenneth Bloomfield, *Stormont in Crisis: A Memoir* (Belfast: Blackstaff Press, 1994), pp. 253–5.

Bloomfield conveyed whatever information he had to the Policy Coordinating Committee – a group composed of the Northern Ireland permanent secretaries and a deputy secretary from the Northern Ireland Office chaired by Bloomfield. Maurice Hayes, who was a member of the committee, detected among its members 'no spirit of animosity to [the proposals], or any desire on anyone's part to resign, or to do anything to make the system unworkable'. He mentions that 'the strong arguments advanced officially to support the agreement were the need to improve the international standing of the United Kingdom with the United States and the European partners by appearing to do something, to end the alienation and disaffection of the Catholic community, and to strengthen the SDLP as the voice of constitutional nationalism against Sinn Féin, and to end the violence by withdrawing support from the IRA by involving the Irish government in the process, both to close off a bolthole to the South and to legitimise the actions of the police in the North.' Maurice Hayes, *Minority Verdict: Experiences of a Catholic Public Servant* (Belfast: Blackstaff Press, 1995) p. 288.

150 I attended a dinner hosted by Secretary of State Tom King at Hillsborough Castle on 11 November 1985. The other guests were from business, commerce and academia. The script could have been written by Lewis Carroll, and Stephen Leacock as our host attempted to take us through a hypothetical exercise based on the assumption that at some day in the future some sort of agreement might be signed between the two governments. He was attempting to gauge what sort of reaction there would be. The message he received was largely negative and, in some cases, hostile.

151 Private information. I acted as UTV's political analyst on their live broadcast and had been contacted only in mid-morning on the day itself. The agreement was signed at 2.00 p.m., but true to the independent television ethos UTV had gone off air for a commercial break.

152 See FitzGerald, *All in a Life*, pp. 494–550, for a detailed account of the negotiations. Thatcher, *Downing Street Years*, pp. 393–402, deals with them much more peremptorily.

153 Shannon, 'Anglo-Irish Agreement', p. 864.

154 *HC Deb.*, vol. 63, col. 80 (2 July 1984).

155 'Continuously we surrender it, we merge it and we blur it when it suits our interest. What is the point of sovereignty if it cannot be used for the benefit of the people? I suggest that the United Kingdom has made the biggest surrender of its sovereignty in its history to the European Court of Human Rights. It has done that without statute, without debate in this House, and without even much interest among hon. Members ... The sovereignty of the United

Kingdom over Northern Ireland is not at issue. The achievement of agreement does not require it. The stability that we seek can come in many guises, provided that we provide the two essential ingredients that the loyalties of both nations need to be satisfied, and the resultant modified union of the Province with the United Kingdom must be underwritten by the Governments and the peoples both of the United Kingdom and of the Republic.' *HC Deb.*, vol. 63, cols. 70–1 (2 July 1984). See the Northern Secretary's remarks on sovereignty as a difficult concept and on the need to keep it in context: Prior, *Balance of Power*, pp. 241–2.

156 *HC Deb*, vol. 63, cols. 23–30 (2 July 1984).

157 Prior, *Balance of Power*, p. 240.

158 T.E. Utley, 'A marriage deranged', *Spectator*, 4 February 1984, pp. 12–13.

159 Quoted in Shannon, 'Anglo-Irish Agreement', p. 863. She mentioned all three options and pronounced each of them 'out'. Television footage reveals that while she was adamant in her rejection she was not so certain about each option: the Northern Secretary, Douglas Hurd, had to prompt her about the third option of joint authority.

160 Jim Cusack, 'Forum "in a burial plot in Chequers"', *Irish Times*, 21 November 1984.

161 Ed Moloney, 'Powell calls for Unionist rejoicing', *Irish Times*, 24 November 1984. In his leader's address the following day James Molyneaux said: 'Exhibiting the qualities of courage and clear sightedness which she displayed in freeing the Falklands, the Prime Minister slapped down the plotters … The Forum assault has been beaten off, but the probing attacks will continue.' See *Irish Times*, 27 November 1984.

162 Ed Moloney and Jim Cusack, 'Mallon comforted on Irish identity', *Irish Times*, 20 November 1984.

163 See Arwel Ellis Owen, *The Anglo-Irish Agreement: The First Three Years* (Cardiff: University of Wales Press, 1994), pp. 15–16.

164 Seán Cronin, 'US papers join in condemnation of Thatcher', *Irish Times*, 26 November 1984.

165 Leonard Doyle, 'Reagan praises Forum effort', *Irish Times*, 3 December 1984. The formulation he used to describe the major players was that which had been devised first in the Carter statement of August 1977. The message was delivered by his friend, the Secretary of the Interior, Bill Clark, who answered that the 'statement speaks for itself' when asked if it could be construed as an attack on Margaret Thatcher for her hard-line stance.

166 Ellis Owen, 'Anglo-Irish Agreement', p. 16. On the information supplied to the Policy Coordinating Committee, see n. 165 above. There had been an earlier sign that Chancellor Helmut Kohl also wanted to use his good offices to heal the rift: see John Cooney, 'Kohl concerned to ease strains', *Irish Times*, 26 November 1984.

167 Private information. The source also referred to 'wall after wall of [other] prejudices and anxieties, against which concepts like consent and sovereignty and alienation hung their heads in shame'.

168 Dick Walsh, 'Barry determined to press ahead on NI initiative', *Irish Times*, 24 November 1984.

169 David McKittrick, 'London expects long-term gains from summit rift', *Irish Times*, 26 November 1984.

170 See Dennis Kennedy, 'British PM has "good news"', *Irish Times*, 5 December 1984.

171 Besides the FitzGerald and Thatcher accounts there are also the accounts of Shannon, 'Anglo-Irish Agreement', and of Ellis Owen, *Anglo-Irish Agreement*.

172 Shannon, 'Anglo-Irish Agreement', p. 863.

173 John Cole, *The Thatcher Years: A Decade of Revolution in British Politics* (London: BBC Books, 1987), pp. 191–2.

174 Clark, *Diaries*, p. 117.

175 *DE Deb.*, 361, 11, col. 2581 (19 November 1985).

176 See, for example, Peter Smith, *Why Unionists Say No* (Belfast: Joint Unionist Working Party, 1986), and E. Haslett, *Ulster Must Say No* (Belfast: Joint Unionist Working Party, 1986).

177 Shannon, 'Anglo-Irish Agreement', p. 850.

178 *Irish Times*, 22 June 1988.

179 Paul Arthur, 'The Anglo-Irish Agreement: Events of 1985–86', in *Irish Political Studies*, 2 (Galway: PSBI Press, 1987), p. 101.

180 *Irish Times*, 6 October 1986. See 'Sinn Féin power moves North', *Irish Press*, 12 November 1983.

181 One of the reasons why the Prime Minister reacted so strongly at Chequers was that it came soon after the Brighton bomb when the IRA tried to kill her and the rest of her cabinet. In interview one of those involved in negotiation (on the British side) suggested to me that she had to demonstrate that she was immovable on the issue of violence.

182 For a powerful critique of the British position see a speech by the Fine Gael TD John Kelly in 'Kelly attacks "bone-headed" British reply', *Irish Times*, 6 February 1984.

183 See Jackson, *Ireland*, pp. 390–2.

184 Quoted in Dick Walsh, *Des O'Malley: A Political Profile* (Dingle, Co. Kerry: Brandon Books, 1986), p. 74. The bill was a proposed amendment to family planning legislation.

CHAPTER 10

1   Richard Murphy, 'Amazement', *The Price of Stone* (London: Faber and Faber, 1985), p. 39. This poem was about the hunger strikes and closes with the lines:
      These are the sacrifice
      A word imprisoned and a word
        could save.

2   From Robert Greacen, 'Procession', *Protestant Without a Horse* (Belfast: Lagan Press, 1997), p. 14. This poem was based on the painting *The Twelfth of July, Portadown* (1928) by Sir John Lavery.

3   Quoted in Oliver MacDonagh, 'What was new in the New Ireland Forum?', *Crane Bag*, 9, 2 (1985), p. 170.

4   Robert L. Rothstein, 'After the Peace: The Political Economy of Reconciliation' (Inaugural Rebecca Meyerhoff Memorial Lecture, Harry S. Truman Institute, Hebrew University, Jerusalem, May 1966), p. 20.

5   Kirsten E. Schulze, 'The Northern Ireland Political Process: A Viable Approach to Conflict Resolution', *Irish Political Studies*, 12 (1997), p. 104. Her remarks are based on the work of William I. Zartman, *Ripe for Resolution: Conflict and Intervention in Africa* (Oxford: Oxford University Press, 1989).

6   His comments can be found in *HC Deb.*, vol. 84, cols. 914–20 (25 November 1985).

7   'McCusker sees a hard fight ahead', *News Letter*, 8 November 1986.

8   Private information.

9   Ann Purdy, *Molyneaux: The Long View* (Antrim: Greystone Books, 1989), pp. 8–9.

10 In separate interviews with me two Whitehall insiders used the same phrase about never forgetting 'the PM's commitment to "our boys"'. Once she realised that there was a commitment by the Taoiseach and his closest advisers and that there was an equal, parallel investment by officials and politicians in London then she had a real anxiety to get things moving. With the (ironic) exception of Edward Heath it is extremely unlikely that any modern Prime Minister would have shown the same determination to face down those opposed to the agreement. Unionism's tactics played to her greater strengths.

11 Quoted in Arwel Ellis Owen, *The Anglo-Irish Agreement: The First Three Years* (Cardiff: University of Wales Press, 1994), p. 25. Much of my commentary on the agreement and resistance to it comes from this source.

12 *ibid.*, p. 26.

13 A.T.Q. Stewart, *The Narrow Ground: The Roots of Conflict in Northern Ireland* (London: Faber and Faber, 1989), p. 2.

14 A.T.Q. Stewart, 'Strikes may mark first anniversary of pact', *Irish Times*, 8 November 1986.

15 Quoted in Ellis Owen, *Anglo-Irish Agreement*, p. 38. The same source gives some flavour of British and international media support for the agreement. In her memoirs Margaret Thatcher claimed that 'only the international dimension became noticeably easier to deal with as a result of the agreement'. Margaret Thatcher, *The Downing Street Years* (London: HarperCollins, 1993), p. 407.

16   Michael Cunningham, 'Conservative Dissidents and the Irish Question: The "Pro-Integrationist" Lobby 1973–94', *Irish Political Studies*, 10 (1995), p. 35.

17   *ibid.*, pp. 36–7.

18   Brendan O'Leary, 'The Conservative Stewardship of Northern Ireland, 1979–97: Sound-bottomed Contradictions or Slow Learning?', *Political Studies*, 44, 4 (September 1997), p. 666.

19   *Spectator*, 29 March 1986.

20   For a touching account of the role of the Friends of the Union see Arthur Aughey, *Under Siege: Ulster Unionism and the Anglo-Irish Agreement* (Belfast: Blackstaff Press, 1989), pp. 144–6. He claims there were 650 members by the autumn of 1986: if so, the vast bulk was moribund.

21   *ibid.*, p. 144.

22   Norman Porter, *Rethinking Unionism: An Alternative Vision for Northern Ireland* (Belfast: Blackstaff Press, 1996), pp. 14–15. Porter deserves the title of visionary, and for those unfamiliar with his personal odyssey it would be well to consult his 'personal notes' at pp. 3–6.

23   Three obvious sources are Aughey, *Under Seige*, Ellis Owen, *Anglo-Irish Agreement*, and Feargal Cochrane, *Unionist Politics and the Politics of Unionism Since the Anglo-Irish Agreement* (Cork: Cork University Press, 1997).

24   Quoted in Paul Dixon, ' "The Usual English Doubletalk": The British Political Parties and the Ulster Unionists 1974–94', *Irish Political Studies*, 9 (1994), p. 37, fn 15, and p. 36.

25   For a summary of the futility of the campaign see Ellis Owen, *Anglo-Irish Agreement*, pp. 110–11; and for its conduct, pp. 50, 67–9, 83 and 104–5. See, too, Michael Connolly and Colin Knox, 'The 1985 Local Government Elections in Northern Ireland', *Irish Political Studies*, 1 (1986), pp. 103–10,

26   Quoted in Ellis Owen, *Anglo-Irish Agreement*, p. 107. For good succinct accounts of the Ulster Clubs and Ulster Resistance see Sydney Elliott and W.D. Flackes, *Northern Ireland: A Political Directory 1968–1999*, 5th edn (Belfast: Blackstaff Press, 1999), pp. 474 and 486.

27   New Ulster Political Research Group, *Common Sense: Northern Ireland – An Agreed Process* (Belfast: New Ulster Political Research Group, 1987). This document was a modification from the same source of a 1979 set of constitutional ideas, *Beyond the Religious Divide*. The 1979 document plumped for Ulster independence as offering the best prospect for peace and stability, and suggested a constitution based on the US system of a separation of powers, a committee system based on proportionality and a bill of rights. It is likely that both documents were influenced by contacts with the Irish-American civil rights lawyer Paul O'Dwyer.

28   Unionist Task Force, *An End to Drift: The Task Force Report* (Belfast: Unionist Task Force, 1987), pp. 6–8.

29   Fionnuala O'Connor, 'True Blue Peter', *Sunday Tribune*, 9 March 1986. See, too, *News Letter* editorial, 'Facing facts', 8 October 1987, on his resignation. While Frank Millar had been a highly effective general secretary, the UUP was a much more professional organisation. Harold McCusker did not resign. He was involved in a long battle against cancer. He died in 1990.

30   See Ed Moloney, 'King-maker King engineers DUP return for Robinson', *Sunday Tribune*, 10 January 1988.

31   Fergus Pyle, 'Present union not protecting Unionist interests – Robinson', *Irish Times*, 15 April 1988.

32   For an account of the election see Ellis Owen, *Anglo-Irish Agreement*, pp. 136–45.

33   Brendan O'Leary, 'The Anglo-Irish Agreement: Folly or Statecraft?', *West European Politics*, 10, 1 (January 1987), pp. 6–7. The argument is developed at pp. 5–32.

34   Heinrich Böll, *Irish Journey: A Traveller's Portrait of Ireland* (London: Abacus, 1983), p. 122.

35   'Haughey suggests separate social laws for North in a united Ireland', *Irish Times*, 10 June 1980.

36   See an interview with Seán O'Rourke in the *Irish Press*, 26 September 1984, and an editorial in the same edition, 'Mr Haughey's view', which examines his sleight of hand on the divorce issue. See, too, Denis Coghlan, 'Fianna Fáil changes

stand on divorce poll', *Irish Times*, 8 September 1984; and Denis Coghlan, 'Anger over FF marital vote', *Irish Times*, 4 October 1984.

37   'Cushnahan snub not our idea – Young FF', *Sunday Tribune*, 30 September 1984.

38   Denis Coghlan, 'Hume, Haughey agree to differ on accord', *Irish Times*, 9 December 1986.

39   See 'O'Malley out', *Irish Times*, 27 February 1985, where the leader-writer speculated that 'Fianna Fáil will be ditched and done in the new Ireland, and consigned to be the most conservative party in the Twenty-six Counties'. See, too, 'It's time to grow up', *Sunday Tribune*, 20 May 1984, on the occasion of O'Malley's expulsion from the Fianna Fáil parliamentary party; this leader complained of a tradition of autocracy and of myopia: 'the Forum Report seems to have prompted an outbreak of political hallucination, notably within Fianna Fáil, which is positively dangerous. To listen to [Fianna Fáil TD] Pádraig Flynn on television on Friday night state, apparently without mischief, that he believed that the unionists would "sit down" shortly to discuss the form of the unitary state we were to have, was despairing.'

40   See John Healy, 'How O'Malley party could sink Haughey', *Irish Times*, 27 July 1985. On 12 July 1989 Haughey was forced into coalition with O'Malley's Progressive Democrats, thus breaking sixty years of settled Fianna Fáil policy and tradition against coalition government. For an account see Shane Kenny, *Go Dance on Somebody Else's Grave* (Dublin: Kildanore Press, 1990).

41   Aughey, *Under Seige*, p. 94.

42   Quoted in Ellis Owen, *Anglo-Irish Agreement*, p. 128.

43   *ibid.*, p. 129. In any case Margaret Thatcher made it clear (*ibid.*, p. 124) after the Irish general election that the agreement would remain in place: 'the Agreement was made between two sovereign countries and not political parties'.

44   Bernadette C. Hayes and Ian McAllister, 'British and Irish Public Opinion Towards the Northern Ireland Problem', *Irish Political Studies*, 11 (1996), p. 77. These changing political preferences mask a much more profound social and cultural change occurring in the Republic. *Pace* Böll (note 34 above) on the pace of change, a series of writers have encapsulated the nature of that change. One could begin with the philosopher's belief that Ireland had witnessed a crisis of culture in the twentieth century – Richard Kearney, *Transitions: Narratives in Modern Irish Culture* (Manchester: Manchester University Press, 1988); the politician's 'anatomy of a changing state' – the subtitle of Gemma Hussey's *Ireland Today* (Dublin: Town House, 1993) – in which she wonders how a healthy economy could still produce 20 per cent unemployment, this just seven years before the Irish government was scouring the world appealing to the Irish diaspora to return home to take up the many unfilled jobs in a booming economy; the novelist's examination of an old republican's challenged certitudes – John McGahern, *Amongst Women* (London: Faber, 1990); the cultural critic's exploration of contemporary Irish life – Fintan O'Toole, *Black Hole, Green Card: The Disappearance of Ireland* (Dublin: New Island Books, 1994); and the playwright's analysis of a forgotten part of contemporary Irish history – Sebastian Barry, *The Steward of Christendom* (London: Methuen, 1995).

45   Hayes and McAllister, 'British and Irish Public Opinion', p. 80.

46   Thatcher, *Downing Street Years*, pp. 403 and 415.

47   Ellis Owen, *Ango-Irish Agreement*, p. 100. Article 8 of the agreement covered administration of justice issues. For a summary of what had (and had not) been achieved see Garret Fitzgerald, *All in a life: An Autobiography* (London: Macmillan, 1991), pp. 571–5. The most succinct summary of the working of the agreement can be found in Patrick Keatinge's annual review of Ireland's foreign relations in *Irish Studies in International Affairs*. See 2, 3 (1987), pp. 103–7, 110–12, 119–38; 2, 4 (1988), pp. 78–81, 85–92, 99–103; 3, 1 (1989), pp. 94–104, 115–23.

48   Ellis Owen, *Anglo-Irish Agreement*, p. 101. *See* the *Tablet*, 19 March 1988,

pp. 332–9 for articles on the state of the agreement by Garret FitzGerald, Paul Arthur, Louis Redmond, Robert McCartney and Cornelius O'Leary. See, too, Gerald Barry, 'The slow death of Hillsborough?' *Sunday Tribune*, 30 August 1987, on the stalemate over reform of the Diplock courts.

49   These figures are taken from the 'Irish Information Partnership' summary of conflict-related fatal casualties in Northern Ireland in 1988.

50   O'Leary, 'Anglo-Irish Agreement', pp. 668–9. I would contend that this process began earlier, especially the decision at the 1983 *ard fheis* to contest Dáil elections and, if successful, to take their seats in the Dáil.

51   *Irish Times*, 19 January 1987.

52   Paragraph 23 of the review bought the functional from what the officials called 'framework meetings' on to centre stage. Following the terminology of Article 3 of the agreement, meetings of the Intergovernmental Conference were categorised as: 'regular' (participation by both nominated ministerial representatives and scheduled to carry forward the main agenda); 'special' (convened at the request of either side to deal with unforeseen business); 'framework' (participation by other ministers without the nominated representatives, covering specific policy areas).

53   See note 22 above.

54   Sasson Sofer, 'The Diplomat as a Stranger', *Diplomacy and Statecraft*, 8 3 (1997), p. 181.

55   Ed Moloney, 'King-maker King engineers DUP return for Robinson', *Sunday Tribune*, 10 January 1988.

56   The details of these talks can be found in Ellis Owen, *Anglo-Irish Agreement*, pp. 172–5.

57   His MCB speech was reported in the *Belfast Telegraph*, 6 December 1989, and his Bangor speech the *Irish Times*, 10 January 1990. Both are cited in Paul Arthur, 'The Brooke Initiative', *Irish Political Studies*, 7 (1992), p. 111.

58   *H.C. Deb.*, vol. 94, cols. 320 and 325 (3 July 1991).

59   Rowntree Reform Trust, *Belfast Telegraph*, 12 July 1991.

60   David Bloomfield, *Political Dialogue in Northern Ireland: The Brooke Initiative 1989–92* (London: St Martin's Press,

1998), p. 179. For more detail on both Brooke and Mayhew see Paul Arthur, 'The Brooke Initiative', *Irish Political Studies*, 7 (1992), pp. 111–15, and Paul Arthur, 'The Mayhew Talks 1992', *Irish Political Studies*, 8 (1993), pp. 138–43.

61   Dean and Virginia Morrison Professor of Population Studies and Economics at Stanford University, W. Brian Arthur, in an interview with Joel Kurtzman, *Strategy and Business*, 11, 2 (1998), p. 103.

62   J.V. Montville, ' "Track Two Diplomacy": The Development of Non-Governmental Peace Promoting Relationships' (Draft paper presented at international conference on peace-building, Irish Peace Institute, Limerick, (28 April – 3 May 1986), p. 1; see, too, J.V. Montville, 'The Arrow and the Olive Branch: A Case for Track Two Diplomacy', in J.W. McDonald Jr and D.B. Bendahmane (eds.), *Conflict Resolution: Track Two Diplomacy* (Washington D.C.: Foreign Service Institute, US Department of State, 1987), pp. 5–21. On its utility to the Northern Ireland conflict see Paul Arthur, 'Negotiating the Northern Ireland Problem: Track One or Track Two Diplomacy?', *Government and Opposition*, 25, 4 (Autumn 1990), pp. 403–8; and Paul Arthur, ' "Quiet Diplomacy and Personal Conversation": Track Two Diplomacy and the Search for a Settlement in Northern Ireland', in Joseph Ruane and Jennifer Todd (eds.), After the Good Friday Agreement: Analysing Political Change in Northern Ireland (Dublin: University College Dublin Press, 1999), pp. 71–95.

63   Patrick Mayhew, speech, University of Ulster, Coleraine, 16 December 1992.

64   See Denzil McDaniel, *Enniskillen: The Remembrance Sunday Bombing* (Dublin: Wolfhound Press, 1997). This can be placed in the post-conflict literature of catharsis.

65   On that last point Hume quoted (tellingly) Wolfe Tone, the secular saint of Irish republicanism, on the distinction between objective and means. The five-page letter is remarkably prescient.

66 For a stimulating analysis of varieties of identity in a changing political landscape see Cathal McCall, *Identity in Northern Ireland: Communities, Politics and Change* (Basingstoke: Macmillan, 1999), especially pp. 84 and 203.

67 A useful 'insider' account of the significance of this dialogue and its impact on the bigger picture can be found in Tim Pat Coogan, *The Troubles: Ireland's Ordeal 1966–1995 and the Search for Peace* (London: Hutchinson, 1995), pp. 325–407. For an account of *Setting the Record Straight* see Paul Arthur, 'Dialogue between Sinn Féin and the British government', *Irish Political Studies*, 10 (1995), pp. 185–91.

68 Hume–Adams joint statement (mimeo), 24 April 1993.

69 Hume–Adams joint statement (mimeo), 25 September 1993.

70 On the 'validity' of the Hume–Adams document and on the nature and intensity of intergovernmental discussions a good source is Fergus Finlay, *Snakes and Ladders* (Dublin: New Ireland Books, 1998), pp. 193–5 and 232–3.

71 *ibid.*, pp. 110–13.

72 There was some surprise in political circles that Labour agreed to go into coalition with Fianna Fáil, and cries of opportunism were raised. When Dick Spring and Albert Reynolds were engaged in negotiation Reynolds informed Spring about the prospects of a breakthrough on Northern Ireland. That had huge significance for Spring because he had devoted so much of his political life to searching for peace in Northern Ireland. Finlay, *Snakes and Ladders*, p. 140, hints as much when he recalls a conversation with Spring after the Reynolds's meeting: ' "We talked about Northern Ireland", Dick said. "I promised him I wouldn't elaborate, but you can take it that there are real possibilities there." '

73 'Fianna Fáil – Labour Programme for a Partnership Government 1993–1997' (Dublin, 1993), p. 4.

74 *HC Deb.*, 234, 20, col. 1071 (15 December 1993). See, too, John Major, *The Autobiography* (London: HarperCollins, 1999), p. 433, where he accepts that he 'knew very little of Northern Ireland and had only once or twice visited any part of the island of Ireland. My previous political offices had not prepared me for the subject, and the conventional wisdom was that prime ministers were well advised to keep their distance.' Reynolds was also adept at claiming credit for being part of the process from the outset. See, for example, Geraldine Kennedy, 'One-page man confounds his critics', *Irish Times*, 31 December 1993.

75 David Goodall, 'Terrorists on the spot', *Tablet*, 25 December 1993/1 January 1994, p. 1676. Goodall supplies a neat précis of the declaration: 'So the central thrust of the declaration lies in the British Government's assurance that "they have no selfish strategic or economic interest in Northern Ireland"; in the Irish Government's stress on the reality of the unionist veto; in the (significantly differentiated) commitments of the two governments to self-determination for the people of Ireland; and in the offer of a place at the negotiating table for Sinn Féin once violence has been brought to an end and definitively renounced. All else is top dressing.'

76 The Downing Street Declaration is reproduced in Appendix II of Cochrane, *Unionist Politics*, pp. 404–8.

77 *ibid.*

78 See Finlay, *Snakes and Ladders*, pp. 236–8 for Reynolds's role in securing the IRA ceasefire.

79 The six points in paragraph 20 are about commitments: a) to democratic and exclusively peaceful means of resolving political issues; b) to the total disarmament of all paramilitary organisations; c) to agree that such disarmament must be verifiable to the satisfaction of an independent commission; d) to renounce for themselves, and to oppose any efforts by others, to use force, or threaten to use force, to influence the course or the outcome of all-party negotiations; e) to agree to abide by the terms of any agreement reached in all-party negotiations and to resort to democratic and exclusively peaceful methods in trying to alter any aspect of that outcome with which they may disagree; and f) to urge that 'punishment' killings and beatings stop and take effective steps to

prevent such actions. At the time of writing an international decommissioning panel, composed of the former ANC leader, Cyril Ramaphosa, and Harri Holkeri, is examining the verification of decommissioning.

80 See Paul Arthur, 'Some Thoughts on Transition: A Comparative View of the Peace Processes in South Africa and Northern Ireland', *Government and Opposition*, 30, 1 (Winter 1995), pp. 48–59; and 'Time, Territory and Tradition and the Anglo-Irish "Peace" Process', *Government and Opposition*, 31, 4 (Autumn 1996), pp. 426–40 for detailed accounts of the problems that arose in the aftermath of the Downing Street Declaration.

81 O'Leary, 'Conservative Stewardship of Northern Ireland', pp. 672–3.

82 Sidney Blumenthal, 'Along the Clinton–Blair axis', *Times*, 5 May 1997.

83 I have examined that role in 'Multiparty Mediation in Northern Ireland', in Chester A. Crocker, Fen Osler Hampson and Pamela Aall (eds.), *Herding Cats: Multiparty Mediation in a Complex World* (Washington D.C.: United States Institute of Peace Press, 1999), pp. 469–501. See, too, George Mitchell, *Making Peace* (London: Heinemann, 1999); Thomas Hennessey, *The Northern Ireland Peace Process: Ending the Troubles?* (Dublin: Gill and Macmillan, 2000); Michael Cox, Adrian Guelke and Fiona Stephen (eds.), *A Farewell to Arms? From 'Long War' to Long Peace in Northern Ireland* (Manchester: Manchester University Press, 2000); and three articles by the former Minister for Foreign Affairs, David

Andrews, 'Unionists in talks went "for the man, not the ball" ', *Irish Times*, 28 August 2000; 'Outlook was bleak as May deadline loomed', 29 August; and 'Sleepless nights and odd bedfellows', 30 August 2000.

84 For a clear-sighted and insider view on the 1998 agreement see John de Chastelain, 'The Good Friday Agreement in Northern Ireland', in Chester A. Crocker, Fen Osler Hampson and Pamela Aall (eds.), *Herding Cats: Multiparty Mediation in a Complex World* (Washington D.C.: United States Institute of Peace Press, 1999), pp. 435–68.

85 Joseph Ruane and Jennifer Todd, 'The Belfast Agreement: Context, Content, Consequences' in Joseph Ruane and Jennifer Todd (eds.), *After the Good Friday Agreement: Analysing Political Change in Northern Ireland* (Dublin: University College Dublin Press, 1999), pp. 71–95.

86 Rothstein, 'After the Peace', p. 7.

87 See Henry McDonald, 'Mandelson is wrong – Shankill war is all about the agreement', *Irish Times*, 23 August 2000.

88 'A New Beginning: Policing in Northern Ireland', *The Report of the Independent Commission on Policing in Northern Ireland* (Norwich: Crown Copyright, September 1999).

89 Gerry Moriarity, 'Level of North–South co-operation "unprecedented" ', *Irish Times*, 30 August 2000.

90 Deaglan de Breadun, 'Cook emphasises lessons of peace process', *Irish Times*, 28 August 2000.

91 Vernon Bogdanor, 'The British–Irish Council and Devolution', *Government and Opposition*, 34, 3 (Summer 1999), pp. 288–9.

BIBLIOGRAPHY

Adams, Gerry, *The Politics of Irish Freedom* (Dingle, Co Kerry: Brandon Books, 1986)

Akenson, Donald, Harman, 'Data: What is Known about the Irish in North America?', in Oliver MacDonagh and W.F. Mandle (eds.), *Ireland and Irish-Australia: Studies in Cultural and Political History* (London: Croom Helm, 1986)

— *Half the World from Home: Perspectives on the Irish in New Zealand 1860–1950* (Ontario: Langdale Press, 1990)

Amnesty International, *Report of an Amnesty International Mission to Northern Ireland (28 November 6 December 1977)* (Amnesty International, 1978)

Apter, David, 'A View from the Bogside', in Hermann Gilomee and Jannie Ganiano (eds.), *The Elusive Search for Peace: South Africa, Israel and Northern Ireland* (Capetown: Oxford University Press, 1990)

Armstrong, David and Hilary Saunders, *A Road Too Wide: The Price of Reconciliation in Northern Ireland* (Basingstoke: Marshall, Morgan and Scott, 1985)

Arnold, Bruce, *What Kind of Country: Modern Irish Politics 1968–1983* (London: Jonathan Cape, 1984)

Arthur, Paul, *The People's Democracy 1968–1972* (Belfast: Blackstaff Press, 1974)

— 'Anglo-Irish Relations Since 1968: A "Fever Chart" Interpretation', *Government and Opposition*, 18, 2 (1983)

— 'Policing and Crisis Politics: Northern Ireland as a Case Study', *Parliamentary Affairs*, 39, 3 (July 1986)

— 'The Media and Politics in Northern Ireland', in Jean Seaton and Ben Pimlott (eds.), *The Media in British Politics* (Aldershot: Gower, 1987)

— 'The Party System in Northern Ireland Since 1945', in A. Seldon (ed.), UK *Political Parties Since 1945* (London: Philip Allen, 1990)

— 'Negotiating the Northern Ireland Problem: Track One or Track Two Diplomacy?', *Government and Opposition,* 25, 4 (Autumn 1990)

— 'The Brooke Initiative', *Irish Political Studies*, 7 (1992)

— 'The Mayhew Talks 1992', *Irish Political Studies*, 8 (1993)

— 'Dialogue between Sinn Féin and the British Government', *Irish Political Studies*, 10 (1995)

— 'Some Thoughts on Transition: A Comparative View of the Peace Processes in South Africa and Northern Ireland', *Government and Opposition*, 30, 1 (Winter 1995)

— 'Time, Territory and Tradition and the Anglo-Irish "Peace" Process', *Government and Opposition*, 31, 4 (Autumn 1996)

— ' "Reading" Violence: Ireland', in David Apter (ed.), *The Legitimization of Violence* (London: Macmillan in association with the United Nations Research Institute for Social Development, 1997)

— 'Multiparty Mediation in Northern Ireland', in Chester A. Crocker, Fen Osler

Hampson and Pamela Aall (eds.), *Herding Cats: Multiparty Mediation in a Complex World* (Washington D.C.: United States Institute of Peace Press, 1999)

— '"Quiet Diplomacy and Personal Conversation": Track Two Diplomacy and the Search for a Settlement in Northern Ireland', in Joseph Ruane and Jennifer Todd (eds.), *After the Good Friday Agreement: Analysing Political Change in Northern Ireland* (Dublin: University College Dublin Press, 1999)

Aughey, Arthur, *Under Siege: Ulster Unionism and the Anglo-Irish Agreement* (Belfast: Blackstaff Press, 1989)

Baker, Susan, 'Nationalist Ideology and the Industrial Policy of Fianna Fáil (1955–72): The Evidence of the *Irish Press*', *Irish Political Studies*, 1 (1986)

Barcroft, Stephen, 'Irish Foreign Policy at the League of Nations 1929–1936', *Irish Studies in International Affairs*, 1, 1 (1979)

Barker, Rodney, *Political Ideas in Modern Britain* (London: Methuen, 1978)

Barnett, Anthony, *Iron Britannia: Why Parliament Waged Its Falklands War* (London: Allison and Busby, 1982)

Barrington, Donal, 'Uniting Ireland', *Tuairim* (Dublin, n.d.)

Barry, Brian, 'Political Accommodation and Consociational Democracy', *British Journal of Political Science*, 5, 4 (1975)

Barry, Sebastian, *The Steward of Christendom* (London: Methuen, 1995)

Barton, Brian, 'Relations between Westminster and Stormont during the Attlee Premiership', *Irish Political Studies*, 7 (1992)

Bax, Mart, *Harpstrings and Confessions: Machine-Style Politics in the Irish Republic* (Assen: Van Gorcum, 1976)

Beckett, J.C., 'Northern Ireland', in B. Crozier and R. Moss (eds.), *The Ulster Debate: Report of a Study Group* (London: Bodley Head, 1972)

Bell, J. Bowyer, 'Aspects of the Dragonworld: Covert Communication and the Rebel Ecosystem', *Intelligence and Counterintelligence*, 3, 1 (1990)

Bell, Sam Hanna, *The Theatre in Ulster* (Dublin: Gill and Macmillan, 1972)

Bell, Sam Hanna (ed.), *The Arts in Ulster: A Symposium* (London: Harrap, 1951)

[Bennett Report] *Report of the Committee of Inquiry into Police Interrogation Procedures in Northern Ireland*, Cmnd 7497 (London: HMSO, 1979)

Bew, Paul, Peter Gibbon and Henry Patterson, *The State in Northern Ireland, 1921–72: Political Forces and Social Classes* (Manchester: Manchester University Press, 1979)

— *Northern Ireland 1921–1996: Political Forces and Social Classes* (London: Serif, 1996)

Bew, Paul and Henry Patterson, *The British State and the Ulster Crisis: From Wilson to Thatcher* (London: Verso, 1985)

— 'The New Stalemate: Unionism and the Anglo-Irish Agreement', in Paul Teague (ed.), *Beyond the Rhetoric: Politics, the Economy and Social Policy in Northern Ireland* (London: Lawrence and Wishart, 1987)

Birch, A.H., 'A Note on Devolution', *Political Studies*, 4, 2 (1956)

— 'Minority Nationalist Movements and Theories of Political Integration', *World Politics*, 30, 3 (1978)

Birrell, Derek and Alan Murie, *Policy and Government in Northern Ireland: Lessons of Devolution* (Dublin: Gill and Macmillan, 1980)

Bland, Byron, *Marching and Rising: The Rituals of Small Differences and Great Violence in*

Northern Ireland (Stanford, Calif.: Center for International Security and Arms Control, Stanford University, 1996)

Bloomfield, David, *Political Dialogue in Northern Ireland: The Brooke Initiative 1989–92* (London: St Martin's Press, 1998)

Bloomfield, Kenneth, 'Constitution-Making in Northern Ireland: A Look Around the Monuments' (Bass Ireland Lecture, University of Ulster, Jordanstown, 28 February 1991)

— *Stormont in Crisis: A Memoir* (Belfast: Blackstaff Press, 1994)

Bogdanor, Vernon, *Devolution* (Oxford: Oxford University Press, 1979)

Böll, Heinrich, *Irish Journal: A Traveller's Portrait of Ireland* (London: Abacus, 1983)

Bowman, John, *De Valera and the Ulster Question 1917–1973* (Oxford: Clarendon Press, 1982)

Boyle, K., T. Hadden and P. Hillyard, *Law and State: The Case of Northern Ireland* (London: Martin Robertson, 1975)

Brett, C.E.B., *Long Shadows Cast Before: Nine Lives in Ulster 1625–1977* (Edinburgh: John Bartholomew, 1978)

— *Buildings of Belfast 1700–1914*, 2nd edn (Belfast: Friars Bush Press, 1985)

— 'The International Fund for Ireland, 1986–1989', *Political Quarterly*, 61, 4 (October–December 1990)

Broder, D.S., *Changing of the Guard: Power and Leadership in America* (Harmondsworth: Penguin Books, 1984)

Bruce, Steve, *God Save Ulster: The Religion and Politics of Paisleyism* (Oxford: Clarendon Press, 1986)

— *The Red Hand: Protestant Paramilitarism in Northern Ireland* (Oxford: Oxford University Press, 1992)

Buckland, Patrick, 'The Unity of Ulster Unionism 1886–1939', *History*, 60 (June 1975)

— *The Factory of Grievances: Devolved Government in Northern Ireland 1921–39* (Dublin: Gill and Macmillan, 1979)

Budge, Ian and Cornelius O'Leary, *Belfast: Approach to Crisis – A Study of Belfast Politics, 1613–1970* (London: Macmillan, 1973)

Bulpitt, J.G., *Territory and Power in the United Kingdom: An Interpretation* (Manchester: Manchester University Press, 1983)

Burke, Edmund, *A Letter to the Sheriffs of Bristol on the Affairs of America* (1777), in B.W. Hill (ed.), *Burke on Government Politics and Society* (London: Fontana, 1975).

Burton, Frank, *The Politics of Legitimacy: Struggles in a Belfast Community* (London: Routledge and Kegan Paul, 1978)

Callaghan, James, *A House Divided: Dilemma of Northern Ireland* (London: Collins, 1973)

Campbell, John, *Edward Heath: A Biography* (London: Jonathan Cape, 1993)

Carson, William A., *Ulster and the Irish Republic* (Belfast: Cleland, 1957)

Carter, Charles, 'Permutations of Government', *Administration*, 20, 4 (Winter 1972)

— *Two Years of Peace, Stability and Reconciliation?: A Commentary on the First Two Years of the Anglo-Irish Agreement* (London: Policy Search and Friends of the Union, 1987)

Carter, Jimmy, *Talking Peace: A Vision for the Next Generation* (New York: Puffin Books, 1995)

Carty, R.K., *Electoral Politics in Ireland: Party and Parish Pump* (Dingle, Co. Kerry: Brandon Books, 1983)

Castle, Barbara, *The Castle Diaries 1974–76* (London: Weidenfeld and Nicolson, 1980)

Cathcart, Rex, *The Most Contrary Region: The BBC in Northern Ireland 1924–1984* (Belfast: Blackstaff Press, 1984)

Catto, Mike, *Art in Ulster: 2* (Belfast: Blackstaff Press, 1977)

Chehabi, H.E., 'Self-Determination, Territorial Integrity, and the Falkland Islands', *Political Science Quarterly*, 100, 2 (1985)

Chossudovsky, Evgeny M., 'The Origins of the Treaty on the Non-proliferation of Nuclear Weapons: Ireland's Initiative in the United Nations (1958–61)', *Irish Studies in International Affairs*, 3, 2 (1990)

Chubb, Basil, *The Government and Politics of Ireland*, 2nd edn (London: Longman, 1982)

Clark, Alan, *Diaries* (London: Weidenfeld and Nicolson, 1993)

Clyde, Tom (ed.), *Ancestral Voices: The Selected Prose of John Hewitt* (Belfast: Blackstaff Press, 1987)

Cochrane, Feargal, *Unionist Politics and the Politics of Unionism Since the Anglo-Irish Agreement* (Cork: Cork University Press, 1997)

Cockfield, Lord, 'The Constitution in Transition: Brussels and Westminster', in Norman Lewis (ed.), *Happy and Glorious: The Constitution in Transition* (Milton Keynes: Open University Press, 1990)

Cohan, A.S., *The Irish Political Elite* (Dublin: Gill and Macmillan, 1972)

— 'The Question of a United Ireland: Perspectives of the Irish Political Elite', *International Affairs*, 53, 2 (1977)

Cole, John, *The Thatcher Years: A Decade of Revolution in British Politics* (London: BBC Books, 1987)

Collins, Martin, Interview with Joe Haines, *New Labour and Ireland*, 2, 5 (1981)

Collins, Stephen, *The Haughey File* (Dublin: O'Brien Press, 1992)

Connolly, Michael and Colin Knox, 'The 1985 Local Government Elections in Northern Ireland', *Irish Political Studies*, 1 (1986)

Connor, Walker, 'A Nation is a Nation, is an Ethnic Group, is a . . .', *Ethnic and Racial Studies*, 1, 4 (1978)

Coogan, Tim Pat, *The Troubles: Ireland's Ordeal 1966–1995 and the Search for Peace* (London: Hutchinson, 1995)

Cook, Chris and Mary Francis, *The First European Elections* (London: Macmillan, 1979)

Corcara, Michael Ó and Ronald J. Hill, 'The Soviet Union in Irish Foreign Policy', *International Affairs*, 58, 2 (1982)

Cremin, Con, 'Northern Ireland at the United Nations August/September 1969', *Irish Studies in International Affairs*, 1, 2 (1980)

Crick, Bernard, 'The Sovereignty of Parliament and the Irish Question', in D. Rea (ed.), *Models of Political Co-operation in Divided Societies* (Dublin: Gill and Macmillan, 1982)

— 'The Concept of Consent and the Agreement', in Charles Townshend (ed.),
     Consensus in Ireland: Approaches and Recessions (Oxford: Clarendon Press,
     1988)

Crocker, Chester A., *High Noon in Southern Africa: Making Peace in a Rough
     Neighborhood* (New York: Norton, 1992)

Cronin, Seán, *Washington's Irish Policy 1916–1986* (Dublin: Anvil Books, 1987)

Crossman, R.H.S., *The Diaries of a Cabinet Minister*, vol. III (London: Hamilton and
     Cape, 1977)

Cunningham, Michael J., *British Government Policy in Northern Ireland: Its Nature and
     Execution* (Manchester: Manchester University Press, 1991)

— 'Conservative Dissidents and the Irish Question: The "Pro-Integrationist" Lobby
     1973–94', *Irish Political Studies*, 10 (1995)

Daly, Cahal, 'War: The Morality, the Reality, the Myths' (Monsignor Arthur H.
     Ryan Memorial Lecture, Queen's University Belfast, 2 February 1984)

Dalyell, Tam, *Devolution: The End of Britain?* (London: Jonathan Cape, 1977)

Daniel, T.K., 'Griffith on his Noble Head: The Determinants of Cumann na
     nGaedheal Economic Policy, 1922–32', *Irish Economic and Social History*, 3 (1976)

Darby, John, *Intimidation and the Control of Conflict in Northern Ireland* (Dublin: Gill and
     Macmillan, 1986)

de Chastelain, John, 'The Good Friday Agreement in Northern Ireland', in Chester
     A. Crocker, Fen Osler Hampson and Pamela Aall (eds.), *Herding Cats: Multiparty
     Mediation in a Complex World* (Washington D.C.: United States Institute of Peace
     Press, 1999)

Dekmejian, R.H., 'Consociational Democracy in Crisis: The Case of Lebanon',
     Comparative Politics, 10 (1978)

Department of Foreign Affairs, *Challenges and Opportunities Abroad: White Paper on
     Foreign Policy* (Dublin: Stationery Office, 1996)

Dixon, Paul, ' "The Usual English Doubletalk": The British Political Parties and the
     Ulster Unionists 1974–94', *Irish Political Studies*, 9 (1994)

Dodd, Philip, 'Englishness and the National Culture', in Robert Colls and Philip
     Dodd (eds.), *Englishness: Politics and Culture, 1880–1920* (London: Croom Helm,
     1986)

Donaldson, A.G., 'The Constitution of Northern Ireland: Its Origins and
     Development', *University of Toronto Law Journal*, 11, 1 (1955)

Donaldson, Jeffrey, 'The U.S.A. Effect', in Ulster Young Unionist Council, *Selling
     Unionism: Home and Away* (Belfast, 1995)

Donoghue, Bernard, *Prime Minister: The Conduct of Policy under Harold Wilson and James
     Callaghan* (London: Jonathan Cape, 1987)

Donoghue, Denis, *Warrenpoint* (London: Jonathan Cape, 1991)

Downey, James, *Them and Us: Britain, Ireland and the Northern Ireland Question
     1969–1982* (Dublin: Ward River Press, 1983)

[Duncan Report] *Report of the Committee on Overseas Representation*, Cmnd 4107
     (London: HMSO, 1969)

Dunlop, John, 'The Self-Understanding of Protestants in Northern Ireland', in Enda
     McDonagh (ed.), *Irish Challenges to Theology* (Dublin: Dominican Publications,
     1986)

Editor's Foreword, 'Northern Ireland: The International Dimension', *Cambridge Review of International Affairs*, 11, 1 (Summer–Fall 1997)

Edwards, Owen Dudley, *Eamon de Valera* (Cardiff: GPC Books, 1987)

Elliott, Sydney and W.D. Flackes, *Northern Ireland: A Political Directory 1968–1999*, 5 edn (Belfast: Blackstaff Press, 1999)

Ellis Owen, Arwel, *The Anglo-Irish Agreement: The First Three Years* (Cardiff: University of Wales Press, 1994)

Enloe, Cynthia, *Ethnic Conflict and Political Development* (Boston: Little, Brown and Co., 1973)

Fahey, Tony, 'Progress or Decline?: Demographic Change in Political Context', in William Crotty and David E. Schmitt (eds.), *Ireland and the Politics of Change* (London: Longman, 1998)

Fairweather, Eileen et al., *Only the Rivers Run Free: Northern Ireland – The Women's War* (London: Pluto, 1984)

Fanagan, John (ed.), *Belling the Cats: Selected Speeches and Articles of John Kelly* (Dublin: Moytura Press, 1992)

Fanning, Ronan, 'London and Belfast's Response to the Declaration of the Republic of Ireland, 1948–49', *International Affairs*, 58, 1 (1981–2)

— *Independent Ireland* (Dublin: Helicon, 1983)

— 'Anglo-Irish Relations: Partition and the British Dimension in Historical Perspectives', *Irish Studies in International Affairs*, 2, 1 (1985)

— 'The Anglo-American Alliance and the Irish Application for Membership of the United Nations', *Irish Studies in International Affairs*, 2, 2 (1986)

Farrell, Brian, *The Founding of Dáil Éireann: Parliament and Nation-Building* (Dublin: Gill and Macmillan, 1971)

Farrell, Brian (ed.), *The Irish Parliamentary Tradition* (Dublin: Gill and Macmillan, 1973)

Farrell, Michael, *Emergency Legislation*, Field Day Pamphlet No. 11 (Derry, 1986)

Faulkner, Brian, *Memoirs of a Statesman* (London: Weidenfeld and Nicolson, 1978)

Finlay, Fergus, *Snakes and Ladders* (Dublin: New Island Books, 1998)

Fisk, Robert, *The Point of No Return: The Strike which Broke the British in Ulster* (London: André Deutsch, 1975)

— *Ireland, Ulster and the Price of Neutrality 1939–1945* (London: André Deutsch, 1983)

FitzGerald, Garret, 'Preconditions for an Irish peace', *London Review of Books*, 8 November 1979

— *All in a Life: An Autobiography* (London: Macmillan, 1991)

FitzGerald, Garret and Paddy Harte, *Ireland – Our Future Together* (Dublin: Fine Gael, 1979)

Fitzpatrick, David, *The Two Irelands 1912–1939* (Oxford: Oxford University Press, 1998)

Foster, R.F., 'Garret's crusade', *London Review of Books*, 21 January–3 February 1982

— *Modern Ireland 1600–1972* (London: Allen Lane, 1988)

Freedman, Lawrence, *Britain and the Falklands War* (Oxford: Basil Blackwell and the Institute of Contemporary History, 1988)

Gallagher, Eamon, 'Anglo-Irish Relations in the European Community', *Irish Studies in International Affairs*, 2, 1 (1985)

Gallagher, Eric and Stanley Worrall, *Christians in Ulster 1968–1980* (Oxford: Oxford University Press, 1982)

Gallagher, John, *The Decline, Revival and Fall of the British Empire* (Cambridge: Cambridge University Press, 1982)

Gallagher, Michael, *The Irish Labour Party in Transition 1957–82* (Manchester: Manchester University Press, 1982)

Garvin, Tom, *The Evolution of Irish Nationalist Politics* (Dublin: Gill and Macmillan, 1981)

— 'The Growth of Faction in the Fianna Fáil Party, 1966–1980', *Parliamentary Affairs*, 34, 1 (1981)

Gibbon, Peter, *The Origins of Ulster Unionism* (Manchester: Manchester University Press, 1975)

Giliomee, Hermann and Jannie Gagiano (eds.), *The Elusive Search for Peace: South Africa, Israel and Northern Ireland* (Cape Town: Oxford University Press, 1990)

Goodall, David, 'Terrorists on the spot', *Tablet*, 25 December 1993/1 January 1994

Government of Northern Ireland: A Working Paper for a Conference, Cmnd 7763 (London: HMSO, 1979)

Government of Northern Ireland: Proposals for Further Discussion, Cmnd 7950 (London: HMSO, 1980)

Greacen, Robert, *Protestant Without a Horse* (Belfast: Lagan Press, 1997)

Greenberg, Stanley B., 'Social Differentiation and Political Violence', *Journal of Conflict Resolution*, 19, 1 (1975)

Haagerup, Niels J., *A Report on Northern Ireland* (Strasbourg: European Parliament, 1984)

Hadfield, Brigid, 'More Reports on Northern Ireland: Panaceas or Pandora's Box?', *Public Law* (Summer 1985)

Hainsworth, Paul, 'Political Parties and the European Community' in A. Aughey, P. Hainsworth and M.J. Trimble, *Northern Ireland in the European Community: An Economic and Political Analysis* (Belfast: Policy Research Institute, 1989)

Hamill, Desmond, *Pig in the Middle: The Army in Northern Ireland 1969–1984* (London: Methuen, 1985)

Harkness, David, *The Restless Dominion: The Irish Free State and the British Commonwealth of Nations 1921–31* (London: Macmillan, 1969)

— *Northern Ireland Since 1920* (Dublin: Helicon, 1983)

— 'The Constitutions of Ireland and the Development of National Identity', *Journal of Commonwealth and Comparative Politics*, 36, 2 (July 1988)

Harris, Rosemary, *Prejudice and Tolerance in Ulster: A Study of Neighbours and 'Strangers' in a Border Community* (Manchester: Manchester University Press, 1972)

Hartley, Stephen, *The Irish Question as a Problem in British Foreign Policy 1914–18* (Basingstoke: Macmillan, 1987)

Harvey, Brian, *Cosgrave's Coalition: Irish Politics in the 1970s* (London: Selecteditions, 1980)

Haslett, E., *Ulster Must Say No* (Belfast: Joint Unionist Working Party, 1986)

Hattersley, Roy, *Who Goes Home? Scenes from a Political Life* (London: Little, Brown and Company, 1995)

Hayes, Bernadette C. and Ian McAllister, 'British and Irish Public Opinion Towards the Northern Ireland Problem', *Irish Political Studies*, 11 (1996)

Hayes, Maurice, *Minority Verdict: Experiences of Catholic Public Servant* (Belfast: Blackstaff Press, 1995)

Healey, Denis, *The Time of My Life* (Harmondsworth: Penguin Books, 1990)

Heaney, Seamus, *North* (London: Faber, 1975)

— 'Among Schoolchildren' (John Malone Memorial Lecture, Queen's University Belfast, 9 June 1983)

— *Station Island* (London: Faber, 1984)

Hennessy, Peter, *Cabinet* (Oxford: Basil Blackwell, 1986)

Heskin, Ken, *Northern Ireland: A Psychological Analysis* (Dublin: Gill and Macmillan, 1980)

Hewitt, John, *Art in Ulster: 1* (Belfast: Blackstaff Press, 1977)

— 'Planter's Gothic', in Tom Clyde (ed.), *Ancestral Voices: Selected Prose of John Hewitt* (Belfast: Blackstaff Press, 1987)

Hill, Dilys M. and Phil Williams, 'The Reagan Presidency: Style and Substance', in Dilys M. Hill, Raymond Moore and Phil Williams (eds.), *The Reagan Presidency: An Incomplete Revolution?* (Basingstoke: Macmillan in association with the Centre for International Policy Studies, University of Southampton, 1990)

Hinsley, F.H., *Sovereignty*, 2 edn (Cambridge: Cambridge University Press, 1986)

Hogan, James, *Election and Representation* (Cork: Cork University Press/Oxford: B.H. Blackwell, 1945)

Holland, Jack, *The American Connection* (New York: Viking Press, 1987)

Holland, Mary, 'Haughey's strategy', *Magill*, August 1983

Horgan, John, *Seán Lemass: The Enigmatic Patriot* (Dublin: Gill and Macmillan, 1997)

Horowitz, Donald, 'Dual Authority Politics', *Comparative Politics*, 14, 3 (1982)

Hume, John, 'The Irish Question: A British Problem', *Foreign Affairs*, 58, 2 (1979)

— *Personal Views: Politics, Peace and Reconciliation in Ireland* (Dublin: Town House, 1996)

[Hunt Report] *Report of the Advisory Committee on Police in Northern Ireland*, Cmd 535 (Belfast: HMSO, 1969)

Hussey, Gemma, *Ireland Today* (Dublin: Town House, 1993)

IBEC Technical Services Corporation, *Industrial Potentials of Ireland: An Appraisal* (New York, 1952)

Ireland, Denis, *From the Jungle of Belfast* (Belfast: Blackstaff Press, 1973)

Irish Episcopal Conference, *Submission to the New Ireland Forum* (Dublin: Veritas Publications, January 1984)

Irvin, Cynthia L., 'Parties against the State: Militant Nationalism in Ireland and Spain' (D.Phil. thesis, Duke University, 1993)

Ivory, Gareth E., 'The Political Parties of the Republic of Ireland and the Northern Ireland Question, 1980–1995' (Ph.D. thesis, University of Wolverhampton, 1999)

Jackson, Alvin, *Ireland 1798–1998* (Oxford: Basil Blackwell, 1999)

Jalland, Patricia, 'United Kingdom Devolution 1910–14: Political Panacea or Tactical Diversion?', *English Historical Review* (October 1979)

Jenkins, Richard, Hastings Donnan and Graham McFarlane, *The Sectarian Divide in*

Northern Ireland Today (London: Royal Anthropological Society of Great Britain and Ireland, Occasional Paper No. 41, 1986)

Jenkins, Roy, *British Foreign Policy Since 1945*, Proceedings of the British Academy (Oxford: Oxford University Press, 1972)

Johnson, D.S., 'The Northern Ireland Economy 1914–39', in L. Kennedy and P. Ollernshaw (eds.), *An Economic History of Ulster, 1820–1940* (Manchester: Manchester University Press, 1985)

Johnson, R.W., 'High Priest of Mumbo-Jumbo', *London Review of Books*, 19, 22 (1997)

Jordan, Robert S. and Werner J. Feld, *Europe in the Balance: The Changing Context of European International Politics* (London: Faber and Faber, 1986)

Joyce, James, *Ulysses* (New York: Random House, 1961)

Joyce, Joe and Peter Murtagh, *The Boss: Charles J. Haughey in Government* (Dublin: Poolbeg Press, 1983)

Kearney, Richard, *Transitions: Narratives in Modern Irish Culture* (Manchester: Manchester University Press, 1988)

Keatinge, Patrick, *A Place Among the Nations: Issues of Irish Foreign Policy* (Dublin: Institute of Public Administration, 1978)

— *A Singular Stance: Irish Neutrality in the 1980s* (Dublin: Institute of Public Administration, 1984)

— 'Unequal Sovereigns: The Diplomatic Dimension of Anglo-Irish Relations', in P.J. Drudy (ed.), *Ireland and Britain Since 1922* (Cambridge: Cambridge University Press, 1986)

— Annual Review of Ireland's Foreign Relations in 1986, *Irish Studies in International Affairs*, 2, 3 (1987)

— Annual Review of Ireland's Foreign Relations in 1987, *Irish Studies in International Affairs*, 2, 4 (1988)

— Annual Review of Ireland's Foreign Relations in 1988, *Irish Studies in International Affairs*, 3, 1 (1989)

Keena, Colm, *Gerry Adams: A Biography* (Cork: Mercier Press, 1990)

Kennedy, Dennis, *The Widening Gulf: Northern Attitudes to the Independent Irish State 1919–49* (Belfast: Blackstaff Press, 1988)

Kennedy, Edward, 'The Protestant Irish Heritage in America', *Congressional Record – Senate*, S513235 – S13237

Kenny, Shane, *Go Dance on Somebody Else's Grave* (Dublin: Kildanore Press, 1990)

Keogh, Dermot, *The Vatican, the Bishops and Irish Politics 1919–1939* (Cambridge: Cambridge University Press, 1986)

[Kilbrandon Commission] *Royal Commission on the Constitution 1969–1973*, Cmnd 5460 (London: HSMO, 1973)

[Kilbrandon Report] *Northern Ireland: Report of an Independent Inquiry* (London, 1984)

Killanin, Lord and Michael V. Duignan, *The Shell Guide to Ireland*, 2nd edn (London: Ebury Press, 1967)

King, Cecil, *The Cecil King Diary 1970–1974* (London: Jonathan Cape, 1975)

Kissinger, Henry, *The White House Years* (London: Weidenfeld and Nicolson, 1979)

Kratochwil, Friedrich, 'Of Systems, Boundaries, and Territoriality: An Inquiry into the Formation of the State System', *World Politics*, 39, 1 (October 1986)

Kurtzman, Joel, Interview with W. Brian Arthur, *Strategy and Business*, 11, 2 (1998)

Lawrence, R.J., S. Elliott and M.J. Laver, *The Northern Ireland General Elections of 1973*, Cmnd 5851 (London: HMSO, 1975)

Lee, J.J., *Ireland 1912–1985: Politics and Society* (Cambridge: Cambridge University Press, 1989)

Lijphart, Arend, 'The Northern Ireland Problem: Cases, Theories and Solutions', *British Journal of Political Science*, 5, 1 (1975)

— *Democracy in Plural Societies: A Comparative Exploration* (New Haven: Yale University Press, 1977)

— 'The Demise of the Last Westminster System? Comments on the Report of New Zealand's Royal Commission on the Electoral System', *Electoral Studies*, 6 (1987)

Loftus, Belinda, *Mirrors: William III and Mother Ireland* (Dundrum: Picture Press, 1990)

Low, D.A., *Eclipse of Empire* (Cambridge: Cambridge University Press, 1991)

Lynch, Jack, 'My Life and Times', *Magill*, November 1979

McCall, Cathal, *Identity in Northern Ireland: Communities, Politics and Change* (Basingstoke: Macmillan, 1999)

McCann, Eamonn, *War and an Irish Town* (Harmondsworth: Penguin Books, 1974)

McCarrick, Billy, 'The British Labour Party, British Politics and Ireland' (D.Phil thesis, University of Ulster, 1992)

McCartney, Robert, QC, *Unionist Review*, 1 (Autumn 1983)

McColgan, John, *British Policy and the Irish Administration 1920–22* (London: Allen and Unwin, 1983)

McDaniel, Denzil, *Enniskillen: The Remembrance Sunday Bombing* (Dublin: Wolfhound Press, 1997)

MacDonagh, Oliver, *Ireland: The Union and its Aftermath* (London: Allen and Unwin, 1977)

— 'Time's Revenges and Revenge's Time: A Review of Anglo-Irish Relations', *Anglo-Irish Studies*, 4 (1979)

— *States of Mind: A Study of Anglo-Irish Conflict 1780–1980* (London: Allen and Unwin, 1983)

— 'What was new in the New Ireland Forum?', *Crane Bag*, 9, 2 (1985)

McGahern, John, *Amongst Women* (London: Faber, 1990)

McGuinness, Frank, *Observe the Sons of Ulster Marching Towards the Somme* (London: Faber, 1986)

McKeown, Michael, *The Greening of a Nationalist* (Dublin: Murlough Press, 1986)

McKittrick, David, 'Biaggi thought the British Army was in the Republic', *Irish Times*, 5 September 1979

— 'Horsemen of the Irish apocalypse', *Irish Times*, 6 September 1979

— *Despatches from Belfast* (Belfast: Blackstaff Press, 1989)

McKittrick, David, Seamus Kelters, Brian Feeney and Chris Thornton, *Lost Lives: The Stories of the Men, Women and Children who Died as a Result of the Northern Ireland Troubles* (Edinburgh: Mainstream Publishing, 1999)

McMahon, Deirdre, *Republicans and Imperialists: Anglo-Irish Relations in the 1930s* (New Haven: Yale University Press, 1984)

McMahon, Sean, *Sam Hanna Bell: A Biography* (Belfast: Blackstaff Press, 1999)

McManus, Fr Seán, Testimony before the Joint Committee of the Finance and State Government of the Pennsylvanian House of Representatives, 15 September 1987 (mimeograph)

MacNeice, Louis, *The Collected Poems of Louis MacNeice*, ed. E. R. Dodds (London: Faber & Faber, 1949)

MacQueen, Norman, 'Ireland's Entry to the United Nations 1946–56', in Tom Gallagher and James O'Connell (eds.), *Contemporary Irish Political Studies* (Manchester: Manchester University Press, 1983)

— 'The Expedience of Tradition: Ireland, International Organization and the Falklands Crisis', *Political Studies*, 33, 1 (1985)

Madden, A.F., 'Constitution-Making and Nationhood: The British Experience – An Overview', *Journal of Commonwealth and Comparative Politics*, 36, 2 (July 1988)

— '"Not For Export": The Westminster Model of Government and British Colonial Practice', *Journal of Imperial and Commonwealth History* 8 (October 1979).

Maidment, R. and A. McGrew, *The American Political Process* (London: Longman, 1986)

Major, John, *The Autobiography* (London: HarperCollins, 1999)

Mallie, Eamon and David McKittrick, *The Fight for Peace: The Secret Story Behind the Irish Peace Process* (London: Heinemann, 1996)

Mansergh, Martin (ed.), *The Spirit of the Nation: The Speeches and Statements of Charles J. Haughey* (Cork: Mercier Press, 1986)

Mansergh, Nicholas, *The Government of Northern Ireland: A Study in Devolution* (London: Allen and Unwin, 1936)

— *Britain and Ireland* (London: Longman, 1942)

— *The Prelude to Partition: Concepts and Aims in Ireland and India*, The 1976 Commonwealth Lecture (Cambridge: Cambridge University Press, 1978)

Mason, Roy, *Paying the Price* (London: Robert Hale, 1999)

Mathias, Charles McC, Jr, 'Ethnic Groups and Foreign Policy', *Foreign Affairs*, 59, 5 (Summer 1981)

Michie, Alistair and Simon Hoggart, *The Pact: The Inside Story of the Lib-Lab Government, 1977–8* (London: Quartet Books, 1978)

Middlemas, Keith, *Politics in Industrial Society: The Experience of the British System Since 1911* (London: André Deutsch, 1979)

Miller, David W., *Queen's Rebels: Ulster Loyalism in Historical Perspective* (Dublin: Gill and Macmillan, 1978)

Miller, Kerby A., 'Emigration, Capitalism and Ideology in Post-Famine Ireland', in Richard Kearney (ed.), *Migrations: The Irish at Home and Abroad* (Dublin: Wolfhound Press, 1990)

[Mitchell Report] *Report of the International Body on Arms Decommissioning* (Belfast: Northern Ireland Office, 24 January 1996)

Moloney, Ed and Andy Pollak, *Paisley* (Dublin: Poolbeg Press, 1986)

Montville, J.V., ' "Track Two Diplomacy": The Development of Non-Governmental Peace Promoting Relationships' (Draft paper presented at international conference on peace-building, Irish Peace Institute, Limerick, 28 April–3 May 1986)

— 'The Arrow and the Olive Branch: A Case for Track Two Diplomacy', in J.W. McDonald Jr. and D.B. Bendahmane (eds.), *Conflict Resolution: Track Two Diplomacy* (Washington D.C.: Foreign Service Institute, US Department of State, 1987)

Morgan, Austen, *Harold Wilson* (London: Pluto Press, 1992)

Morgan, Janet (ed.), *The Backbench Diaries of Richard Crossman* (London: Hamilton and Cape, 1981)

Morris, Edmund, *Dutch: A Memoir of Ronald Reagan* (New York: Random House, 1999)

Moss, David, 'Analysing Italian Political Violence as a Sequence of Communicative Acts: The Red Brigades, 1970–1982', *Social Analysis*, 13 (May 1983)

Mount, Ferdinand (ed.), *The Inquiring Eye: A Selection of the Writings of David Watt* (Harmondsworth: Penguin Books, 1988)

Moynihan, Daniel, 'The Irish Among Us', *Reader's Digest*, January 1985

Muldoon, Paul (ed.), *The Faber Book of Contemporary Irish Poetry* (London: Faber, 1986)

Mulloy, Eanna, *Emergency Legislation: Dynasties of Coercion*, Field Day Pamphlet No. 10 (Derry, 1986)

Munger, Frank, *The Legitimacy of Opposition: The Change of Government in Ireland in 1932*, Contemporary Political Sociology Series, vol. 1 (London: Sage Professional Papers, 1975)

Murphy, John A., *Ireland in the Twentieth Century* (Dublin: Gill and Macmillan, 1975)

Murphy, Richard, *The Price of Stone* (London: Faber and Faber, 1985)

Murray, Gerard, *John Hume and the SDLP: Impact and Survival in Northern Ireland* (Dublin: Irish Academic Press, 1998)

Nairn, Tom, *The Breakup of Britain: Crisis and Neo-nationalism* (London: New Left Books, 1977)

— *The Enchanted Glass: Britain and its Monarchy* (London: Radius Books, 1988)

Needham, Richard, *Battling for Peace* (Belfast: Blackstaff Press, 1998)

New Ireland Forum, *Report of Proceedings* (Dublin: Stationery Office, 1983–4)

— *Report*, (Dublin: Stationery Office, 2 May 1984)

— *The Cost of Violence Arising from the Northern Ireland Crisis Since 1969* (Dublin: Stationery Office, 1984)

— *The Macroeconomic Consequences of Integrated Economic Policy, Planning and Co-ordination in Ireland* (Dublin: Stationery Office, 2 May 1984)

New Ulster Political Research Group, *Common Sense: Northern Ireland – An Agreed Process* (Belfast: New Ulster Political Research Group, 1987)

Newsam, Frank, *The Home Office* (London: Allen and Unwin, 1955)

Newsom, David D., 'US–British Consultation: An Impossible Dream?', *International Affairs*, 63, 2 (1987)

Nordlinger, Eric A., *Conflict Regulation in Divided Societies* (Cambridge, Mass.: Center for International Affairs, Harvard University, 1972)

Northern Ireland: A Framework for Devolution, Cmnd 8541 (London: HMSO, 1982)

Northern Ireland: Statement by the National Executive Committee to the 1981 Conference (London: Labour Party, 1981)

O'Brien, Conor Cruise, 'Imagination and Politics', in Conor Cruise O'Brien and

William Dean Vanech, *Power and Consciousness* (London: London University Press, 1969)

— *States of Ireland* (London: Hutchinson, 1972)

— *Memoir: My Life and Themes* (London: Profile Books, 1998)

O'Clery, Conor, *The Greening of the White House: The Inside Story of How America Tried to Bring Peace to Ireland* (Dublin: Gill and Macmillan, 1996)

O'Duffy, Brendan and Brendan O'Leary, 'Violence in Northern Ireland, 1969–June 1989', in John McGarry and Brendan O'Leary (eds.), *The Future of Northern Ireland* (Oxford: Oxford University Press, 1990)

O'Faolain, Sean and Paul Henry, *An Irish Journey* (London: Readers' Union, 1941)

O'Halloran, Clare, *Partition and the Limits of Irish Nationalism* (Dublin: Gill and Macmillan, 1987)

O'Halpin, Eunan, 'Intelligence and Security in Ireland, 1922–45', *Intelligence and National Security*, 5, 1 (1990)

O'Hanlon, Ray, *The New Irish Americans* (Boulder, Colo.: Roberts Rinehart, 1998)

O'Keeffe, T.M., 'Suicide and Self-starvation', *Philosophy*, 59, 229 (1984)

O'Leary, Brendan, 'The Anglo-Irish Agreement: Folly or Statecraft?', *West European Politics*, 10, 1 (January 1987)

— 'The Conservative Stewardship of Northern Ireland, 1979–97: Sound-bottomed Contradictions or Slow Learning?', *Political Studies*, 44, 4 (September 1997)

O'Leary, Brendan and John McGarry, *The Politics of Antagonism: Understanding Northern Ireland* (London: Athlone Press, 1993)

O'Leary, Cornelius, *Irish Elections 1918–1977: Parties, Voters and Proportional Representation* (Dublin: Gill and Macmillan, 1979)

O'Leary, Cornelius, Sydney Elliott and R.A. Wilford, *The Northern Ireland Assembly 1982–1986: A Constitutional Experiment* (London: Hurst, 1988)

O'Leary, Olivia, 'The John Hume Show', *Magill*, March 1984

Oliver, John A., *Working at Stormont: Memoirs* (Dublin: Institute of Public Administration, 1978)

O'Malley, Padraig, *The Uncivil Wars: Ireland Today* (Belfast: Blackstaff Press, 1983)

— *Biting at the Grave: The Irish Hunger Strikes and the Politics of Despair* (Belfast: Blackstaff Press, 1990)

O'Toole, Fintan, *Black Hole, Green Card: The Disappearance of Ireland* (Dublin: New Island Books, 1994)

Ó Tuama, Seán, and Thomas Kinsella (eds.), *An Duanaire: Poems of Dispossessed 1600–1900* (Portlaoise: Dolmen, 1981)

Ó Tuathaigh, M.A.G., 'Religion, Nationality and a Sense of Community in Modern Ireland', in M.A.G. Ó Tuathaigh (ed.), *Community, Culture and Conflict: Aspects of the Irish Experience* (Galway: Galway University Press, 1986)

Palley, Claire, *The Evolution, Disintegration and Possible Reconstruction of the Northern Ireland Constitution* (Belfast: Barry Rose Publishers in conjunction with the Institute of Irish Studies, 1973)

Parry, Geraint, 'Tradition, Community and Self-determination', *British Journal of Political Science*, 12, 4 (October 1982)

Partridge, P.H., *Consent and Consensus* (London: Macmillan, 1971)

Paulin, Tom, *Ireland and the English Crisis* (Newcastle upon Tyne: Bloodaxe Books, 1985)
— *Fivemiletown* (London: Faber, 1987)
Peck, John, *Dublin from Downing Street* (Dublin: Gill and Macmillan, 1978)
[Plowden Report] *Report of the Committee on Representational Services Overseas*, Cmnd 2276 (London: HMSO, 1964)
Pocock, J.G.A., 'The Limits and Divisions of British History: In Search of the Unknown Subject', *American History Review*, 87, 2 (1982)
Popper, Karl, *The Open Society and its Enemies* (London: Routledge, 1960)
Porter, Norman, *Rethinking Unionism: An Alternative Vision for Northern Ireland* (Belfast: Blackstaff Press, 1996)
Prior, James, *A Balance of Power* (London: Hamish Hamilton, 1986)
Pro Mundi Vita, 'The Irish Conflict and the Christian Conscience', *The Furrow*, 24, 9 (September 1973)
Purdie, Bob, 'The Irish Anti-Partition League, South Armagh and the Abstentionist Tactic 1945–58', *Irish Political Studies*, 1 (1986)
— *Politics in the Streets: The Origins of the Civil Rights Movement in Northern Ireland* (Belfast: Blackstaff Press, 1990)
Purdy, Ann, *Molyneaux: The Long View* (Antrim: Greystone Books, 1989)
Quigley, George, 'Of Three Minds', in Richard Kearney (ed.), *Migrations: The Irish at Home and Abroad* (Dublin: Wolfhound Press, 1990)
Rees, Merlyn, *Northern Ireland: A Personal Perspective* (London: Methuen, 1985)
Regan, Donald T., *For the Record: From Wall Street to Washington* (London: Hutchinson, 1988)
Reynolds, David, 'A "Special Relationship"?: America, Britain and the International Order Since the Second World War', *International Affairs*, 62, 1 (1985–6)
— 'Rethinking Anglo-American Relations', *International Affairs*, 65, 1 (1988–9)
Roche, Richard, 'The High Cost of Complaining Irish Style', *Irish Business and Administrative Research*, 12 October 1982
Ronsley, J. (ed.), *Myth and Reality in Irish Literature* (Waterloo, Ontario: Winfrid Laurier University Press, 1977)
Rose, Richard, *Governing Without Consensus: An Irish Perspective* (London: Faber and Faber, 1971)
Rosten, Leo, *The Joys of Yiddish* (Harmondsworth: Penguin Books, 1971)
Rothstein, Robert L., 'After the Peace: The Political Economy of Reconciliation' (Inaugural Rebecca Meyerhoff Memorial Lecture, Harry S. Truman Institute, Hebrew University, Jerusalem, May 1966)
Ruane, Joseph and Jennifer Todd, *The Dynamics of Conflict in Northern Ireland: Power, Conflict and Emancipation* (Cambridge: Cambridge University Press, 1996)
— 'The Belfast Agreement: Context, Content, Consequences' in Joseph Ruane and Jennifer Todd (eds.), *After the Good Friday Agreement: Analysing Political Change in Northern Ireland* (Dublin, University College Dublin Press, 1999)
Sacks, Paul, *The Donegal Mafia: An Irish Political Machine* (New Haven: Yale University Press, 1976)

Salmon, T.C., *Unneutral Ireland: An Ambivalent and Unique Security Policy* (Oxford: Clarendon Press, 1989)

[Scarman Report] *Violence and Civil Disturbances in Northern Ireland: Report of Tribunal of Inquiry*, Cmd 566 (Belfast: HMSO, 1972)

Schulze, Kirsten E., 'The Northern Ireland Political Process: A Viable Approach to Conflict Resolution', *Irish Political Studies*, 12 (1997)

Shannon, William, 'The Anglo-Irish Agreement', *Foreign Affairs*, 64, 4 (1986)

Shea, Patrick, *Voices and the Sound of Drums: An Irish Autobiography* (Belfast: Blackstaff Press, 1981)

Shearman, Hugh, *How Northern Ireland is Governed* (Belfast: HMSO, 1963)

Shultz, George P., *Turmoil and Triumph: My Years as Secretary of State* (New York: Scribners, 1993)

Sinnott, Richard, *Irish Voters Decide: Voting Behaviour in Elections and Referendums Since 1918* (Manchester: Manchester University Press, 1993)

Smith, Hedrick, *The Power Game: How Washington Works* (New York: Ballentine Books, 1996)

Smith, Peter, *Why Unionists Say No* (Belfast: Joint Unionist Working Party, 1986)

Smith, Trevor and Alison Young, *The Fixers: Crisis Management in British Politics* (Aldershot: Dartmouth, 1996)

Sofer, Sasson, 'The Diplomat as a Stranger', *Diplomacy and Statecraft*, 8, 3 (1997)

Stewart, A.T.Q., *The Narrow Ground: The Roots of Conflict in Northern Ireland* (London: Faber and Faber, 1989)

Symmons, Clive R., 'The Anglo-Irish Agreement and International Precedents: A Unique Experiment in Inter-State Co-operation on Minority Rights', in J. Hayes and P. O'Higgins (eds.), *Lessons from Northern Ireland* (Belfast: Servicing the Legal System Publishers, 1990)

Taylor, A.J.P., *English History 1914–1945* (Oxford: Oxford University Press, 1965)

Thatcher, Margaret, *The Downing Street Years* (London: HarperCollins, 1993)

Theroux, Paul, *The Kingdom by the Sea* (Harmondsworth: Penguin Books, 1984)

Thompson, J.L.P., 'Ethnicity, Class and Incorporation: Political Mobilisation and Social Structures in Northern Ireland' (unpublished manuscript)

Tolstoy, Leo, *War and Peace* (Harmondsworth: Penguin Books, 1971)

Townshend, Charles, *Political Violence in Ireland: Government and Resistance Since 1848* (Oxford: Oxford University Press, 1983)

Tugendhat, Christopher, *Making Sense of Europe* (Harmondsworth: Viking, 1986)

Ulster Unionist Party, *Devolution and the Northern Ireland Assembly: The Way Forward – A Discussion Paper* (Belfast: Ulster Unionist Council, 1984)

Unionist Task Force, *An End to Drift: The Task Force Report* (Belfast: Unionist Task Force, 1987)

Urban, Mark, *Big Boys' Rules: The Secret Struggle against the IRA* (London: Faber, 1992)

Utley, T.E., *Lessons of Ulster* (London: Dent, 1975)

Van Voris, W.H., *Violence in Ulster: An Oral Documentary* (Amherst: Massachusetts University Press, 1975)

Vital, David, *The Making of British Foreign Policy* (London: Allen and Unwin, 1968)

Wallace, Martin, *Northern Ireland: 50 Years of Self-Government* (Newton Abbot: David and Charles, 1971)

Wallace, William, *The Foreign Policy Process in Britain* (London: Royal Institute of International Affairs, 1975)

— 'What Price Independence? Sovereignty and Interdependence in British Politics', *International Affairs*, 62, 3 (1986)

— 'Foreign Policy and National Identity in the United Kingdom', *International Affairs*, 67, 1 (1991)

Wallis, R., S. Bruce and D. Taylor, *No Surrender! Paisleyism and the Politics of Ethnic Identity in Northern Ireland* (Belfast: Department of Social Studies, Queen's University Belfast, 1986)

Walsh, Dick, *Des O'Malley: A Political Profile* (Dingle, Co. Kerry: Brandon Books, 1986)

— *The Party: Inside Fianna Fáil* (Dublin: Gill and Macmillan, 1986)

Webb, Keith, *The Growth of Nationalism in Scotland* (Harmondsworth: Pelican, 1978)

Weiler, Joseph H.H., 'The European Community in Change: Exit, Voice and Loyalty', *Irish Studies in International Affairs*, 3, 2 (1990)

Wheeler, Marcus, 'The Dublin–Moscow Accord', *The World Today*, 29, 11 (November 1973)

— 'Soviet Interest in Ireland', *Survey: A Journal of East and West Studies*, 21, 3 (1975)

White, Barry, *John Hume: Statesman of the Troubles* (Belfast: Blackstaff Press, 1984)

Whyte, John, *Church and State in Modern Ireland 1923–1979*, 2nd edn (Dublin: Gill and Macmillan, 1980)

— *Catholics in Western Democracies: A Study in Political Behaviour* (Dublin: Gill and Macmillan, 1981)

— 'The Permeability of the United Kingdom–Irish Border: A Preliminary Reconnaissance' (unpublished paper, 1983)

— *Interpreting Northern Ireland* (Oxford: Clarendon Press, 1990)

Williams, David, *A History of Modern Wales* (London: John Murray, 1977)

Wills, Gary, *The Kennedy Imprisonment: A Meditation on Power* (Boston: Little, Brown and Company, 1981)

— 'Goodbye Columbus', *New York Review of Books*, 37, 18 (22 November 1990)

Wilson, Andrew J., *Irish America and the Ulster Conflict 1968–1995* (Belfast: Blackstaff Press, 1995)

Wilson, Harold, *Final Term: The Labour Government 1974–1976* (London: Weidenfeld and Nicolson and Michael Joseph, 1979)

Wilson, Tom, *Ulster: Conflict and Consent* (Oxford: Oxford University Press, 1989)

Winchester, Simon, *In Holy Terror* (London: Faber, 1974)

Windlesham, Lord, 'Ministers in Ulster: The Machinery of Direct Rule', *Public Administration*, 51 (Autumn 1973)

Wootton, Barbara, *Contemporary Britain* (London: Allen and Unwin, 1971)

Wright, Frank, *Northern Ireland: A Comparative Analysis* (Dublin: Gill and Macmillan, 1987)

INDEX